Tonkawa Texts

Tonkawa Texts
A New Linguistic Edition

Compiled by Harry Hoijer

Translated and Edited by Thomas R. Wier

University of Oklahoma Press : Norman

Published through the Recovering Languages and Literacies of the Americas initiative, supported by the Andrew W. Mellon Foundation

Library of Congress Cataloging-in-Publication Data
Names: Hoijer, Harry, 1904–1976, compiler. | Wier, Thomas R., 1979– editor, translator.
Title: Tonkawa texts : a new linguistic edition / compiled by Harry Hoijer ; translated and edited by Thomas R. Wier.
Description: First edition. | Norman, OK : University of Oklahoma Press, [2018] | Includes bibliographical references and index. | Text in English and Tonkawa.
Identifiers: LCCN 2017023313| ISBN 978-0-8061-5899-0 (hardcover : alk. paper) | ISBN 978-0-8061-5988-1 (pbk. : alk. paper)
Subjects: LCSH: Tonkawa Indians—Folklore. | Tonkawa language—Grammar. | Tonkawa language—Texts.
Classification: LCC E99.T75 T65 2018 | DDC 398.20897—dc23
LC record available at https://lccn.loc.gov/2017023313

RECOVERING LANGUAGES & LITERACIES OF THE AMERICAS

This book is published as part of the Recovering Languages and Literacies of the Americas initiative. Recovering Languages and Literacies is generously supported by the Andrew W. Mellon Foundation.

The paper in this book meets the guidelines for permanence and durability of the Committee on Production Guidelines for Book Longevity of the Council on Library Resources, Inc. ∞

1 2 3 4 5 6 7 8 9 10

Contents

PART III. TONKAWA TEXTS: OLD STORIES · 237

Map and Tables

Map

Tables

Preface

The creation of a corpus for an extinct language entails problems distinct from creating corpora for living languages. Unless some new recording has been discovered, corpora of dead languages are always based on preexisting corpora in some way, whether they be unedited texts, collations of separate edited texts, or even already published corpora. Thus it is probably appropriate to say a few words on why a new corpus of Tonkawa might be needed.

First, although a reasonable body of texts exists for Tonkawa, all the available materials for the language—grammar, dictionary, text collections, and a handful of theoretical papers, none of which are particularly widely available on paper much less in electronic format—are written in prephonemic notation, provide no morphological glossing, use archaic terminology that is opaque to modern linguists, or (mis)analyze the language in a way that we today would find inappropriate. Through no fault of their own, the existing materials also fail to discuss many phenomena (e.g., obviation, binding, control and raising constructions, long-distance dependencies) that were unknown or poorly understood at the time of writing but are today central to much linguistic theorizing. This is unfortunate in the case of Tonkawa, because the language not only is a language isolate, and therefore of interest to phylogenetic studies, but also manifests a quite baroque polysynthetic morphological structure that challenges many theories about the relationship that word-structure bears to the wider domains of the clause or discourse. If a modern description were properly prepared, Tonkawa could become a citation language in many such discussions.

That having been said, we are still largely dependent on the decades of dedication and research carried out by one man, Harry Hoijer, without whom the language would have been utterly lost to us for the most part. In this collection of texts, I rely largely on Hoijer's own *Tonkawa Texts* (1972). Hoijer generally did not annotate or gloss his texts and translated only each word, with no free English translation of full clauses, so I have not only added morphological glossing for each Tonkawa word but also (where necessary) indicated where phonological processes significantly obscure a more complex underlying morphology and provided a free English translation for each line of text. Where discourse structure is not fully obvious (proximate and further obviatives are morphologically unmarked, while obviative arguments bear overt marking), I have supplied notes to explain shifts in obviation status.

Part I

Tonkawa Sketch Grammar

ONE

Introduction

The first mention of the Tonkawa Tribe comes almost from the dawn of historical writing in the New World. By 1536, after years of wandering through then largely uncharted lands along the Gulf Coast, the Spanish conquistador Álvar Núñez Cabeza de Vaca (1490–1557) had seen just about everything. The fleet carrying him and three hundred other Spaniards under the command of Pánfilo de Narváez in search of the Fountain of Youth ran ashore near present-day Tampa Bay, Florida, forcing him and the rest of the crew to seek a route back to Mexico City by land. Along the way, most of them succumbed to disease, drowning, or attacks from hostile tribes. By the time they made their way to Texas, only forty of them were left. Cabeza de Vaca and his Moorish slave Estevanico spent the better part of seven years living enslaved as medicinemen among the Karankawas, then escaped, only to be captured by the Tonkawas near present-day Llano, Texas. Although the tale is probably apocryphal, it is said that they were tied to a tree at the top of Enchanted Rock, an enormous granite rock formation at the rim of the Edwards Plateau in central Texas, which the Tonkawas and other tribes revered as sacred. Late at night, Cabeza de Vaca and Estevanico managed to escape once again without being detected, leading the Tonkawas to believe that they had escaped into the rock itself. When the Spaniards next came into contact with the Tonkawas over 150 years later, the Tonkawas reported the incident to the incredulous Europeans, who promptly named the rock *piedra encantada* in the conquistador's honor.

1.1. Genetic Affiliation

The superficiality of the encounter with Cabeza de Vaca and the repeated failures in communication through half-understood rumors and reports over the centuries to come are emblematic of the larger lack of knowledge about the languages and cultures of the indigenous population of Texas. Although our knowledge of Tonkawa is relatively complete compared to some other languages (the entire corpus of texts, word-lists, and discussion of Coahuilteco, Comecrudan, Maratino, Atakapan, Aranama, and Karankawa in Swanton 1940 is a thin 137 pages), allowing us to understand most basic and many detailed facts about Tonkawa morphology and phonology, much remains wholly unclear. Foremost among such questions must surely be its genetic affiliation. Tonkawa has been connected to more than half a dozen major linguistic phyla of the New World, often based on little more than assumption and guesswork. It has even been speculated that it could even be an "Amerind-Na-Dene *Mischsprache*" (Manaster-Ramer 1996b, 276), but it is safe to say that the academic consensus is that it has no clear connection to any known or attested indigenous language of the New World (Goddard 1979; Manaster-Ramer 1996b; Mithun 2001), as shown in table 1.1.

Table 1.1. Proposed linguistic affiliations of Tonkawa

Suspected linguistic affiliation	Source
1. Hokan-Coahuiltecan	Sapir (1920)
2. Penutian	Hymes (1987, 55–56)
3. Algonquian	Haas (1959, 1967, 1993)
4. Algonquian-Gulf	Haas (1958, 231, f. 2)
5. Na-Dene	Manaster-Ramer* (1996a)
6. Pakawan**-Karankawa	Powell (1890); cf. Manaster-Ramer (1996b)
7. Amerind	Greenberg (1987)

* Manaster-Ramer (1996b) posits this more as a foil to the claims of Greenberg (1987) than as a claim to the actual origins of Tonkawa as such.

** Pakawan is Manaster-Ramer's term that includes Comecrudan, Cotoname, and Maratino but excludes Karankawa, Atakapan, and Tonkawa. Powell's original term "Coahuiltecan" has since been applied to so many languages as to lose terminological focus.

Directly related to the question of genetic affiliation is the question of whether Tonkawa has always been spoken in its historically attested ranges. The earliest historical records often do not directly record which Indian tribe European settlers and missionaries came into contact with, but evidence suggests that the Tonkawas have long occupied the extreme southern fringe of the Great Plains, a grassy area then rich in bison, deer, and pronghorns that transitions to blackforest prairie, which today constitutes most of central Texas from around Austin northeast toward Dallas. It is also possible that they once occupied much of the

Edwards Plateau before being pushed onto the plains by the Lipan Apaches and Comanches within the protohistorical period (ca. sixteenth and seventeenth centuries; Newlin 1981, 4). Other tribes or bands such as the Meyeys, Yojaunes, and Ervipianes perhaps also spoke Tonkawa, or languages related to Tonkawa, but essentially nothing is known of their speech. Indeed, it is indicative of the lack of information about this people that the very name "Tonkawa" is not Tonkawa in origin; rather, it stems from a Waco word *tonkawéya* meaning 'they stay together' (Hoijer 1933, 1, citing Gatschet).

The Tonkawas themselves referred to their tribe as *tickanwa·tic* 'the real people.' Unlike people in eastern Texas, or farther west at the height of the Rio Grande, the

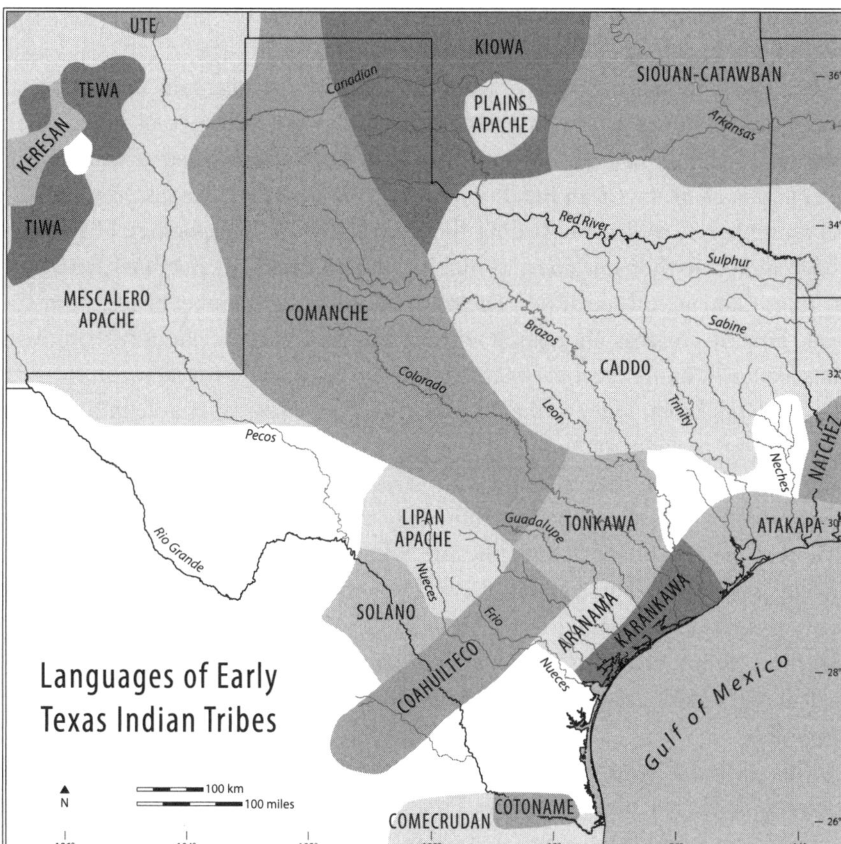

Languages of Early Texas Indian Tribes. Map by Carol Zuber-Mallison.

Tonkawas practiced an essentially migratory hunter-gatherer mode of subsistence. When encouraged to settle by Stephen F. Austin, they specifically refused on the grounds of their wolf ancestry (the wolf being their totemic animal) and an injunction by the Great Spirit not to engage in agriculture (Newlin 1981, 23).

1.2. Previously Published Materials

Although words and phrases in Tonkawa had been recorded sporadically for centuries (Goddard 1979, 359–61), the first significant fieldwork on Tonkawa was carried out by Albert Gatschet (1876). Unfortunately, it consists of little more than word elicitations and a few paradigms. Work on kinship terminology was also carried out by Alexander Lesser and on body-part terms from "Old Tonkawa" (to use Manaster-Ramer's term for the earliest attestations from the nineteenth century) by Goddard (1979).

But by far the most extensive work on Tonkawa is Hoijer's doctoral dissertation, pursued at the University of Chicago under the guidance of Franz Boas, Edward Sapir, and Leonard Bloomfield, which he later published as volume 3 of the *Handbook of American Indian Languages* (Hoijer 1933). The dissertation covers a number of subjects regarding the phonology and morphology of the language, almost to the exclusion of syntax, argument structure, anaphora, discourse structure, and lexical semantics. The work suffers from a number of general problems. First, it presents phonology without any reference to phonemic contrast, thus losing an entire level of generalization (a flaw that Hoijer later corrected in *An Analytical Dictionary of the Tonkawa Language* [1949a] and *Tonkawa Texts* [1972]). More problematic than this and its lack of general organization (all questions of both clause structure and word structure are dealt with in a chapter on "morphology") is its idiosyncratic terminology influenced by antimentalist attitudes then prevalent in American Structuralism, whereby a root or stem is a "theme" and an "element" is a level of structure above the phoneme that lacks meaning and does not necessarily correspond to a syllable or a foot (so that CV, CVCV, and CVC are all potential "simple elements" despite appearances to the contrary). Such terminological and analytical problems make understanding the text difficult even for specialists.

This revised collection of Tonkawa texts and the grammatical sketch addresses such problems in a number of ways. First, all texts have been normalized with a standard phonemic transcription system. This means that transcriptions are based on specific alternations within the language and abstracted from surface phonetic facts. Where the underlying morphology would otherwise be too obscure to identify, as happens frequently with some verb forms, the surface form has been set on an additional tier within the textual corpus. Furthermore, each line of text has been broken down into morphological strings and English glosses of such strings, in each case abiding by the Leipzig Convention on linguistic glossing. Thus each morph in the morphological tier corresponds to the extent possible with a single gloss on the glossing tier, separated by a hyphen. Where forms are cliticized and not fully affixal, they are separated by "=." Discontinuous constituents and compound verbs are marked with subscript numerals, and roots of uncertain meaning are sometimes indicated with superscript question marks. Paralinguistic uses of language (e.g., whining or laughing) occasionally found in the Tonkawa texts are noted in the English. In the grammatical sketch and texts, nouns are singular in number and bear nominative case where not otherwise noted. Likewise, verbal person and number markers agree with the subject unless otherwise marked for some other grammatical relation.

1.3. Glossing Abbreviations

1 first person; 2 second person; 3 third person; ABL ablative; ACC accusative; ADESS adessive; ADV adverbial; ALL allative; ASS assertive mood; AUG augmentative; C consonant; CAUS causative; CIS cislocative; COM comitative; COMP comparative; COND conditional mood; CONS consecutive; CONT continuous aspect; DECL declarative mood; DEF definite; DEON deontic mood; DET determiner; DS different subject; DU dual; EP epenthetic material without semantic content; EVID evidential; FUT future; GEN genitive; GER gerund; HORT hortative mood; IMP imperative mood; INDEF indefinite; INGR ingressive; INST instrumental; INTENT intentive mood; INTER interrogative mood; JUSS jussive mood; LOC locative; MIR mirative mood; NEG negative; NOM nominative; NP noun phrase; NSIM non-simultaneous; OBJ object; OBV obviative; PART participle; PAST past tense; PERF perfective aspect; PL plural; POSS possessive; PRES present tense; Q secondary question paradigm (used only with participial forms); RECIP reciprocal voice; RED reduplication; REFL reflexive voice; RES resultative aspect; SBJ subject; SG singular; SIM simultaneous; SS same subject; SUP superlative; TH thematic prefix; V vowel; * not attested.

TWO

Phonology

We can begin our discussion of Tonkawa grammar with a discussion of the phonology of Tonkawa: its segmental inventory, its rules of syllabification, and the various morphophonological rules that affect surface forms.

2.1. Consonant and Vowel Inventory

The inventory of phonemes in Tonkawa has changed with almost every succeeding publication on the work. Gatschet (1876) was the first to articulate a list of distinctive sounds, which differed in quite a number of ways from Hoijer (1933) and again from Hoijer (1972), both in terms of the phonological categories used and in terms of the phonetic variants possible. Gatschet, for example, notes the existence of some kind of rhotic consonant /r/, which he says is rare (but whether it is a tap, trill, or English-style retroflex he does not say). His analysis also entirely lacks any contrast between glottalic and pulmonic series of consonants (table 2.1). Hoijer (1933), in contrast, does not mention a retroflex consonant and argues for extensive sets of glottalized obstruents and resonants, no contrast between /s/ and /š/, and a series of labiovelar obstruents. He changes this in his later works (Hoijer 1949a, 1972) by totally eliminating phonemically glottalized consonants, on the assumption that all phonetically glottalized consonants are actually underlying a sequence of a consonant plus a glottal stop, a segment that is independently needed anyway (table 2.2).

Table 2.1. Consonant inventory in Gatschet 1876

	Labial	Coronal	Palatal	Velar	Glottal
'Explosive' (vl)	p	t		k	
'Explosive' (vd)	b	d		g	
Affricate		č <tch>			
Fricative		s	š	x	h
Nasal	m	n			
Approximant	w <v>		y		
Liquids		l, r			

Table 2.2. Consonant inventory in Hoijer 1933 and 1972

	Labial	Coronal	Dorsal		Glottal
Stop	p	t	k	k^{w}	ʔ
Stop, glott.		*t'*	*k'*	$k^{w'}$	
Affricate		c			
Affricate, glott.		*c'*			
Fricative		s	x	x^{w}	h
Fricative, glott.		*s'*	*x'*	$x^{w'}$	
Nasal	M	n			
Nasal, glott.	*m'*	*n'*			
Approximant		l	y	w	
Approximant, glott.		*l'*	*y'*	*w'*	

Positional Contrasts

	/p/	/t/	/k/	/kʷ/	/ʔ/
Initial	*pa n*	*tan*	*kana*	*kwa·n*	*ʔana*
	'bread'	'tail'	'all right'	'woman'	'look!'
Medial	*pa·pa q*	*kataʔ*	*kokon*	*yakwan*	*taʔane*
	'set'	'grandfather'	'chief'	'bucket'	'grasp'
Final	*s'apep*	*ʔekat*	*ʔoʔatak*	*na·kw*	*heyʔ*
	'empty'	'grandfather'	'last night'	'now!'	'okay'

			/k'/
Initial			*kʔame-* 'bend'
Medial			*na-kʔame-* 'gnaw'
Final			*

	/c/	/s/	/x/	/xʷ/
Initial	*cakaw*	*samox*	*xawak*	*xwete-*
	'river'	'red'	'onion'	'put belt on'
Medial	*pa·ca*	*xasis*	*to·xa-*	*sa·xwa*
	'pile'	'clear'	'finish'	'be hoarse'
Final	*we·tic*	*pas*	*pax*	*cʔaxw*
	'like this'	'a while'	'only'	'blanket'

	/c'/	/s'/	/x'/
Initial	*cʔa*	*sʔaycec*	*
	'oak tree'	'lungs'	
Medial	*hecʔeyʔeyewa*	*pasʔaxe*	*poxʔoc*
	'be jealous of s.o.'	'burst'	'night hawk'
Final	*	*	*

	/m/	/n/	/y/	/l/
Initial	*makay*	*naʔas*	*yamas*	*loskoy*
	'yellow'	'daylight'	'lips'	'upper thigh'
Medial	*hemaxan*	*Hanil*	*hayon*	*kalak*
	'turkey'	'wood rat'	'itch'	'other'
Final	*	*tan*	*teyey*	*tekal*
		'tail'	'liver'	'hardwood'

	/m'/	/n'/	/y'/	/l'/
Initial	*mʔaye-*	*nʔa·n-*	*yʔoco-*[*]	
	'set fire to'	'grind up'	'pinch'	
Medial	*mamʔe-*	*kwenʔamayʔan*	*mayʔan*	*walʔe*
	'salt food'	'a whine'	'prairie turtle'	'fish'
Final	*	*	*	*

So what can we take away from these disagreements in the literature? Some of Gatschet's claims quite possibly result from insufficient exposure to the language and/or the lack of any way to record speech in the mid-nineteenth century. This possibly explains his failure to detect glottalized variants of consonants—it is noteworthy in this respect that he does not identify the glottal stop as a distinct consonant. But other aspects of Gatschet's summary possibly result from a change in the language itself. The rarity of /r/ at the time of Gatschet's writing and its complete absence by the time of Hoijer (1933) might reflect this, as liquids have a limited distribution in Tonkawa, with only a handful of exceptional words having word-initial /l/ even in Hoijer's work. In the case of Hoijer's reassessment of his earlier analyses, the elimination of glottalized series does make the phonological system "cleaner," but it does not come without its own problems. For one thing, it creates syllable-initial consonant clusters (Cʔ) in a language that would otherwise not have syllable-internal clusters at all. Maybe more pointedly, in pluractional reduplication constructions that copy the first CV of the root, the consonant plus glottalized release patterns as a unit:

(1a)	*na-k'am'e-*	*na-k'a-k'am'e-*	'gnaw'
(1b)	*na-s'oka-*	*na-s'o-s'oka-*	'squeeze'

That is, if the glottalized consonants are in fact clusters, then we must make an exception of CCV reduplication precisely when glottalization functions as part of the onset of a root. This text therefore adopts a modified form of Hoijer's (1933) analysis in which glottalized consonants are unit phonemes. In a larger sense, what we might be seeing here is evidence of a language in transition: losing liquids as a phonological category on the one hand and the incipient phonologization of glottalization on the other.

The inventory of vowel segments is somewhat more straightforward. Gatschet's analysis argued for a typologically commonplace five vowel system: /i/, /e/, /a/, /o/, and /u/. Hoijer's (1933) analysis introduced evidence for length contrasts and eliminated /u/ as a vowel quality (table 2.3).

Table 2.3. Vowel inventory

<table>
<tr><th></th><th>Front</th><th></th><th>Back</th></tr>
<tr><td>High</td><td>i, i·</td><td rowspan="2"></td><td rowspan="2">o~u, o·~u</td></tr>
<tr><td>Mid</td><td>e, e·</td></tr>
<tr><td>Low</td><td></td><td>a, a·</td><td></td></tr>
</table>

All of these are found in all positions except syllable-initially, where they are otherwise preceded by a glottal stop. Notably, Hoijer (1933, 69) argues that Tonkawa had three levels of syllable weight: light, heavy, and superheavy. The distinction between the latter two syllable weights, however, arises only in unusual circumstances, such as when three distinct morphological units collide:[1]

(2a) [yakpa·kwa]
/yakapa-V·kwa/
strike-when
'when he hit him'

(2b) [yakpa:kwa]
/yakapa-V·-V·kwa/
strike-2OBJ-when
'when he hit you'

In the form in (2a), the root *yakapa-* 'strike' ends in a simple light syllable, which is then lengthened by a suffix *-V·kwa* 'when'; the third-person object is simply not marked at all. However, when the same verb indicates a second-person object, which is marked only by the insertion of an extra mora, a trimoraic verb can occur, as in (2b).

In his later work, Hoijer (1949b) and (1972) changes some of these analyses. For one thing, he reintroduces the /u/ vowel, presumably because of its liminal use in words like *hecu·* 'what,' where the /u/ vowel appears only word-finally. Another change is that he does not (implicitly at least) acknowledge three levels of syllable weight, presumably on the grounds that only two syllable weights are distinguished underlyingly.

2.2. Syllable Structure and Prosody

Possibly more has been written about Tonkawa syllable structure than about any other aspect of Tonkawa. This is because, as in Semitic languages, the

1. In these examples "V" stands for any vowel.

superficial variation in root structure seems to interact with syllabification in ways that posed problems for mid-twentieth century generative treatments of phonological rule ordering. To cite just a few examples used by C. M. Kisseberth (1970):[2]

(3a)	notxoʔ	<	notoxo-we-ʔe	'he hoes it'
(3b)	wentoxoʔ	<	we-notoxo-we-ʔe	'he hoes them'
(3c)	notxonoʔ	<	notoxo-no-we-ʔe	'he is hoeing it'
(3d)	wentoxonoʔ	<	we-notoxo-no-we-ʔe	'he is hoeing them'
(3e)	notox	<	notoxo	'a hoe'
(4)	notx-, -ntoxo-, notxo-, -ntoxo, notox			

What this illustrates clearly is that the language is seeking to maximize realization of a consonantal tier. To achieve syllabification of maximally CVC syllables from the left, vowels are regularly deleted where this would not create otherwise illicit syllables (an elision rule; see 2.3). Possibly related to this process, Hoijer (1933, 22) reports that "each syllable receives substantially the same accentuation[, but] a slightly heavier accent may be noted for the penult." As such, Tonkawa was probably a syllable-timed language that had recently shifted from a stress-timed language; such stress-timed languages are known to be susceptible to vowel reduction processes (Roach 1982).

2.3. Morphophonological Alternations

The relationship between the morphological content of words in Tonkawa and their overt phonological expression is usually fairly transparent. However, a number of important (morpho)phonological rules intervene to create sometimes opaque surface structures. As discussed in Kisseberth (1970) and Wier (n.d.), at least four distinct phonological rules are needed to piece apart surface from underlying representations:[3]

(5)	a. Conflation	/awe/ & /owe/ → /o/	
	b. Word-final vowel deletion	$V \rightarrow \emptyset \,/\, \_\_\#$	
	c. Vowel elision	$V \rightarrow \emptyset \,/\, CVC\_C\,[V_{\text{STEM}}]$	(*iterative*)
	d. Vowel harmony	$/V_1ʔV_2/ \rightarrow /V_1ʔV_1/$	

2. Kisseberth misanalyzed the morphological structure of these finite forms: for two distinct suffixes (*-we* and *-ʔe*) he assumed a single unanalyzable *-oʔ*. In most forms this analysis works, but when the extra mora provided by the second-person object agreement is present, it blocks the conflation rule of *(a/o)we* > *o*. I have provided the corrected forms in section 2.3.

3. Rules 5b–c from Kisseberth (1970); rules 5a and 5d from Wier (n.d.). Brackets denote extrametrical syllables refashioned by analogy.

(6) /yakapa-wesʔa-we-ʔei-[no]/
hit-1/2.SUBJ.PL-DECL-PAST-2SUBJ
'Y'all hit him'

Conflation	yakap-osʔ-o-ʔei-no
Deletion	yakap-osʔ-o-ʔei-n
Elision	yakp-osʔ-o-ʔei-n
Harmony	yakp-osʔ-o-ʔoi-n
Attested form	yakposʔoʔoino

Rule 5a converts any sequence of /awe/ or /owe/ to a simple /o/. Thus in the example in (6), the second-person plural subject marker conflates to /osʔ/, as does the declarative suffix, because both happen to involve sequences of /awe/ (even though crossing morphological boundaries). After this rule applies come rules 5b–d. Kisseberth's rules (5b–c) were one early generative attempt to explain the behavior of vowel reduction, though some of them might well be morphologically dependent or might well be reinterpreted as historical sound laws. Rule 5b, for example, is necessary to account for forms like (6) *yakposʔoʔoino,* but its failure to operate in this tense might be explained by reference to the particular tense suffix *-no,* or by the grammaticalization of *-no* after deletion ceased to operate, or even by analogical restoration of *-no* by reference to other forms (see the verbal paradigms in chapter 3).

Like any phonological rule, the rules only operate when their initial conditions apply. Thus, when the extra mora of the second-person object agreement is inserted, the rule of conflation is bled, producing rather different surface forms, as in (7):

(7)	/picena-we-ʔe/ cut-DECL-PRES 'He cuts it'	/picena-V·-we-ʔe/ cut-2OBJ-DECL-PRES 'He cuts you'
Deletion	picena-we-ʔ	picena-··-we-ʔ
Elision	picna-we-ʔ	picna-··-we-ʔ
Surface realization	[picnoʔ]	[picna·weʔ]

In any event, the system includes some combination of historical sound laws, synchronic phonological rules conspiring to create a particular kind of prosodic structure, and synchronic rules that are sensitive to particular morphological patterns.

THREE

Morphology

Tonkawa word-structure comes close to the ideal notion of a polysynthetic language: verbal phrasal heads inflect for multiple categories, including person, number, tense, aspect, mode, negation, and evidentiality. With great regularity, both verbs and nouns also incorporate nominals, verbs, particles, even entire clauses, making the distinction between words and phrases a rather weak one. Descriptively at least, Tonkawa verbs might consist of a dozen or so distinct slots in something like the following template:

(8) Tonkawa Verbal Template
OBJ.AGR-OBJ.PL-CAUS-TH-RED-[**ROOT**]-NEG-FUT-DU/PL-CONT-DECL-SUBJ.AGR

(9) [kenesta·ʔa·tonoʔ]
ke-nes-ta·ʔ-a·tewa-no-we-ʔe (TT 1.6)
1.OBJ-CAUS-marry-FUT-CONT-DECL-PRES.3.SG
'They will force me to marry her!'

3.1. Nominal Morphology

Tonkawa nominals inflect for number, case, the person and number of a possessor, definiteness, and obviation status. Like verbs, they also inflect according to a specific template:

(10a) [ROOT$_1$—(*STEM$_2$*, *STEM$_3$*, etc.)]$_{\text{STEM}}$—Poss—OBV—DEF—NUM—CASE

(10b) ha·ʔako·n-osas-[[neswalʔan-[k-e-ykewʔ-a·to-nwaʔ]]-no-no]-wa·-ʔa·-la (TT 23.4)
man-young-[[fish-[1.OBJ-REFL-make-FUT-COND]]-say-CONT]-OBV-DEF-NOM.SG
'The young man who said he'd be turned into a fish.'

This form, which involves a phonologically full clause *yakewʔa-* 'make, turn into' incorporating the object *neswalʔan* 'fish,' which in turn is incorporated into form of *no-* 'say,' illustrates how complex morphological nouns might be in Tonkawa.[4]

3.1.1. *Pronouns*

Personal pronouns in Tonkawa inflect for mostly the same categories as regular nouns, except that pronouns also explicitly mark a dual number and inflect for discourse features that regular nouns cannot, as in table 3.1: *sa·xwa* 'I too' but **ha·ʔako·n-xwa* 'the man too.'

Table 3.1. Personal pronouns

		NOMINATIVE	ACCUSATIVE	GENITIVE	'too'	'by oneself'
SINGULAR	1	sa·ya	sa·sik	sa·ken	sa·xwa	sa·cos
	2	na·ya	na·yak	na·xen	na·xwa	na·cos
	3	ʔaye·la	ʔaye·lak	ʔa·xen	ʔa·xwa	ʔa·cos
DUAL	1	kewsa·ya	kewsa·sik	*	*	*
	2	wena·ya	wena·yak	*	*	*
	3	ʔawe·la	ʔawe·lak	*	*	*
PLURAL	1	kewsa·ka	kewsa·sak	kewsa·ken	kewsa·xwa	kewsa·cos
	2	wena·ka	wena·yak	nawenexen	wena·xwa	wena·cos
	3	ʔawe·ka	ʔawe·kak	ʔawxen	ʔawaxwa	ʔawacos

Source: Hoijer 1933, 122–23.

* Not attested.

In addition to personal pronouns, Tonkawa also has a limited number of demonstrative and interrogative pronouns, as well as indefinites derived from them (table 3.2).

With the exception of three interrogative pronouns—*hecu·* 'who?, what?,' *hecu·ʔet* 'why?,' and *hetwan* 'how many'—all other interrogatives are formed by

4. For more discussion of wordhood in Tonkawa, see section 3.5 on incorporation.

Table 3.2. Demonstrative pronouns

TERM	SUBSTANTIVE	PLACE *-ca*	DIRECTION *-l*	MANNER *-c, -tic*
wa- 'this [OBV]'	wa·ʔa·la, wa·ka, etc.	wa·ca	*	*
te- 'this'	te·la, etc.	te·ca	te·l	te·c
he·ʔe- 'that'	he·ʔela, etc.	he·ʔeca	he·ʔel	he·c
we- 'yonder'	*	*	we·ʔil	we·tic

Source: Hoijer 1933, 124.

* Not attested.

the addition of *he-* plus a demonstrative: *hete·l* 'whither,' *hete·c* 'how,' and so forth. Indefinites are formed by the suffixation of *-ʔax*: *hetwanʔax* 'any number,' *hecu·ʔax* 'anyone, anything,' and so forth.

3.1.2. *Nouns*

Tonkawa nouns inflect for seven cases (table 3.3): nominative, accusative, allative, adessive, instrumental, genitive, and ablative; two numbers: singular and plural; (in)definiteness; and proximate or obviative status.

Table 3.3. Nominal case suffixes

NOMINATIVE	(null)
ACCUSATIVE	-k
ALLATIVE	-yʔik
ADESSIVE	-wʔan
INSTRUMENTAL	-s, -es, -ʔas, -lʔas, -las; -y (INST.PL)
GENITIVE	-lʔan, -ʔan[1]
ABLATIVE	-nan[2]

Source: Hoijer 1933, 113.

[1] Not identified by Hoijer.

[2] A grammatical *hapax legomenon*, found only in TT 27.1.

Nouns typically distinguish two numbers by means of distinct overt suffixes: *-la* for singulars and *-ka* for plurals. Some nouns, however, also indicate groups by reduplication of the initial syllable:

(11)	kwa·-kwan-ka	noho·-na·ʔe·-kla		(TT 4.6)
	RED-woman-NOM.PL	fetch.wood-go.off-DS.NSIM		

'The women went off to fetch wood'

(12)	kwa·-kwan-la	ketay-ta	ma-mka-nes-no-k-laknoʔo.	(TT 7.3)
	RED-woman-NOM.SG	two-DET	RED-weep-DU-CONT-PART-EVID	

'Both women kept on crying, supposedly.'

The fact that nominal reduplication is sometimes used in addition to a plural suffix and sometimes used with a singular suffix indicates that these are formally separate morphological processes and not formally linked in a single process of syntactic agreement.

Definite noun forms are formally marked with a suffix *-ʔa·* coming immediately before the number suffixes; indefinites are marked by the absence of a definite suffix. The glottal stop of this suffix is systematically lost when it is not preceded by an obviative marker and the stem of the noun ends in /k/:

(13)	ʔo·ca-ʔa·-la-k	hacip-kalak-a·-wʔan	we-ta[·]-ta-kxo-na-k-laknoʔo.	(TT 11.3)
	children-DEF-SG-ACC	hole-other-DEF-ADESS	OBJ.PL-COM-move.PL-in-ABL-PART-EVID	

'[Mouse] took her children into the other hole.'

Like definites and indefinites, proximate and obviative NPs (noun phrases) contrast by the presence of an obviative suffix *-wa·* and the absence of any overt proximate suffix. As in Algonquian and some other language families of North America, obviation marking reflects relative discourse salience: proximate arguments have more salience in the discourse, while obviative arguments have less salience. In some languages, only two levels of obviation are realized (e.g., Kutenai), while others have three or more levels (e.g., Plains Cree, Meskwaki, and others). Morphologically, Tonkawa belongs to the former group, inasmuch as proximate arguments are never overtly marked and primary obviative arguments always are. However, there is some reason to believe that there might be a secondary class of further obviatives, which, like proximates, are morphologically unmarked, resulting in a covert three-way contrast of proximate~obviative~further obviative (Wier 2012).

In earlier literature (e.g., Hoijer 1933) *-wa·* was identified as meaning 'aforementioned,' but this is problematic in two senses. First, definiteness and *-wa·* can be marked independently of each other, as in (14a–d), with the implication that, although all aforementioned arguments are identifiable, some arguments marked with *-wa·* nonetheless are not marked for definiteness:

(14a) **No definite marking, no obviative marking**

ha·ʔako·n-osas-la saxʔay-ka-k ʔe-ʔeyo·-no-k-laknoʔo. (TT 3.2)
man-young-NOM.SG arrow-PL-ACC RED-make-CONT-PART-EVID
'A young man was making arrows.'

(14b) **Definite marking, no obviative marking**

ha·ʔako·n-osaʔas-ʔa·-la sikit-ita taʔan-ce-ta (TT 21.5)
man-young-DEF-NOM.SG four-DET grasp-up-SS.NPURP

saxwa-k-laknoʔo
run.away.PL-PART-EVID
'Four young men grabbed hold of him and ran away.'

(14c) **No definite marking, obviative marking**

ha·ʔako·n-osaʔas-wa·-ka "ya·c-xwe·l-ape-we·sʔe-w," no·-no-n-k-laknoʔo. (TT 13.2)
man-young-OBV-NOM.PL look-miss-NEG-1/2.SBJ.PL-IMP say-CONT-PART-PART-EVID
'The young men were saying: "Watch him closely." '

(14d) **Definite marking, obviative marking**

ha·ʔako·n-osas-wa·-ʔa·-la ya-txw-an-samox-ʔa·-la-k (TT 21.7)
man-young-OBV-DEF-NOM.SG TH-fill.pipe-GER-red-DEF-SG-ACC

ya-txo-k-laknoʔo
TH-fill-PART-EVID
'The young man filled his red pipe.'

These two categories are thus morphologically independent of each other. Another problem with assigning the status of 'aforementioned' to what we are calling an obviative suffix is that there are actually instances of *-wa·-* that have not been mentioned before in a text. For example, in TT 4.2, the first mention of the woman in the story is marked *kwa·n**wa·**ʔa·la,* which is unexpected if this suffix marks only the given information. Another problem is that many aforementioned NPs are not marked with *-wa·* ('fence' in TT 1.3, 'hand' in TT 1.4, 'tree' in TT 1.10, etc.). This suffix is thus not even weakly associated with 'aforementionedness' (see chapter 5 for more discussion).

One nominal category that has not received full attention in the previous literature is possession. Tonkawa nominals may optionally inflect for a pronominal possessor; sometimes these markers of possession take the form of incorporated genitival pronouns, but sometimes they use special possessive suffixes seen nowhere else in Tonkawa morphology:

(15)	Ha·csokonay-la	"saxʔay-na·xen-coʔ,"	no-k-laknoʔo.	(TT 3.13)
	Coyote-NOM.SG	arrow-2.SG.POSS-RES	say-PART-EVID	

'Coyote said: "Here is your arrow."'

(16)	Ha·csokonay-la	helʔeya-kxo-na-t	"ʔen	kwa·n-ke-la?"	(TT 4.21)
	Coyote-NOM.SG	peer-in-ABL-SS.CONS	and	woman-1.POSS-NOM.SG	

no-k-laknoʔo.
say-PART-EVID
'Coyote peered in and said: "[Where is] my wife?"'

(17)	ʔe··kla	kalak-la	xa··xa-t	ka·x-wa··ʔa··la-k	(TT 25.16)
	be-DS.NSIM	other-NOM.SG	AUG.move.SG-AUG-SS.CONS	blind-OBV-DEF-SG-ACC	

"ta··h-e··pano··na·xen-ke-la-k	ya·lo·na-kwa,"	no-k-laknoʔo.
COM-REFL-TH-narrate-2.SG.GEN-2.SG-ACC	kill-MIR	say-PART-EVID

'So the other guy came over to the blind man and said: "They killed your friend."'

(18)	ʔewas-ʔa··l=ʔon	xʔay-ʔa··l=ʔen	"henox	ʔe··no-k-coʔ,"	(TT 4.22)
	father-DEF-3.POSS-and	mother-DEF-3.POSS-and	well	do-CONT-PART-RES	

no-k-laknoʔo.
say-PART-EVID
'Her father and mother said: "You did the right thing."'

The incorporated genitival pronouns are identical to the free forms mentioned above; the extant texts suggest that the shorter possessive markers only distinguish first- and second-person as opposed to third-person possessors and do not distinguish singular from plural (table 3.4; cf. TT 4.21; TT 17.23; TT 19.4; TT 25.8; TT 25.16).

Table 3.4. Nominal possessive markers

PERSON	MARKER
1	-ke
2	
3	-ʔa·l

3.1.3. *Adnominals*

Although syntactically predicative and attributive nominals modifying other nominals are much like other nominals, they can be morphologically distinguished from them by markers of comparison (*-nʔa*) and superlative (*-tak*) degrees:

(19) kwa·lo·-nʔa he-ykoʔo-k-laknoʔo. (TT 17.2)
big-COMP REFL-make-PART-EVID
'He got bigger.'

(20) "kwa·lo·-tak-la na·ce-w." (TT 17.23)
big-SUP-NOM.SG bite-IMP
'Bite the biggest one.'

3.2. Verbal Morphology

By far the most complicated part of Tonkawa morphology is the structure of verbs. Verbs inflect for the person and number of both subjects and objects, but the features of these categories are distributed across verb forms in different places in different paradigms. Like pronouns, verbal subjects indicate singular, dual, and plural numbers; verbal objects only distinguish singular and plural. In terms of order, in most cases, the verbal stem is followed by any negation, which is followed by any future marking, which is in turn followed by dual or plural marking of subjects.

(21)	Different verb templates across modes (Hoijer 1933, 81):
Declarative:	STEM-NEG-FUT-DU/PL-TENSE(PRES/PAST)-***PRON***
Interrogative:	STEM-NEG-FUT-DU/PL-TENSE(PRES/PAST)-***PRON***-INTERR
Assertive mode:	STEM-NEG-FUT-DU/PL-CONT-ASS-***PRON***
	STEM-NEG-CONT-ASS
	STEM-***1***-ASS
Intentive	STEM-NEG-DU/PL-MODE-***PRON***
Imperative	STEM-NEG-DU/PL-MODE-***PRON***
Potential	STEM-NEG-DU/PL-MODE-***PRON***
Hortatory	STEM-NEG-***PRON***-k-MODE

3.2.1. *Finite Verb Forms*

The most basic modality of verbs is that of declarative verbs, used to make statements about actions or states of being. Declarative verbs are overtly marked with a suffix—*we,* which is, however, frequently absorbed by surrounding suffixes because of the rule of conflation (see section 2.3). Likewise, tense suffixes sometimes display distinctions for person. Hoijer 1933 describes Tonkawa as having four tenses, but in fact, morphologically speaking, Tonkawa has two tenses, present (*-ʔe*) and past (*-ʔe·/ʔei/ʔe*). The use of the future suffix *-a·tewa* with these two tenses renders near future and remote future readings, respectively. Morphologically, however, these future forms are no more distinct tenses than English's modal auxiliary "will" creates a future tense in English; "future" might thus better be rendered as a kind of "prospective" aspect. On top of this, each "tense" can be marked for continuous aspect with *-no,* resulting in eight possible tense-aspect readings (tables 3.5, 3.6, 3.7, and 3.8).

In addition to suffixal aspect, Tonkawa also has a highly productive system of reduplicative pluractional aspect based on a CV template (Hoijer 1933, 61; Gouskova 2007):

(22a)	topo- 'cut'	to-topo- 'cut several times'
(22b)	lopaw- 'dive'	lo-lopaw- 'dive over and over'
(22c)	sola- 'drip'	so-sola- 'keep dripping'
(22d)	yʔoco- 'pinch'	yʔo-yʔoco- 'pinch over and over'

These two systems of aspect are in principle distinct from each other, standing in neither morphological nor semantic dependence on each other:

Table 3.5. Present tense verb paradigm

NUMBER	PERSON	PRESENT *(-ʔe)*	PRESENT CONTINUOUS *(-no- . . . -ʔe)*
SINGULAR	1	/yakapa-we-ʔe-s/ [yakpoʔs] 'I hit it,' etc.	/yakapa-no-we-ʔe-s/ †[yakpanoʔs] 'I am hitting it,' etc.
	2	/yakapa-we-·-ka/ [yakpo·ka]	/yakapa-no-we-·-ka/ †[yakpano·ka]
	3	/yakapa-we-ʔe/ [yakpoʔ]	/yakapa-no-we-ʔe/ †[yakpanoʔ]
DUAL	1	/yakapa-nesʔa-we-ʔe-s/ [yakpanesʔoʔs]	/yakapa-nesʔa-no-we-ʔe-s/ †[yakpanesʔanoʔs]
	2	/yakapa-nesʔa-we-·-ka/ [yakpanesʔo·ka]	/yakapa-nesʔa-no-we-·-ka/ †[yakpanesʔano·ka]
	3	/yakapa-nesʔa-we-ʔe/ [yakpanesʔoʔ]	/yakapa-nesʔa-no-we-ʔe/ †[yakpanesʔanoʔ]
PLURAL	1	/yakapa-wesʔa-we-ʔe-s/ [yakpo·sʔoʔs]	/yakapa-wesʔa-no-we-ʔe-s/ †[yakpo·sʔanoʔs]
	2	/yakapa-wesʔa-we-·-ka/ [yakpo·sʔo·ka]	/yakapa-wesʔa-no-we-·-ka/ †[yakpo·sʔano·ka]
	3	/yakapa-we-ʔe-yuk/ [yakpoʔoyuk]	/yakapa-no-we-ʔe-yuk/ †[yakpanoʔoyuk]

† Form not attested in texts, elicited from native speakers, or found in previous publications but consistent with the grammar.

(23a) **With continuous marker, no reduplication:**

Ha·csokonay-la "saxʔay-e·-ka-k henox (TT 3.16)
Coyote-NOM.SG arrow-yonder-PL-ACC good

yaknanoʔ
yaka-na-no-we-ʔe," no-k-laknoʔo.
shoot-ABL-CONT-DECL-NP say-PART-EVID
'Coyote said: "One is shooting the arrows well." '

Table 3.6. Past tense verb paradigm

NUMBER	PERSON	RECENT PAST	RECENT PAST CONTINUOUS
		(*-ʔe·/ʔei/ʔe*)	(*-no- . . . -ʔe·/ʔei/ʔe*)
SINGULAR	1	/yakapa-we-ʔe·-ʔ/ [yakpoʔo·ʔ] 'I hit it,' etc.	/yakapa-no-we-ʔe·-ʔ/ †[yakpanoʔo·ʔ] 'I used to hit, was hitting it,' etc.
	2	/yakapa-we-ʔei-no/ [yakpoʔoino]	/yakapa-no-we-ʔei-no/ †[yakpanoʔoino]
	3	/yakapa-we-ʔe/ [yakpoʔo]	/yakapa-no-we-ʔe/ †[yakpanoʔo]
DUAL	1	/yakapa-nesʔa-we-ʔe·-ʔ/ [yakpanesʔoʔo·ʔ]	/yakapa-nesʔa-no-we-ʔe·-ʔ/ †[yakpanesʔanoʔo·ʔ]
	2	/yakapa-nesʔa-we-ʔei-no/ [yakpanesʔoʔoino]	/yakapa-nesʔa-no-we-ʔei-no/ †[yakpanesʔanoʔoino]
	3	/yakapa-nesʔa-we-ʔe/ [yakpanesʔoʔo]	/yakapa-nesʔa-no-we-ʔe/ †[yakpanesʔanoʔo]
PLURAL	1	/yakapa-wesʔa-we-ʔe·-ʔ/ [yakpo·sʔoʔo·ʔ]	/yakapa-wesʔa-no-we-ʔe·-ʔ/ †[yakpo·sʔanoʔo·ʔ]
	2	/yakapa-wesʔa-we-ʔei-no/ [yakpo·sʔoʔoino]	/yakapa-wesʔa-we-ʔei-no/ †[yakpo·sʔanoʔoino]
	3	/yakapa-we-ʔe-lok/ [yakpoʔolok]	/yakapa-no-we-ʔe-lok/ †[yakpanoʔolok]

† Form not attested in texts, elicited from native speakers, or found in previous publications but consistent with the grammar.

(23b) **With no continuous marker, but reduplication:**

ʔa·x-ʔa·-yʔik	ta-kla-na-t	lo-lopo·-nesʔe-k-laknoʔo.	(TT 3.14)
water-DEF-ALL	move.DU-down-ABL-SS.CONS	RED-dive-DU-PART-EVID	

'Both of them went down and kept diving into the water, supposedly.'

Table 3.7. Near future tense verb paradigm

NUMBER	PERSON	NEAR FUTURE (=FUT+PRES)	NEAR FUTURE CONTINUOUS
SINGULAR	1	/yakapa-a·tewa-we-ʔe-s/ [yakpa·tewo·ʔs] 'I am about to hit it,' etc.	/yakapa-a·tewa-no-we-ʔe-s/ [yakpa·tono·ʔs] 'I am about to be hitting it,' etc.
	2	/yakapa-a·tewa-we-·-ka/ †[yakpa·tewo·ka]	/yakapa-a·tewa-no-we-·-ka/ †[yakpa·tono·ka]
	3	/yakapa-a·tewa-we-ʔe/ †[yakpa·tewoʔ]	/yakapa-a·tewa-no-we-ʔe/ †[yakpa·tonoʔ]
DUAL	1	/yakapa-a·tewa- nesʔa-we-ʔe-s/ †[yakpa·to·nesʔoʔs]	/yakapa-a·tewa-nesʔa-no-we-ʔe-s/ †[yakpa·to·nesʔanoʔs]
	2	/yakapa-a·tewa- nesʔa-we-·-ka/ †[yakpa·tonesʔo·ka]	/yakapa-a·tewa- nesʔa-no-we-·-ka/ †[yakpa·tonesʔano·ka]
	3	/yakapa-a·tewa-nes'a-we-ʔe/ †[yakpa·to·nesʔoʔ]	/yakapa-a·tewa-nes'a-no-we-ʔe/ †[yakpa·to·nesʔanoʔ]
PLURAL	1	/yakapa-a·tewa-wesʔa-we-ʔe-s/ †[yakpa·tewo·sʔoʔs]	/yakapa-a·tewa-wesʔa-no-we-ʔe-s/ †[yakpa·tewo·sʔanoʔs]
	2	/yakapa-a·tewa-wesʔa-we-·-ka/ †[yakpa·tewo·sʔo·ka]	/yakapa-a·tewa-wesʔa-no-we-·-ka/ †[yakpa·tewo·sʔano·ka]
	3	/yakapa-a·tewa-we-ʔe-yuk/ †[yakpa·tewoʔoyuk]	/yakapa-a·tewa-no-we-ʔe-yuk/ †[yakpa·tonoʔoyuk]

† Form not attested in texts, elicited from native speakers, or found in previous publications but consistent with the grammar.

(23c) **With both continuous marker and reduplication:**

"we·lʔa	hexalʔoy-a·ʔas	ʔe-no-k!	k-e·-na-naco·-no-kwa!"	(TT 3.8)
Ouch	ant-many	be-CONT-MIR	1.OBJ-REFL-RED-bite-CONT-MIR	

'Ouch! There are a bunch of ants! They keep biting me over and over!'

In some cases, reduplication has been lexicalized as part of the stem:

Table 3.8. Remote future tense verb paradigm

NUMBER	PERSON	DISTANT FUTURE (=FUT+PAST)	DISTANT FUTURE CONTINUOUS
SINGULAR	1	/yakapa-a·tewa-we-ʔe·-ʔ/ [yakpa·tewoʔo·ʔ] 'I will hit it'	/yakapa-a·tewa-no-we-ʔe·-ʔ/ [yakpa·tonoʔo·ʔ] 'I will be hitting it'
	2	/yakapa-a·tewa-we-ʔei-no/ †[yakpa·tewoʔoino]	/yakapa-a·tewa-no-we-ʔei-no/ †[yakpa·tonoʔoino]
	3	/yakapa-a·tewa-we-ʔe/ †[yakpa·tewoʔo]	/yakapa-a·tewa-no-we-ʔe/ †[yakpa·tonoʔo]
DUAL	1	/yakapa-a·tewa-nesʔa-we-ʔe·-ʔ/ †[yakpa·tonesʔoʔo·ʔ]	/yakapa-a·tewa-nesʔa-no-we-ʔe·-ʔ/ †[yakpa·tonesʔanoʔo·ʔ]
	2	/yakapa-a·tewa-nesʔa-we-ʔei-no/ †[yakpa·tonesʔoʔoino]	/yakapa-a·tewa-nesʔa-no-we-ʔei-no/ †[yakpa·tonesʔanoʔoino]
	3	/yakapa-a·tewa-nesʔa-we-ʔe/ †[yakpa·tonesʔoʔo]	/yakapa-a·tewa-nesʔa-no-we-ʔe/ †[yakpa·tonesʔanoʔo]
PLURAL	1	/yakapa-a·tewa-wesʔa-we-ʔe·-ʔ/ †[yakpa·tewo·sʔoʔo·ʔ]	/yakapa-a·tewa-wesʔa-no-we-ʔe·-ʔ/ †[yakpa·tewo·sʔoʔo·ʔ]
	2	/yakapa-a·tewa-wesʔa-we-ʔei-no/ †[yakpa·tewo·sʔoʔoino]	/yakapa-a·tewa-wesʔa-no-we-ʔei-no/ †[yakpa·tewo·sʔoʔoino]
	3	/yakapa-a·tewa-we-ʔe-lok/ †[yakpa·tewoʔolok]	/yakapa-a·tewa-no-we-ʔe-lok/ †[yakpa·tewoʔolok]

† Form not attested in texts, elicited from native speakers, or found in previous publications but consistent with the grammar.

(24) ʔe·-ta ha·-na-ci-cxile-xey-ne-k-laknoʔo. (TT 6.14)
be-SS.NPURP move.SG-ABL-RED-run-far-LOC-ABL-PART-EVID
'Then they went and ran far off.'

Finally, Tonkawa also indicates the person and number of objects in the first and second person and the number of objects in the third person (table 3.9).

Unlike subject markers, object markers never vary for tense or modality; also unlike subject markers, object markers are not found in dedicated templatic slots. The first-person object prefix *ke-*, for example, is found before any reflexive, caus-

Table 3.9. Object agreement

PERSON	SINGULAR	PLURAL
1	ke-	ke-we- [kew]
2	-V·-	we- . . . -V·-
3	Ø	we-

ative, or thematic prefix, generally at the beginning of the word; the *we-* object pluralizer is found immediately after *ke-*:

(25) kewya·lo·nto·xa·to·notaʔa (TT 10.5)
hemaxan-we·ʔis "ke-we-ya·lo·n-to·x-a·tewa-no-t-aʔa!" no-k-laknoʔo
turkey-one 1.OBJ-OBJ.PL-kill-finish-FUT-CONT-EP-3.ASS say-PART-EVID
'One turkey said: "He's going to finish us all off!"'

The only exception when *ke-* does not stand immediately at the beginning of a word is when the agreement marker is stranded between two verb roots compounded together, as in (26) and (27):

(26) ʔe·-kla ʔawas-ayon-wa·-ʔa·-la "ya-mʔacx-an te·l (TT 16.18)
be-DS.NSIM buffalo-itch-OBV-DEF-NOM.SG TH-sneeze-GER here

so·l-**ke**-to·xa-kwa!" no-k-laknoʔo.
drip-**1.OBJ**-finish-MIR say-PART-EVID
'Then the itchy buffalo said: "Something has dripped onto my nose!"'

(27) "ya·c-**ke**-xwel-pe-w," no-k-laknoʔo. (TT 7.6)
watch-**1.OBJ**-miss-NEG-IMP say-PART-EVID
'"Don't lose sight of me," [the alligator] said.'

Second-person objects, however, are marked only by the insertion of an extra mora and are found immediately after the future suffix *-a·tewa-* in positive polarity forms or immediately preceding the negative suffix in negative polarity forms (Hoijer 1933, 69):

(28a) [yaca·tonoʔs]
yac-a·tewa-no-we-ʔe-s
see-FUT-CONT-DECL-PRES-1.SBJ
'I will be seeing him.'

(28b) [yacatewa·noʔs]
yac-a·tewa-·-no-we-ʔe-s
see-FUT-2.OBJ-CONT-DECL-PRES-1.SBJ
'I will be seeing you.'

(29a) [yacapa·tonoʔs]
yac-ap-a·tewa-no-we-ʔe-s
see-NEG-FUT-CONT-DECL-PRES-1.SBJ
'I won't be seeing him.'

(29b) [yaca·pa·tonoʔs]
yac-ap-·-a·tewa-no-we-ʔe-s
see-NEG-2.OBJ-FUT-CONT-DECL-PRES-1.SBJ
'I won't be seeing you.'

Because the rule of conflation is sensitive to the moraic quantity of the vowels it applies to, the insertion of this extra mora has the effect of bleeding this rule. Even more interestingly, when the second-person object agreement moves forward in the verb form to be after the negator, the conflation rule affecting the future suffix goes into effect as usual. Second-person object agreement thus poses an interesting rare example of morphology that not only is mobile (itself a grammatical *rarum*) but whose effect interacts with phonology to create dissimilar surface paradigms.

3.2.2. *Modality*

Tonkawa features a rather rich array of modal paradigms expressing a variety of different kinds of epistemic and deontic modal readings: interrogative, assertive, deontic, intentive, jussive, imperative, and mirative. Some paradigms, such as the interrogative and imperative, exist only in certain person-number combinations, while others have full paradigms, such as the assertive. Some moods exist in multiple tenses and aspects (e.g., the interrogative), while others are morphologically tenseless (e.g., the imperative). Although all of these are more marked than the declarative in the sense that they are more infrequent in texts, from a morphological perspective they usually have the same amount of morphological expression: an overt modal affix plus one or more person-number affixes specific to that mood.

The **interrogative**, used to create questions, is typical in this sense (table 3.10). Instead of a *-we* suffix found in the declarative, the interrogative is formed with a glottal stop in that templatic slot as well as another in final position, with person-number affixes falling in between. It takes both present and past tense forms as well as prospective and continuous aspect markers (*yakpa·toʔkaʔ, yakpanoʔkaʔ,* etc.).

Table 3.10. Interrogative verb paradigm

		INTERROGATIVE PRESENT	INTERROGATIVE PAST
SINGULAR	2	/yakapa-ʔ-ka-ʔe/ [yakpaʔkaʔ] 'Do you hit it?' etc.	/yakapa-ʔei-no-ʔ/ [yakpeynoʔ] 'Did you hit it?' etc.
DUAL	2	/yakapa-nesʔe-ʔ-ka-ʔe/ [yakpanesʔeʔkaʔ]	/yakapa-nesʔe-ʔei-no-ʔ/ [yakpanesʔeynoʔ
PLURAL	2	/yakapa-wesʔe-ʔ-ka-ʔe/ [yakpo·sʔeʔkaʔ]	/yakapa-wesʔe-ʔei-no-ʔ/ [yakpo·sʔeynoʔ]

Source: Hoijer 1933, 89.

(30) (TT 18.8)

kwa·n-la	wa·-teca	ha-kla-ta-k-e·-la-k	ya·c-ape-[ʔ]-ka-ʔ
woman-NOM.SG	this-place	move.SG-down-CIS-PART-this-SG-ACC	see-NEG-INTER-2.SG-INTER

'A woman came down this way. Didn't you see her?'

The **assertive** mood is used to indicate that the speaker believes the statement to be a true fact, a kind of antidubitative (Hoijer 1933, 86; table 3.11). Its marker *-ʔa·* or *-ʔaʔa* follows any future or continuous suffix and precedes any person-number marker.

(31) (TT 16.21)

ʔe·-kwa	ʔawase-pay-xwet-an-wa·-ʔa·-la	"sa·ya
be-DS.SIM	buffalo-bead-wear-GER-OBV-DEF-NOM.SG	1.SG.NOM

ʔe·-n-a·-nʔe-s!	ke-cn-o·sʔe-w!"
be-CONT-ASS-1/2.ASS-1	1.OBJ-leave-1/2.SBJ.PL-IMP

'Meanwhile, the buffalo woman said: "It really is me! Spare me!"'

Hoijer (1933, 86, 93) lists assertive and potential moods separately, but it is clear from the paradigms he lists that these two moods are distinguished only by the additional suffix *-ilʔa* in the third-person forms of the potential: *yakpaylʔa* 'he

Table 3.11. Assertive paradigm

		ASSERTIVE
SINGULAR	1	/yakapa-ʔa·-nʔe-s/ [yakpaʔa·nʔes] 'I do hit it,' etc.
	2	/yakapa-ʔa·-nʔe-i/ [yakpaʔa·nʔey]
	3	/yakapa-ʔaʔa/ [yakpaʔa]
DUAL	1	/yakapa-nesʔa-ʔa·-nʔe-s/ [yakpaʔnesʔa·nʔes]
	2	/yakapa-nesʔa-ʔa·-nʔe-i/ [yakpanesʔa·ney]
	3	/yakapa-nesʔa-ʔaʔa/ [yakpanesʔaʔa]
PLURAL	1	/yakapa-wesʔa-ʔa·-nʔe-s/ [yakpo·sʔa·nʔes]
	2	/yakapa-wesʔa-ʔa·-nʔe-i/ [yakpo·sʔa·ney]
	3	*not attested*

might strike him.' It is likely that this suffix is in fact a recently grammaticalized clitic that attaches to assertive paradigm forms, rather than being part of a completely separate potential paradigm.

Another modal form with a full paradigm is the **deontic** mood, which indicates that the subject should or ought to perform some action or be in some state. Called the "declarative-assertive" mood by Hoijer (1933), presumably because he argued that it grammaticalized from a combination of declarative and assertive mood affixes, it is characterized by the suffix *-nwa·* or *-nwaʔa* (table 3.12).

A number of moods are confined to particular combinations of person and number.

Two morphological mood paradigms, the **jussive** and the **imperative**, both serve to issue commands to third-person and second-person members of the

Table 3.12. Deontic paradigm

		DEONTIC *(-nwa / -nwaʔa)*
SINGULAR	1	/yakapa-nwa·-sʔ/ [yakpanwa·s'] 'I should hit it,' etc.
	2	/yakapa-nwa·-nʔei/ [yakpanwa·nʔei]
	3	/yakapa-nwa·-ʔe/ [yakpanwaʔ]
DUAL	1	/yakapa-nes'e-nwa·-s'/ [yakpanes'enwa·s']
	2	/yakapa-nes'e-nwa·-nʔei/ [yakpanes'enwa·nʔei]
	3	/yakapa-nes'e-nwa·-ʔe/ [yakpanes'enwaʔ]
PLURAL	1	/yakapa-we·s'e-nwa·-s'/ [yakpo·s'enwa·s']
	2	/yakapa-we·s'e-nwa·-nʔei/ [yakpo·s'enwa·nʔei]
	3	/yakapa-nwaʔa-nik/ [yakpanwaʔanik]

discourse, respectively. In other languages (e.g., Ancient Greek), paradigmatic similarities would motivate treating them as members of a single paradigm, but the Tonkawa forms bear only similar semantics and otherwise have completely separate modal affixes, *-e·l* and—*w*, so it is probably best to treat them morphologically as separate moods (table 3.13).

(32) (TT 4.8)

	ʔo·sʔow		
ma·tan	ʔe-we·sʔa-w	ya-coxʔ-an-te·-la	naw-e·l
quick	move-1/2.SBJ.PL-IMP	TH-camp-GER-this-NOM	burn-JUSS

'Be quick! Let this camp burn!'

Table 3.13. Jussive and imperative paradigms

	Person	JUSSIVE	*Person*	IMPERATIVE
SINGULAR	3	/yakapa-e·l/ [yakpe·l] 'Let him hit it,' etc.	2	/yakapa-w/ [yakpaw] '[You] hit it!' etc.
DUAL	3	/yakapa-nesʔe-e·l/ [yakpanesʔe·l]	2	/yakapa-nesʔe-w/ [yakpanesʔew]
PLURAL	3	/yakapa-wesʔa-e·l / [yakpo·sʔe·l]	2	/yakapa-wesʔa-w/ [yakpo·sow]

Source: Hoijer 1933, 92, 93.

Another mode mostly limited to a single person-number combination is the **mirative** suffix *-kwa*, used to express surprising or unexpected actions or states:

(33) yo·mʔa·to·nokwa! (TT 1.9)

"ya·ce-w!	kwa·low	yo·mʔ-a·tewa-no-kwa!"	no-k-laknoʔo.
look-IMP	big	rain-FUT-CONT-MIR	say-PART-EVID

'"Look! It's going to be raining a lot!" [Rabbit] said.'

Hoijer (1933, 89) indicates one textual *hapax* of a first-person mirative form: *hoʔoxawe·kwaʔas* 'I have stolen it!'

Another kind of modal paradigm is the **intentive** suffix *-a·haʔa*, which exists only in the first person and indicates that the speaker has plans to perform some action (table 3.14).

Table 3.14. Intentive paradigm

	Person	INTENTIVE
SINGULAR	1	/yakapa-a·haʔa/ [yakpa·haʔa] 'I'm going to hit it, intend to hit it,' etc.
DUAL	1	/yakapa-nesʔe-a·haʔa/ [yakpanesʔa·haʔa]
PLURAL	1	/yakapa-wesʔe-a·haʔa/ [yakapo·sʔa·haʔa]

Unlike the other moods, according to Hoijer (1933) the intentive is not compatible with the future suffix *-a·tewa.*[5]

Two modal paradigms attach not to the regular verb stem but to the participial stem. The **hortative** is marked with *-(ʔ)e·* and is used to make urgent suggestions:

(34) ʔe··kla Ha·csokonay-la "saxʔay-te··las yake-xamyo··se-k-e!" (TT 3.12)
be-DS.NSIM Coyote-NOM.SG arrow-this-INST do-arrow.contest-1-PART-HORT
'Then Coyote [said]: "Let's have an shooting contest with this arrow!"'

Another paradigm used abundantly in the extant texts is the **evidential**, which sets the speaker at one remove from confirming the veracity of the statement and can usually be translated by 'supposedly.' It is formed by suffixing *-laknoʔo* to the *-k* or *-n* participle forms of verbs:

(35) ha-txil-na-k-laknoʔo ʔe··t he-co-cxo··-k-wa··ʔa··la-k (TT 17.24)
move.SG-out-ABL-PART-EVID be-SS.CONS REFL-RED-fear-PART-OBV-DEF-SG-ACC

nexel-ci-cxwa-no-k-laknoʔo.
$drag_1$-RED-$drag_2$-CONT-PART-EVID
'So he went out and dragged the monster around.'

(36) ʔe··t xa·ya-t lasas-a·tak he-pcana-n-laknoʔo. (TT 17.32)
be-SS.CONS move.SG.AUG-SS.CONS bald-very REFL-sheer-PART-EVID
'So they arrived and shaved themselves very bald.'

3.3. Morphological Valence Markers

One feature of many highly polysynthetic languages is that most roots do not bear any underlying specification for transitivity. In such languages most roots are rather built up from more basic primitives in which surface patterns of transitivity are explicitly marked with overt affixal morphology. Tonkawa's verbal morphology is a fairly typical example of such a language: a root can take multiple verbal operators that increase, decrease, or leave unaltered the number of participants in an action while still altering argument structure. In many cases, the valency affixes have been lexicalized so that surface meanings are no longer semantically compositional.

5. Hoijer (1933, 91) says that the intentive is not found with the continuous marker *-no*. However, at least one occurrence of the continuous intentive is found in TT 4.16.

Tonkawa relies on a number of valence increasing affixes of different origins and different levels of productivity. The most basic, as well as the most productive, is a **causative** affix *nes-*, which can attach to underlyingly transitive (37) as well as underlyingly intransitive (38) predicates:

(37) "taxas-wa·ta-ʔas | Ka·nos-e-pay-xwet-an-la-k | henox-la-k (TT 1.6)
be.day-this.time-INST | Mexican-REFL-bead-wear-GER-SG-ACC (='Mexican woman') | pretty-SG-ACC

kenesta·ʔa·tonoʔ
ke-nes-ta·ʔ-a·tewa-no-we-ʔe."
1.OBJ-CAUS-take.hold-FUT-CONT-DECL-PRES
'This very day they will make me marry a pretty Mexican woman.'

(38) kewnescoxnapa·to·noʔ (TT 3.10)
"ke-we-[nes-coxn]-ap-a·tewa-no-we-ʔ," no-k-laknoʔo.
1.OBJ-OBJ.PL-[CAUS-sleep]-NEG-FUT-CONT-DECL-PRES say-PART-EVID
'"They won't let us fall asleep," [the woman] said supposedly.'

In addition to *nes-*, other markers of lesser productivity are also attested: *ʔe·(y)-* and *ya-*:

(39) we·ʔis-pax ʔey-kana-txil-na-k-laknoʔo. (TT 13.9)
one-just CAUS-take-out-ABL-PART-EVID

ʔe·-kla ya·lo·na-k-laknoʔo ʔe·-t yaxa-no-n-laknoʔo.
be-DS.NSIM kill-PART-EVID be-SS.CONS eat-CONT-PART-EVID
'He took out just one [buffalo], killed it, and ate it.'

(40) ʔe·-kla Tanmaslak-la "ya-kwlaxe-w," no-k-laknoʔo. (TT 1.7)
be-DS.NSIM Rabbit-NOM.SG TH-open-IMP CONT-PART-EVID
'Then Rabbit said: "Open it."'

These alternative causative markers probably belong to different periods of grammaticalization and productivity. The marker *ya-* belongs to an old semi-productive series of thematic markers, relics of an older stratum of grammatical particles that altered valence and semantic properties of the predicate and in many cases is no longer truly separable from the root. By contrast, *ʔe(y)-* belongs to a very recent layer of verb-verb compounds and probably means little more than 'do X.' Neither is as productive as *nes-*.

Another kind of affix that increases transitivity is the comitative affix *ta·-*, which functions as a kind of **applicative**:

(41) Ha·ʔako·n-osas-la ʔekaka·-la-k (TT 16.1)
man-young-NOM.SG maternal.grandmother-SG-ACC

ta·-ya-coxʔa-no-k-laknoʔo.
COM-TH-camp-CONT-PART-EVID
'A young man was living with his mother's mother.'

There is some evidence that the comitative affix in some words undergoes back-copying of the vowel length or, contrarily, induces dissimilation if the following syllable is identical:

(42a) wetataxkoʔs (TT 17.28)
we-ta-ta-xka-we-ʔe-s
OBJ.PL-COM-move.PL-back-DECL-PAST-1
'I brought them [here].'

(42b) ʔe·-kla kwa·-kwan-wa·-ka ta-sa-ta-na-n-laknoʔo (TT 17.27)
be-DS.NSIM RED-woman-OBV-NOM.PL COM-RED-move.PL-ABL-PART-EVID

ya-cox-ʔan-ʔa·-yʔik.
TH-camp-GER-DEF-ALL
'So the women went back to the camp with him.'

In (42b), the reduplicant ought to be realized as *ta-*, because the verbal root is *ta-*. In this case, however, the addition of the comitative with backcopying would create three identical syllables in a row, which Tonkawa phonology apparently avoids.

Tonkawa also has morphology that reduces valence. By far the most frequent is the **reflexive** affix *he-*, which comes in the slot immediately before the verb root (43a), unless the verb root has been reduplicated (43b):

(43a) ʔe·-t xa·ya-t lasas-a·tak he-pcana-n-laknoʔo. (TT 17.32)
be-SS.CONS move.SG.AUG-SS.CONS bald-very REFL-sheer-PART-EVID
'They arrived and shaved themselves very bald.'

(43b)	ʔekwan-esxa-wa·-ka	ta-kla-ta-t	he-xa-xano·-no-k-laknoʔo.	(TT 6.14)
	dog-big-OBV-NOM.PL	move.PL-down-CIS-SS.CONS	REFL-RED-drink-CONT-PART-EVID	

'The horses came down and kept on drinking for themselves.'

However, this most basic use of the reflexive to indicate coreference between a subject and an object is less frequent than its use to indicate the subject's non-agentivity:

(44)	ʔey-kana-kxo-n-a·to-k-a·-la	samox-a·tak	(TT 17.33)
	CAUS-throw-in-ABL-FUT-PART-DEF-NOM.SG	red-very	

he-yace-no-k-laknoʔo.
REFL-look-CONT-PART-EVID
'The [buffalo] about to throw [Little One] into [the fire] was looking very red.'

In some cases, both true reflexives and passive-like uses of the reflexive are used in the same clause. In (45) below, the first example relates how some young men go down to a river to bathe themselves, after which they are magically transformed back into their original forms (geese). Because the narrator does not know or wish to relate by what means the young men are transformed, he uses a passive-like reflexive:

(45)	ʔe·-kla	losos-ʔita	ta-kla-na-t	he-pnonoxo·-t	(TT 17.36)
	be-DS.NSIM	all-DET	move.PL-down-ABL-SS.CONS	REFL-bathe.PLUR-SS.CONS	

waʔanwa·ʔal	he-ykoʔo-n-laknoʔo.
just.as.before	REFL-make-PART-EVID

'So they all went down and bathed themselves and were turned into what they were before.'

Another kind of valence morphology is that used to indicate **reciprocals**. This consists of a prefix *he(·)-* plus a suffix *-V·yewa-*, frequently with verb root reduplication (Hoijer 1933, 76–77):

(46a) [henpapasxa·yewoʔ]
/he-na-pa-pasaxa-V·yewa-we-ʔe/
RECIP$_1$-TH-RED-play.shinny-RECIP$_2$-DECL-PRES
'They play shinny with each other.'

(46b) [he·ʔatna·yewoʔ]
/he·-ʔatanawa-V·yewa-we-ʔe/
RECIP$_1$-love-RECIP$_2$-DECL-PRES
'They love each other.'

(46c) [hetatxa·yewoʔ]
/he·-ta-taxa-V·yewa-we-ʔe/
RECIP$_1$-RED-talk-RECIP$_2$-DECL-PRES
'They talk among themselves.'

(46d) [hecocoxa·yewoʔ]
/he-co-coxana-V·yewa-we-ʔe/
RECIP$_1$-RED-sleep-RECIP$_2$-DECL-PRES
'They sleep with each other.'

3.4. Mixed Categories and Derivational Morphology

One side effect of polysynthesis is that many nominals that in other languages would be underived are in Tonkawa derived from verbal forms. In particular, nominalizations and participial forms stand out for both the frequency and ubiquity of their use. A very large number of Tonkawa nouns are derived from underlyingly verbal stems with an *-(a)n* suffix; in the corpus of texts these are marked as **gerunds**.

(47a) ya-tmax-an-la-k (TT 1.1)
TH-shatter-GER-SG-ACC
'a watermelon ' (lit. 'shattering thing')

(47b) Ka·nos-e-pay-xwet-an-la-k (TT 1.6)
Mexican-REFL-bead-wear-GER-SG-ACC
'a Mexican woman' (lit. 'Mexican bead-wearer')

(47c) he-ylapa-n-ʔa·yay-te·-ca (TT 1.9)
REFL-stand-GER-inside-this-place
'here inside the tree' (lit. 'thing that stands')

(47d) ya-talp-an-kwa·low-la (TT 1.11)
TH-fry-GER-big-NOM.SG
'a big fry-bread' (lit. 'fried thing')

As one can readily see, the nominalizations have generally undergone significant semantic shift as a result of their lexicalization.

Like gerunds, **participles** are derived from verbs, formally through four different means: the addition of suffixes *-k* or *-n*, the lengthening of the vowel that precedes the participial slot, or no overt marking. Like gerunds, participles allow the addition of otherwise purely nominal morphological categories such as obviation, definiteness, number, and case.

(48) ***k*-participle**

"ʔekwan-esxaw-yax-an-aklanan-e-co-cxo·-**k̲**-la-k (TT 19.10)
dog-big-eat-GER-sharp-REFL-RED-fear-**P̲A̲R̲T̲**-SG-ACC

ʔey-ka-kayc-a·to-k-noʔo."
CAUS-RED-cut.off.at.joint-FUT-PART-EVID
'"That frighteningly sharp grass ought to be cut down."'

(49) ***n*-participle**

He-co-cxo·-k-wa·-ʔa·-la-k	he-wle-t	(TT 4.7)
REFL-RED-fear-PART-OBV-DEF-SG-ACC	REFL-catch-SS.CONS	

ta·-he·-sok-yo·-no-**n̲**-laknoʔo.
PVB-REFL-fight-RECIP-CONT-**P̲A̲R̲T̲**-EVID
'[A bunch of wolves] cornered the monster and were fighting with him.'

(50) **Vowel length participle**

kwa·ko·-tak	pancale-k-laknoʔo	ʔa·x-wa·ʔal-sokona-·-la	(TT 17.19)
wide-very	open.mouth-PART-EVID	water-time-own-**P̲A̲R̲T̲**-NOM.SG	

ʔe·-t	wixwan-wa·-ʔa·-la-k	wa-wana-ta
be-SS.CONS	small-OBV-DEF-SG-ACC	RED-swallow-SS.NPURP

'the One Who Owns All the Water opened up his mouth real wide, swallowed up the Little One'

(51) **Null participle**

ʔe·-kla	Ha·csokonay-la	"neykanak-xa·-xa-no-**[̲Ø̲]̲**-ʔa·-la	(TT 12.5)
be-DS.NSIM	Coyote-NOM.SG	first-move.SG.AUG-AUG-CONT-**P̲A̲R̲T̲**-DEF-NOM.SG	

xa·-ʔa·-la-k	losos	to·x-a·to-nwa-ʔ."
fat-DEF-SG-ACC	all	finish-FUT-DEON-DEON.3

'So Coyote said: "The first one to get there gets to finish off the fat."'

Unlike participles in English and most European languages, participles in Tonkawa can inflect for the person and number of the internal subject (Hoijer 1933, 100; see table 3.15).

Table 3.15. Participial paradigm

		PARTICIPLE
SINGULAR	1	/yakapa-se-k/ [yakpasek] 'I who hit it,' etc.
	2	/yakapa-ne-k/ [yakpanek]
	3	/yakapa-k/ [yakpak]
DUAL	1	/yakapa-nesʔe-se-k/ [yakpaʔnesʔesek]
	2	/yakapa-nesʔe-ne-k/ [yakpanesʔenek]
	3	/yakapa-nesʔe-k/ [yakpanesʔek]
PLURAL	1	/yakapa-wesʔe-se-k/ [yakpo·sʔesek]
	2	/yakapa-wesʔe-ne-k/ [yakpo·sʔenek]
	3	/yakapa-n/ [yakpan]

3.5. Incorporation

While nominalizations and participles fit somewhat well into cross-linguistic expectations about what a "word" might look like, Tonkawa quite regularly and freely incorporates a wide-range of materials into both nominal and verbal heads. In some cases, these incorporated elements are highly lexicalized and not semantically compositional, while in other cases they appear to be spontaneous formations by the speaker. The most common kind of incorporation represent substantives that have been incorporated into verbal predicates or nominal roots, as in (52):

Substantive incorporation

(52a) he-pay-xwet-an-la xa·-xa-k-laknoʔo (TT 16.1)
REFL-bead-wear-GER-NOM.SG move.SG.AUG-AUG-PART-EVID
'The woman [lit. 'bead-wearing one'] came [to them]'

(52b) "heʔe-ca maslak-a·ʔako·n-la kwa·low-la he-cn-a·we" (TT 1.16)
DIST-LOC buffalo-man-NOM.SG big-NOM.SG TH-lie-PERF
'Over yonder is a big bull buffalo'

(52c) "xecwa[l]-la he-ynaw-kapay-ʔ-aʔa." (TT 7.3)
alligator-NOM.SG REFL-win.game-nothing-do-ASS.3.SG
'"The alligator can't be beat."'

Like substantives, predicates can also be incorporated into other predicates. Resultative predication seems to consist entirely of incorporation of such verb-verb incorporation (53). The line in TT 7.3 quoted above, for example, is followed by the verb-verb incorporation in (54):

Resultative predication by incorporation

(53a) ne-kel-nacka-k-laknoʔo. (TT 3.15)
TH-drown-kill-PART-EVID
'He drowned him to death.'

(53b) kwe·-la-k taʔane-t yaxwe-ncaka-k-laknoʔo. (TT 9.7)
club-SG-ACC grasp-SS.CONS club-kill-PART-EVID
'He grabbed his club and clubbed him to death.'

(53c) xʔop-co-cow-nacka-k-laknoʔo. (TT 18.16)
fart_1-RED-fart_2-kill-PART-EVID
'He killed him by farting.'

(54) kewya·lo·nto·xanoʔ
ke-we-ya·lo·n-to·xa-no-we-ʔe. (TT 7.3)
1OBJ-OBJ.PL-kill-finish-CONT-DECL-PRES
'He is killing us all off.'

Although, in some cases, it seems to have been grammaticalizing toward a new kind of marker of perfective aspect, this root is nonetheless still an autonomous verb:

(55) wetoxanoʔo (TT 4.2)
“Hc co cxo· k·la we-toxa-no-we-ʔe.”
REFL-RED-fear-PART-NOM.SG OBJ.PL-finish-CONT-DECL-PAST
‘“A monster finished them off.”’

Predicative stems also frequently become incorporated into nominal heads. Though single incorporatees are most frequent (56), multiple predicative incorporatees are not uncommon (57):

Predicative incorporation (single incorporatee)

(56a) ʔe[·]-kla ta-na-nesʔe-k-laknoʔo. cakaw-kwa·low-ʔa·-yʔik. (TT 19.15)
be-DS.NSIM move.PL-ABL-DU-PART-EVID river-big-DEF-ALL
‘So the two of them went off to the big river.’

(56b) Ha·csokonay-la ha-kla-na-t ya-coxʔ-an-a·naxok-wa·-yʔik. (TT 4.1)
Coyote-SG.NOM move.SG-down-ABL-SS.PURP TH-camp-GER-big-OBV-ALL
‘Coyote went down to the big camp.’

Predicative incorporation (multiple incorporatees)

(57a) ʔe·-kla ʔekwan-esxaw-maslak-pax-wa·-ʔa·-la (TT 19.4)
be-DS.NSIM dog-big-white-only-OBV-DEF-NOM.SG

“na·kw sa·sik k-a·-yoxo-w,” no-k-laknkoʔo.
all.right 1.SG.ACC 1.OBJ-TH-ride-IMP say-PART-EVID
‘So the horse that was white all over supposedly said: “All right, ride me.”’

(57b) “kokon-ke-la ha·csokonay-eykaʔay-samox-ka-k (TT 19.4)
chief-1.SG.POSS-NOM.SG wolf-big-red-PL-ACC

[k]e-nes-ʔe-y-wey-coʔ,”
1.OBJ-CAUS-CAUS-TH-bind-RES
‘My chief has made me catch big red wolves.’

Taken to an extreme, this process of predicate incorporation can consume entire sentences, such as the one quoted above in (10b). Another example is:

(58) Ka·nos-[[ya-tmax-an]-wa·-ʔa·-la-k-sokano]-ʔa·-la (TT 1.5)
Mexican-[[TH-shatter-GER]-OBV-DEF-SGACC-own]-DEF-NOM.SG
'The Mexican who owned the watermelon'

Without access to native speakers, how do we know that these long agglutinations are truly morphological words? Are the nominal grammatical suffixes, in other words, really affixes attaching to nominal stems or are they clitics? The theoretical literature on wordhood holds no universal consensus about what exactly are the criteria that identify "words," crosslinguistically, capable of distinguishing these possibilities. However, in an extended discussion on whether such a crosslinguistic definition is possible, M. Haspelmath (2011, 38) identified ten criteria often mentioned in the literature on morphosyntactic wordhood:

(59) a. Potential pauses
b. Free occurrence
c. External mobility and internal fixedness
d. Uninterruptibility
e. Nonselectivity
f. Noncoordinatability
g. Anaphoric islandhood
h. Nonextractability
i. Morphophonological idiosyncrasies
j. Deviations from biuniqueness

For most of these criteria, it is clear that the Tonkawa data single out definite nominal grammatical suffixes as affixes and not clitics. Negative evidence is not directly available from corpora, but there are no attestations of their occurrence on their own (60a). Thus they are also not extractable or coordinable; nor do they take scope over multiple noun phrases (60b):

(60a) *wa·-ʔa·-la ha·ʔako·n
OBV-DEF-NOM.SG man
'the man'

(60b) * ha·ʔako·n ʔen kwa·n-wa·-ʔa·-la
man and woman-OBV-DEF-NOM.SG
'The man and the woman'

The obviative and definite suffixes are highly selective: they otherwise attach exclusively to noun stems and never to verbs or other parts of speech. They are also rigidly fixed with respect to one another, since the order of the affixes is always invariant:

Table 3.16. Numerals

NUMERAL	CARDINAL	ORDINAL	ADVERBIAL
1	we·ʔis-pax	neykanak	we·ʔis-ʔis-pax
2	ketay	yaxkosan	ketaya-ʔas
3	metis	mets-ay	mets-ʔas
4	sikit	sikt-ay	sikt-ʔas
5	kaskwa	†kaskw-ay	kaskwa-ʔas
6	sikwa·law	†sikwa·law-ay	†sikwa·law-ʔas
7	sikyeʔestaw	†sikyeʔestaw-ay	†sikyeʔestaw-ʔas
8	sikitye·ʔes	†sikitye·ʔes-ay	†sikitye·ʔes-ʔas
9	sikwe·ʔisxwe·lʔa	†sikwe·ʔisxwe·lʔa-ay	†sikwe·ʔisxwe·lʔa-ʔas
10	sik-pax	†sik-ay-pax	†sik-ʔas-pax
11	†sik-pax-ʔen we·ʔis-pax-ʔen		
12	†sik-pax-ʔen ketay-ʔen		
20	sik-pax-xʔa·la ketay		
100	se·nto we·ʔis-pax		
1000	se·nto sik-pax		

† Form not attested in texts, elicited from native speakers, or found in previous publications but consistent with the grammar.

(61) *kwa·n-ʔa·-wa·-la
woman-DEF-OBV-NOM.SG
'the woman'

As noted above, there is one notable phonological idiosyncrasy, the loss of the glottal stop of the definite suffix after stems ending in /k/; this rather reinforces the affix-like rather than clitic-like character of these suffixes. The only criterion, in fact, that gives one pause is the violation of the putative anaphoric island: the obviation and definite markers modifying 'watermelon' are buried inside a larger morphological complex and should be invisible to external interpretation. In fact, it is now widely recognized that anaphoric islands are violable in many languages (Sadock 1980, 1986; Harris 2006; etc.), so this ought not be taken as too serious a problem. Instead, probably the best analysis is that examples like (58) represent a phonologically null participle, analogous to (51).

3.6. Numerals and Quantifiers

Numerals in Tonkawa are formed according to a decimal primary base with a subbase of four. Numerals from one to five are basic, while numerals between five and ten are constructed with ten as a base, with the exception of eight, which is derived from four (Hoijer 1933, 121–22; see table 3.16).

FOUR

Syntax

Tonkawa constitutes a fairly standard example of nonconfigurational syntax, in that syntactic constituents of clauses, as well as any constituents of noun phrases, may surface in any order. There is remarkably little evidence for syntactic asymmetries below the level of the clause. To begin with, transitive sentences with overt arguments are rare, and most permutations of basic word order appear in the corpus:

(62a) **SVO**

Ha·csokonay-la [. . .]	ya·ce-no-k-laknoʔo [. . .]	ha·ʔako·n-wa·-ʔa·-la-k.	(TT 14.5)
Coyote-NOM.SG [. . .]	see-CONT-PART-EVID [. . .]	man-OBV-DEF-SG-ACC	

'Coyote . . . was seeing the man.'

(62b) **SOV**

ha·ʔako·n-wa·-ʔa·-la	kwe·-ʔa·-la-k	ta·kona-no-k-laknoʔo.	(TT 14.8)
man-OBV-DEF-NOM.SG	club-DEF-SG-ACC	search-CONT-PART-EVID	

'The man was looking for his club.'

(62c) **OVS**

ʔawakcʔe·k-la-k	wa·-lʔas	Ka·nos	yakoʔot yaka-we-ʔe-t	(TT 1.2)
gum-SG-ACC	that-INST	Mexican	make-DECL-PAST-SS.CONS	

nes-e-ylapa-k-lakno?o.
CAUS-REFL-be.upright-PART-EVID
'The Mexican made the gum with it and stood it up.'

(62d) **OSV**

ʔawas-wa·-ʔa-la-k	ʔexwa-la	losos	ha-wa-wne-k-laknoʔo.	(TT 8.6)
meat-OBV-DEF-SG-ACC	buzzard-NOM.SG	all	TH-RED-pack-PART-EVID	

'Buzzard packed all the meat.'

(62e) **VOS**

ka·-na-k-laknoʔo	yanʔa·nwan-kwa·lo-wa·-ʔa·-la-k	Xecwal-wa·-ʔa·-la.	(TT 7.11)
throw-ABL-PART-EVID	iron-big-OBV-DEF-SG-ACC	Alligator-OBV-DEF-NOM.SG	

'Alligator threw the big piece of iron.'

4.1. Phrase Structure

Determining phrase structure asymmetries in an extinct language like Tonkawa, without native speaker judgments, can be challenging. For one thing, we cannot derive categorical negative judgments from corpora, only statistical generalizations. Another reason is that many of the tests that one would use to determine headedness in other languages are lacking or liminal in Tonkawa. For example, determiners like definite articles, obviation markers, and even deictic pronouns, which in English and other languages are freestanding words, in Tonkawa are usually rigidly suffixed. Likewise, as discussed in section 3.5, predicational modifiers also very freely incorporate into the nominal phrase. When nominal nongenitival modifiers surface outside this morphological matrix, they may surface either before or after the modified substantive as in (63) and (64), though they usually occur after:

(63a) **Incorporated modifier**

	ha·na·tewoʔs	(TT 4.9)
"ya-coxʔ-an-**kalak**-eʔe·-k	ha·-na-a·tewa-we-ʔe-s,"	
TH-camp-GER-**other**-yonder-ACC	move.SG-ABL-FUT-DECL-PRES-1	

no-k-laknoʔo	Ha·csokonay-la.
say-PART-EVID	Coyote-NOM.SG

'Coyote said: "I'm going to the other camp over yonder." '

(63b) **Free modifier**

ʔe·-kwa **kalak** tansa·le-wa·-ʔa·-la (TT 22.9)
be-DS.SIM **other** chicken.hawk-OBV-DEF-NOM.SG

ne-nxas-ʔan-kakn-aʔa.
TH-ignite-GER-go.off.for-ASS
'So the other chicken hawk really went off to find firewood.'

(64a) **Incorporated modifier**

ʔe·-kla ha·ʔako·n-osas-wa·-ʔa·-la caka-**wixwan**-ʔa·-yʔik (TT 16.10)
be-DS.NSIM man-young-OBV-DEF-NOM.SG river-**small**-DEF-ALL

he-nkwaya-k-laknoʔo.
REFL-run-PART-EVID
'So the young man ran to the small river.'

(64b) **Free modifier**

no-noto·-n we·ʔis-pax naxc-an-ʔa·-la (TT 14.9)
RED-touch-GER one-just build.fire-GER-DEF-NOM.SG

wixwan-tak ye·la-k-laknoʔo.
small-very sit-PART-EVID
'A tiny little spark lay [on] just one finger.'

One special class of nominal modifiers, numerals and other quantifiers, always surfaces postnominally. With few exceptions, such quantifiers usually select a nominal that is morphologically singular, as in (65): *wewxa·yon**la** ketayta* 'two children.' Only occasionally do we see overt plural forms after quantifiers, as in (67): *ha·ʔako·nosaʔas**ka** sikitita* 'four young men.'

(65) he-ylap-an-[n]e-kam-an we-wxa·-yo-n-la (TT 9.5)
REFL-stand-GER-TH-gnaw-GER RED-grow.up-INGR-PART-NOM.SG
(='beaver') (='children')

ketay-ta he-kta·we-nes-no-k-laknoʔo.
two-DET REFL-count-DU-CONT-PART-EVID
(='play')
'Two beaver children were playing.'

(66) ʔo·ʔa-ʔa·-la-k metis coxn-ape-no-k-laknoʔo. (TT 14.5)
night-DEF-SG-ACC three sleep-NEG-PART-EVID
'He didn't sleep for three nights.'

(67) ha·ʔako·n-osaʔas-ka sikit-ita ya-coxʔo-no-n-laknoʔo. (TT 17.1)
man-young-NOM.PL four-DET TH-camp-CONT-PART-EVID
'Four young men were setting up camp.'

(68) tickan-ʔa·-la ha·naxok ha·-na-ci-cxile-k-laknoʔo. (TT 4.8)
people-DEF-SG many move.SG-ABL-RED-run-PART-EVID
'Many people went off running.'

(69) ʔaw-ʔa·-la ha·ʔas-ʔita heykew-ta-k-laknoʔo. (TT 6.2)
deer-DEF-NOM.SG many-DET move.as.group.PL-CIS-PART-EVID
'Many deer are coming.'

(70) ʔe·-kla he-pay-xwet-an-osas-wa·-ʔa·-la xa·-wa·-ʔa·-la-k (TT 26.8)
be-DS.NSIM REFL-bead-wear-GER-young-OBV-DEF-NOM.SG fat-OBV-DEF-SG-ACC

losos taʔane-ta yakca-k-a·-yʔik xa-ka-ta-k-laknoʔo.
all take-SS.NPURP sit.PL-PART-DEF-ALL AUG-throw-CIS-PART-EVID
'So the woman took all the fatty meat to where they were sitting and threw it around in a circle.'

Like many other grammatical categories, quantifiers may be incorporated into the noun, and thus not all quantified substantives constitute syntactically complex phrases (71). In other cases, both incorporated and nonincorporated quantifiers are used in the same phrase (72).

(71) "we·lʔa hexalʔoy-**a·ʔas** ʔe·-no-kwa! K-e·-na-naco·-no-kwa!" (TT 3.9)
Ouch ant-**many** be-CONT-MIR 1.OBJ-REFL-RED-bite-CONT-MIR
'Ouch, there are a bunch of ants here! They keep on biting me!'

(72) ya-coxʔ-an-**a·naxok**-wa·-ʔa·-la **ca·cxok** he·malo·-no-k-laknoʔo (TT 7.2)
TH-camp-GER-**many**-OBV-DEF-NOM.SG **half** dance-CONT-PART-EVID

ʔenik ca·cxok he·-ma-ma·ko·-no-k-laknoʔo.
and half REFL-RED-weep-CONT-PART-EVID
'[Coyote saw that] half of the many camps were dancing, and half were weeping.'

Like nongenitival modifiers, genitival modifiers may occur either before or after the head noun, but, unlike them, genitival modifiers tend strongly to occur before the head noun, as in (73a–c), rather than after it, as in (73d):

(73a)	ʔe·-kla	"kokon-wa·-lʔan	ʔahan-ʔa·-la		**(TT 2.2)**
	be-DS.NSIM	chief-OBV-GEN	daughter-DEF-NOM.SG		
	wa·-tel	ʔe·-n-w-a·-sʔ,"	no-k-laknoʔo.		
	OBV-ADV	be-CONT-DECL-ASS-1	say-PART-EVID		
	'So she said: "I am that very chief's daughter!"'				
(73b)	"Ha·csokonay-ʔan	ta·ʔe·-k-la!"			(TT 4.12)
	Coyote-GEN	grasp-PART-NOM.SG			
	'[She is] Coyote's wife!'				
(73c)	Ha·csokonay-la	kwa·-kwan-wa·-lʔan	hexwit-la-k	ho·ʔoxo·-k-laknoʔo.	(TT 8.2)
	Coyote-NOM.SG	RED-woman-OBV-GEN	belt-SG-ACC	steal-PART-EVID	
	'Coyote stole the women's belt.'				
(73d)	wixwan-wa·-ʔa·-la	we-mama-ta			(TT 17.8)
	small-OBV-DEF-NOM.SG	OBJ.PL-carry-SS.NPURP			
	ha·-na-k-laknoʔo	ya-cox-ʔan	hosaʔas-wa·-lʔan.		
	move.SG-ABL-PART-EVID	TH-camp-GER	young-OBV-GEN		
	'Little One carried them and went off to the camp of the young people.'				

The evidence for distinct adpositional phrases in Tonkawa is relatively weak. Like some languages of Mesoamerica (see, e.g., Campbell et al. 1986), instead of prepositions or postpositions, Tonkawa makes use of relational nouns that are often incorporated into the nominal matrix:

(74a)	maslak-a·ʔako·n-wa·-ʔa·-la	he-[y]lap-an-**ʔa·yay**-ʔa·-y'ik	(TT 1.17)
	buffalo-man-OBV-DEF-NOM.SG	[TH-stand.up-GER]-**under**-DEF-ALL (='tree')	

he-cne·la-k-lakno?o lak.
TH-lie-PART-EVID there
'The bull buffalo lay down there underneath the tree.'

(74b) ?awas-wa·-ka ya·c-ayco-na-l-?ok he-ylap-an-**c?el**-?a·-y?ik (TT 16.18)
meat-OBV-NOM.PL look-up-ABL-3-when REFL-stand-GER-**top**-DEF-ALL

yele·la-k-lakno?o.
sit-PART-EVID
'When the buffalo looked up, he was sitting on top of the tree.'

(74c) yox-an-xa·-xa-t kilix-pax-**a·cin**-wa·-y?ik (TT 9.4)
fly-GER-move.SG.AUG-AUG-SS.CONS river-high-**near**-OBV-ALL

he-cne-k-lakno?o.
REFL-lie-PART-EVID
'He arrived flying near to the high riverbank and lay down.'

(74d) ha-kxo-na-ta xa·pcet-an-**?a·yay**-?a·-w?an Ka·nos-wa·-?a·-la-k (TT 1.3)
move.SG-in-ABL-SS.NCONS fence-GER-**under**-DEF-ADESS Mexican-OBV-DEF-SG-ACC
'[Rabbit] came in under the fence and . . .'

Like regular incorporated nouns, these nouns are within the scope of obviation, definiteness, number, and case markers. When these relational nouns stand alone as free forms, they never take obviation, though they can take definiteness marking, and usually follow the dependent noun as postpositions, with the noun always taking accusative case, as in (75a and 75b).

(75a) kilix-pax-la-k ?a·yay-?a·-y?ik he-cne-t (TT 25.6)
river.bank-high-SG-ACC under-DEF-ALL REFL-lie-SS.CONS

ma·ka-no-k-lakno?o ka·x-wa·-?a·-la.
weep-CONT-PART-EVID blind-OBV-DEF-NOM.SG
'The blind man was lying under the high riverbank and crying.'

(75b) nex?ew-?a·-la-k losos noko-ta hakay-ta-?a·-y?ik (TT 26.12)
gun-DEF-SG-ACC all pick-SS.NPURP side.of-CIS-DEF-ALL

he·topow-la-k	hewle-k-a··yʔik	yate-l-ʔok	he-cne·la-k-laknoʔo.
Osage-SG-ACC	capture-PART-DEF-ALL	come-3-when	REFL-be.lying-PART-EVID

'They picked up all their guns and when they came to the side [of] the Osage whom they had captured, he was just lying there.'

(75c)

caka-wa··ʔa··la-k	ha·cin-tak	nakwto··k-laknoʔo.	(TT 8.11)
river-OBV-DEF-SG-ACC	close-just	approach-PART-EVID	

'He approached right close to the river.'

Very frequently, the directional force of relational nouns is redundant, in that directional suffixes of verbs of motion indicate motion, with relational nouns merely specifying additional details. In the example (76), the relational noun *cʔel-* 'top, summit, up' could normally surface immediately after the noun *na·ton* 'mountain,' but in this instance surfaces at the end of the clause with a motion verb suffixed with *-(a)yco* 'up.'

(76)

na·ton-away-ʔa··yʔik	ha-yco-na-k-laknoʔo	cʔel-ʔa··yʔik.	(TT 7.1)
mountain-tall-DEF-ALL	move.SG-up-ABL-PART-EVID	summit-DEF-ALL	

'[Coyote] went up the tall mountain to the summit.'

If the evidence for other phrasal categories is weak, the evidence for verb phrases is most conflicted. NPs do not clearly form a constituent with verbs, but *verba loquendi* almost always take a clausal complement immediately before, even when such a constituent is quite heavy:

(77a)

ʔe··kwa	Ha·csokonay-la	xa··xa-k-laknoʔo	ʔe··t	(TT 8.4)
be-DS.SIM	Coyote-NOM.SG	AUG.move.SG-AUG-PART-EVID	be-SS.CONS	

"tickan-ʔa··ka	ha··xey-ta-kwaʔ?"	no-k-laknoʔo.
person-DEF-NOM.PL	move.SG-LOC-CIS-MIR	say-PART-EVID

'So Coyote got there and said: "Did anyone really come by?!"'

(77b)

"hexwit-wa··ʔa··la-k	tickan-e··ka	ha··xey-ta-t
belt-OBV-DEF-SG-ACC	people-that-NOM.PL	move.SG-LOC-CIS-SS.CONS

nahawa··lʔok	hepak-ape-w,"	no-k-laknoʔo.	(TT 8.2)
ask.about-if	tell-NEG-IMP	say-PART-EVID	

'"If those people come by and ask about the belt, don't tell them," [Coyote] said.'

4.2. Grammatical Functions

Grammatical functions like subject and object constitute a different kind of syntax not wholly congruent with phrase structure (indeed in some theories a completely different domain of grammar). As one kind of test of grammatical functions, agreement in Tonkawa largely concerns the categories of person and number on verbal predicates, since modifier nominals ("adjectives"), adpositions, and other parts of speech do not participate in any kind of agreement process. However, even with verbs, agreement is by no means a straightforward test of grammatical functions, as many grammatical paradigms (e.g., the evidential) do not change for person or number or other nominal categories. A more serious problem is that there are numerous verbs in which object morphology is used where its English translation would naturally be translated with an English subject (Hoijer 1933, 70):

(78)	kaʔacoʔ	kewʔacoʔ
	ke-ʔace-we-ʔe	ke-we-ʔace-we-ʔe
	1OBJ-be.ill-DECL-PRES	1OBJ-OBJ.PL-be.ill-DECL-PRES
	'I'm sick'	'We're sick'

	ʔace·weʔ	waʔace·weʔ
	ʔace-··-we-ʔe	we-ʔace-··-we-ʔe
	be.ill-2.OBJ-DECL-PRES	OBJ.PL-be.ill-2.OBJ-DECL-PRES
	'You are sick'	'Y'all are sick'

	ʔacoʔ	waʔacoʔ
	ʔace-we-ʔe	we-ʔace-we-ʔe
	be.ill-DECL-PRES	OBJ.PL-be.ill-DECL-PRES
	'He's sick'	'They're sick'

In some cases, such object-oriented predicates can take either subject or object morphology depending on interpretation:

(79a) hecnoʔs
he-cane-we-ʔe-s
REFL-lie.down-DECL-PRES-1
'I lie down [willingly]'

(79b) kecnoʔ
k-e-cane-we-ʔe
1OBJ-REFL-lie.down-DECL-PRES
'I fall over'

As such, Tonkawa appears to have had a Fluid-S alignment in verb agreement in which some classes of intransitive predicates pattern either like transitive subjects or like transitive objects, depending on their semantic interpretation. Tonkawa also has object-oriented predicates, mainly verbs of possession and psychological predicates, that encode the possessor or experiencer as object:

(80)	saxʔay	ya-kew-ʔ-a·to-l-ʔila	xalʔo·-n-ka-k	(TT 12.3)
	Arrow	TH-make-do-FUT-3-DS.SIM	cut.with.knife-GER-PL-ACC	

k-e·-kpayo·-l-kaʔak
1OBJ-REFL-have.nothing-3-but
'I was going to make arrows, but I don't have any knives.'

Some of these object-oriented predicates might provide evidence that they are morphological in character or might not apply to other syntactic classes. For example, a verb showing object agreement need not necessarily be accompanied by an overt pronoun in the accusative case (81):

(81)				kexacno·noʔo	(TT 11.2)
	"sa·ya	o·ca-te-la	we-nes-yakwa-l-ʔila	ke-xacno·-no-we-ʔe,"	
	1.SG.NOM	child-this-NOM.SG	OBJ.PL-CAUS-dance-3-as	1OBJ-belong-CONT-DECL-PRES	

no-k-laknoʔo	hanilesʔaw-la.
say-PART-EVID	mouse-NOM.SG

'"What makes these children dance belongs to me," said Mouse.'

In this example, a kind of headless subordinate clause serves as the subject of the matrix verb *kexacno·noʔo* 'it belongs to me.' Surprisingly, the overt pronoun takes nominative case rather than accusative case expected of most objects. Likewise, full NPs need not be marked in the accusative if they are subjects of psychological predicates identified by Hoijer (1933, 71) as object-oriented:

(82)	ʔe·-kwa	kwa·n-wa·-ʔa·-la	so-sko·na-t	xaclo·-k-laknoʔo.
	be-DS.SIM	woman-OBV-DEF-NOM.SG	RED-hear-SS.CONS	be.angry-PART-EVID

'So the woman heard him and got angry.'

In (82), the full NP *kwa·nwa·ʔa·la* 'woman' participates in two psychological predicates, *sosko·na-* 'hear' and *xaclo·-* 'be angry,' but is nonetheless not marked in the accusative.

This also reflects the alignment of full noun phrases in Tonkawa as a whole: full NPs have accusative alignments, with the subjects of both transitive and intransitive predicates being unmarked for nominative case and the objects of transitives being marked for accusative case.

(83) *Ha·csokonay-la* ha·-na-no-k-laknoʔo.[6] (TT 3.1)
Coyote-NOM.SG move.SG-ABL-CONT-PART-EVID
'Coyote went off.'

(84) *Ha·csokonay-la* yake-k-laknoʔo ʔe·-t kwa·n-wa·-ʔa·-la-k
Coyote-NOM.SG shoot-PART-EVID be-SS.CONS woman-OBV-DEF-SG-ACC
ya·lo·na-k-laknoʔo. (TT 3.16)
kill-PART-EVID
'Coyote shot and killed the woman.'

Likewise, ditransitive predicates also set off objects as opposed to subjects. Although the available corpus only rarely marks both first and second objects with explicit full noun phrases because it can omit arguments freely (85), it is clear that Tonkawa makes use of a double-object construction, treating each object identically (86):

(85) kwa·n-kosʔa-wa·-ʔa·-la ʔeke-k-laknoʔo hexwit-wa·-ʔa·-la-k. (TT 8.3)
woman-old-OBV-DEF-NOM.SG give-PART-EVID belt-OBV-DEF-SG-ACC
'The old woman gave [her] the belt.'

(86) Ha·csokonay-la-k tica·cxok-a·-yʔik yatexan-la-k nes-kwite-k-laknoʔo. (TT 1.12)
Coyote-SG-ACC waist-DEF-ALL stone-SG-ACC CAUS-tie-PART-EVID
'[Rabbit] made Coyote tie a stone to his waist.'

Without access to native speaker judgments it is impossible to say definitively whether this double object construction also carried over to function-changing processes like passivization or antipassivization.

6. Italicized arguments are grammatical subjects, while boldfaced arguments are grammatical objects.

4.3. Relative Clauses

If one defines a relative clause in a Eurocentric way, with an external head and relative pronoun inside a subordinate clause coreferential with it, then Tonkawa does not have relative clauses. However, if defined semantically as a clause with a head noun whose extension is restricted in some way by a proposition, then relative constructions are rife. This is because, although Tonkawa does not have full subordinate relative clauses, nominals can be modified by participial constructions that have the same functional role as European-style subordinate relative clauses. For example, in (87), the participial phrase *xa·xakla* 'who arrived' modifies the subject *wixwanwa·ʔa·la* 'Little One' (a trickster folk-hero):

(87) wixwan-wa·-ʔa·-la xa·-xa-k-la (TT 17.11)
small-OBV-DEF-NOM.SG move.SG.AUG-AUG-PART-NOM.SG

"ha-kla-na-t panxo-w," no-k-laknoʔo.
move.SG-down-ABL-SS.CONS bathe-IMP say-PART-EVID
'Little One, who arrived, said: "Go down and bathe."'

Though this might be the most canonical form of relative clause, most participial forms in the available texts serve other functions. Example (88), for instance, represents a locative adjunct 'toward where the woman was lying,' and in (89) a phrase that at first appears to be a preposed relative clause in fact is an accusative absolute: 'as one settling down in a big camp':

(88) ʔe·-kla Ha·csokonay-la ha-cxo-t waʔasay-ʔa·-wʔan (TT 3.9)
be-DS.NSIM Coyote-NOM.SG move.SG-up-SS.CONS one.side-DEF-ADESS

[kwa·n-la he-cne-k-a·-wʔan] he-cne-k-laknoʔo.
woman-NOM.SG REFL-lie.down-PART-DEF-ADESS REFL-lie.down-PART-EVID
'So Coyote got up and lay down toward one side, toward where the woman was lying down.'

(89) yacoxʔanoklak (TT 27.1)
[ya-cox-ʔan-a·xok-a·-yʔik ya-coxʔa-no-k-la-k] tickan-wa·c-la
TH-camp-GER-large-DEF-ALL TH-camp-CONT-PART-SG-ACC person-real-NOM.SG

ha·ʔako·n-osas-la saxʔay-ka-k ʔe[y]-ʔe-yo·-no-k-laknoʔo.
man-young-NOM.SG arrow-PL-ACC CAUS-do-INGR-CONT-PART-EVID

'A young Tonkawa man who was settling down in a big camp was making arrows.'

It is probable that some participial constructions either originated as or were biclausal, with a higher extraposed question word and a participial form, as in (90):

(90) "hete-ca ya-mka-·-k-ye na·ya-k?" (TT 3.3)
what-place TH-call-2.OBJ-PART-Q 2.SG-ACC
'Where is it that they called you?'

In some cases, participial forms with null heads serve effectively as finite forms, as with (91), where *ka·lwa·nasek* '[It is I] who am going off to gamble' has no overt main clause head:

(91) "taxso·-k-la ʔacxo·ne·-wʔan ka·lw-a·-na-se-k." (TT 4.16)
be.dawn-PART-NOM.SG north-ADESS gamble-move.SG-ABL-1-PART
'I'm going up north to gamble tomorrow.'

Another finite-like verb form that relies on participial morphology is the resultative, as in (92):

(92) "ʔe·-ta ke-yace-w! ʔe·-la we·-tic-aʔa ya·lo·na-t (TT 6.6)
be-SS.NPURP 1.OBJ-watch-IMP be-NOM.SG this-SIM-3ASS kill-SS.CONS
yax-a·to-ne-k-coʔ," no-k-laknoʔo ʔokmaʔek-wa·-ʔa·-la.
eat-FUT-2-PART-RES say-PART-EVID Tiger-OBV-DEF-NOM.SG
'"So, watch me! With someone killing just like this you will eat your fill," Tiger said.'

FIVE

Anaphora, Reference, and Discourse Structure

Perhaps the most complicated aspect of Tonkawa grammar is anaphora and reference tracking. Tonkawa possesses a wide array of deictic devices, including demonstratives, definite suffixes, obviation markers, and most famously switch-reference markers on verbs—and all of these pattern separately grammatically. As in English, definite suffixes in Tonkawa single out identifiable entities in a discourse, though identifiability is sometimes culturally contingent as in English. Obviation, as discussed in section 3.1, is morphologically and anaphorically distinct from definiteness, in that nouns can be formed with and without definiteness marking and with and without obviation marking. Switch-reference markers are a third category of reference-tracking, in which most clauses are marked for whether the subject of the clause refers to the same or a different subject NP in the prior discourse. Like other languages with switch-reference, these markers are also marked for unrelated temporal properties of the clause (as in table 5.1).

Table 5.1. Switch-reference markers

	SAME SUBJECT	DIFFERENT SUBJECT
CONSECUTIVE/ NONSIMULTANEOUS	-t	-kla
SIMULTANEOUS/ NONCONSECUTIVE	-ta	-kwa

All three types of reference tracking can be illustrated in the following two opening lines of an Uncle Remus–like narrative:

(93)	Ka·nos-la	ya-tmax-an-la-k	ya-wye-k-laknoʔo.	ʔe··-kla	(TT 1.1)
	Mexican-NOM.SG	TH-shatter-GER-SG-ACC	TH-plant-PART-EVID	be-DS.NSIM	

Tanmaslak-awʔis-la	ho·ʔoxo·-no-laknoʔo	ya-tmax-an-wa·-ʔa·-la-k.
Rabbit-small-NOM.SG	steal-CONT-EVID	TH-shatter-GER-OBV-DEF-SG-ACC

'A Mexican planted a watermelon, and then a little rabbit was stealing the watermelons.'

In the two clauses in (93), the first two noun phrases *Ka·nosla* 'a Mexican' and *yatmaxanlak* 'watermelon' are both new items in the discourse and are not identifiable from previous discourse (being the beginning of the discourse). The second clause opens up with a form of the verb 'be,' which is very frequent in Tonkawa texts as a host for switch reference markers. Because the second clause has a noncoreferential noun phrase (NP) *Tanmaslakawʔisla* 'a little rabbit' as subject, this form of 'be' has an SR marker *-kla* to denote that the subject is not the same and the action is not simultaneous with the previous clause's verb. The subject of the second clause is also not identifiable from previous discourse and therefore does not bear a definite suffix. This stands it in contrast with the second instance of 'watermelon,' which is now both definite (by being identifiable) and obviative (by being nonsalient).

This illustrates how saliency here does not function identically to paradigm examples of obviation systems from Algonquian languages. For one thing, in Algonquian languages, obviation is obligatorily marked in every clause as long as there is more than one third-person noun phrase. In Tonkawa, although the first clause in (93) contains two third-person NPs, neither is marked as obviative. In the second clause, which also contains two third-person NPs, the subject is morphologically unmarked (i.e., proximate or nonobviative), while the second NP is overtly marked as obviative. The following clauses from the same text provide further detail about the working of this system. In (94), the aforementioned *Ka·nosokanoʔa·la* 'Mexican who owns' is marked as definite, and the *yatmaxanwa·ʔa·lak* 'watermelon' is marked as both definite and obviative. The succeeding clause is opened with another marker of switch-reference, *ʔe·t*, to indicate that the subject remains the same between clauses, and is followed by a postpositional phrase, *ʔawakcʔe·klak wa·lʔas* 'with some gum,' which is marked as neither definite nor obviative. The subject of this next clause is *Ka·nos* 'Mexican,' again marked as neither definite nor obviative.

(94) ʔe·-no-k-la | Ka·nos-[s]okano-[Ø]-ʔa·-la | (TT 1.2)
be-CONT-PART-NOM.SG | Mexican-own-PART-DEF-NOM.SG

ya-tmax-an-wa·-ʔa·-la-k | xa-cl-o·-k-laknoʔo
TH-shatter-GER-OBV-DEF-SG-ACC | AUG-angry-INGR-PART-EVID

ʔe·-t | ʔawakcʔe·k-la-k | wa·-lʔas
be-SS.CONS | gum-SG-ACC | that-INST

	yakoʔot	
Ka·nos	yaka-we-ʔe-t	nes-e-ylapa-k-laknoʔo.
Mexican	make-DECL-PAST-SS.CONS	CAUS-REFL-be.upright-PART-EVID

'Then the Mexican who owned the watermelons got angry and with some gum fixed them [to the ground].'

The significance of these patterns of marking is that both definiteness and obviation pick out particular entities in the discourse, but they do so in different ways at different times. Definites are not necessarily salient, but they are always likely to be identifiable by the hearer, while NPs marked as obviative are singled out in contrast to other more salient main characters. Thus the obviative marker behaves somewhat like a contrastive focus marker but, unlike focal markers in other languages, occurs very frequently, in almost every clause, and occurs in all kinds of positions in the clause. This might indicate that this particular morphological patterning was evolving from something that marked contrastive focus toward an Algonquian-style obviation system, though it crucially had not actually achieved this.

Part II

Tonkawa Texts

Night Stories

1. Coyote and Rabbit

(1)

Ka·nos-la	ya-tmax-an-la-k	ya-wye-k-lakno?o.	?e·-kla
Mexican-NOM.SG	TH-shatter-GER-SG-ACC	TH-plant-PART-EVID	be-DS.NSIM

Tanmaslak-aw?is-la	ho·?oxo·-no-lakno?o	ya-tmax-an-wa·-?a·-la-k
Rabbit-small-NOM.SG	steal-CONT-EVID	TH-shatter-GER-OBV-DEF-SG-ACC

(2)

?e·-no-k-la	Ka·nos-[s]okano-[Ø]-?a·-la
be-CONT-PART-NOM.SG	Mexican-own-PART-DEF-NOM.SG

ya-tmax-an-wa·-?a·-la-k	xa-cl-o·-k-lakno?o
TH-shatter-GER-OBV-DEF-SG-ACC	AUG-angry-INGR-PART-EVID

?e·-t	?awakc?e·k-la-k	wa·-l?as
be-SS.CONS	gum-SG-ACC	that-INST

	yako?ot	
Ka·nos	yaka-we-?e-t	nes-e-ylapa-k-lakno?o
Mexican	make-DECL-PAST-SS.CONS	CAUS-REFL-be.upright-PART-EVID

(3)

?e·-kla	Tanmaslak-la	ke·sxa-ya-·kwa	ho·?oxawa·-ta-t
be-DS.NSIM	Rabbit-NOM.SG	be.evening-INGR-DS.SIM	steal-CIS-SS.CONS

xa·pcet-an-?a·-y?ik	xa·-xa-l-?ok	Ka·nos-la
build.fence-GER-DEF-ALL	AUG.move.SG-AUG-3-SS.SIM	Mexican-NOM.SG

he-ylapa-·-la-k.
REFL-be.upright-PART-SG-ACC

ha-kxo-na-ta	xa·pcet-an-?a·yay-?a·-w?an	Ka·nos-wa·-?a·-la-k
move.SG-in-ABL-SS.NCONS	fence-GER-under-DEF-ADESS	Mexican-OBV-DEF-SG-ACC

ya-tmax-an-ka-k	he-s?eke-no-k-lakno?o.	?e·-l-?ok
TH-shatter-GER-PL-ACC	REFL-ask.for-CONT-PART-EVID	be-3-when

hetatxanapa?a	
he-ta-taxana-ape-a?a	he-ylapa-no-k-lakno?o.
REFL-RED-speak-NEG-ASS3SG	REFL-be.upright-CONT-PART-EVID

(4) ʔe·-kla Tanmaslak-wa·-ʔa·-la "ya·ce-w! yakon-ack-a·tewa·-nes,"
be-DS.NSIM Rabbit-OBV-DEF-NOM.SG look-IMP beat-down[?]-FUT-2.OBJ-1

no-k-lakno?o ʔe·-l-ʔok he·txanapaʔa he·-taxan-ape-aʔa
say-PART-EVID be-3-when TH-speak-NEG-ASS.3SG

he-ylapa-no-k-laknoʔo heyʔey-ʔa·-wʔan-ta
REFL-be.upright-CONT-EVID right.side-DEF-ADESS-SS.NCONS

yakona-k-laknoʔo ʔe·-kla ʔawakcʔe·k-wa·-ʔa·-la
punch-PART-EVID be-DS.NSIM gum-OBV-DEF-NOM.SG

han-kapya-ce-k-laknoʔo nonoto·n-ʔa·-la-k ʔe·-kla
TH-be.fastened-tight-PART-EVID hand-DEF-SG-ACC be-DS.NSIM

ʔasa·hey-ʔa·-wʔan-ta yakona-k-laknoʔo
left.side-DEF-toward-SS.NCONS punch-PART-EVID

Ka·nos-wa·-ʔa·-la-k ʔe·-kla han-kapya-k-laknoʔo
Mexican-OBV-DEF-SG-ACC be-DS.NSIM TH-be.fastened-PART-EVID

nonoto·n-ʔa·-la-k. ʔe·-kla yakwa-k-laknoʔo ʔe·-t
hand-DEF-SG-ACC be-DS.NSIM kick-PART-EVID be-SS.CONS

han-kapya-k-laknoʔo ʔe·-kla ʔecinʔe yakwa-k-laknoʔo
TH-be.fastened-PART-EVID be-DS.NSIM then kick-PART-EVID

ʔe·-t han-kapya-cona-no-k-laknoʔo
be-SS.CONS TH-be.fastened-hung-CONT-PART-EVID

(5) ʔe·-no-k-la-k taxso·-kwa
be-CONT-PART-SG-ACC be.dawn-when

Ka·nos-[[ya-tmax-an]-wa·-ʔa·-la-k-sokano]-ʔa·-la
Mexican-[[TH-shatter-GER]-OBV-DEF-SGACC-own]-DEF-NOM.SG

ha·-xey-ta-k-laknoʔo ʔe·-t ya·ce-k-laknoʔo
move.SG-LOC-CIS-PART-EVID be-SS.CONS look.at-PART-EVID

Tanmaslak-wa·-ʔa·-la-k
Rabbit-OBV-DEF-SG-ACC

ʔe·-t xʔaxʔayʔa-no-k-laknoʔo "wa·-tel he-wl-a·tewa-·-t
be-SS.CONS laugh-CONT-EVID OBV-ADV REFL-catch-FUT-2.OBJ-SS.CONS

ʔo-ʔs," no-k-laknoʔo. ʔe-ta Tanmaslak-wa·-ʔa·-la-k
do-1 say-PART-EVID be-SS.NCONS Rabbit-OBV-DEF-SG-ACC

taʔane-ta na:hon-wixwan-ʔa·-yʔik xa·-xa-k-laknoʔo.
pick.up-SS.NCONS house-small-DEF-ALL AUG.move.SG-AUG-PART-EVID

ʔe·-t ʔa·yay-ʔa·-yʔik cane-k-laknoʔo
be-SS.NCONS inside-DEF-ALL put-PART-EVID

(6) ʔe·-no-k-la-k hetwan-ʔax he-cna-·kwa Ha·csokonay-la
be-CONT-PART-SG-ACC several-INDEF REFL-leave-when Coyote-SG.NOM

xa·-xa-k-laknoʔo. ʔe·-kla Tanmaslak-la "ya·ce-w!"
AUG.move.SG-AUG-PART-EVID be-DS.NSIM Rabbit-NOM.SG look-IMP

no-k-laknoʔo. "taxas-wa·ta-ʔas Ka·nos-e-pay-xwet-an-la-k
say-PART-EVID be.day-this.time-INST Mexican-REFL-bead-wear-GER-SG-ACC
(='Mexican woman')

kenesta·ʔa·tonoʔ
henox-la-k ke-nes-ta·ʔ-a·tewa-no-we-ʔe," no-k-laknoʔo
pretty-SG-ACC 1.OBJ-CAUS-take.hold-FUT-CONT-DECL-PRES say-PART-EVID

Tanmaslak-la. "ʔe·-l-ʔok k-a·-tola-no-ʔ,"[1] no-k-laknoʔo
Rabbit-NOM.SG be-3-when 1-move.SG-in.vain-CONT-3.SG say-PART-EVID

Tanmaslak-la.
Rabbit-NOM.SG

"na·ya ha-kxo-ta-t ta·ʔe-w!" no-k-laknoʔo.
2.SG move.SG-in-CIS-SS.CONS grasp-IMP say-PART-EVID

1. /k(e)-(h)a·-/ > [ka·-].

ʔe··kla Hacsokonay-la "hehe·ʔ," no-k-laknoʔo
be-DS.NSIM Coyote-NOM.SG yes say-PART-EVID

"ʔ-a·to··nes," no-k-laknoʔo.
do-FUT-1.SG say-PART-EVID

(7) ʔe··kla Tanmaslak-la "ya-kwlaxe-w," no-k-laknoʔo.
be-DS.NSIM Rabbit-NOM.SG TH-open-IMP CONT-PART-EVID

ʔe:-kla Ha·csokonay-la ya-kwlaxe-laknoʔo.
be-DS.NSIM Coyote-NOM.SG TH-open-EVID

ʔe··kla Tanmaslak-la ha-txil-na-k-laknoʔo.
be-DS.NSIM Rabbit-NOM.SG move.SG-out-ABL-PART-EVID

ʔe··ta Ha·csokonay-la-k "ya·ce-w! naʔas kwa·n-wa··ʔa··la-k
be-SS.NCONS Coyote-SG-ACC look-IMP just.as woman-OBV-DEF-SG-ACC

ʔe[y]-ta-l-ʔok nexʔew-ka-k nes-wa-wan-a·to-nwa-ʔ,"
CAUS-move.PL-3-when gun-PL-ACC CAUS-RED-shoot-FUT-DEON-3

no-k-laknoʔo. ʔe··kwa heʔe··la-k ya·koxo-we··ka-k
CONT-PART-EVID be-DS.SIM that-SG-ACC box-that-PL-ACC

nesma·ka·tonwaʔ
ʔey-ne-ti-txewa-w. ʔe-yo-ʔok henox nes-ma·k-a·tewa-nwa-ʔ,"
do-TH-RED-poke-IMP do-2-when pretty CAUS-wail-FUT-DEON-

no-k-laknoʔo. ʔe··kla Ha·csokonay-la "hehe·ʔ
CONT-PART-EVID be-DS.NSIM Coyote-NOM.SG yes

ʔa·to·nes
ʔ-atewa-no-s," no-k-laknoʔo.
do-FUT-CONT-1 CONT-PART-EVID

(8) ʔe··kwa Tanmaslak-la ha··na-k-laknoʔo.
be-DS.SIM Rabbit-NOM.SG move.SG-ABL-PART-EVID

ʔe··kwa nexʔew-ʔa··la he-xwe-no-k-laknoʔo.
be-DS.SIM gun-DEF-NOM.SG TH-hear-CONT-PART-EVID

ʔe··kla	Ha·csokonay-la	ya·koxo··wa··ka-k
be-DS.NSIM	Coyote-NOM.SG	box-OBV-PL-ACC

ʔey-ni-txoʔo-k-laknoʔo.	ʔe··kla	pixa·taka··la
do-TH-poke-PART-EVID	be-DS.NSIM	bee-NOM.SG

yo-xa-nxil-na-t	Ha·csokonay-la	he··na-naco··k-laknoʔo.
TH-AUG-go.SG-ABL-SS.CONS	Coyote-NOM.SG	REFL-RED-sting-PART-EVID

ʔe-kla	Ha·csokonay-la	so·paknacka-t	he-cne-no-k-laknoʔo.
be-DS.NSIM	Coyote-NOM.SG	swell.up-SS.CONS	TH-lie-CONT-PART-EVID

ʔe··kwa	Ka·nos-wa··ʔa··la	xa··xa-k-laknoʔo	e··t
be-DS.SIM	Mexican-OBV-DEF-NOM.SG	AUG-move.SG-AUG-PART-EVID	be-SS.CONS

Ha·csokonay-la-k	taʔane-t	kaltey-ʔa··yʔik	ka··na-k-laknoʔo.
Coyote-SG-ACC	pick.up-SS.CONS	outside-DEF-ALL	throw-ABL-PART-EVID

ʔe··kla	he-cne-no-la	ʔaco··t	"heheeʔ	Tanmaslak!"
be-DS.NSIM	TH-lie-CONT-NOM.SG	revive-SS.CONS	yes	Rabbit.VOC

		ke·sya·ceyoʔok
no-k-laknoʔo.	"hetecaʔax	ke-he-sya·ce-yo-ʔok
say-PART-EVID	wherever	1.OBJ-REFL-permit-2-when

ya·lo·n-a·tewa-··nes!"	no-k-laknoʔo.	ʔe··ta
kill-FUT-2.OBJ-1	say-PART-EVID	be-SS.NPURP

ha··na-k-laknoʔo.
move.SG-ABL-PART-EVID

(9)

ʔe··kwa	Tanmaslak-wa··ʔa··la	he-cne·la-k-laknoʔo
be-DS.SIM	Rabbit-OBV-DEF-NOM.SG	TH-lie-CONT-PART-EVID

lak	Ha·csokonay-la	"ya·lo·na-··yuk	newe··we-ʔe··ʔ,"
3SG.ACC	Coyote-NOM.SG	kill-2.OBJ-3PL	say.to-DECL-PAST-1

no-k-laknoʔo.	ʔe··kla	Tanmaslak-la	"ʔa·kay!"
say-PART-EVID	be-DS.NSIM	Rabbit-NOM.SG	no

no·k-laknoʔo.
say-PART-EVID

		yo·mʔa·to·nokwa!	
"ya·ce-w!	kwa·low	yo·mʔ-a·tewa-no-kwa!"	no·k-laknoʔo.
look-IMP	big	rain-FUT-CONT-MIR	say-PART-EVID

			sokna·s	
"na·kw	ʔe-w	ʔoyu-te·-ca	sokna-·-s,"	no·k-laknoʔo.
Now	come-IMP	sack-this-here	put-2.OBJ-1	say-PART-EVID

		yatxalka·s
"ʔe·-ta	he-[y]lap-an-eʔe-ca	ya-taxalka-·-s,"
be-SS.NPURP	REFL-stand-GER-that-place (='tree')	TH-hang-2.OBJ-1

no·k-laknoʔo Tanmaslak-la.
say-PART-EVID Rabbit-NOM.SG

"ʔe·-ta	sa·-xwa	he-ylapa-n-ʔa·yay-te·-ca	ʔ-a·haʔa,"
be-SS.NPURP	I-also	TH-stand.up-GER-inside-this-place (='tree')	be-INTENT

no·k-laknoʔo.
say-PART-EVID

ʔe·-kla	Ha·csokonay-la	"heheeʔ,"	no·k-laknoʔo.
be-DS.NSIM	Coyote-NOM.SG	okay	say-PART-EVID

(10)

ʔe·-kla	ya-txalka-k-laknoʔo	he-ylap-an-ʔa·-yʔik.
be-DS.NSIM	TH-hang-PART-EVID	TH-stand.up-GER-DEF-ALL (='tree')

ʔe·-ta	Tanmaslak-la	yatexan-wa·-ka-s
be-SS.NPURP	Rabbit-NOM.SG	stone-OBV-PL-INST

yal-nacka-k-laknoʔo	Ha·csokonay-la-k.	ʔe·-ta
throw-die-PART-EVID	Coyote-SG-ACC	be-SS.NPURP

ha·-na-k-laknoʔo.
move.SG-ABL-PART-EVID

ʔe·-no-k-la-k	Ha·csokonay-la	ʔaco·-t
be-CONT-PART-SG-ACC	Coyote-NOM.SG	be.revived-SS.CONS

"hehee? Tanmaslak!" no-k-lakno?o. "he-te-ca-?ax
all.right Rabbit.VOC say-PART-EVID what-this-place-INDEF

ke·sya·ceyo?ok ya·lo·na·tewa:nes
ke-hes-ya·ce-yo-?ok ya·lo·n-a·tewa·-·-nes!" no-k-lakno?o.
1.OBJ-CAUS-see-2-when kill-FUT-2.OBJ-1.SG say-PART-EVID

(11) ?e·-ta ha·-na-·kwa Tanmaslak-la he-cne·la-k-lakno?o
be-SS.NPURP move.SG-ABL-when Rabbit-NOM.SG TH-be.lying-PART-EVID

lak Ha·csokonay-la "ya·lo·na-·-yuk newe-·-we-?e·-?,"
3SG.ACC Coyote-NOM.SG kill-2.OBJ-3.PL tell-2.OBJ-DECL-PAST-1

no-k-lakno?o ?e·-kla Tanmaslak-la "?a·kay,"
say-PART-EVID be-DS.NSIM Rabbit-NOM.SG no

no-k-lakno?o. "ya·ce-w!" no-k-lakno?o. "he?e-ca
say-PART-EVID look-IMP say-PART-EVID that-place

ya-talp-an-kwa·low-la he-cn-a·we Lak
TH-fry-GER-big-NOM.SG REFL-lie-PERF 3SG.ACC

ke·sta?anpeno?
ke-hes-ta?ane-ape-no-we-?e-?,"
1.OBJ-TH-get.hold.of-NEG-CONT-DECL-PRES-1

no-k-lakno?o. "na·ya ta?ane-t ke-ta[·]-yaxa-w,"
say-PART-EVID 2.SG.NOM get.hold.of-SS.CONS 1.OBJ-COM-eat-IMP

no-k-lakno?o. ?e·-kla Ha·csokonay-la "hehe·?
say-PART-EVID be-DS.NSIM Coyote-NOM.SG Okay

?a·to·nes
?-a·tewa-nes," no-k-lakno?o.
do-FUT-1 say-PART-EVID

(12) ?e·-ta ta-na-nes?e-k-lakno?o cakaw-ixwan-?a·-y?ik
be-SS.NPURP move.PL-ABL-DU-PART-EVID river-small-DEF-ALL

?e·-l?ok ?a·x-?ayay-?a·-y?ik na?as-?o-?o-tel?a·t-la
be-when water-under-DEF-ALL light-moon-this-NOM.SG

hew?ax ya-talp-an he-cne·la-k-lakno?o.
just.like TH-fry-GER REFL-lie-PART-EVID

ʔe·-kla	Ha·csokonay-la-k	tica·cxok-a·-yʔik
be-DS.NSIM	Coyote-SG-ACC	waist-DEF-ALL

yatexan-la-k	nes-kwite-k-laknoʔo
stone-SG-ACC	CAUS-tie-PART-EVID

ʔe·-ta	ka·-na-kla-na-k-laknoʔo	ʔa·x-ʔa·-yʔik.
be-SS.NPURP	throw-ABL-down-ABL-PART-EVID	water-DEF-ALL

ʔe·-kla	Ha·csokonay-la	he-wawa-k-laknoʔo.
be-DS.NSIM	Coyote-NOM.SG	REFL-die-PART-EVID

ʔe·-kla	Tanmaslak-la	ha·-na-k-laknoʔo.
be-DS.NSIM	Rabbit-NOM.SG	move-ABL-PART-EVID

(13)

ʔe·-no-k-la-k	Ha·csokonay-la	ʔaco·-t
be-CONT-PART-SG-ACC	Coyote-NOM.SG	resurrect-SS.CONS

ta·kona-no-k-laknoʔo
seek-CONT-PART-EVID

Tanmaslak-la-k.	ʔe·-lʔok	wa·-yʔik	he-cne·la-k-laknoʔo
Rabbit-SG-ACC	be-WHEN	OBV-ALL	TH-lie-PART-EVID

Tanmaslak-wa·-ʔa·-la	lak.	Ha·csokonay-la	ya·ce-t
Rabbit-OBV-DEF-NOM.SG	3SG.ACC	Coyote-NOM.SG	see-SS.CONS

"ya·lo·na-·-yuk	newe·-we-ʔe·-ʔ,"	no-k-laknoʔo.
kill-2.OBJ-3.PL	tell-2.OBJ-DECL-PAST-1	say-PART-EVID

"ʔa·kay,"	no-k-laknoʔo.	"ya·ce-w!"	no-k-laknoʔo.
no	say-PART-EVID	look-IMP	say-PART-EVID

"heʔe-ca	xa·-ka-k	nasox-an	ke-ke-·kwa	yaxas-ʔok
that-place	fat-PL-ACC	cook-GER	1.OBJ-give-when	eat-if

na·xwa	he·-nawʔace-t	ke-ta·xa-w,"	no-k-laknoʔo.
2.SG.also	TH-ask.for-SS.CONS	1.OBJ-eat-IMP	say-PART-EVID

ʔe·-kla	Ha·csokonay-la	"hehe·ʔ,"	no-k-laknoʔo.
be-DS.NSIM	Coyote-NOM.SG	okay	say-PART-EVID

(14)

ʔe·-ta	ta-na-nesʔe-k-laknoʔo.	ʔe·-l-ʔok	hacip-a·-la [*sic*]
be-SS.NPURP	move.DU-ABL-PART-EVID	be-3-when	hole-DEF-NOM.SG

ye·la-k-lakno?o lak. Ha·csokonay-la
sit-PART-EVID 3SG.ACC Coyote-NOM.SG

he·tya-na-kxo-na-k-lakno?o ha·cip-wa·-y?ik.
reach-GER-in-ABL-PART-EVID hole-OBV-ALL

?e·-kla se·nantak-la nace-k-lakno?o.
be-DS.NSIM rattlesnake-NOM.SG bite-PART-EVID

?e·-kla so·pak-nacka-t he-cne·-no-k-lakno?o.
be-DS.NSIM swell.up-die-SS.CONS TH-lie-PART-EVID

?e·-kla Tanmaslak-la ha·-na-k-lakno?o.
be-DS.NSIM Rabbit-NOM.SG move.SG-ABL-PART-EVID

(15) ?e·-kla Ha·csokonay-la ?aco·-k-lakno?o.
be-DS.NSIM Coyote-NOM.SG resurrect-PART-EVID

?e·-t "hehe·? Tanmaslak," no-k-lakno?o.
be-SS.CONS okay Rabbit.VOC say-PART-EVID

ya·lo·n-a·te·wa·-nes wa·-ta?as," no-k-lakno?o
kill-FUT-2.OBJ-1 this-time say-PART-EVID

Ha·csokonay-la.
Coyote-NOM.SG

?e·-ta ha·-na-·kwa Tanmaslak-la he-cne·la-k-lakno?o
be-SS.NPURP move.SG-ABL-when Rabbit-NOM.SG TH-be.lying-PART-EVID

lak Ha·csokonay-la "ya·lo·na·-yuk newe·-we-?e·-?,"
3SG Coyote-NOM.SG kill-2.OBJ-3.PL tell-2.OBJ-DECL-PAST-1

no-k-lakno?o. ?e·-kla Tanmaslak-la
say-PART-EVID be-DS.NSIM Rabbit-NOM.SG

"?a·kay," no-k-lakno?o. "ya·ce-w!
No say-PART-EVID look-IMP

c?elay-te·-la xa-wan-a·to·-no-kwa! ke-taple-w
sky-this-NOM.SG AUG-fall-FUT-CONT-MIR 1.OBJ-help-IMP

ya-kex-ayco-na-se-k-e!" no-k-laknoʔo Tanmaslak-la.
TH-push-up-ABL-1-PART-HORT say-PART-EVID Rabbit-NOM.SG

ʔe·-kla Ha·csokonay-la "hehe·ʔ," no-k-laknoʔo.
be-DS.NSIM Coyote-NOM.SG okay say-PART-EVID

ʔe·-kwa Ha·csokonay-la ya-kex-ayco-na-·kwa
do-DS.SIM Coyote-NOM.SG TH-push-up-ABL-when

Tanmaslak-la ha·-na-k-laknoʔo.
Rabbit-NOM.SG move.SG-ABL-PART-EVID

(16) ʔe·-no-k-la-k Ha·csokonay-la "hehe·ʔ Tanmaslak,"
be-CONT-PART-SG-ACC Coyote-NOM.SG okay Rabbit.VOC

no-k-laknoʔo. "ya·lo·n-a·tewa-·-nes!" no-k-laknoʔo
say-PART-EVID kill-FUT-2.OBJ-1 say-PART-EVID

ʔe·-ta ha·-na-·kwa Tanmaslak-la he-cne·-no-k-laknoʔo
be-SS.NPURP move.SG-ABL-when Rabbit-NOM.SG TH-lie-CONT-PART-EVID

ʔe·-kla Ha·csokonay-la "ya·lo·na-·-yuk newe-·-we-ʔe·-ʔ,"
be-DS.NSIM Coyote-NOM.SG kill-2.OBJ-3.PL tell-2.OBJ-DECL-PAST-1

no-k-laknoʔo. ʔe·-kla Tanmaslak-la "ʔa·kay,"
say-PART-EVID be-DS.NSIM Rabbit-NOM.SG okay

no-k-laknoʔo. "ya·ce-w," no-k-laknoʔo.
say-PART-EVID look-IMP say-PART-EVID

"heʔe-ca maslak-a·ʔako·n-la kwa·low-la he-cn-a·we,"
DIST-LOC buffalo-man-NOM.SG big-NOM.SG TH-lie-PERF

no-k-laknoʔo. "kana-kxo-na-w ʔe·-t ʔey-kelʔaxe-w
say-PART-EVID throw-in-ABL-IMP be-SS.CONS CAUS-shatter-IMP

ʔe·-t ke-ta·xa-w,"
be-SS.CONS 1.OBJ-heat-IMP

no-kla Ha·csokonay-la "hehe·ʔ," no-k-laknoʔo.
say-DS.NSIM Coyote-NOM.SG okay say-PART-EVID

(17) ʔe·-ta ta-na-nesʔe-·kwa maslak-a·ʔako·n-wa·-ʔa·-la
be-SS.NPURP move.PL-ABL-DU-when buffalo-man-OBV-DEF-NOM.SG

he-[y]lap-an-ʔa·yay-ʔa·-yʔik he-cne·la-k-laknoʔo lak
TH-stand.up-GER-under-DEF-ALL TH-lie-PART-EVID 3SG.ACC
(='tree')

Ha·csokonay-la kan-akxo-na-k-laknoʔo.
Coyote-NOM.SG throw-in-ABL-PART-EVID

ʔe·-ta tica·cxok-a·-yʔik he-nes-kwite-k-laknoʔo.
be-SS.NPURP waist-DEF-ALL TH-CAUS-tie-PART-EVID

ʔe·-ta "we·-ʔil!" no-k-laknoʔo. "ʔey-nesexa-w,"
be-SS.NPURP now! say-PART-EVID CAUS-fear-IMP

no-k-laknoʔo.
say-PART-EVID

ʔe·-kla Tanmaslak-la ʔey-nesexa-k-laknoʔo.
be-DS.NSIM Rabbit-NOM.SG CAUS-fear-PART-EVID

ʔe·-kla maslak-a·ʔako·n-wa·-ʔa·-la Ha·csokonay-la-k
be-DS.NSIM buffalo-male-OBV-DEF-NOM.SG Coyote-SG-ACC

nexel-ci-cwa-ta yan-ci-cxa·-xey-ne-k-laknoʔo
$drag_1$-RED-$drag_2$-SS.NPURP TH-RED-run-far-LOC-ABL-PART-EVID

maslak-a·ko·n-wa·-ʔa·-la.
buffalo-male-OBV-DEF-NOM.SG

(18) he·pano·noʔo
naʔa he·panewa-no-we-ʔe we·-tic.
so narrate-CONT-DECL-PRES.3SG yon-like[2]

Coyote and Rabbit: Free English Translation

[1] A Mexican planted a watermelon, and then a little rabbit was stealing the watermelons. [2] This being so, the Mexican who owned the watermelons got

2. The similitive suffix: 'like, as.' Here 'like' is used to avoid confusion with SIM (simultaneous) switch-reference markers.

angry and with some gum fixed them [to the ground]. [3] Then when evening came Rabbit came to the fence that the Mexican had set up to steal. [Rabbit] came in under the fence and asked the Mexican for a watermelon. And he kept on standing there not speaking. [4] Then he told the rabbit: "I'll knock you unconscious!" and when he did so, not speaking, he was standing upright and punched [Rabbit's] right side and his hand got stuck. And he [Rabbit] punched the Mexican on his left side, and [his] hand got stuck. Then [Rabbit] kicked it, and he got stuck. Then again he kicked it, and he was hung up, fastened to it. [5] This having happened, when it was morning, the Mexican who owned the watermelons came there and looked at the rabbit, and he was laughing: "Just like that I was about to catch you!" And then picking him up, he came to a small house and put him [the Rabbit] into it. After this, when several days had passed, Coyote arrived. Then Rabbit said: "Look here!" [6] Then, after several [days] had passed, Coyote arrived. Then Rabbit said: "Look! This very day they will make me marry a pretty Mexican woman," he said. "When they do so, I'll refuse," Rabbit said. "[How about] you come in and marry her!" he said. Then Coyote said: "Yes, I'll do it," he said. [7] Then Rabbit said: "Open it!" Then Coyote opened it. Then Rabbit went out and said to Coyote: "Look! Right when they bring her, they will shoot guns. When they do so, poke those boxes [=phonograph?] over there. When you do, they will play pretty music," he said. Then Coyote said: "All right, I'll do it." [8] Then Rabbit went far off. Then [Coyote] heard gun noises and poked the box. Then, with bees rushing out, Coyote got stung all over, and he just lay there swelling up and dying. Then the Mexican arrived and, picking Coyote up, threw him outside. Then the one lying down came back to life and said: "All right! Rabbit, wherever you allow me to see you, I'll kill you!" Then he [Coyote] went away. [9] As he left, Rabbit was lying down there, and Coyote [came up] and said: "I told you I would kill you!" Then Rabbit said: "No! Look! It's going to rain down a lot! Now come, I'll put you into this here sack," he said, "and then I will hang you in the tree here," Rabbit said. "And I too will be right under the tree." Then Coyote said: "Okay." [10] Then he hung him onto the tree, and Rabbit pounded Coyote to death with the stones. Then he went away. Then Coyote came back to life and said: "All right, Rabbit! Wherever you let me catch sight of you, I'll kill you!" he said. [11] And then when he left, Rabbit was lying down [there], and Coyote said: "I told you I was going to kill you!" Then Rabbit said: "No! Look over there! There's a big loaf of fry-bread over there, I can't get hold of it. You pick it up, eat it with me," he said. Then Coyote said "All right, I'll do it. [12] And then they both went off to a small river. When they did, the moon up there [looked] just like fry-bread lying under the water. [Rabbit] made Coyote tie a stone to his waist and throw it down into the water. Then Coyote died, and Rabbit went off. [13] As such, Coyote came back to life and went searching for Rabbit. As he did so, Rabbit was just lying there in the same place. Seeing him, Coyote said: "I told you that I'd kill you!" Rabbit said: "No! Look there!" He said: "When they give me the fats for cooking over there, if I eat any, you can eat with me too!" Then Coyote said: "Okay." [14] Then both of them went off, and as they did so a hole appeared. Coyote reached his arm into the hole, and a rattlesnake bit him! Swelling up and dying, he lay there [lifeless]. Then Rabbit went off. [15] Then Coyote came back to life and said: "All right, Rabbit! I'll kill you this time!" Then when he went away, Rabbit was just lying there, and Coyote said: "I told you that I would kill you!" Then Rabbit said: "No! Look here! The sky is about to fall right down, help me push it up!" Then Coyote said: "All right." Then when Coyote was pushing [the sky] up, Rabbit buggered off. [16] Then Coyote said: "All right, Rabbit! I'm going to kill you!" And then he went off. Rabbit was just lying there, and Coyote said: "I told you I'd kill you!" Then Rabbit said: "No! Look here! Over yonder is a big bull [buffalo], rope him and break his neck and heat him up for me," he said. Coyote said: "All right." [17] And when they both went off, the bull [buffalo] was lying under a tree. Coyote lassoed him and then tied it to himself. And then he tied [the buffalo] to his waist. Then [Coyote] said: "Now! Get him scared!" Then Rabbit scared him, and the bull ran off, dragging him along, that bull [did]. [18] So they have always told it. So it goes.

2. Coyote and Jackrabbit

(1) Ha csokonay-la ha -na-no-k-laknoʔo xamʔal-ʔa -yʔik.
Coyote-NOM.SG move.SG-ABL-CONT-PART-EVID prairie-DEF-ALL

ʔe·-kwa Tanmasla-kwa·low he-cne·la-k-laknoʔo lak.
be-DS.SIM Rabbit-big TH-lie-PART-EVID there

Ha·csokonay-la "ʔo·c!" no-k-laknoʔo.
Coyote-NOM.SG "oh!" say-PART-EVID

"ʔekwan-esxaw sa·ken nen-xale-s!" [*sic*][3] no-k-laknoʔo.
dog-big 1.SG.GEN TH-find-1 say-PART-EVID

ʔe·-ta Tanmasla-kwa·lo-wa·-ʔa·-la-k he-wle-k-laknoʔo.
be-SS.NPURP Rabbit-big-OBV-DEF-SG-ACC TH-catch-PART-EVID

ʔe·-t nes-yacxa-n-ʔa·-la-k ya-caska-k-laknoʔo
be-SS.CONS CAUS-torso-GER-DEF-SG-ACC TH-put.on.back-PART-EVID
(='saddle')

ʔe·-ta yakaw-ʔa·-la-k he-yweye-k-laknoʔo
be-SS.NPURP spur-DEF-SG-ACC REFL-fasten-PART-EVID

ʔe·-ta Tanmasla-kwa·lo-wa·ʔa·-la-k ha-yxo-k-laknoʔo
be-SS.NPURP Rabbit-big-OBV-DEF-SG-ACC move.SG-across.SG-PART-EVID

ʔe·-ta yakwa-no-k-laknoʔo.[4]
be-SS.NPURP TH-kick-CONT-PART-EVID

ʔe·-l-kaʔak Tanmasla-kwa·low-la cʔetxa-na-no-laknoʔo.
be-3-while Rabbit-big-NOM.SG jump-ABL-CONT-EVID

ʔe·-l-kaʔak "wo·!" no-no-k-laknoʔo
be-3-while "whoa!" say-CONT-PART-EVID

ʔe·-ta taʔan-ayco-na-no-k-laknoʔo.
be-SS.NPURP grasp-up-ABL-CONT-PART-EVID

3. Cf. Hoijer (1972, 25): *nenxʔale-* 'to find (it); to guard, watch over (it).'

4. Note that *yakaw* 'spur' and *yakwa-* 'kick' are cognates (also *yakwa-n-* 'leg').

(2) ʔe -kwa ka nos-kwa n-la ha -na-k-la
be-DS.SIM Mexican-woman-NOM.SG move.SG-ABL-PART-NOM.SG

nes-yan-ci-cxil-xa·xa-k-laknoʔo.
CAUS-TH-RED-run-DIST-PART-EVID

ʔe·-t "kokonʔa·-la he-teca ʔe· -no-kwa," no-k-laknoʔo.
be-SS.CONS chief-NOM.SG this-place be-CONT-MIR say-PART-EVID

ʔe·-kla "kokon-wa·-lʔan ʔahan-ʔa·-la
be-DS.NSIM chief-OBV-GEN daughter-DEF-NOM.SG

wa·-tel ʔe·-n-w-a·-sʔ," no-k-laknoʔo.
OBV-ADV be-CONT-DECL-ASS-1 say-PART-EVID

ʔe·-kla "ʔax-ka-k ke-nes-xane-w!"
be-DS.NSIM water-PL-ACC 1.OBJ-CAUS-drink-IMP

ʔe·-kla "wilʔa!" no-k-laknoʔo.
be-DS.NSIM no say-PART-EVID

(3) ʔe -kla "ya ce-w!" no-k-laknoʔo Ha csokonay-la.
be-DS.NSIM look-IMP say-PART-EVID Coyote-NOM.SG

yancicxelenoʔo
"ʔekwan-esxaw-sa·ken-te·-la cikew yan-ci-cxele-no-we-ʔe,"
dog-big-my-this-NOM.SG fast TH-RED-run-CONT-DECL-PRES

no-k-laknoʔo.
say-PART-EVID

"nes-ya·nsxile·-s-ʔok ke-yace-w!" no-k-laknoʔo.
CAUS-run-1-if 1.OBJ-watch-IMP say-PART-EVID

ʔe·-kla kwa·n-wa·-ʔa·-la "heyʔ," no-k-laknoʔo.
be-DS.NSIM woman-OBV-DEF-NOM.SG okay say-PART-EVID

Ha·csokonay-la nes-yan-ci-cxile-k-laknoʔo xamʔal-ʔa·-yʔik
Coyote-NOM.SG CAUS-TH-RED-run-PART-EVID prairie-DEF-ALL

ʔe·-t cʔawʔal henkwa·-n-ʔan kilix-pax-ʔa·-yʔik
be-SS.CONS far.away run-ABL-GER river.bank-high-DEF-ALL

ha·cin-ʔa·-yʔik.
nearby-DEF-ALL

ʔe·-ta	he-y-cane-nxo·-t	Tanmaslak-la-k
be-SS.NPURP	REFL-TH-leave-abruptˀ-SS.CONS (=‘turn [e.g., a horse] sharply while running’)	Rabbit-SG-ACC

ʔe·-kla	ne-klaxe-k-laknoʔo.
be-DS.NSIM	TH-throw.off-PART-EVID

ʔe·-kla	kilix-wa·-yʔik	wa·-na-t	he-wawa-k-laknoʔo.
be-DS.NSIM	river.bank-OBV-ALL	fall-ABL-SS.CONS	REFL-kill-PART-EVID

ʔe·-kla	Tanmasla-kwa·low-ʔa·-la	yan-ci-cxila·-xey-ne-k-laknoʔo
be-DS.NSIM	Rabbit-big-DEF-NOM.SG	TH-RED-run-far-LOC-ABL-PART-EVID

we·-tic.
yon-like

Coyote and Jackrabbit: Free English Translation

[1] Coyote went off to the prairie, and when he did Jackrabbit was lying there. Coyote said: “Oh! I’ve found my horse.” Then he caught Jackrabbit and put the saddle on his back, fastened his spurs on himself, mounted Jackrabbit, and was spurring him. While Jackrabbit was jumping, [Coyote] kept saying: “Whoa!” and pulling him up. [2] As he did so, he made Jackrabbit run way over to a Mexican woman walking along. Then he said: “Where is the chief living?” Then she said: “I am that very chief’s daughter.” Then [Coyote said]: “Give me water to drink!” Then she said “No!” [3] Then Coyote said: “Look here! This horse of mine always runs fast. When I make him run, watch me!” Then the woman said: “Okay.” Coyote made him run to the prairie and far away near a high riverbank. While turning sharply, he was thrown off [Jackrabbit’s back], and falling over the bluff he was killed. Then Jackrabbit ran far off. So it goes.

3. Coyote, Rabbit, and Eagle's Daughter

(1) Ha·csokonay-la ha·-na-no-k-lakno?o. ?e·-no-·-la
Coyote-NOM.SG move.SG-ABL-CONT-PART-EVID do-CONT-PART-NOM.SG

na·to·n-?a·y-?a·-y?ik [*sic*] ha-yco-na-ta yela-no-k-lakno?o.
mountain-below-DEF-ALL move.SG-up-ABL-SS.NPURP sit-CONT-PART-EVID

?e·-kwa yacox?an-?a·-la na·to·n-?a·yay-wa·-y?ik
be-DS.SIM camp-DEF-NOM.SG mountain-base-OBV-ALL

yacox?an-a·naxok ye·la-k-lakno?o lak.
camp-large be.located-PART-EVID 3SG.ACC

Ha·csokonay-la ha-kla-na-k-lakno?o.
Coyote-NOM.SG move.SG-down-ABL-PART-EVID

?e·-t yacox?an-ca·cxoka-y?ik yacox?an-away-?a·-y?ik
be-SS.CONS camp-center-ALL tipi-tall-DEF-ALL

kwa·low-?a·-y?ik xa·-xa-t nes-kap-an-?a·-la-k
big-DEF-ALL go.SG-AUG-SS.CONS CAUS-close-GER-DEF-SG-ACC (='tipi flap')

ta?an-xa-ycon-ta hel?eya-kxo-na-k-lakno?o.
grasp-AUG-raise-SS.NPURP peer-in-ABL-PART-EVID

(2) ?e·-l?ok ha·?ako·n-osas-la sax?ay-ka-k ?e-?eyo·-no-k-lakno?o.
do-when man-young-NOM.SG arrow-PL-ACC RED-make-CONT-PART-EVID

?e·-kla Ha·csokonay-la ha-kxo-na-k-lakno?o ?e·-t
be-DS.NSIM Coyote-NOM.SG move.SG-in-ABL-PART-EVID be-SS.CONS

"hecu· ?e·-no-kwa?" no-k-lakno?o.
what do-CONT-MIR say-PART-EVID

?e·-kla ha·?ako·n-osas-wa·-?a·-la "he?e·-w?an
be-DS.NSIM man-young-OBV-DEF-NOM.SG that-ADESS

yacoxʔan-a·naxok-eʔe·-k kwa·n-la-k ke-nes-ta·ʔe·-t
camp-big-yon-ACC woman-SG-ACC 1.OBJ-CAUS-grasp-SS.CONS (='marry')

keymakoʔo
ke-yamaka-we-ʔe," no-k-laknoʔo. ʔe·-kla Ha·csokonay-la
1.OBJ-call-DECL-PRES say-PART-EVID be-DS.NSIM Coyote-NOM.SG

n-oʔo
"ʔoc," no-k-laknoʔo. "sa·-xwa we·c no-we-ʔe," no-k-laknoʔo.
oh say-PART-EVID 1.SG-also yon.PLACE speak say-PART-EVID

ʔe·-ta Ha·cosokonay-la cakaw-ixwan-ʔa·-yʔik
be-SS.NPURP Coyote-NOM.SG river-small-DEF-ALL

ha-kla-na-t
move.SG-down-ABL-SS.CONS

saxʔay ya-koʔo-no-k-laknoʔo.
arrow TH-make-CONT-PART-EVID

ʔe·-ta ha-yco-ta-t ʔe·-kwa ha·ʔako·n-osas-wa·-ʔa-la
be-SS.NPURP move.SG-up-CIS-SS.CONS be-DS.SIM man-young-OBV-DEF-NOM.SG

"we·ʔil," no-k-laknoʔo.
okay say-PART-EVID

(3) ʔe·-kla ta-na-nesʔe-k-laknoʔo ʔe·-t
be-DS.NSIM move.DU-ABL-DU-PART-EVID be-SS.CONS

na·ton-cʔel-ʔa·-yʔik ta-yco-na-nesʔe-k-laknoʔo.
mountain-top-DEF-ALL move.DU-up-ABL-DU-PART-EVID

ʔe·-kwa ha·ʔako·n-osas-wa·-ʔa·-la
be- DS.SIM man-young-OBV-DEF-NOM.SG

"we·ʔil," no-k-laknoʔo "hete-ca
okay say-PART-EVID what-place

yamka·ka·kyeʔ,"
ya-maka-·-ka·-k-yeʔ"
TH-call-2.OBJ-INTER.2.SG-PART-Q

no·k-laknoʔo. ʔe·-kla Ha·csokonay-la "na·ya no-w,"
say-PART-EVID be-DS.NSIM Coyote-NOM.SG 2.SG.NOM say-IMP

no·k-laknoʔo. "hete-ca ya-mka-·-k-ye na·ya-k?"
say-PART-EVID what-place TH-call-2.OBJ-PART-Q 2.SG-ACC

no·k-laknoʔo Ha·csokonay-la. ʔe·-kla ha·ʔako·n-osas-wa·-ʔa·-la
say-PART-EVID Coyote-NOM.SG be-DS.NSIM man-young-OBV-DEF-NOM.SG

"ʔalʔ helʔa·t yacoxʔan-ca·cxok-eʔe·-k
all.right over.there camp-center-yon-ACC

yacoxʔan-away-kwa·low-eʔe·-k we·-yʔik keymakoʔo
ke-yamaka-we-ʔe,"
camp-tall-big-yon-ACC yon-ALL 1.OBJ-call-DECL-PRES

no·k-laknoʔo Haʔako·n-osas-wa·-ʔa·-la. ʔe·-kla Ha·csokonay-la
say-PART-EVID man-young-OBV-DEF-NOM.SG be-DS.NSIM Coyote-NOM.SG

"he·ʔ we·-yʔik
yes yon-ALL

noʔo
no-we-ʔe sa·-xwa," no-k-laknoʔo ʔe·-kla "we·ʔil,"
say-DECL-PRES 1.SG-also say-PART-EVID be-DS.NSIM all.right

no-k-laknoʔo ʔe·-ta ta-kla-nesʔe-k-laknoʔo
say-PART-EVID be-SS.NPURP move.DU-down-DU-PART-EVID

na·to·n-wa·-ʔa·-la-k.
mountain-OBV-DEF-SG-ACC

(4) ʔe·-t yacoxʔan-a·naxok-wa·-yʔik xa-t-xa-nesʔe-k-laknoʔo
be-SS.CONS camp-large-OBV-ALL AUG-move.DU-AUG-DU-PART-EVID

yacoxʔan-away-kwa·lo-wa·-yʔik. ʔe·-lʔok cʔa·pxan-ʔa·-la
camp-tall-big-OBV-ALL do-when bed-DEF-NOM.SG

kwa·lo·-tak ye·la-k-lakno?o lak. Ha·csokonay-la
big-SUP be.located-PART-EVID 3SGACC Coyote-NOM.SG

c?a·pxan-wa·-y?ik he-cne-k-lakno?o
bed-OBV-ALL REFL-lie.down-PART-EVID

?e·-ta ha·?ako·n-osas-wa·-?a·-la-k "na·ya-k he?a·-co?,"
be-SS.NPURP man-young-OBV-DEF-SG-ACC 2.SG-ACC there-RES

no-k-lakno?o. ?e·-kla ha·?ako·n-osas-wa·-?a·-la yela-k-lakno?o.
say-PART-EVID be-DS.NSIM man-young-OBV-DEF-NOM.SG sit-PART-EVID

(5) ?e·-kwa kwa·n-wa·-?a·-la ha-kxo-ta-k-lakno?o.
do-DS.SIM woman-OBV-DEF-NOM.SG move.SG-in-CIS-PART-EVID

?e·-l-?ok kwa·n-enoxa·-tak ye·la-k-lakno?o.
be-3-if woman-beauty-SUP be.located-PART-EVID

Ha·csokonay-la-k "ha-cxo-w!"
Coyote-SG-ACC move.SG-up-IMP

no-k-lakno?o. "na·ya-k hel?at=a·we!" no-k-lakno?o.
say-part-EVID 2.SG-ACC over.there=PERF say-PART-EVID

?e·-kla Ha·csokonay-la "?al?," no-k-lakno?o.
be-DS.NSIM Coyote-NOM.SG all.right say-PART-EVID

"hey?," no-k-lakno?o.
yes say-PART-EVID

ha-cxo-t kalak-a·-y?ik yela-k-lakno?o.
move.SG-up-SS.CONS other-DEF-ALL be.located-PART-EVID

?e·-kla Ha·?ako·n-osas-wa·-?a·-la c?a·pxan-wa·-y?ik
do-DS.NSIM man-young-OBV-DEF-NOM.SG bed-OBV-ALL

he-cne-k-lakno?o.
REFL-lie.down-PART-EVID

(6) ?e·-kwa kwa·n-wa·-?a·-la yaxa-n-?a·-la-k
be-DS.SIM woman-OBV-DEF-NOM.SG eat-GER-DEF-SG-ACC

ʔe-ʔey-o·-tanpil-ta-k-laknoʔo.
RED-CAUS-do-away-CIS-PART-EVID

ʔe·-kla	Ha·csokonay-la-k	"na·kw!	yaxa-w!"	no-k-laknoʔo.
be-DS.NSIM	Coyote-SG-ACC	okay!	eat-IMP	say-PART-EVID

ʔe·-kla	Ha·csokonay-la	yaxa-no-k-laknoʔo
be-DS.NSIM	Coyote-NOM.SG	eat-CONT-PART-EVID

ʔe·-ta	waʔanpax	ʔe·-kwa	yakwan-ʔa·-la-k
be-SS.NPURP	as.soon.as	be-when	dish-DEF-SG-ACC

noko-tanpil-na-k-laknoʔo.
pick-take-ABL-PART-EVID

ʔe·-ta	kwa·n-wa·-ʔa·-la	ha-kxo-ta-k-laknoʔo.
be-SS.NPURP	woman-OBV-DEF-NOM.SG	move.SG-in-ABL-PART-EVID

ʔe·-kwa	ʔo·ʔo·-t-la	he-cne-nesʔe-k-laknoʔo.
be-DS.SIM	night-PART-NOM.SG	REFL-lay-DU-PART-EVID

ʔe·-kla	Ha·csokonay-la	ha·c-ʔa·-yʔik
be-DS.NSIM	Coyote-NOM.SG	ground-DEF-ALL

kwa·n-wa·-ʔa·-la	na-wle-t
woman-OBV-DEF-NOM.SG	TH-spread.out-SS.CONS

ʔeke-k-laknoʔo.	Ha·csokonay-la-k	"he-cne-w!"	no·-t
give-PART-EVID	Coyote-SG-ACC	REFL-lie-IMP	say-SS.CONS

ʔe·-kla	Ha·csokonay-la	he-cne-k-laknoʔo.
be-DS.NSIM	Coyote-NOM.SG	REFL-lie-PART-EVID

(7)

He-cne-t	papasanʔe	he-cn-an	"ʔehehehe!"
REFL-lie-SS.CONS	little.while	REFL-lie-GER	ahahaha

no-no-k-laknoʔo.
say-CONT-PART-EVID

"we·lʔa!"	no-no-k-laknoʔo.	"hexalʔoy
oh!	say-CONT-PART-EVID	ants

ke-nce-no-kwa!"	no-no-k-laknoʔo.
1.OBJ-bite-CONT-MIR	say-CONT-PART-EVID

(8) ʔe·kla ha·ʔako·n-osas-wa·-ʔa·-la "ha-yco-ta-w,"
be-DS.SIM man-young-OBV-DEF-NOM.SG move.SG-up-CIS-IMP

no-k-laknoʔo.
say-PART-EVID

ʔe·-kla Ha·csokonay-la ha-yco-na-k-laknoʔo
be-DS.NSIM Coyote-NOM.SG move.SG-up-ABL-PART-EVID

ʔe·-t he-cne-k-laknoʔo cʔa·px-an-wa·-yʔik.
be-SS.CONS REFL-lay.down-PART-EVID make.bed-GER-OBV-ALL

ʔe·-t papasanʔe he-cn-an "ʔehehehe!"
be-SS.CONS little.while REFL-lay.down-GER ouch!

no-k-laknoʔo. "we·lʔa! hexalʔoy-a·ʔas ʔe-no-k!"
say-PART-EVID oh! ant-many be-CONT-MIR

no-k-laknoʔo. "k-e·-na-naco·-no-kwa!" no-k-laknoʔo.
say-PART-EVID 1OBJ-REFL-RED-bite-CONT-MIR say-PART-EVID

(9) ʔe·-kla ha·ʔako·n-osas-wa·-ʔa·-la "na·kw!" te·-wʔan
be-DS.NSIM man-young-OBV-DEF-NOM.SG okay this-ADESS

he-cne-w! no-k-laknoʔo
REFL-lay.down-IMP say-PART-EVID

ʔe·-kla Ha·csokonay-la ha-cxo-t waʔasay-ʔa·-wʔan
be-DS.NSIM Coyote-NOM.SG move.SG-up-SS.CONS one.side-DEF-ADESS

kwa·n-la he-cne-k-a·-wʔan he-cne-k-laknoʔo.
woman-NOM.SG REFL-lie.down-PART-DEF-ADESS REFL-lie.down-PART-EVID

ʔe·-kla kwa·n-wa·-ʔa·-la ha-cxo-t
be-DS.NSIM woman-OBV-DEF-NOM.SG move.SG-UP-SS.CONS

kalak-a·-yʔik He-cne-k-laknoʔo. ʔe·-kla Ha·csokonay-la
other-DEF-ALL REFL-lie.down-PART-EVID be-DS.NSIM Coyote-NOM.SG

"ʔehehehe," no-k-laknoʔo.
ehhehehehe say-PART-EVID

"we·lʔa hexalʔoy-a·ʔas ʔe·-no-kwa! K-e·-na-naco·-no-kwa!"
Ouch ant-many be-CONT-MIR 1OBJ-REFL-RED-bite-CONT-MIR

no-k-laknoʔo.
say-PART-EVID

(10) ʔe·-kla kwa·n-wa·-ʔa·-la
be-DS.NSIM woman-OBV-DEF-NOM.SG

kewnescoxnapa·to·noʔ
"ke-we-[nes-coxn]-ap-a·tewa-no-we-ʔ," no-k-laknoʔo.
1.OBJ-OBJ.PL-[CAUS-sleep]-NEG-FUT-CONT-DECL-PRES say-PART-EVID

"ke-ta-ta-na-w Ha·csokonay-te·-la coxna·-kwa," no-k-laknoʔo
1.OBJ-RED-take-ABL-IMP Coyote-this-NOM.SG sleep-DS.SIM say-PART-EVID

taxse-w-a·to·-kwa
ʔe·-kwa taxse-wa-a·tewa-kwa Ha·csokonay-la coxna-k-laknoʔo.
be-DS.SIM morning-INGR-FUT-DS.SIM Coyote-NOM.SG fall.asleep-PART-EVID

ʔe·-kla "we·ʔil!" no-k-laknoʔo. ta·-ta-na-k-laknoʔo
be-DS.NSIM all.right say-PART-EVID COM-move.PL-ABL-PART-EVID

kwa·n-wa·-ʔa-la-k. cʔawʔal ta·-ta-na-k-laknoʔo.
woman-OBV-DEF-SG-ACC far.away COM-move.PL-ABL-PART-EVID

(11) ʔe·-kwa Ha·csokonay-la ʔanco·-k-laknoʔo
be-DS.SIM Coyote-NOM.SG awake-PART-EVID

ʔe·-t kapay-la-k.
be-SS.CONS no.one-SG-ACC

ha-txil-na-k-laknoʔo yaltey-ʔa·-yʔik ʔe·-t
move.SG-out-ABL-PART-EVID outside-DEF-ALL be-SS.CONS

wecʔelʔe·-k-laknoʔo.
pursue-PART-EVID

ʔe·-t cʔawʔal ta-na-nesʔe-k-latoy
be-SS.CONS far.away move.SG-ABL-DU-PART-although

yan-ci-cxil-xa·xa-k-laknoʔo
TH-RED-run-DIST-PART-EVID

ʔe·-t no-k-laknoʔo "hecu
be-SS.CONS say-PART-EVID what

ʔe-t k-e·-pak-apa-nesʔe-kaʔ" ʔe·-kla
be-SS.CONS 1OBJ-REFL-tell-NEG-DU.SBJ-2 be-DS.NSIM

ha·ʔako·n-osas-wa·-ʔa·-la "na·ya coxna-no·-ka," no-k-laknoʔo.
man-young-OBV-DEF-NOM.SG 2.SG sleep-CONT-2.SG say-PART-EVID

(12) ʔe·-kla Ha·csokonay-la "saxʔay-te·-las yake-xamyo·-se-k-e,"
be-DS.NSIM Coyote-NOM.SG arrow-this-INST do-arrow.contest-1-PART-HORT

no-k-laknoʔo. ʔe·-kla "heyʔ," no-k-laknoʔo.
say-PART-EVID be-DS.NSIM Okay say-PART-EVID

"we·ʔil," no-k-laknoʔo.
all.right say-PART-EVID

(13) ʔe·-kla Ha·ʔako·n-osas-wa·-ʔa·-la yak-na-k-laknoʔo
be-DS.NSIM man-young-OBV-DEF-NOM.SG shoot-ABL-PART-EVID

ʔe·-t na·to·n-wa·-ʔa·-la-k neskaltey-ʔa-wʔan [*sic*]
be-SS.CONS mountain-OBV-DEF-SG-ACC far.side-DEF-ADESS

yak-xa-ylapa-k-laknoʔo.
shoot-AUG-stick.in.ground-PART-EVID

ʔe·-kla Ha·csokonay-la na·to·n-wa·-ʔa·-la-k hakayta-ʔa·-yʔik
be-DS.NSIM Coyote-NOM.SG mountain-OBV-DEF-SG-ACC near.side-DEF-ALL

yak-xa-ylapa-k-laknoʔo. ʔe·-kla xaya-k-laknoʔo.
shoot-AUG-stick.in.ground-PART-EVID be-DS.NSIM go.there-PART-EVID

saxʔay-na·xen-coʔ
Ha·csokonay-la "saxʔay-na·xen-coʔ," no-k-laknoʔo.
Coyote-NOM.SG arrow-2.SG.POSS-RES say-PART-EVID

ʔe·-kla ha·ʔako·n-osas-wa·-ʔa·-la "a·kay," no-k-laknoʔo.
be-DS.NSIM man-young-OBV-DEF-NOM.SG no say-PART-EVID

"sa·ken kap-a·we," no-k-laknoʔo. ʔe·-ta na·ʔe·-t
1.SG.GEN be.not-PERF say-PART-EVID be-SS.NPURP go.on-SS.CONS

na·to·n-ʔa·-la-k ʔa·yay-wa·-yʔik na·ʔe·-kwa
mountain-DEF-SG-ACC other.side-OBV-ALL come-DS.SIM

ha·ʔako·n-osas-wa·-ʔa·-la saxʔay-ʔa·xen-ʔa·-la-k
man-young-OBV-DEF-NOM.SG arrow-3.SG.GEN-DEF-SG-ACC

taʔane-k-laknoʔo.
pick.up-PART-EVID

(14) ʔe·-ta cakaw-ʔa·-yʔik ta-kla-na·-kwa Ha·csokonay-la
be-SS.NPURP river-DEF-ALL move.PL-down-ABL-DS.SIM Coyote-NOM.SG

"lopaw-xa·me-no-[Ø]-ʔa·-la ta·ʔe·-k kwa·n-te·-la-k,"
dive-defeat-CONTPART-DEF-NOM.SG[5] marry-PART woman-that-SG-ACC

no-k-laknoʔo.
say-PART-EVID

ʔe·-kla ha·ʔako·n-osas-wa·-ʔa·-la "we·ʔil," no-k-laknoʔo.
be-DS.NSIM man-young-OBV-DEF-NOM.SG okay say-PART-EVID

ʔe·-ta ʔa·x-ʔa·-yʔik ta-kla-na-t
be-SS.NPURP water-DEF-ALL move.DU-down-ABL-SS.CONS

lo-lopo·-nesʔe-k-laknoʔo.
RED-dive-DU-PART-EVID

(15) pasʔe·-kwa Ha·csokonay-la xa-ytele-xa-k-laknoʔo.
time.pass-DS.SIM Coyote-NOM.SG AUG-come.up-AUG-PART-EVID.

ʔe·-kla kwa·n-wa·-ʔa·-la "xa-ytele-xa-kwa!"
be-DS.NSIM woman-OBV-DEF-NOM.SG AUG-come.up-AUG-MIR

5. In Hoijer's original text, this word featured two case suffixes, an instrumental *-les* followed by the regular (nominative) singular suffix *-la*: *lopaw-xa·me-no-[Ø]-ʔa·-les-la*. This probably represents a speaker error in which the speaker changed his or her mind in mid-discourse. It has been amended here to just *-la*.

no-k-laknoʔo.
say-PART-EVID

ʔe·-l-ʔok ha·ʔako·n-osas-wa·-ʔa·-la sosko·n-ape
be-3-when man-young-OBV-DEF-NOM.SG hear-NEG

no-k-laknoʔo. ʔe·-kla Ha·csokonay-la xa-cl-o·-t
say-PART-EVID be-DS.NSIM Coyote-NOM.SG AUG-angry-INGR-SS .CONS

he-wle-k-laknoʔo ha·ʔako·n-wa·-ʔa·-la-k
TH-catch.hold.of-PART-EVID man-OBV-DEF-SG-ACC

ʔe·-t ne-kel-nacka-k-laknoʔo. ʔe·-ta Ha·csokonay-la
be-SS.CONS TH-drown-kill-PART-EVID be-SS.NPURP Coyote-NOM.SG

"we·ʔil!" no-k-laknoʔo.
okay say-PART-EVID

kwa·n-wa·-ʔa·-la-k ta·-ta-na-k-laknoʔo.
woman-OBV-DEF-SG-ACC COM-move.PL-ABL-PART-EVID

(16) xamʔal-ʔa-y·ik ta-nesʔe-·kwa Ha·csokonay-la "saxʔay-e·-ka-k
prairie-DEF-ALL move.PL-DU-when Coyote-NOM.SG arrow-yonder-PL-ACC

yaknanoʔ
henox yaka-na-no-we-ʔe," no-k-laknoʔo. "heʔe·-k
good shoot-ABL-CONT-DECL-NP say-PART-EVID yonder-ACC

he-ylapa-w. yake·-s," no-k-laknoʔo.
REFL-stand-IMP shoot-1 say-PART-EVID

ʔe·-kla kwa·n-wa·-ʔa·-la ha·-na-t cʔawʔal-ʔa·-yʔik
be-DS.NSIM woman-OBV-DEF-NOM.SG move.SG-ABL-SS.CONS distance-DEF-ALL

xeylapakla
xa-he-yalapa-k-la Ha·csokonay-la yake-k-laknoʔo
AUG-REFL-stand-PART-NOM.SG Coyote-NOM.SG shoot-PART-EVID

ʔe·-t kwa·n-wa·-ʔa·-la-k ya·lo·na-k-laknoʔo.
be-SS.CONS woman-OBV-DEF-SG-ACC kill-PART-EVID

(17) Ha·csokonay-la xa·xa·t sax?ay-?a·-la-k x?e·pa-ta
Coyote-NOM.SG go.SG-SS.CONS arrow-DEF-SG-ACC pull.out-SS.NPURP

ma·ka-no-k-lakno?o. ?e·-ta kwa·n-wa·-?a-la-k
weep-cont-PART-EVID be-SS.NPURP woman-OBV-DEF-SG-ACC

kes?acan-?a·-w?an
lower.body-DEF-ADESS

topo-k-lakno?o. ?e·-t ha-wa-wne-ta
cut.off-PART-EVID be-SS.CONS TH-RED-carry-SS.NPURP

ha·-na-k-lakno?o yacox?an-?a·-y?ik.
move.SG-ABL-PART-EVID camp-DEF-ALL

(18) taxas-?a·-la ha-kla-na-·kwa yacox?an-wa·-y?ik
sun-DEF-NOM.SG move.SG-down-ABL-when camp-OBV-ALL

xa·xa-k-lano?o.
go.to-PART-EVID

naxackanwo?o?
?e·-t "[naxac-kan-we]-we-?e-?," no-k-lakno?o.
be-SS.CONS [as.friend-possess-INGR]-DEC-PAST-3 say-PART-EVID

"ya-cox?a-w," no-k-lakno?o.
TH-erect.tipi-IMP say-PART-EVID

"xa·xa-t ta·-ta-?-a·ha?a. kwa·n-sa·ken-?a·-la
go.to-SS.CONS COM-move.PL-EP-INTENT woman-1.SG.GEN-DEF-NOM.SG

he-ytisa-n-a·we," no-k-lakno?o
REFL-be.bashful-CONT-PERF say-PART-EVID

(19) ?e·-ta ha·-na-·kwa yacox-?o·-k-lakno?o.
be-SS.NPURP move.SG-ABL-when tipi-do-PART-EVID

?e·-t papasan?e
be-SS.CONS a.little.while

?e·-kwa yacox?an-wa·-y?ik [laughing], no-no-k-lakno?o.
be-DS.SIM camp-OBV-ALL [laughing] say-CONT-PART-EVID

?e·-kla ha·?ako·-s?atic-?a·-la "we·-y?ik
be-DS.NSIM man-old[?]-DEF-NOM.SG that-ALL

ta·taxkoʔo
ta·-ta-xka-we-ʔei," no-k-laknoʔo
COM-move.PL-back-DECL-PAST say-PART-EVID

ʔo·ʔa-wa·-lʔas ʔe-ʔeyo·-t ʔe·-tanpil-ta-t
night-OBV-INST.SG RED-prepare-SS.CONS do-carry-CIS-SS.CONS

nes-yaxa-k-la Ha·csokonay-la yax-to·xa-k-laknoʔo
CAUS-eat-PART-NOM.SG Coyote-NOM.SG eat-finish-PART-EVID

xatyaw-la-k.
sweet.potato-SG-ACC

(20) ʔe·-ta taxso·-kwa "he-teca ye·la-k-ye
be-SS.NPURP be.dawn-DS.SIM what-place sit-PART-Q

xatyaw-te·-laʔ," no-k-laknoʔo.
sweet.potato-this-NOM.SG say-PART-EVID

ʔe·-kla "we·-wʔan cakaw-eʔe·-k ha·we,"
be-DS.NSIM that-ADESS river-that-ACC exist.3SG

no-k-laknoʔo.
say-PART-EVID

(21) Taxso·-kla Ha·csokonay-wa·-ʔa·-la neskaysanan-ʔoyuk-la-k
be.dawn-DS.NSIM Coyote-OBV-DEF-NOM.SG yucca-sack-SG-ACC

taʔane-ta ha·-na-[Ø]-la ʔoyuk-wa·-ʔa·-la-k
take-SS.NPURP move.SG-ABL-PART-NOM.SG sack-OBV-DEF-SG-ACC

xatyaw-ʔa·-la-k nes-pece-ta
sweet.potato-DEF-SG-ACC CAUS-full-SS.NPURP

ha-wa-wne-ta-xka-k-laknoʔo. ʔe·-ta
TH-RED-carry-move.PL-back-PART-EVID be-SS.NPURP

mʔe·yc-a·to-no-k-laknoʔo Ha·csokonay-la.
urinate-FUT-CONT-PART-EVID Coyote-NOM.SG

(22) ʔe·-t ha-txil-na-t cʔawʔal-ʔa·-yʔik
be-SS.CONS move.SG-out-ABL-SS.CONS distance-DEF-ALL

mʔe·yca-·kwa he-payxwet-an-wixwan-la
urinate-while REFL-dress.as.female-GER-small-NOM.SG

yan-ci-cxil-tanpila-k-laknoʔo
TH-RED-run-move.DU-away-PART-EVID

yacoxʔan-wa·-yʔik. ʔe·-t cʔaxw-ʔa·-la-k
camp-OBV-ALL be-SS.CONS tipi.curtain-DEF-SG-ACC

taʔan-xa-[a]ycona-lʔok kwa·n-wa·-ʔa·-la kawcew-pax
grasp-AUG-pull-when woman-OBV-DEF-NOM.SG maggot.covered-quite

ye·la-k-laknoʔo lak. he-payxwet-an-wixan-ʔa·-la
sit-PART-EVID 3SG.ACC REFL-dress.as.female-GER-small-DEF-NOM.SG

he-xsasa-ta ya-lxil-na-k-laknoʔo
REFL-scream-SS.NPURP TH-run.off-ABL-PART-EVID

xʔay-ʔa·-la-k he-pake-k-laknoʔo.
mother-DEF-SG-ACC REFL-tell-PART-EVID

(23) ʔe·-kla kwe·-ʔa·-la-k taʔane-ta
be-DS.NSIM club-DEF-SG-ACC take-SS.NPURP

ha-n-pil-na-k-laknoʔo.
move.SG-TH-another.place-ABL-PART-EVID

ʔe·-lok Ha·csokonay-la yel-e·la-k-laknoʔo lak.
be-when Coyote-NOM.SG sit-be.located-PART-EVID 3SG.ACC

kwa·n-wa·-ʔa·-la Ha·csokonay-la-k hesʔacan-ʔa·-yʔik
woman-OBV-DEF-NOM.SG Coyote-SG-ACC body's.lower.half-DEF-ALL

ya-xwce-k-laknoʔo.
TH-beat-PART-EVID

ʔe·-kla Ha·csokonay-la xacolta-ta
be-DS.NSIM Coyote-NOM.SG defecate-SS.NPURP

yan-ci-cxil-a·xey-na-k-laknoʔo.
TH-RED-run-far-ABL-PART-EVID

(24)		he·pano·noʔo	
	naʔa	he·panewa-na-we-ʔei	ʔo·ʔo·-panon-wa·-ka-k.
	So	narrate-CONT-DECL-PAST	night-story-OBV-PL-ACC

Coyote, Rabbit, and Eagle's Daughter: Free English Translation

[1] Coyote was going along, and, as he did so, he climbed up a mountain and was sitting there. When he did so, there was a camp at the foot of the mountain—there was a large camp. Coyote went down to the center of the camp to a big, tall tipi and, going up and grasping the tipi flap, he peered inside. [2] When he did so, a young man was making arrows. Then Coyote went in and said: "What are you doing?" Then the young man said: "Over there they have asked me to marry a woman in that big camp." Then Coyote said: "Oh, I too was talking [to them] over there." Then Coyote went down to a small river and made arrows. Then he went up and, when he did so, the young man said: "Okay." [3] Then they both went off and went up to the top of a mountain. When they did, the young man said: "Let's go. Where did they call you to?" Coyote said: "You say [first], to what place did they call *you*?" Then the young man said: "Okay, they called me over to the big tall tipi in the center of camp." Then Coyote said: "Yes, they called me over there too." Then [the young man] said: "Let's go," and the two went down the mountain. [4] And the two arrived at the large camp, at the big tall tipi. When they did, there was a very big bed there. Coyote lay down on the bed. The young man said: "It's right there for you." Then the young man sat down. [5] When he did so, the woman came in. As the beautiful woman sat down, she said to Coyote: "Get up!" she said. "For you it's over there!" Then Coyote said: "All right, yes." Getting up, he sat down on the other side, and the young man lay down on the bed. [6] After this, the woman prepared some food and brought it in, and Coyote said: "Okay, eat!" Then Coyote ate, and after he finished she picked up the plates. Then the woman went in, and when it was night they both lay down. Then, with Coyote on the ground, the woman spread out [a bed] for him and said: "Lie down!" and then Coyote lay down. [7] Lying down for a little while, he kept on saying: "Ouch! Ants are biting me!" [8] Then the young man said: "Get up," and Coyote got up and lay down on the bed. After a little while lying down, he cried out: "Ouch! There are a bunch of ants! They keep on biting me!" [9] Then the young man said: "All right, lie down on this side!" Then Coyote got up and lay down toward one side, toward where the woman was lying. Then the woman got up and lay down on the other side, and Coyote said: "Ouch! There are a bunch of ants! They keep on biting me!" [10] Then the woman said: "He won't let us sleep! Take me away when Coyote falls

asleep." When it was about to be morning, Coyote fell asleep. Then the woman said: "Let's go!" and the two went far away together. [11] Then Coyote woke up, and no one was there. He went outside and went after them. Although the two had gone a long way, he ran and caught up with them. He said: "So why didn't you tell me?" Then the young man said: "You were sleeping." [12] Then Coyote said: "Let's have an arrow-shooting contest with these arrows." Then [the young man] said: "Okay, let's do it." [13] Then the young man shot off [an arrow] toward the far side of the mountain so that it stuck in the ground. Then Coyote shot off [an arrow] to the near side of the mountain so that it stuck into the ground. Then they went there, and Coyote said: "Here is your arrow." Then the young man said: "No, it's not mine." Then they went on to the other side of the mountain, and when they arrived the young man picked up his arrow. [14] Then when they went down to a river, Coyote said: "Whoever defeats the other in diving marries that woman." Then the young man said: "All right," and the two dived down into the water. [15] After time had passed, Coyote came up. Then the woman said: "He's really come up!" When she did so, the young man didn't hear her. Then Coyote got angry and grabbed the man and killed him by drowning. Then Coyote said: "All right!" and took the woman away with him. [16] When they both went off to the prairie, Coyote said: "I shoot arrows pretty well. Stand over there, I'll shoot at you." Then the woman went off to a distance and stood. Coyote shot at her, and he killed the woman. [17] Coyote then went to her and, pulling the arrow out, was weeping. Then he cut off the lower half of the woman's body and carried it to camp as he went. [18] When the sun was going down, he went to the camp, and said: "I've gotten married! Put up a tipi. I'm going to bring her her here. My wife is very shy." [19] Then when he went off they put up a tipi and after a little while there was laughing in the tipi. Then the old man said: "He has come back with her," he said. During the night he prepared [food] and brought it and gave it to him to eat. Coyote ate all of the sweet potatoes up. [20] Then when it was morning, he said: "Where are the sweet potatoes to be found?" Then [the old man] said: "They're over yonder at the creek over there." [21] The next day Coyote took a sack made of yucca and went off and filled the sack with sweet potatoes and then was going to take a piss. [22] Going off a bit, while he was peeing, a little girl ran up around to where the tipi was. Then when she lifted the tipi tentflap, there was the woman covered with maggots! The little girl ran off screaming and told her mother. [23] Then taking her club with her, she ran over there. When she did, Coyote was just sitting there. Then woman beat him all over the lower part of his body, and Coyote ran away shitting all over the place. [24] They've always told night stories like that.

4. Coyote and Eagle's Daughter

(1) Ha·c-sokonay-la ha·-na-no-k-lakno?o ?e·-no·-la
Coyote-SG.NOM move.SG-ABL-CONT-PART-EVID be-CONT-PART-NOM.SG

na·ton-?a·-y?ik ha-yco-na-t he-ylapa-no-k-lakno?o
mountain-DEF-ALL move.SG-up-ABL-SS.CONS REFL-stand-CONT-PART-EVID

?e·-l-?o·k na·ton-wa·-?a·-la-k ?a·yay-?a·-y?ik
be-3-when mountain-OBV-DEF-SG-ACC below-DEF-ALL

[ya-cox?-an]-a·naxok ye·la-k-lakno?o lak
TH-camp-GER-large sit-PART-EVID 3SGACC

Ha·csokonay-la ha-kla-na-t ya-cox?-an-a·naxok-wa·-y?ik
Coyote-SG.NOM move.SG-down-ABL-SS.PURP TH-camp-GER-big-OBV-ALL

xa·xat xa·xal?ok
xa-ha·-xa-t holaw-?a·-y?ik xa-ha·-xa-l-?ok
DIST-move.SG-DEST-SS.PURP end-DEF-ALL DIST-move.SG-AUG-3-when

ya-cox?-an-?a·yay-?a·-y?ik ma·ka-no-k-lakno?o
TH-tipi-GER-under-DEF-ALL weep-CONT-PART-EVID

(2) ?e·-kla Ha·csokonay-la ha-kxo-na-t
be-DS.NSIM Coyote-SG.NOM move.SG-in-ABL-SS.PURP

"hecu ?e·-kwa?" no-k-lakno?o
What be-MIR say-PART-EVID

?e·-kla kwa·n-wa·-?a·-la[6] "te·-wan ya-cox?-an-ta-na-te·-la
be-DS.NSIM woman-OBV-DEF-SG.NOM this-ADESS TH-camp-GER-go.PL-ABL-this-SG.NOM

6. Hoijer calls the *-wa·* suffix "aforementioned," but this form is evidence that it is really an obviative suffix, because the woman has not yet been mentioned in the story.

tickan-ʔa·-ka ka·p-a·we," no-k-laknoʔo "He-co-cxo·-k-la
people-DEF-NOM.PL nothing-PERF CONT-PART-EVID REFL-RED-fear-PART-NOM.SG

wetoxanoʔo
we-toxa-no-we-ʔe," no-k-laknoʔo
OBJ.PL-finish-CONT-DECL-PAST say-PART-EVID3SG

(3)
ma·kapow
ʔe·-kla Ha·c-sokonay-la "na·kw, ma·ka-ape-w,"
be-DS.NSIM Coyote-NOM.SG well weep-NEG-IMP

no-k-laknoʔo "taxso·-l-ʔok ta·-he·-sok-yaw-a·haʔa,"
CONT-PART-EVID day.break-3-when COM-REFL-fight-RECIP-

no-k-laknoʔo
CONT-PART-EVID

ʔe·-kla kwa·n-wa·-ʔa·-la kaltey-ʔa·-yʔik
be-DS.NSIM woman-OBV-DEF-SG.NOM outside-DEF-ALL

ha-txil-na-ta "Ha·csokonay-la
move.SG-out-ABL-SS.NPURP Coyote-SG.NOM

ta·he·sokyawa·toyow
taxso·-l-ʔok ta·-he·-sok-yaw-a·tewa-yow,"
day.break-SUB3SG-when COM-REFL-fight-RECIP-FUT-?

no·-n-aʔa no-k-laknoʔo
say-CONT-ASS say-PART-EVID

yaxilnapow
(4) "taxso·-l-ʔok ta·-he·-sok-yawa·-s-ʔok ya-xila-na-ape-w,"
day.break-SUB3SG-when COM-REFL-fight-RECIP-1-when TH-run-ABL-NEG-IMP

yackexwʔelapow
no-k-laknoʔo "yac-ke-xwʔel-ape-w," no-k-laknoʔo
say-PART-EVID see-1.OBJ-miss-NEG-IMP say-PART-EVID

ʔe·-kla "hehey," no-k-laknoʔo
be-DS.NSIM yes say-PART-EVID

(5) ke·sxaya-·kwa cakaw-ʔa·-yʔik ha-kla-na-t
night.fall-when river-DEF-ALL move.SG-down-ABL-SS.CONS

tekal-la-k yaxw-kayce-t
hard.wood-SG-ACC strike-chop.off-SS.PURP

kaxaw nes-amʔamʔa-ta soko-ta coxna-k-laknoʔo
black CAUS-burn-SS.NPURP put.away-SS.NPURP go.to.sleep-PART-EVID

ʔe·-t hos-taxso·-n ha-cxo-t kaltey-ʔa·-yʔik
be-SS.PURP early-dawn.break-GER move.SG-up-SS.PURP outside-DEF-ALL

ha-txil-na-ta taxas-ha-yco-ta-k-e·-wʔan
move.SG-out-ABL-SS.NPURP be.dawn-move.SG-up-CIS-PART-that-ADESS

hawa·tak
yel-na-ta hawa(y)-hatak he-xsasa-k-laknoʔo
sit-ABL-SS.NPURP tall/loud-very REFL-yell-PART-EVID

ʔe·-ta yantan-away-e·-wʔan yel-na-ta he-xsasa-k-laknoʔo
be-SS.NPURP wind-long-that-ADESS sit-DEST-SS.NPURP REFL-howl-PART-EVID

ʔe·-ta ʔecinʔe taxas-[h]a-kla-na-k-e·-wʔan
be-SS.NPURP again sun-move.SG-down-ABL-PART-this-ADESS

ʔecinʔe he-xsasa-k-laknoʔo
again REFL-howl-PART-EVID

ʔe·-ta holaw-ʔa·-la-k ʔacxo·n-te·-wʔan
be-SS.NPURP last-DEF-SG-ACC bad.weather-this-ADESS

yel-na-ta he-xsasa-k-laknoʔo
sit-ABL-SS.NPURP REFL-howl-PART-EVID

(6) ʔe·-kwa kwa·-kwan-ka noho·-na·ʔe·-kla
be-DS.SIM RED-woman-NOM.PL fetch.wood-go.off-DS.NSIM

Ha·csokonay-la he-tayʔo-k-laknoʔo
Coyote-NOM REFL-join-PART-EVID

ʔe·-kwa "we·lʔa-t ʔey-t-e·l," no-k-laknoʔo
be-DS.SIM that-SS.PURP do-move.PL-JUSS say-PART-EVID

ʔe·-kwa he-co-cxo·-k-wa·-ʔa·-la xokos-ʔa·-wʔan
be-DS.SIM REFL-RED-fear-PART-OBV-DEF-NOM.SG above.waist-DEF-ADESS

samox ye·la-k-laknoʔo ʔenik kesʔacan-ʔa·-wʔan
red sit-PART-EVID and below.waist-DEF-ADESS

kaxaw ye·la-k-laknoʔo
black be.PAST-PART-EVID

ʔe·-kla kwa·-kwan-wa·-ka saxwa-k-laknoʔo
be-DS.NSIM RED-woman-OBV-PL run.away-PART-EVID

ʔe·-kwa Ha·csokonay-la cʔa·pe-k-laknoʔo
be-DS.SIM Coyote-NOM hide-PART-EVID

(7) ʔe·-kwa wa·til henkwa·-ta-kla Ha·csokonay-la
be-DS.SIM that.one run-CIS-DS.NSIM Coyote-NOM.SG

ta·-he·sokyo·-k-laknoʔo He-co-cxo·-k-wa·-ʔa·-la-k
COM-REFL-fight-PART-EVID REFL-RED-fear-PART-OBV-DEF-SG-ACC

ʔe·-kwa ha·csokonay-yeykaʔay-ʔa·-la ha·naxok-ʔita
be-DS.SIM Coyote-big-DEF-NOM.SG many-DET

He-co-cxo·-k-wa·-ʔa·-la-k he-wle-t
REFL-RED-fear-PART-OBV-DEF-SG-ACC REFL-catch-SS.CONS

ta·-he·-sok-yo·-no-n-laknoʔo
PVB-REFL-fight-RECIP-CONT-PART-EVID

ʔe·-no-·-ka ya·lo·na-n-laknoʔo He-co-cxo·-k-wa·-ʔa·-la-k
be-CONT-PART-NOM.PL kill-PART-EVID REFL-RED-fear-PART-OBV-DEF-SG-ACC

ʔe·-ta ha·csokonay-yeykaʔay-wa·-ka na·ʔe·-k-laknoʔo
be-SS.NPURP coyote-big-OBV-NOM.PL go.off-PART-EVID

(8) ʔe·-kla Ha·csokonay-la ya-coxʔ-an-e·-wʔan tickan-kapay-eʔe·-la-k
be- DS.NSIM Coyote-NOM TH-camp-GER-that-ADESS people-no-that-SG-ACC

"ya-coxʔ-an-eka·t-ka-k	ta·mow	nes-esk-apo-w,"	no-k-laknoʔo
TH-camp-GER-toward-PL-ACC	tight	CAUS-close-NEG-IMP	say.PAST-PART-EVID

ya-coxʔ-an-wa·-ʔa·-la-k	losos	nes-esk-apa-k-laknoʔo
TH-camp-GER-OBV-DEF-SG-ACC	all	CAUS-close-NEG-PART-EVID

ʔenik	Ha·csokonay-la	te·ca-ʔa·-yʔik
and	Coyote-NOM	here-DEF-ALL

ha·-na-ta	yan-ci-cxil-ta-ʔan
move.SG-ABL-SS.NPURP	TH-RED-run-CIS-GER

	ʔo·sʔow		
"ma·tan	ʔe-we·sʔa-w	ya-coxʔ-an-te·-la	naw-e·l,"
quick	move-1/2[SUBJ]PL-IMP	TH-camp-GER-this-NOM	burn-JUSS

no-k-laknoʔo	ʔe·-l-ʔok	kapay	ʔe·-no-k-laknoʔo
say.PAST-PART-EVID	be-3-when	nothing	happen-CONT-PART-EVID

ʔe·-kla	ʔe·cinʔe	ha·-na-ta	yan-ci-cxil-ta-ʔ-an
be-DS.NSIM	again	move.SG-ABL-SS.NPURP	TH-RED-run-CIS-EP-GER

	ʔo·sʔo-w		
"hetan-ʔok	ʔe-we·sʔa-w	ya-coxʔ-an-te·-la	naw-e·l,"
hurry-if	be-1/2PL-IMP	TH-camp-GER-this-NOM.SG	burn-JUSS

no-k-laknoʔo	ʔe·lʔok	kapay	ʔe·-k-laknoʔo
say.PAST-PART-EVID	but	nothing	happen-PART-EVID

ʔe·-kla	ʔecinʔe	ha·-na-ta	henkwa·-ta-n
be-DS.NSIM	then	move.SG-ABL-SS.NPURP	run-CIS-GER

	ʔo·sʔo-w		
"hetan-ʔok	ʔe-we·sʔa-w	ya-coxʔ-an-te·-la	naw-e·l,"
hurry-if	be-1/2PL-IMP	TH-camp-GER-this-NOM.SG	burn-JUSS

no-k-laknoʔo	ʔe·-kla	kapay	ʔe·-k-laknoʔo
say-PART-EVID	be-DS.NSIM	nothing	happen-PART-EVID

ʔe·-kla	holaw-ʔa·-la-k	ha·-na-ta	he-nkwa·-ta-n
be-DS.NSIM	end-DEF-SG-ACC	move.SG-ABL-SS.NPURP	REFL-run-CIS-GER

ʔo·sʔow
"hetan-ʔok ʔe-we·sʔa-w ya-coxʔ-an-te·-la naw-e·l,"
hurry-if be-1/2PL-IMP TH-camp-GER-this-NOM.SG burn-JUSS

no-k-laknoʔo ʔe·-kla tickan-ʔa·-la ha·naxok
say.PAST-PART-EVID be-DS.NSIM people-DEF-SG many

ha·-na-ci-cxile-k-laknoʔo ʔe·-kla Ha·csokonay-la-k
move.SG-ABL-RED-run-PART-EVID be-DS.NSIM Coyote-SG-ACC

kwa·n-enox-la-k nes-ta·ʔe·-k-laknoʔo
woman-pretty-SG-ACC CAUS-grasp-PART-EVID

(9) ʔe·-kla pasʔe·-no-[Ø]-la kwa·n-wa·-ʔa·-la-k
be-SS.NSIM time.pass-CONT-PART-NOM.SG woman-OBV-DEF-SG-ACC

ha·na·tewoʔs
"ya-coxʔ-an-kalak-eʔe·-k ha·-na-a·tewa-we-ʔe-s,"
TH-camp-GER-other-yonder-ACC move.SG-ABL-FUT-DECL-PRES-1

no-k-laknoʔo Ha·csokonay-la. ʔe·-kla
say-PART-EVID Coyote-NOM.SG be-SS.NSIM

kwa·n-wa·-ʔa·-la we·lʔa no-k-laknoʔo. "ha·-n-ape-w!"
woman-OBV-DEF-NOM.SG oh! say-PART-EVID move.SG-ABL-NEG-IMP

no-k-laknoʔo. ʔe·-kla Ha·csokonay-la "pasʔ-a·p-a·ʔ,"
say-PART-EVID be-DS.NSIM Coyote-NOM.SG spend.time-NEG-1.INT

no-k-laknoʔo. "ketay he-cne-ta ʔe·-t-aha·ʔ,"
say-PART-EVID two REFL-lie.down-SS.NPURP be-EP-1.INT

no-k-laknoʔo. ʔe·-kla kwa·n-wa·-ʔa·-la "ʔeye-w,"
say-PART-EVID be-DS.NSIM woman-OBV-DEF-NOM.SG do-IMP

no-k-laknoʔo.
say-PART-EVID

(10) ʔe·-kla Ha·csokonay-la ha·-na-k-laknoʔo.
be-DS.NSIM Coyote-NOM.SG move.SG-ABL-PART-EVID

ʔe·-t ya-coxʔ-an-a·naxok-wa·-yʔik xa·-xa-t
be-SS.CONS TH-camp-GER-big-OBV-ALL AUG.move.SG-AUG-SS.CONS

pasʔe·-no-k-laknoʔo. ʔe·-no-k-la kwa·n-wa·-ʔa·-la
time.pass-CONT-PART-EVID be-CONT-PART-NOM.SG woman-OBV-DEF-NOM.SG

cʔelʔe·-k-laknoʔo. xa·-xa-t ya-coxʔ-an-a·naxok-wa·-yʔik
follow-PART-EVID AUG.move.SG-AUG-SS.CONS TH-camp-GER-big-OBV-ALL

"ʔen Ha·csokonay-laʔ" no-k-laknoʔo.
and Coyote-NOM.SG say-PART-EVID

ʔe·-kla "helʔat hetayʔo·ka·lwenoʔ he-tayʔo·-ka·lwe-no-we-ʔe," no-k-laknoʔo.
be-DS.NSIM over.yonder REFL-join-gamble-CONT-DECL-PRES say-PART-EVID

(11) ʔe·-kla ha·cin-ʔa·-yʔik xa·-xa-ta
be-DS.NSIM near-DEF-ALL AUG.move.SG-AUG-SS.NPURP

ya-coxʔ-an-ʔa·-yʔik ha-kxo-na-t
TH-camp-GER-DEF-ALL move.SG-in-ABL-SS.CONS

"a·x-ka-k," no-k-laknoʔo. ʔe·-kla
water-PL-ACC say-PART-EVID be-DS.NSIM

"kap-a·we," no-k-laknoʔo. ʔe·-kla
nothing-PERF say-PART-EVID be-DS.NSIM

yakw-an-ʔa·-la-k taʔane-ta yakwa·-na-k-laknoʔo.
fetch.water-GER-DEF-SG-ACC (='bucket') pick.up-SS.NPURP fetch.water-ABL-PART-EVID

(12) ʔe·-kwa he-kalwe-k-wa·-yʔik we·ʔis ha·ʔako·n-osas-la
be-DS.SIM REFL-gamble-PART-OBV-ALL one man-young-NOM.SG

"o·c!" no-k-laknoʔo. "Ha·csokonay-ʔan ta·ʔe·-k-la!"
whoa! say-PART-EVID Coyote-GEN grasp-PART-NOM.SG (='wife')

no-k-laknoʔo. "te·-l xa·ne·-l!" no-k-laknoʔo.
say-PART-EVID this-DIR go.off-JUSS say-PART-EVID

ʔe·-kla Ha·csokonay-la ya·ce-t xʔaxʔayʔa-no-k-laknoʔo.
be-DS.NSIM Coyote-NOM.SG look-SS.CONS laugh-CONT-PART-EVID

caneneknoʔo
ʔe·-kla Ha·ʔako·n-osaʔas-wa·-ka "cane-ne-k-no-we-ʔe,"
be-DS.NSIM man-young-OBV-NOM.PL leave-2-PART-CONT-DECL-PRES

no·-no-n-laknoʔo.
say-CONT-PART-EVID

ʔe·-kla Ha·csokonay-la "o·ko," no-k-laknoʔo.
be-DS.NSIM Coyote-NOM.SG no say-PART-EVID

ke-yaca-we·sʔa-w
"ke-yac-o·sʔo-w!" no-k-laknoʔo.
1.OBJ-see-1/2PL-IMP say-PART-EVID

"ʔa·x-ka-k ke-nes-xan-a·to-nwa-ʔ," no-k-laknoʔo.
water-PL-ACC 1.OBJ-CAUS-drink.water-FUT-DEON-DEON3 say-PART-EVID

(13) ʔe·-ta kwa·n-la ʔe·-k-wa·-yʔik xa·-xa-ta
be-SS.NPURP woman-NOM.SG be-PART-OBV-ALL AUG.move.SG-AUG-SS.NPURP

ʔey-ne-txewʔa-k-laknoʔo. ʔe·-kla kwa·n-wa·-ʔa·-la
CAUS-TH-poke-PART-EVID be-DS.NSIM woman-OBV-DEF-NOM.SG

Ha·csokonay-la-k ya·ce-t "ke-cne-w!" no-k-laknoʔo.
Coyote-SG-ACC see-SS.CONS 1.OBJ-leave-IMP say-PART-EVID

ʔe·-kla Ha·csokonay-la "ke-nes-xane-w!" no-k-laknoʔo.
be-DS.NSIM Coyote-NOM.SG 1.OBJ-CAUS-drink-IMP say-PART-EVID

ʔe·-kla kwa·n-wa·-ʔa·-la nes-xan-ape-ta
be-DS.NSIM woman-OBV-DEF-NOM.SG CAUS-drink-NEG-SS.NPURP

ha·-na-k-laknoʔo.
move.SG-ABL-PART-EVID

(14) ʔo·ʔo·-kwa xa·-xa-t kwa·n-wa·-ʔa·-la-k
be.night-DS.SIM AUG.move.SG-AUG-SS.CONS woman-OBV-DEF-SG-ACC

ta·-he·-pano·-kwa haʔako·n-osaʔas-ka "Ha·csokonay-la-k
COM-REFL-narrate-DS.SIM man-young-NOM.PL Coyote-SG-ACC

nes-coxn-ape-no-n ʔo·ʔa-wa·-tak," no·-no-n-laknoʔo.
CAUS-sleep-NEG-CONT-PART night-this-very say-CONT-PART-EVID

"kwa·n-ʔa·-la-k ho·ʔoxo·-no-n," no·-no-n-laknoʔo.
woman-DEF-SG-ACC steal-CONT-PART say-CONT-PART-EVID

(15) ʔe·-ta ʔo·ʔo·-k-la ta·-he·malo·-no-n-laknoʔo ʔe·-t
be-SS.NPURP be.night-PART-NOM.SG COM-dance-CONT-PART-EVID be-SS.CONS

nes-coxn-ape-·kwa taxso·-k-laknoʔo Ha·csokonay-la-k.
CAUS-sleep-NEG-when be.dawn-PART-EVID Coyote-SG-ACC

ʔe·-kla kwa·n-wa·-ʔa·-la xaclo·-k-laknoʔo
be-DS.NSIM woman-OBV-DEF-NOM.SG be.angry-PART-EVID

ha·na·tewoʔs
ʔe·-t "ha·-na-a·tewa-we-ʔe-s," no-k-laknoʔo.
be-SS.CONS move.SG-ABL-FUT-DECL-PRES-1 say-PART-EVID

(16) Ha·csokonay-la "ʔac[x]o·ne·-wʔan[7] ka·lwe-n-a·haʔa," no-k-lakoʔo.
Coyote-NOM.SG north-ADESS gamble-CONT-INTENT say-PART-EVID

ʔe·-t ha·-na-k-laknoʔo Ha·csokonay-la. ʔe·-t
be-SS.CONS move.SG-ABL-PART-EVID Coyote-NOM.SG be-SS.CONS

ya-coxʔ-an-a·naxok-a·-yʔik xa·-xa-ta "ʔacxo·ne·-wʔan
TH-camp-GER-big-DEF-ALL AUG.move.SG-AUG-SS.NPURP north-ADESS

ka·lw-a·-na-[s]e-k," no-k-laknoʔo. ʔe·-ta ha·-na-t
gamble-move.SG-ABL-1-PART say-PART-EVID be-SS.NPURP move.SG-ABL-SS.CONS

7. Hoijer's original text has: *ʔacso·ne·wʔan.*

ya-coxʔ-an-a·naxok-a·-yʔik xa·-xa-k-laknoʔo. ʔe·-t
TH-camp-GER-big-DEF-ALL AUG.movc.SG-AUG-PART-EVID be-SS.CONS

taxso·-k-la "ʔacxo·ne·-wʔan ka·lw-a·-na-se-k,"
be.dawn-PART-NOM.SG north-ADESS gamble-move.SG-ABL-1-PART

no-k-laknoʔo Ha·csokonay-la. taxso-k-la
say-PART-EVID Coyote-NOM.SG be.dawn-PART-NOM.SG

ha·-na-k-laknoʔo. ya-coxʔ-an-a·naxok-a·-yʔik.
move.SG-ABL-PART-EVID TH-camp-GER-big-DEF-ALL

xa·-xa-t he-tayʔo·-ka·lwe-no-k-laknoʔo.
AUG.move.SG-AUG-SS.CONS REFL-join-gamble-CONT-PART-EVID

(17) ʔe·-kwa kwa·n-wa·-ʔa·-la "Ha·csokonay-la-k
be-DS.SIM woman-OBV-DEF-NOM.SG Coyote-SG-ACC

cʔelʔeya·tonʔes
cʔelʔey-a·tewa-no-ʔe-s," no-k-laknoʔo. ʔe·-t
follow-FUT-CONT-PRES-1 say-PART-EVID be-SS.CONS

cʔelʔe·-k-laknoʔo. ya-coxʔ-an-a·naxok-a·-yʔik
follow-PART-EVID TH-camp-GER-big-DEF-ALL

xa·-xa-t "ʔen Ha·csokonay-laʔ," no-k-laknoʔo.
AUG.move.SG-AUG-SS.CONS and Coyote-NOM.SG say-PART-EVID

ka·lwa·noʔo
ʔe·-kla "ʔacxaw-tak-e·-wʔan ka·lwe-ha·-na-we-ʔe,"
be-DS.NSIM north-quite-that-ADESS gamble-move.SG-ABL-DECL-PRES

no-k-laknoʔo. ʔe·-kla kwa·n-wa·-ʔa·-la cʔelʔe·-k-laknoʔo.
say-PART-EVID be-DS.NSIM woman-OBV-DEF-NOM.SG follow-PART-EVID

ʔe·-t ʔecinʔe ya-coxʔ-an-a·naxok-a·-yʔik xa·-xa-t
be-SS.CONS then TH-camp-GER-big-DEF-ALL AUG.move.SG-AUG-SS.CONS

"ʔen Ha·csokonay-laʔ" no-k-laknoʔo. ʔe·-kla
and Coyote-NOM.SG say-PART-EVID be-DS.NSIM

	ka·lwa·noʔo	
"ʔacxaw-tak-e·-wʔan	ka·lwe-ha·-na-we-ʔe,"	no-k-laknoʔo.
north-quite-that-ADESS	gamble-move.SG-ABL-DECL-PRES	say-PART-EVID

ʔe·-kla	kwa·n-wa·-ʔa·-la	cʔelʔe·-k-lakno.
be-DS.NSIM	woman-OBV-DEF-NOM.SG	follow-PART-EVID

ʔe·-t	ya-coxʔ-an-a·nxok-a·-yʔik	xa·-xa-t
be-SS.CONS	TH-camp-GER-big-DEF-ALL	AUG.move.SG-AUG-SS.CONS

"ʔen	Ha·csokonay-laʔ,"	no-k-laknoʔo.
and	Coyote-NOM.SG	say-PART-EVID

		ka·lwa·noʔo
ʔe·-kla	"ʔacxaw-tak-e·-wʔan	ka·lw-ha·-na-we-ʔe,"
be-DS.NSIM	north-quite-that-ADESS	gamble-move.SG-ABL-DECL-PRES

no-k-laknoʔo.	ʔe·-kla	kwa·n-wa·-ʔa·-la	cʔelʔe-k-laknoʔo.
say-PART-EVID	be-DS.NSIM	woman-OBV-DEF-NOM.SG	follow-PART-EVID

ʔe·-t	ya-coxʔ-an-a·naxok-a·-yʔik	xa·-xa-t
be-SS.CONS	TH-camp-GER-big-DEF-ALL	AUG.move.SG-AUG-SS.CONS

"ʔen	Ha·csokonay-laʔ,"	no-k-laknoʔo.
and	Coyote-NOM.SG	say-PART-EVID

		ka·wenoʔ [*sic*]	
ʔe·-kla	"te·ca	ka·[l]we-no-we-ʔe,"	no-k-laknoʔo.
be-DS.NSIM	this-place	gamble-CONT-DECL-PRES	say-PART-EVID

(18)	ʔe·-k-la	"xa·-xa-t	he-pake-w
	be-PART-NOM.SG	AUG.move.SG-AUG-SS.CONS	REFL-tell-IMP

ʔe·-ta-w!"	no-k-laknoʔo.	ʔe·-kla	xa·-xa-t
be-CIS-IMP	say-PART-EVID	be-DS.NSIM	AUG.move.SG-AUG-SS.CONS

	yamka·noʔ	
"kwa·n-[n]a·xen-la	ya-maka-·-no-we-ʔe,"	no-k-laknoʔo.
woman-2.SG.GEN-NOM.SG	TH-cry-2.OBJ-CONT-DECL-PRES	say-PART-EVID

ʔe·-kla Ha·csokonay-la "to·na-no-·nwa-nʔey," [*sic*]
be-DS.NSIM Coyote-NOM.SG lie-CONT-DEON-DEON2

noʔs
no-k-laknoʔo. ʔe·-kla "wa·xes no-we-ʔe-s," no-k-laknoʔo.
say-PART-EVID be-DS.NSIM true say-DECL-PRES-1 say-PART-EVID

"na·kw ʔe·-ta-w!" no-k-laknoʔo.
all.right be-CIS-IMP say-PART-EVID

(19) ʔe·-kla Ha·csokonay-la ta-saʔe·-k-laknoʔo. [*sic*]
be-DS.NSIM Coyote-NOM.SG COM-enter-PART-EVID

xa-t-xa-nesʔe-k-laknoʔo ya-coxʔ-an-ʔa·-yʔik
AUG-move.PL-AUG-DU-PART-EVID TH-camp-GER-DEF-ALL

ʔe·noʔ
"te·-ca ʔe·-no-we-ʔe," no-k-laknoʔo.
this-place be-CONT-DECL-PRES say-PART-EVID

(20) ʔe·-kla Ha·csokonay-la helʔeya-kxo-na-k-laknoʔo.
be-DS.NSIM Coyote-NOM.SG peer-in-ABL-PART-EVID

ʔe·-kla kwa·n-wa·-ʔa·-la "ha-kxo-ta-w!" no-k-laknoʔo.
be-DS.NSIM woman-OBV-DEF-NOM.SG move.SG-in-CIS-IMP say-PART-EVID

ʔe·-kla Ha·csokonay-la ha-kxo-n-ape-ta
be-DS.NSIM Coyote-NOM.SG move.SG-in-ABL-NEG-SS.NPURP

xʔaxʔayʔa-no-k-laknoʔo. ʔe·-kla ʔecinʔe
laugh-CONT-PART-EVID be-DS.NSIM then

"ha-kxo-ta-w!" no-k-laknoʔo.
move.SG-in-CIS-IMP say-PART-EVID

ʔe·-kla Ha·csokonay-la ha-kxo-n-ape-ta
be-DS.NSIM Coyote-NOM.SG move.SG-in-ABL-NEG-SS.NPURP

xʔaxʔayʔa-no-k-laknoʔo. ʔe·-kla ʔecinʔe kwa·n-wa·-ʔa·-la
laugh-CONT-PART-EVID be-DS.NSIM then woman-OBV-DEF-NOM.SG

ha-kxo-ta-w no-k-laknoʔo. ʔe·-kla Ha·csokonay-la
move.SG-in-CIS-IMP say-PART-EVID be-DS.NSIM Coyote-NOM.SG

ha-kxo-n-ape-ta xʔaxʔayʔa-no-k-laknoʔo. ʔecinʔe
move.SG-in-ABL-NEG-SS.NPURP laugh-CONT-PART-EVID then

helʔeya-kxo-na-k-la "ha-kxo-ta-w!" no-k-laknoʔo.
peer-in-ABL-PART-NOM.SG move.SG-in-CIS-IMP say-PART-EVID

ʔe·-kla Ha·csokonay-la xʔaxʔayʔa-·kwa kwa·n-wa·-ʔa·-la
be-SS.NSIM Coyote-NOM.SG laugh-MIR woman-OBV-DEF-NOM.SG

"ha·-n-a·to·-nʔes," no-k-laknoʔo. "he-ce-co·-nʔ," [*sic*]
move.SG-ABL-FUT-1 say-PART-EVID REFL-RED-back-GER

no-k-laknoʔo.
say-PART-EVID

(21) ha-txil-na-n yox-na-k-laknoʔo. ʔe·-kla Ha·csokonay-la
move.SG-out-ABL-GER fly-ABL-PART-EVID be-DS.NSIM Coyote-NOM.SG

helʔeya-kxo-na-t "ʔen kwa·n-ke-laʔ?" no-k-laknoʔo.
peer-in-ABL-SS.CONS and woman-1.POSS-NOM.SG say-PART-EVID

ha·noʔ
ʔe·-kla "ha·-no-we-ʔe," no-k-laknoʔo. ʔe·-kla
be-DS.NSIM move.SG-CONT-DECL-PRES say-PART-EVID be-SS.NSIM

Ha·csokonay-la yan-ci-cxil-ta-no-k-laknoʔo he-ce-co·-n.
Coyote-NOM.SG TH-RED-run-CIS-CONT-PART-EVID REFL-RED-back-GER

(22) ʔe·-kwa kwa·n-wa·-ʔa·-la xa·-xa-t
be-DS.SIM woman-OBV-DEF-NOM.SG AUG.move.SG-AUG-SS.CONS

canoʔs
"cane-ʔe-s," no-k-laknoʔo. ʔe·-kla
leave-PAST-1 say-PART-EVID be-DS.NSIM

ʔewas-ʔa·-l=ʔon xʔay-ʔa·-l=ʔen "henox ʔe·-no-k-coʔ,"
father-DEF-3.POSS-and mother-DEF-3.POSS-and well do-CONT-PART-RES

no-k-laknoʔo.	"na·ʔe·-no-n,"	no-k-laknoʔo.
say-PART-EVID	go-CONT-GER	say-PART-EVID

ʔe·-t	cʔelʔ-te·-ca	we-ta-yu-yuxa·-na-k-laknoʔo.
be-SS.CONS	up-this-place	OBJ.PL-COM-RED-fly-ABL-PART-EVID

ko·lʔa·-tak-la	ʔe·-no-k-laknoʔo.	we·-tic.
bird-great-NOM.SG (='eagle')	be-CONT-PART-EVID	this-like

Coyote and Eagle's Daughter: Free English Translation

[1] Coyote was going along [and], climbing up to a mountain, was standing there. When he did so, there lay a large camp at its foot. Going down, Coyote went down to the big camp and when he got to the last one, there was weeping inside the tipi. [2] Then Coyote went in and said: "What is it?" Then the woman said: "All over here in this camp there are no people. A monster finished them off." [3] Then Coyote said: "Now, now, don't cry. Tomorrow I'll fight with him." Then the woman went outside and said: "Coyote just was saying that he would fight with him." [4] "Tomorrow when I fight with him, don't run away," Coyote said. "Don't lose sight of me." Then she said: "Yes." [5] When night fell, he went down to the river and chopped off a piece of hard wood, burned it black, put it away, and went to sleep. At daybreak, he got up, went outside, and sitting toward the east howled very loudly. Then sitting toward the south he howled. Then sitting toward the west he howled again. Then at last sitting toward the north he howled. [6] Then afterward there were women going to fetch wood, and Coyote joined them. Then they said: "Let him come!" When they did, the monster was red above the waist and black below the waist. Then those women were frightened and Coyote hid. [7] When Coyote came running off that way, he fought the monster, and when he did, a whole bunch of wolves cornered the monster and were fighting with him. The ones fighting him killed [him] and then the wolves went off. [8] Then Coyote said toward the camp where there were no people: "Tightly close all those tipis!" and they tightly closed the tipis. Then Coyote came running up here and said: "Come quickly! The camp is on fire!" Then nothing happened. Then again he went off running and said: "Come hurry! This camp is burning!" Then nothing happened. Then he went off running and said: "Come hurry! This camp is on fire!" Then nothing happened. And finally he went off running and said: "Get going! This camp is on fire!" Then a whole bunch of people ran out. Then they made her marry Coyote. [9] Then some time passed and and Coyote said to the woman: "I'm

going to go to that other camp over yonder." Then the woman said: "Oh! Don't go!" Then Coyote said: "I don't plan on spending much time there. I'll be back in two days." Then the woman said: "Fine." [10] Then Coyote went off. After he arrived at the large camp, a lot of time went by. As such, the woman went after him. She arrived in the big camp and said: "And Coyote?" Then they said: "He went over yonder to join a group gambling." [11] Then when she got near to the camp there, she went in and said: "[Give me some] water." They said: "There is none." Then she picked up the bucket up and went off to fetch water. [12] When she did, at the place where they were gambling, one young man said: "Oh wow, Coyote's wife! Let her go on through!" Then Coyote saw her and was laughing. Then the young men were saying: "We heard that you left her." Then Coyote said: "Oh no, y'all watch me! She'll give me some water to drink." [13] Then he came to where the woman was and poked her, and then she said to Coyote: "Leave me alone!" Then Coyote said: "Give me something to drink!" But the woman didn't give him anything to drink and went away. [14] When night came he came down and the young men were talking with the woman and were saying: "Let's not let Coyote sleep tonight; let's steal the woman!" [15] Then that night they were dancing together and they did not let Coyote sleep until dawn. Then the woman got angry and said: "I'm going [home]." [16] Coyote said: "I'm going to gamble up north." And Coyote went off. Moving along, he arrived at a big camp and said: "I'm going to gamble up north." Then he went off to a big camp, and when he arrived the next day, he said: "I'm going to gamble up north." The next day he went off to a big camp and when he arrived he joined a group gambling. [17] After all this, the woman said: "I'm going after Coyote!" So she followed him. After she arrived at a big camp, she said: "And Coyote?" They said: "He's gone up north to gamble." So she followed him some more and then reached a big camp and said: "And Coyote?" They said: "He's going up north to gamble." Then the woman followed him some more and reaching a big camp she said: "And Coyote?" They said: "He's gone north to gamble." Then the woman followed him some more and reaching a big camp she said: "And Coyote?" They said: "He's gambling here." [18] Then she said: "Go tell him to come here! Your wife is crying out for you." Then Coyote said: "You're lying." Then [the messenger] said: "I'm telling the truth." [So Coyote said:] "All right, come along!" [19] Then Coyote went in with [the messenger] and they arrived at her tipi. "She's staying here," they said. [20] Then Coyote peered inside, and the woman said: "Come in!" Then Coyote didn't go in and was laughing. Then again she said: "Come in!" And Coyote didn't go in and was laughing. Then again the woman said: "Come in!" and Coyote didn't go in and was laughing. Then as he was peering in, she said: "Come in!" and Coyote laughed. So the woman said: "I'm going away," she said, "back home." [21] Going outside she flew off. Peering in, Coyote said: "[Where is] my wife?" Then they said: "She went off." Then Coyote ran back home. [22] When the woman arrived home, she said: "I left him." Then her father and her mother said: "You've done the right thing." They said: "Let's go." Then she flew right up with them: she was an eagle. So it goes.

5. Coyote and Tiger

(1) ʔokmaʔek-la Ha·csokonay-la henox ta·-ʔe·-n
Tiger-NOM.SG Coyote-NOM.SG good COM-be-GER

ye·la-k-laknoʔo. ʔawe·-ka-k ya·lo·na-l-ʔila
be-PART-EVID deer-PL-ACC kill-3-DS.SIM

ta·-yaxa-no-k-laknoʔo.
COM-eat-CONT-PART-EVID

(2) ʔe·-no-k-la-k ʔokmaʔek-wa·-ʔa·-la
be-CONT-PART-SG-ACC tiger-OBV-DEF-NOM.SG

xil-ʔip-a·-na-t x-e·-cne-k-laknoʔo.
cut-animal$^{?}$-move.SG-ABL-SS.CONS AUG-REFL-leave-PART-EVID

ʔe·-kla Ha·csokonay-la "hecu· ʔe·-kwaʔ?"
be-DS.NSIM Coyote-NOM.SG what happen-MIR

no-k-laknoʔo. "xil-ʔip-a·-na-t xe·cnoʔ xa-he·-cane-we-ʔe,"
say-PART-EVID cut-animal-go.SG-ABL-SS.CONS AUG-REFL-leave-DECL-PRES

(3) ʔe·-kla Ha·csokonay-la cʔelʔe·-k-laknoʔo. ʔe·-lʔok
be-DS.NSIM Coyote-NOM.SG follow-PART-EVID be-when

na·to·n-ʔa·-yʔik yele·la-k-laknoʔo xa·-xa-k-laknoʔo.
mountain-DEF-ALL be.seated-PART-EVID AUG.RED-move.SG-PART-EVID

"ya-mk-a·ta-·-we-ʔ-s," no-k-laknoʔo.
TH-summon-go.after-2.OBJ-DECL-PRES-1.SG say-PART-EVID

ʔe·-kla ʔokmaʔek-la "he-co-cxo·-k-la ke·wiloʔo ke-he-wila-we-ʔei."
be-DS.NSIM Tiger-NOM.SG TH-RED-fear-PART-NOM.SG 1.OBJ-REFL-catch-DECL-PAST

ʔe·-kla Ha·csokonay-la "ya·lo·n-a·haʔa," no-k-laknoʔo.
be-DS.NSIM Coyote-NOM.SG kill-INTENT say-PART-EVID

(4)

ʔe·-kwa	wa·-tel	ha-yco-ta-k-laknoʔo.
be-DS.SIM	obv-DIR	TH-move.up-VENT-PART-EVID

ʔe·-kla	Ha·csokonay-la	ya·lo·na-k-laknoʔo.
be-DS.NSIM	Coyote-NOM.SG	kill-PART-EVID

ʔe·-ta	ta·-ta-na-k-laknoʔo	ʔokmaʔek-wa·-ʔa·-la-k.
be-SS.NPURP	COM-move.PL-ABL-PART-EVID	Tiger-OBV-DEF-SG-ACC

ʔa·cana·ʔaxol-we·c-la	ʔokmaʔek-wa·-ʔa·-la-k
wasp-that.manner-NOM.SG	Tiger-OBV-DEF-SG-ACC

he-wle-k-laknoʔo.	we·-tic.
REFL-catch-PART-EVID	this-like

Coyote and Tiger: Free English Translation

[1] Tiger and Coyote were good friends. Whenever Tiger killed deer, he [always] ate with him. [2] One day Tiger went off to hunt and failed to return. Then Coyote said: "What happened? He went off to hunt and failed to return." [3] Then Coyote followed after him. When he found him sitting on a mountain, he went up to him and said: "I came to get you." Then Tiger said: "A monster has caught me." Then Coyote said: "I'm going to kill him." [4] When he said this, he went up to him and killed him. Then he went off with Tiger. Apparently a wasp of some kind had caught Tiger. So it goes.

6. Coyote, Tiger, and Buzzard

(1) Ha·csokonay-la silwe-no-k-laknoʔo. yax-ap-aʔa
Coyote-NOM.SG wander-CONT-PART-EVID eat-NEG-ASS

ʔe·-no-k-la-k na·to·n-ʔa·-yʔik ha-yco-na-·kwa
be-CONT-PART-SG-ACC mountain-DEF-ALL move.SG-up-ABL-when

ʔokmaʔe-kwa·low-la ta·-ha-ho·-k-laknoʔo
tiger-big-NOM.SG COM-move.SG-meet-PART-EVID

Ha·csokonay-wa·-ʔa·-la-k. ʔe·t "hecu·
Coyote-OBV-DEF-SG-ACC be-SS.CONS what

ʔeye·-no-k-ye?" no-k-laknoʔo ʔokmaʔek-wa·-ʔa·-la.
happen-CONT-PART-Q say-PART-EVID Tiger-OBV-DEF-NOM.SG

yaxoʔo·ʔ
ʔe·-kla "tina·tak pax yaxa-we-ʔe·-ʔ," no-k-laknoʔo.
be-SS.NSIM long.time quite eat-DECL-PAST.1.SG-1 say-PART-EVID

Ha·csokonay-la
Coyote-NOM.SG

ʔe·-kla ʔokmaʔek-la no-k-laknoʔo "ke-yace-w
be-DS.NSIM Tiger-NOM.SG say-PART-EVID 1.OBJ-look-IMP

he·tya-na-n-te·-la-k. sa·ya ʔe·-si-k te·-c
reach-ABL-GER-this-SG-ACC 1.SG.NOM do-1.SG-PART this-manner

ʔe·noʔo
/ʔe·-no-we-ʔe/ ha·ʔako·n-ʔa·-ka," no-k-laknoʔo
be-CONT-DECL-PRES man-DEF-NOM.PL cont-PART-EVID

ʔokmaʔek-wa·-ʔa·-la. ʔe·-ta "na·kw ʔe·-ta-w!"
Tiger-OBV-DEF-NOM.SG be-SS.NPURP all.right be-CIS-IMP

no-k-laknoʔo. "ʔawas-enox-ka-k ya·lo·na·-s-ʔok [*sic*]
say-PART-EVID meat-good-PL-ACC kill-1-when

yaxa-w!" no-k-laknoʔo ʔokmaʔek-wa·-ʔa·-la
eat-IMP say-PART-EVID Tiger-OBV-DEF-NOM.SG

Ha·csokonay-la-k.
Coyote-SG-ACC

(2) ʔe·-ta ta·-ta-na-k-laknoʔo cakaw-kwa·low-ʔa·-yʔik.
be-SS.NPURP COM-move.DU-ABL-PART-EVID river-big-DEF-ALL

ʔe·-ta "na·kw ha·-na-t yawʔeca-w!" no-k-laknoʔo.
be-SS.NPURP look move.SG-ABL-SS.CONS watch.for-IMP say-PART-EVID

ʔe·-kla Ha·csokonay-la na·to·n-ʔa·-yʔik ha-yco-na-k-laknoʔo.
be-DS.NSIM Coyote-NOM.SG mountain-DEF-ALL move.SG-up-ABL-PART-EVID

ʔe·-kwa ʔaw-ʔa·-la ha·ʔas-ʔita heykew-ta-k-laknoʔo.
be-DS.SIM deer-DEF-NOM.SG many-DET move.as.group.PL-CIS-PART-EVID

xa·xat
ʔe·-kla Ha·csokonay-la xa-ha·-xa-t he-pake-k-laknoʔo
be-DS.NSIM Coyote-NOM.SG AUG-move.SG-AUG-SS.CONS REFL-tell-PART-EVID

ʔokmaʔek-wa·-ʔa·-la-k. "ʔaw-ʔa·-la ha·ʔas
Tiger-OBV-DEF-SG-ACC deer-DEF-NOM.SG many

yaʔa-·kwa!" no-k-laknoʔo.
move.along.PL-MIR say-PART-EVID

(3) ʔe·-kla ʔokmaʔek-wa·-ʔa·-la "wa·ka ʔawas ʔix
be-DS.NSIM Tiger-OBV-DEF-NOM.SG that.OBV-PL meat bad

ʔe·noʔo
ʔe·-no-we-ʔe," no-k-laknoʔo. "kalak-a-k yawʔeca-w!"
be-CONT-DECL-AOR3SG say-PART-EVID other-PL-ACC look.for-IMP

no-kla ha·-na-k-laknoʔo.
say-DS.NSIM move.SG-ABL-PART-EVID

(4) ʔe·-kwa maslaka·-la heykew-ta-k-laknoʔo.
be-DS.SIM cattle-NOM.SG move.as.group-CIS-PART-EVID

	xa·xat	
ʔe·-kla	xa-ha·-xa-t	hepake-k-laknoʔo.
be-DS.NSIM	AUG-move.SG-AUG-SS.CONS	tell-PART-EVID

ʔokmaʔek-wa·-ʔa·-la-k.
Tiger-OBV-DEF-SG-ACC

				ʔe·noʔo
ʔe·-kla	"maslak-wa·-ka	ʔawas	ʔix	ʔe·-no-we-ʔe,"
be-DS.NSIM	cattle-OBV-NOM.PL	meat	bad	be-CONT-DECL-PAST.3SG

no-k-laknoʔo.	"kalak-[k]a-k	yawʔeca-w!"	no-k-laknoʔo.
say-PART-EVID	other-PL-ACC	look.for-imp	say-PART-EVID

(5)	ʔe·-kla	ha·-na-k-laknoʔo.	ʔe·-kwa	ʔawas-atak-a·-la
	be-DS.NSIM	move.SG-ABL-PART-EVID	be-DS.SIM	meat-great-PL-NOM (='buffalo')

heykew-ta-k-laknoʔo.	ʔe·-kla	Ha·csokonay-la
move.as.group-CIS-PART-EVID	be-DS.NSIM	Coyote-NOM.SG

xa·xat	
xa-ha·-xa-t	he-pake-k-laknoʔo.
AUG-move.SG-AUG-SS.CONS	REFL-tell-PART-EVID

				ʔe·noʔo
ʔe·-kla	"wa·ka	ʔawas	ʔix	ʔe·-no-we-ʔe,"
be-DS.NSIM	that.OBV	meat	bad	be-CONT-DECL-PAST.3SG

no-k-laknoʔo.	"kalak-a-k	yawʔeca-w!"	no-kla
say-PART-EVID	other-PL-ACC	look.for-IMP	say-DS.NSIM

ha·-na-k-laknoʔo.
move.SG-ABL-PART-EVID

(6)	ʔe·-t	ʔekwan-esxaw-ka	heykew-ta-k-laknoʔo.
	be-SS.CONS	dog-big-NOM.PL (='horse')	move.as.group-CIS-PART-EVID

ʔe··kla	Ha·csokonay-la	ya·ce-t	xa·xat xa-ha·-xa-t
be-DS.NSIM	Coyote-NOM.SG	see-SS.CONS	AUG-move.SG-AUG-SS.CONS

he-pake-k-laknoʔo.
REFL-tell-PART-EVID

ʔokmaʔek-wa·-ʔa·-la-k.	"ʔekwan-esxaw-ʔa·-la	ha·ʔas
Tiger-OBV-DEF-SG-ACC	horse-big-DEF-NOM.SG	many

heykew-ta-kwa!"	no-k-laknoʔo.	e··kla	"heheyʔ,"
go.en.masse-CIS-MIR	say-PART-EVID	be-DS.NSIM	okay

no-k-laknoʔo	ʔokmaʔek-wa·-ʔa·-la.	"tekek-eʔe··k	cʔa·pe-w
say-PART-EVID	Tiger-OBV-DEF-NOM.SG	bush-that-ACC	hide-IMP

"ʔe··ta	ke-yace-w!	ʔe··la	we··tic-aʔa	ya·lo·na-t
be-SS.NPURP	1.OBJ-watch-IMP	be-NOM.SG	this-like=3ASS	kill-SS.CONS

yax-a·to-ne-k-coʔ,"[8]	no-k-laknoʔo	ʔokmaʔek-wa·-ʔa·-la.
eat-FUT-2-PART-RES	say-PART-EVID	Tiger-OBV-DEF-NOM.SG

(7)

ʔe··kwa	ʔekwanesxa-wa·-ka	ha·-n-ci-cxil-ta-k-la-tat[9]
be-DS.SIM	horse-OBV-NOM.PL	move.PL-TH-RED-run-CIS-PART-NOM.SG-SS.CONS

he-xaxno·-no-k-laknoʔo.	ʔe··kwa	ʔokmaʔek-la	mo·laʔek-la
TH-drink-CONT-PART-EVID	be-DS.SIM	Tiger-NOM.SG	mule-NOM.SG

cʔetxa-na-t	hewle-k-laknoʔo.	ʔe··t	cʔel-ʔa·-yʔik
jump-ABL-SS.CONS	catch-PART-EVID	be-SS.CONS	peak-DEF-ALL

ha·-na-ci-cxil-ta-ycona-·kwa	ya-klʔaxe-k-laknoʔo
move.PL-ABL-RED-run-CIS-up-when	TH-break-PART-EVID

ya-klʔaxa-n-ʔa·-la-k	ʔe··t	ya·lo·na-k-laknoʔo.
TH-break-GER-DEF-SG-ACC	be-SS.CONS	kill-PART-EVID

8. The resultative enclitic. See Hoijer (1933, 104).

9. Possibly a mistranscription for *ha·ncicxiltaklataʔ*.

ʔe·-ta yakosa-no-k-laknoʔo. “newey!” no·-no-k-laknoʔo
be-SS.NPURP whistle-CONT-PART-EVID Come on! say-CONT-PART-EVID

ʔokmaʔek-wa·-ʔa·-la “na·kw yaxa-w!” no·-no-k-laknoʔo.
Tiger-OBV-DEF-NOM.SG okay eat-IMP say-CONT-PART-EVID

(8) ʔe·-kla Ha·csokonay-la somʔaxe-no-k-laknoʔo.
be-DS.NSIM Coyote-NOM.SG skin-CONT-PART-EVID

naxce-ta ʔawas-ʔa·-la-k nawlʔ-an yaxa-no-k-laknoʔo.
build.fire-SS.NPURP meat-DEF-SG-ACC cook-GER eat-CONT-PART-EVID

“teyey-ʔa·-la-k yax-ape-w,” no-k-laknoʔo ʔokmaʔek-wa·-ʔa·-la.
liver-DEF-SG-ACC eat-NEG-IMP say-PART-EVID Tiger-OBV-DEF-NOM.SG

“sa·ya yaxa-aʔ,” [*sic*] no-k-laknoʔo. ʔe·-k-latoy
1.SG.NOM eat-INT.1.SG SAY-PART-EVID be-PART-despite

Ha·csokonay-la wixwan yaxa-k-laknoʔo teyey-wa·-ʔa·-la-k.
Coyote-NOM.SG little eat-PART-EVID liver-OBV-DEF-SG-ACC

ʔe·-kla ʔokmaʔek-wa·-ʔa·-la “ix ʔe·-ne-k-a·we,”
be-DS.NSIM Tiger-OBV-DEF-NOM.SG wrong be-2-PART-PERF

no-k-laknoʔo. “na·ya yaxa-w!” no-k-laknoʔo
say-PART-EVID 2.SG.NOM eat-IMP say-PART-EVID

ʔokmaʔek-wa·-ʔa·-la ha·-na-k-laknoʔo.
Tiger-OBV-DEF-NOM.SG move.SG-ABL-PART-EVID

(9) ʔe·-kla Ha·csokonay-wa·-ʔa·-la xawa·takweta xa[·]-wa·-hatak-we-ta [*sic*]
be-DS.NSIM Coyote-OBV-DEF-NOM.SG fat-INGR-very-INGR-SS.NPURP

ha·-na-k-laknoʔo ʔe·-t ʔexwa-la-k
move.SG-ABL-PART-EVID be-SS.CONS buzzard-SG-ACC

ta·-ha-ho·-k-laknoʔo. ʔe·t “hecu· ʔeye-·-no-k-yeʔ,”
COM-RED-move.SG-PART be-SS.CONS what happen-2.OBJ-CONT-PART-Q

no-k-laknoʔo ʔexwa-wa·-ʔa·-la-k.
say-PART-EVID buzzard-OBV-DEF-SG-ACC

ʔe·-kla "tin-a·tak pax yaxa-ta yaxapenoʔo·ʔ yaxa-ape-no-we-ʔe·-ʔ,"
be-DS.NSIM long.ago-very only eat-SS.NPURP eat-NEG-CONT-DECL-AOR.1-1

no-k-laknoʔo.
say-PART-EVID

ʔe·-kla Ha·csokonay-la "na·kwa ʔe·-ta-w!
be-DS.NSIM Coyote-NOM.SG all.right move-CIS-IMP

ya·lo·na-·s-ʔok yaxa-w ʔawas-enox-ka-k!" no-k-laknoʔo.
kill-1-when eat-IMP meat-good-PL-ACC say-PART-EVID

(10) ʔe·-ta ta·-ta-na-k-laknoʔo ʔexwa-la-k
be-SS.NPURP COM-move.DU-ABL-PART-EVID buzzard-SG-ACC

caka-wa·-yʔik. ʔe·-ta "na·kw ha·-na-t
river-OBV-ALL be-SS.NPURP all.right move.SG-ABL- SS.CONS

yawʔeca-w!" no-kla ʔexwa-la
watch.out.for-IMP say-DS.NSIM buzzard-NOM.SG

ha·-na-k-laknoʔo.
move.SG-ABL-PART-EVID

(11) ʔe·-kwa maslaka·-la heykew-ta-k-laknoʔo.
be-DS.SIM cattle-NOM.SG move.as.group-CIS-PART-EVID

ʔe·-kla ha·-xey-ta-t he-pake-k-laknoʔo.
be-DS.NSIM move.SG-LOC-CIS-SS.CONS REFL-tell-PART-EVID

ʔe·-kla "wa·ka ʔawas ʔix ʔe·noʔo ʔe·-no-we-ʔe. kala-ka-k ʔe-w!"
be-DS.NSIM cow meat bad be-CONT-DECL-PRES other-PL-ACC go-IMP

no-k-laknoʔo. ʔe·-kla ha·-na-k-laknoʔo.
say-PART-EVID be-DS.NSIM move.SG-ABL-PART-EVID

(12) ʔe-kwa ʔawas-atak-a·-la heykew-ta-kla
be-DS.SIM meat-great-DEF-NOM.SG move.as.group-CIS-DS.NSIM

he-ce-co·-n xa·-xa-t
REFL-RED-back-GER go.SG-AUG-SS.CONS

he-pake-k-laknoʔo. "ʔawas-atak-a·-la
REFL-tell-PART-EVID meat-great-DEF-NOM.SG

heykew-ta-k-la!" no-kla "ʔawas ʔix
move.as.group-CIS-PART-NOM.SG say-DS.NSIM meat bad

ʔe·noʔo
ʔe·-no-we-ʔe," no-k-laknoʔo.
be-CONT-DECL-PAST say-PART-EVID

ʔe·-kla ha·-na-k-laknoʔo.
be-DS.NSIM move.SG-ABL-PART-EVID

(13) ʔe·-la [*sic*] he-ce-co·-n xa·-xa-t "ʔekwan-esxaw-ʔa·-la
be-NOM.SG REFL-RED-back-GER go.SG-AUG-SS.CONS dog-big-DEF-NOM.SG (='horse')

ha·ʔas heykew-ta-kwa!" no-k-laknoʔo.
many move.as.group-CIS-MIR say-PART-EVID

ʔe·-kla "heheyʔ," no-k-laknoʔo Ha·csokonay-wa·-ʔa·-la. "cʔape-w
be-DS.NSIM all.right say-PART-EVID Coyote-OBV-DEF-NOM.SG hide-IMP

ʔe·-ta ke-yace-w! ʔe·-la
be-SS.NPURP 1.OBJ-watch-IMP be-NOM.SG

we·-tic-aʔa yax-a·to-ne-k-coʔ," no-k-laknoʔo.
that-like=ASS eat-FUT-2-PART-RES say-PART-EVID

Ha·csokonay-wa·-ʔa·-la.
Coyote-OBV-DEF-NOM.SG

(14) ʔe·-kwa ʔekwan-esxa-wa·-ka ta-kla-ta-t
be-DS.SIM dog-big-OBV-NOM.PL move.PL-down-CIS-SS.CONS

he-xa-xano·-no-k-laknoʔo.
REFL-RED-drink-CONT-PART-EVID

ʔe·-kwa Ha·csokonay-la cʔetxa-na-t he-wle-k-laknoʔo
be-DS.SIM Coyote-NOM.SG jump-ABL-SS.CONS REFL-catch-PART-EVID

mo·la-ʔa·-la-k. ʔe·-kla mo·la-wa·-ʔa·-la heklaxe-ta
mule-DEF-SG-ACC be-DS.NSIM mule-OBV-DEF-NOM.SG buck.off-SS.NPURP

yakaw-nacka-k-laknoʔo.
kick-die-PART-EVID

ʔe·-ta ha·-na-ci-cxile-xey-ne-k-laknoʔo.
be-SS.NPURP move.SG-ABL-RED-run-far-LOC-ABL-PART-EVID

(15) ʔe·-kla ʔexwa-wa·-ʔa·-la "ʔix ʔe·-kwa," no-k-laknoʔo.
be-DS.NSIM buzzard-OBV-DEF-NOM.SG bad be-MIR say-PART-EVID

"hecu· ʔ-a·to-lʔa," no-k-laknoʔo. "nemtanxa·-te·-la-k
what be-FUT-POT.3.SG say-PART-EVID eye.fat-this-SG-ACC

pax yax-a·haʔa," no-k-laknoʔo. ʔexwa-wa·-ʔa·-la.
just eat-INTENT say-PART-EVID buzzard-OBV-DEF-NOM.SG

ʔe·-t yaxa-k-laknoʔo. nemtanxa·-ʔa·-la-k
be-SS.CONS eat-PART-EVID eye.fat-DEF-SG-ACC

ʔe·-ta ha·-na-k-laknoʔo.
be-SS.NPURP move.SG-ABL-PART-EVID

(16) he·pano·noʔo.
naʔa he·panewa-na-we-ʔey we·-tic.
So narrate-CONT-DECL-PAST this-like

Coyote, Tiger, and Buzzard: Free English Translation

[1] Coyote was wandering about and hadn't really eaten. He climbed up a mountain where a big tiger met Coyote and asked: "What's going on?" Coyote responded: "I haven't eaten in quite a long time." Then Tiger said: "Look at these arms of mine; they act like men do." Then Tiger said to Coyote: "All right, come on! When I've killed some good meat, eat!" [2] Then both of them went off to a big river and [Tiger] said: "Look, go off and look for game!" Then Coyote climbed up a mountain and as he was climbing up many deer were coming en masse. Then Coyote got back and told Tiger about it. "Many deer are coming!" he said. [3] Then, as he was going off, Tiger said: "That meat is bad. Look for other meat!" [4] Then cattle appeared driving forward, and he got back to tell Tiger about it. Then [Tiger] said: "Those cattle are bad meat, go look for something else!" [5] Then he went off, when buffalo were were thronging forward, and so Coyote went back to tell [Tiger]. Then [Tiger] said: "That meat is bad, go look for something else!" he said, going off. [6] Then there were horses swarming forward, and Coyote seeing them went back [to Tiger] to tell him about it. He said to Tiger: "There are herds of horses swarming forward!" Then Tiger said: "Okay, hide in that bush and watch me. With someone killing just like this you will eat your fill." [7] Then the horses came running down and were drinking. As they did so, Tiger jumped out to catch a mule, and when the horses ran back up to the mountain peak, he broke its neck and killed it. Then he whistled and kept on saying: "Come on!" [Then] Tiger kept on saying: "Okay, eat!" [8] Then Coyote skinned it, built a fire, cooked it, and ate it. Tiger said: "Don't eat the liver," but [Coyote] said: "I'm gonna eat it" and ate a little bit of liver. Then Tiger said: "You've done wrong! Go ahead and eat it!" and Tiger went off. [9] Then Coyote got real fat and went off and met Buzzard. Then [he said] to Buzzard: "What happened to you?" Then [Buzzard replied:] "I haven't eaten since a very long time ago." Then Coyote said: "Come on, when I kill something, you'll eat good meat!" [10] So he went off with Buzzard to the river. Then he said: "All right, go off and be on the look out for game." So Buzzard went off. [11] When he did, cattle swarmed forward, and after coming back he told [Coyote], and he replied: "Cattle meat is bad; go look for something else!" Then [Buzzard] went off. [12] When all that meat was herding back this way, he came back and told him: "A whole bunch of cattle is herding this way!" Then [Coyote] said: "That meat is bad." And [Buzzard] went off. [13] As such, he headed back and said: "There's a whole bunch of horses herding this way!" Coyote said: "All right, hide and watch me! Then you'll eat as I do." [14] Then a herd of horses came swarming

down to drink, and when they did Coyote jumped out and caught a mule. The mule bucked him off and kicked him to death. Then all the horses ran away. [15] Then Buzzard said: "[The meat] really is bad! What could there be to eat? I'll just eat this eye-fat here." Then he ate the eye-fat and went off. [16] That's the way they've always told it. So it goes.

7. Coyote and Alligator

(1) Ha·csokonay-la silwe-no-k-lakno?o. ?e·-no-la
Coyote-NOM.SG wander-CONT-PART-EVID be-CONT-NOM.SG

na·ton-away-?a·-y?ik ha-yco-na-k-lakno?o c?el-?a·-y?ik
mountain-tall-DEF-ALL move.SG-up-ABL-PART-EVID summit-DEF-ALL

?e·-t yaw?eca-no-k-lakno?o. ?e·-l-?ok
be-SS.CONS look.around-CONT-PART-EVID be-3-when

na·tona-wa·-?a·-la-k ?a·yay-?a·-y?ik ya-cox?-an-?a·-la
mountain-OBV-DEF-SG-ACC base-DEF-ALL TH-camp-GER-DEF-NOM.SG

ha·naxok ye·la-k-lakno?o lak.
great.many sit-PART-EVID 3SGACC

(2) Ha·csokonay-wa·-?a·-la ha-kla-na-k-lakno?o ?e·-t
Coyote-OBV-DEF-NOM.SG move.SG-down-ABL-PART-EVID be-SS.CONS

ya-cox?-an-a·?as-wa·-?a·-la-k ha·cin-?a·-y?ik
TH-camp-GER-big-OBV-DEF-SG-ACC nearby-DEF-ALL

xa·xaklakno?o
xa·-xa-k-lakno?o. ?e·-kwa
AUG.move.SG-AUG-RED-AUG-PART-EVID be-DS.SIM

ya-cox?-an-a·naxok-wa·-?a·-la
TH-camp-GER-many-OBV-DEF-NOM.SG

ca·cxok he·malo·-no-k-lakno?o ?enik
half dance-CONT-PART-EVID and

ca·cxok he·-ma-ma·ko·-no-k-lakno?o.
half REFL-RED-weep-CONT-PART-EVID

(3) ?e·-kla Ha·csokonay-wa·-?a·-la ya-cox?-an-ol?aw-?a·-y?ik.
be-DS.NSIM Coyote-OBV-DEF-NOM.SG TH-camp-GER-edge-DEF-ALL

xa·xaklakno?o
xa·-xa-k-lakno?o. ?e·-l-?ok
AUG.move.SG-AUG-PART-EVID be-3-when

ya-coxʔ-an-wixwan-ʔa·-yʔik. kwa·-kwan-la
TH-camp-GER-small-DEF-ALL RED-woman-NOM.SG

ketay-ta[10] ma-mka-nes-no-k-laknoʔo.
two-DET RED-weep-DU-CONT-PART-EVID

ʔe·-kla Ha·csokonay-la ha-kxo-na-k-laknoʔo
be-DS.NSIM Coyote-NOM.SG move.SG-in-ABL-PART-EVID

mamkanesno·ka
ʔe·-t "hecu ʔe·-l-ʔila ma-maka-nes-no-we-·-kaʔ?"
be-SS.CONS what be-3-since RED-weep-DU-CONT-DECL-PRES-2

no-k-laknoʔo.
say-PART-EVID

ʔe·-kla "xecwa[l]-la he-ynaw-kapay-ʔ-aʔa.
be-DS.NSIM Alligator-NOM.SG REFL-win.game-nothing-do-ASS.3.SG

kewya·lo·nto·xanoʔ
ke-we-ya·lo·n-to·xa-no-we-ʔe," no-k-laknoʔo
1.OBJ-OBJ.PL-kill-finish-CONT-DECL-PRES say-PART-EVID

kwa·n-wa·-ʔa·-la.
woman-OBV-DEF-NOM.SG

ʔe·-kla Ha·csokonay-la "hehe·ʔ!" no-k-laknoʔo.
be-DS.NSIM Coyote-NOM.SG all.right say-PART-EVID

"taxso·-kwa ta·-ka·lw-a-haʔa," no-k-laknoʔo.
be.dawn-DS.SIM COM-have.contest-INTENT say-PART-EVID

ʔe·-kla kwa·n-wa·-ʔa·-la kaltey-ʔa·-yʔik
be- DS.NSIM woman-OBV-DEF-NOM.SG outside-DEF-ALL

ha-txil-na-ta
move.SG-out-ABL-SS.NPURP

Ha·csokonay-la "ta·-ka·lwa·-t-ok n-aʔa," no-k-laknoʔo.
Coyote-NOM.SG COM-have.contest-EP-as say-ASS say-PART-EVID

10. Likely a shortening of *ketay-ita* two-DET, as the determiner *-ita* frequently occurs on quantifiers.

(4) ʔe·-k-la-k ho·s-taxso·-n caka-wixwan-ʔa·-yʔik
be-PART-SG-ACC young-be.dawn-GER river-small-DEF-ALL

heykewa-kla-na-k-laknoʔo. ya·ca·-ato-l-ʔila
move.as.group-down-ABL-PART-EVID see-FUT-3-DS.SIM

Ha·csokonay-la ka·lwe-lʔok. ʔe·-kwa Ha·csokonay-la
Coyote-NOM.SG have.contest-when be-DS.SIM Coyote-NOM.SG

ha-kla-na-k-laknoʔo caka-wa·-yʔik ʔe·-t
move.SG-down-ABL-PART-EVID river-OBV-ALL be-SS.CONS

"hete-l-ʔila xecwal-wa·-ʔa·-laʔ" no-k-laknoʔo.
where-3-DS.NSIM alligator-OBV-DEF-NOM.SG say-PART-EVID

ʔe·-kwa "we·lʔat ʔe·-ta-h-e·l!" no-k-laknoʔo.
be-DS.SIM yonder-place move-CIS-EP-JUSS say-PART-EVID

ʔe·-kwa xecwal-wa·-ʔa·-la ha·-xey-ta-k-laknoʔo
be-DS.SIM alligator-OBV-DEF-NOM.SG move.SG-LOC-CIS-PART-EVID

ʔe·-t we·ʔil no-k-laknoʔo.
be-SS.CONS all.right say-PART-EVID

(5) ʔe·-kla Ha·csokonay-la "waʔana·lesok,"[11] no-k-laknoʔo
be-DS.NSIM Coyote-NOM.SG just.a.moment say-PART-EVID

Ha·csokonay-wa·-ʔa·-la ʔe·-ta caka-wixwan-ʔa·-yʔik
Coyote-OBV-DEF-NOM.SG be-SS.NCONS river-small-DEF-ALL

ha-kla-na-l-ʔok xecwal-kwa·n-ko·sʔa-tic-la
move.SG-down-ABL-3-when alligator-woman-old-like-NOM.SG

he-cne·la-k-laknoʔo.
REFL-lie-PART-EVID

keta·plew
"ke-ta·haple-w xecwa-la-k ta·-ka·lw-a·to-no-s-ʔok,"
1.OBJ-help-IMP alligator-SG-ACC COM-have.contest-FUT-CONT-1-when

11. Possibly decomposable into *waʔan-* 'moment' and *a·le-* 'block,' 'delay' *-s* '1st person,' *-ok* 'as': 'as I delay a moment.' Cf. *yakw-alana*, lit. water-block 'river dam.'

no-k-laknoʔo.
cont-PART-EVID

ʔe·-kla xecwal-ko·sʔa-wa·-ʔa·-la "hehe·ʔ," no-k-laknoʔo.
be-DS.NSIM alligator-old-OBV-DEF-NOM.SG all.right say-PART-EVID

"hete-wʔan he-ylap-a·to-ʔa," no-k-laknoʔo. ʔe·-kla
what-ADESS REFL-stand-FUT-ASS say-PART-EVID be-DS.NSIM

Ha·csokonay-la "heʔey te·-wʔan he-ylap-a·haʔa,"
Coyote-NOM.SG all.right this-ADESS REFL-stand-INTENT

no-k-laknoʔo Ha·csokonay-wa·-ʔa·-la. ʔe·-kla
say-PART-EVID Coyote-OBV-DEF-NOM.SG be-DS.NSIM

xecwal-ko·sʔa-wa·-ʔa·-la "hehe·ʔ. kana·," no-k-laknoʔo.
alligator-old-OBV-DEF-NOM.SG all.right go.ahead say-PART-EVID

(6) ʔe·-kla Ha·csokonay-la xa·-xa-k-laknoʔo. ʔe·-kwa
be-DS.NSIM Coyote-NOM.SG AUG.move.SG-AUG-PART-EVID be-when

xecwal-a·ʔako·n-wa·-ʔa·-la. "we·ʔil!" no-k-laknoʔo.
alligator-man-OBV-DEF-NOM.SG go.ahead say-PART-EVID

ʔe·-kla Ha·csokonay-la "na·yane-yka-na-k ʔe-w,"
be- DS.NSIM Coyote-NOM.SG 2.SG.NOM TH-shoot-ABL-PART be-IMP

no-k-laknoʔo. ʔe·-kla xecwa[l]-la "hehe·ʔ," no-k-laknoʔo.
say-PART-EVID be-DS.NSIM alligator-NOM.SG all.right say-PART-EVID

"ya·c-ke-xwel-pe-w,"[12] no-k-laknoʔo.
watch-1.OBJ-miss-NEG-IMP say-PART-EVID

(7) ʔe·-ta cʔetxan-x-ayco-na-k-laknoʔo. ʔe·-ta ʔax-ʔa·-yʔik
be-SS.NPURP jump-AUG-up-ABL-PART-EVID be-SS.NPURP water-DEF-ALL

12. This word is unusual in two respects. First, the person agreement comes between two halves of the complex predicate 'try not to miss" (= watch closely). Second, although the negative element is cognate with the normal morphonegator in this case it is probably lexicalized as part of the verb stem; otherwise it would be **xwel-ape-*.

wa·-na-k-laknoʔo.	ʔe·-t	wa·-na-kxo-n-ape-ta
fall-ABL-PART-EVID	be-SS.CONS	fall-ABL-in-CONT-NEG-SS.NPURP

ʔa·x-cʔel-ʔa·-yʔik	wans-ayco-na-no-k-laknoʔo.
water-surface-DEF-ALL	bounce-up-ABL-CONT-PART-EVID

ʔe·-t	ha-yco-ta-k-laknoʔo.
be-SS.CONS	move.SG-up-CIS-PART-EVID

ʔe·t	"we·ʔil.	na·-xwa,"	no-k-laknoʔo	Ha·csokonay-la-k.
be-SS.CONS	all.right	2.SG-also	say-PART-EVID	Coyote-SG-ACC

(8)

ʔe·-kla	Ha·csokonay-la	ʔa·x-wa·-yʔik	wa·-na-k-laknoʔo.
be-DS.NSIM	Coyote-NOM.SG	water-OBV-ALL	fall-ABL-PART-EVID

ʔe·-t	ʔa·x-cʔel-ʔa·-yʔik	xe·cne-k-laknoʔo.
be-SS.CONS	water-surface-DEF-ALL	fall.forcefully-PART-EVID

ʔe·t	sikt-as	wan-xayco-na-no-k-laknoʔo
be-SS.CONS	four-times	bounce-up-ABL-CONT-PART-EVID

ʔa·x-cʔel-ʔa·-yʔik.
water-surface-DEF-ALL

ʔe·-ta	ha-yco-ta-k-laknoʔo.	xecwal-kwa·n-ko·sʔa-tic-la
be-SS.NPURP	move.SG-up-CIS-PART-EVID	alligator-woman-old-like-NOM.SG

Ha·csokonay-wa·-ʔa·-la-k	ta·-haple-no-k-laknoʔo.
Coyote-OBV-DEF-SG-ACC	COM-have.contest-CONT-PART-EVID

(9)

ʔe·-kla	hes-ke-kete-nesʔe-k-laknoʔo	Xecwal-wa·=lʔen
be-DS.NSIM	CAUS-RED-count-DU-PART-EVID	Alligator-OBV=and

Ha·csokonay=ʔen.
Coyote=and

(10)

ʔe·-kla	Xecwa-la	no-k-laknoʔo	"we·ʔis-pax
be-DS.NSIM	Alligator-NOM.SG	say-PART-EVID	one-just

xestew-e·l!"
contest-JUSS

no·k-lakno?o.	"?a·x-kwa·low-e?ek	yan?a·nwan-la-k
say-PART-EVID	water-big-yonder	iron-SG-ACC

ka·-n-a·to-nes?-a·-n?es,"	no·k-lakno?o.
throw-ABL-FUT-DU-POT-POT1	say-PART-EVID

?e·kwa	?a·x-kwa·lo-wa·-?a·-la-k
be-when	water-big-OBV-DEF-SG-ACC

c?el-?a·-y?ik	ta·-notso-k-lakno?o	Ha·csokonay-la-k.
above-DEF-ALL	COM-stand.PL-PART-EVID	Coyote-SG-ACC

(11)

Xecwal-wa·-?a·-la	yan?a·nwan-kwa·low-tak-la-k
Alligator-OBV-DEF-NOM.SG	iron-big-last-SG-ACC

ta?ane-k-lakno?o	?e·-ta	"ke-yace-w!"	no·k-lakno?o
grasp-PART-EVID	be-SS.NPURP	1.OBJ-watch-IMP	say-PART-EVID

xecwal-wa·-?a·-la.
alligator-OBV-DEF-NOM.SG

?e·-kla	Ha·csokonay-la	ya·ce-·kwa	ka·-na-k-lakno?o
be-DS.NSIM	Coyote-NOM.SG	watch-when	throw-ABL-PART-EVID

yan?a·nwan-kwa·lo-wa·-?a·-la-k	Xecwal-wa·-?a·-la.
iron-big-OBV-DEF-SG-ACC	Alligator-OBV-DEF-NOM.SG

?e·-t	?a·x-kwa·lo-wa·-?a·-la-k	ha·cin-?a·-y?ik
be-SS.CONS	water-big-OBV-DEF-SG-ACC	nearby-DEF-ALL

kan-xacne-k-lakno?o.	?e·-ta	Ha·csokonay-la-k
throw-far-PART-EVID	be-SS.NPURP	Coyote-SG-ACC

"we·?il	na·-xwa,"	no·k-lakno?o	Xecwal-wa·-?a·-la.
Now	2.SG-also	say-PART-EVID	Alligator-OBV-DEF-NOM.SG

(12)

?e·-kla	Ha·csokonay-la	yan?a·nwan-?a·-la-k	ha·c-?a·-y?ik
be-DS.NSIM	Coyote-NOM.SG	iron-DEF-SG-ACC	ground-DEF-ALL

na·tkana-kxo-na-k-lakno?o.	?e·-ta	tickan-yasxaw?a-la-k
press[?]-in-ABL-PART-EVID	be-SS.NPURP	people-frighten-SG-ACC (='quail')

ta?ane-ta	ka·-na-k-lakno?o	?a·x-kwa·low-e?e·k.
grasp-SS.NPURP	throw-ABL-PART-EVID	water-big-that

ʔe·-kla tickan-yasxawʔa-ʔa·-la ʔa·x-kwa·low-elʔat-la-k
be-DS.NSIM people-frighten-DEF-NOM.SG water-big-yonder-SG-ACC

yoxan-ayxc-na-k-laknoʔo.
fly-across-ABL-PART-EVID

(13) ʔe·-kla Xecwa-la no-k-laknoʔo
be-DS.NSIM Alligator-NOM.SG say-PART-EVID

"na·kw ke-ya·lo·na-w!" no-k-laknoʔo.
well 1.OBJ-kill-IMP say-PART-EVID

ʔe·-kla Ha·csokonay-la "sa·ya
be-DS.NSIM Coyote-NOM.SG 1.SG.NOM

ya·lo·napenoʔo·ʔ
tickan-e·-ka-k ya·lo·n-ape-no-we-ʔe·-ʔ," no-k-laknoʔo.
person-that-PL-ACC kill-NEG-CONT-DECL-PAST.1.SG-1 say-PART-EVID

ʔe·-kla kalak-a·-ka ya·lo·na-k-laknoʔo. ʔe·-ta
be-DS.NSIM other-DEF-NOM.PL kill-PART-EVID be-SS.NPURP

ha·naxok he·malo·-no-k-laknoʔo. ʔe·-kwa
many dance-CONT-PART-EVID be-DS.SIM

waʔasay-ʔa·-wʔan he-ma-ma·ko·-no-k-laknoʔo.
one.side-DEF-ADESS REFL-RED-weep-CONT-PART-EVID

(14) he·pano·noʔ
naʔa he·panewa-na-we-ʔei ʔo·ʔa-he·pano·n-wa·-ʔa·-la.
So narrate-CONT-DECL-PAST night-narrate-OBV-DEF-NOM.SG

we·-tic.
this-like

Coyote and Alligator: Free English Translation

[1] Coyote was wandering about and, as he was, went up a tall mountain to its top and was looking around. When he did, he saw a big camp at the foot of the mountain. [2] Coyote went on down and got close to the camp. When he did, he saw that half of the people were dancing and half of the people were weeping. [3]

When Coyote got to the edge of the camp, there were two women who were weeping, and as Coyote entered he said: "Why are you two crying like this?" Then one of the women said: "An unbeatable alligator is killing us all off." Then Coyote said: "All right, when it's dawn, I'm going to have a fight with him." Then the woman went outside and said: "Coyote said he's going to fight with [the alligator]." [4] Having done this, at daybreak they all went down to the small river to see how Coyote would fight with him. So Coyote went on down to the river and said: "Where is the alligator?" At that, they said "He's come over there!" And Alligator came that way, and Coyote said: "All right." [5] Then Coyote said: "Just a minute," and when he went down to the small river, an old alligator woman was lying there. "Help me while I'll be fighting with an alligator." Then the old alligator woman said: "Okay, on which side [of the river] will you be standing?" So Coyote responded: "Great, I'll be standing on this side [of the river]." Then the old alligator said: "All right, go ahead." [6] Then Coyote arrived and when he did the alligator man said: "Go ahead!" Then Coyote said: "Why don't *you* be the first to shoot!" Then Alligator said: "Okay, keep an eye on me." [7] Then he jumped way up [into the air] and fell back to the water, but he did not fall into it but bounced up and down off the water surface. Then he came back up [onto land], and said to Coyote: "Well, not it's your turn." [8] Then Coyote fell off into the water, and crashed down onto the water surface. He bounced up and down four times on the water surface, and then came back up on land—the old alligator woman had been helping him. [9] So the two were even, Coyote and Alligator. [10] Then Alligator said: "Come on, let's compete just one more time! We could throw a big ol' piece of iron into the ocean over there." Just then he was standing with Coyote above the the ocean. [11] Alligator picked up a very big piece of iron and said: "Watch me!" Then while Coyote watched him, Alligator threw the big piece of iron—he threw it far off, close to the ocean. Then Alligator turned to Coyote and said: "Now it's your turn!" [12] Then Coyote pressed the iron into the ground and grabbed a quail and threw it away to the ocean over yonder. Then the quail flew across the ocean. [13] Then Alligator said: "Now kill me!" And Coyote said: "I haven't killed those people." So the others killed him, and there many were dancing, and others were weeping. [14] They've always told night stories that way. So it goes.

8. Coyote and the Duck Women

(1) Ha·csokonay-la ʔekak-a·-la-k ta·-yacoxʔa-no-k-laknoʔo.
Coyote-NOM.SG maternal.gmother-DEF-SG-ACC COM-camp-CONT-PART-EVID

ʔe·-no-k-la-k Ha·csokonay-la cakaw-ʔa·-yʔik[13]
be-CONT-PART-SG-ACC Coyote-NOM.SG river-OBV-ALL

silwe-no-k-laknoʔo. ʔe·-kwa caka-wa·-yʔik
wander-CONT-PART-EVID be-DS.SIM river-OBV-ALL

he·-xʔa-xʔayʔo·-no-k-laknoʔo. ʔe·-kla
REFL-RED-laugh-CONT-PART-EVID be-DS.NSIM

Ha·csokonay-la he-ylap-an-a·cin-ʔa·-yʔik
Coyote-NOM.SG REFL-stand-GER-near-DEF-ALL (='near a tree')

he-ylapa-ta he-lʔeya-kla-na-k-laknoʔo. ʔe·-lʔok
REFL-stand-SS.NPURP REFL-peer-down-ABL-PART-EVID be-when

kwa·-kwan-ka sikit-ita he-pnonoso·-no-k-laknoʔo
RED-woman-NOM.PL four-DET REFL-bathe-CONT-PART-EVID

he-payxwet-an kapay-ta.
REFL-dress.as.female-GER nothing-DET

(2) ʔe·-kla Ha·csokonay-la kwa·-kwan-wa·-lʔan
be-DS.NSIM Coyote-NOM.SG RED-woman-OBV-GEN

hexwit-la-k ho·ʔoxo·-k-laknoʔo ʔe·-ta ha·-na-k-laknoʔo
belt-SG-ACC steal-PART-EVID be-SS.NPURP move.SG-ABL-PART-EVID

yacoxʔan-ʔa·-yʔik. ʔe·-t xa·-xa-k-laknoʔo ʔe·-t
camp-DEF-ALL be-SS.CONS move.SG-AUG-PART-EVID be-SS.CONS

13. Hoijer's original text has *cakawʔa·yʔis*, probably a typographical error.

ʔekak-wa·-ʔa·-la-k „te·-la-k soko-w," no-k-laknoʔo.
maternal.gmother-OBV-DEF-SG-ACC this-SG-ACC put.away-IMP say-PART-EVID

"hexwit-wa·-ʔa·-la-k tickan-e·-ka ha·-xey-ta-t
belt-OBV-DEF-SG-ACC people-that-NOM.PL move.SG-LOC-CIS-SS.CONS

nahawa·-lʔok hepak-ape-w," no-k-laknoʔo
ask.about-if tell-NEG-IMP say-PART-EVID

Ha·csokonay-wa·-ʔa·-la. ʔe·-kla ʔekak-wa·-ʔa·-la
Coyote-OBV-DEF-NOM.SG be-DS.NSIM maternal.gmother-OBV-DEF-NOM.SG

"hehe·ʔ," no-k-laknoʔo. ʔe·-kwa Ha·cosokonay-la
all.right say-PART-EVID be-DS.SIM Coyote-NOM.SG

ha·-xey-ne-k-laknoʔo.
move.SG-LOC-ABL-PART-EVID

(3) ʔe·-kwa kwa·n-la xa·-xa-k-laknoʔo yacoxʔan-wa·-yʔik
be-DS.SIM woman-NOM.SG move.SG-AUG-PART-EVID camp-OBV-ALL

ʔe·-t naho·-k-laknoʔo hexwit-wa·-ʔa·-la-k. ʔe·-kla
be-SS.CONS ask.about-PART-EVID belt-OBV-DEF-SG-ACC be-DS.NSIM

ya·capenoʔo·ʔ
kwa·n-ko·sʔa-wa·-ʔa·-la "ya·c-ape-no-we-ʔe·-ʔ," no-k-laknoʔo.
woman-old-OBV-DEF-NOM.SG see-NEG-CONT-DECL-PAST.1-1 say-PART-EVID

ʔe·-kla kwa·n-wa·-ʔa·-la "to·na-no-·ka," no-k-laknoʔo.
be-DS.NSIM woman-OBV-DEF-NOM.SG lie-CONT-2.SG say-PART-EVID

"wa·-te-ca k-e·s-toxwano·-no-ʔ," no-k-laknoʔo. "to·na
OBV-this-place 1OBJ-CAUS-smell-CONT-3 say-PART-EVID just

ke-nes-ya·ce-w," no-k-laknoʔo. "we·-ʔat-la-k te·-c
1.OBJ-CAUS-show-IMP say-PART-EVID yon-place-SG-ACC this-way

ʔe·noʔo·ʔ
ʔe·-no-ʔe·-ʔ," no-k-laknoʔo kwa·n-wa·-ʔa·-la.
do-CONT-PAST.1-1 say-PART-EVID woman-OBV-DEF-NOM.SG

ʔe··kla	kwa·n-kosʔa-wa··ʔa··la	ʔeke-k-laknoʔo
be-DS.NSIM	woman-old-OBV-DEF-NOM.SG	give-PART-EVID

hexwit-wa··ʔa··la-k.	ʔe··kla	kwa·n-wa··ʔa··la	taʔa-n
belt-OBV-DEF-SG-ACC	be-DS.NSIM	woman-OBV-DEF-NOM.SG	grasp-GER

hexwte-t	kap-yukusʔe-k-laknoʔo.
belt-SS.CONS	close-transform?-PART-EVID

(4)

ʔe··kla	ko·sʔa-tic-wa··ʔa··la	yela-no-k-laknoʔo.
be-DS.NSIM	old-like-OBV-DEF-NOM.SG	sit-CONT-PART-EVID

ʔe··kwa	Ha·csokonay-la	xa··xa-k-laknoʔo	ʔe··t
be-DS.SIM	Coyote-NOM.SG	AUG.move.SG-AUG-PART-EVID	be-SS.CONS

"tickan-ʔa··ka	ha··xey-ta-kwaʔ?"	no-k-laknoʔo.
person-DEF-NOM.PL	move.SG-LOC-CIS-MIR	say-PART-EVID

ʔe··kla	ko·sʔa-tic-wa··ʔa··la	"kwa·n-la	ha··xey-ta-t
be-DS.NSIM	old-like-OBV-DEF-NOM.SG	woman-NOM.SG	move.SG-LOC-CIS-SS.CONS

hexwit-wa··ʔa··la-k	taʔame-ta	ha·xeynoʔ ha··xey-no-we-ʔe,"
belt-OBV-DEF-SG-ACC	grasp-SS.NPURP	move.SG-LOC-CONT-DECL-PRES

no-k-laknoʔo.	ʔe··kla	Ha·csokonay-la	"ʔe··ta
say-PART-EVID	be-DS.NSIM	Coyote-NOM.SG	be-SS.NPURP

hete-wʔan	ʔe··kwaʔ"	no-k-laknoʔo.	ʔe··kla
where-ADESS	be-MIR	say-PART-EVID	be-DS.NSIM

ko·sʔa-tic-wa··ʔa··la	"heʔe·wa,"	no-k-laknoʔo.
old-like-obv-def-nom.sg	not.know.1.SG	say-PART-EVID

ʔe··kla	Ha·csokonay-la	ha··na-t	na·to·n-ʔa··yʔik
be-DS.NSIM	Coyote-NOM.SG	move.sg-ABL-SS.CONS	mountain-DEF-ALL

he-cne-t	ma·ka-no-k-laknoʔo	sikit	he-cn-an.
REFL-lie-SS.CONS	weep-CONT-PART-EVID	four	REFL-lie-GER (='day')

(5) ʔe·-kwa ʔexwa-la xa·-xa-k-laknoʔo ʔe·-t "hecu
be-DS.SIM buzzard-NOM.SG move.SG-AUG-PART-EVID (='arrive') be-SS.CONS what

ʔe·-l-ʔila ma·ka-no-·kaʔ?" no-k-laknoʔo.
be-3-DS.SIM weep-CONT-2.SG say-PART-EVID

"he-tec ʔ-a·-n-ʔok ya·c-a·to-ne-k-ye," no-k-laknoʔo
what-like do-POT-2-when see-FUT-2.SG-PART-Q say-PART-EVID

"ma·ka-no-ne-k-wa·-ʔa·-la-k?" cʔelay neskaltey
weep-CONT-2-PART-OBV-DEF-SG-ACC sky other.side

ʔe·-k-a·we. ʔe·-kla Ha·csokonay-la "ke-ta-ta-yco-na-w,"
be-PART-PERF be-DS.NSIM Coyote-NOM.SG 1.OBJ-RED-move.DU-up-ABL-IMP

no-k-laknoʔo. ʔe·-kla ʔexwa-la "cʔelay-sa·xal-eʔe-k
say-PART-EVID be-DS.NSIM buzzard-NOM.SG sky-hole-that-ACC

neskaltey-ʔa·-yʔik h-a·-we," no-k-laknoʔo.
other.side-DEF-ALL be-ASS-DECL say-PART-EVID

yakoʔow
"ʔawas yakewa-w," no-k-laknoʔo. "ʔoyuk-a·-la-k
meat prepare-IMP say-PART-EVID bag-DEF-SG-ACC

sikit," no-k-laknoʔo ʔexwa-la. "ʔe·-ye-·n
four say-part-evid buzzard-NOM.SG do-2-GER

ta·-ta-yco-n-a·tewa-·-nwa-sʔ," no-k-laknoʔo ʔexwa-la.
COM-move.DU-up-ABL-FUT-2.OBJ-DEON-1.SBJ say-PART-EVID buzzard-NOM.SG

(6) ʔe·-kla Ha·csokonay-la ʔawas-ka-k ya·lo·n-ʔan
be-DS.NSIM Coyote-NOM.SG buffalo-PL-ACC kill-GER

ʔoyuk-a·-la-k sikit nes-pece-k-laknoʔo ʔawas-ʔa·-la-k.
bag-DEF-SG-ACC four CAUS-FULL-PART-EVID meat-DEF-SG-ACC

ʔe·-kwa ʔexwa-la xa·-xa-k-laknoʔo. "weʔil,"
be-DS.SIM buzzard-NOM.SG move.SG.AUG-AUG-PART-EVID all.right

no-k-laknoʔo. ʔe·-kla ʔawas-wa·-ʔa-la-k
say-PART-EVID be-DS.NSIM meat-OBV-DEF-SG-ACC

ʔexwa-la losos ha-wa-wne-k-laknoʔo ʔenik
buzzard-NOM.SG all TH-RED-pack-PART-EVID and

Ha·csokonay-la ha-yxo-k-laknoʔo ʔexwa-la-k.
Coyote-NOM.SG TH-mount-PART-EVID buzzard-SG-ACC

ʔe·-kwa yoxana-cso-k-laknoʔo[14] [*sic*] ʔe·-t yoxana-yco-na-k-laknoʔo.
be-DS.SIM fly-rise-PART-EVID be-SS.CONS fly-up-ABL-PART-EVID

“waʔanes hetewʔanʔax wa·-na-·kwa-nes ke-nes-yasna-w
as.soon.as in.any.direction fall-ABL-when-1 1.OBJ-CAUS-put.in.mouth-IMP

ʔawas-eʔe·-la-k,” no-k-laknoʔo. “ʔe·-y-ʔok sitix
meat-this-SG-ACC say-PART-EVID do-2-when straight

“k-e·sa-yco-n-a·to-nwa-ʔ,” no-k-laknoʔo.
1OBJ-point-up-ABL-FUT-DEON-DEON3 say-PART-EVID

(7) ʔe·-kla Ha·cosokonay-la ʔexwa-la-k
be-DS.NSIM Coyote-NOM.SG buzzard-SG-ACC

nes-yaxa-ta-yco-na-no-k-laknoʔo ʔe·t ʔoyuk-a·-la
CAUS-eat-move.DU-up-ABL-CONT-PART-EVID be-SS.CONS bag-DEF-NOM.SG

we·ʔis-pax he-toxa-k-laknoʔo. ʔe·-kla metis
one-just REFL-finish-PART-EVID be-DS.NSIM three

xa-sto·-k-laknoʔo. ʔe·-kla ʔecinʔe ʔoyuk-a·-la-k
AUG-remain-PART-EVID be-DS.NSIM then bag-DEF-SG-ACC

we·ʔis ya-kwlaxe-t nes-yaxa-ta-yco-na-no-k-laknoʔo.
one TH-open-SS.CONS CAUS-eat-move.DU-up-ABL-CONT-PART-EVID

14. Hoijer (1972, 45 [entry 552.8]): *yoxan-acxo-*.

ʔe··kwa ʔecinʔe he-toxa-k-laknoʔo. ʔe··kla
be-DS.SIM then REFL-finish-PART-EVID be-DS.NSIM

ʔecinʔe we·ʔis ya-kwlaxe-k-laknoʔo ʔe··t
then one TH-open-PART-EVID be-SS.CONS

nes-yaxa-ta-yco-na-no-k-laknoʔo. ʔe··kwa ʔecinʔe
CAUS-eat-move.DU-up-ABL-CONT-PART-EVID be-DS.SIM then

holaw-ʔa··la-k ya-kwlaxe-k-laknoʔo ʔe··t
last-DEF-SG-ACC TH-open-PART-EVID be-SS.CONS

nes-yaxa-ta-yco-na-no-k-laknoʔo. ʔe··kwa cʔelay-wa··ʔa··la
CAUS-eat-move.DU-up-ABL-CONT-PART-EVID be-DS.SIM sky-OBV-DEF-NOM.SG

sa·xal-ʔa··la wa··tel ha·cin-tak xasto··kwa
hole-DEF-NOM.SG that-way near-very remain-when

ʔawas-ʔa··la he-toxa-k-laknoʔo.
meat-DEF-NOM.SG REFL-finish-PART-EVID

(8) ʔe··kla Ha·csokonay-la "ʔawas-ʔa··la he-toxa-kwa,"
be-DS.NSIM Coyote-NOM.SG meat-DEF-NOM.SG REFL-finish-MIR

no-k-la ʔexwa-la "ʔo·c!" no-k-laknoʔo. "na·kw
say-PART-NOM.SG buzzard-NOM.SG oh! say-PART-EVID Now

he-tec ʔ-a·to-y-aʔaʔ?" no-k-laknoʔo. ʔe··kla
what-way do-FUT-2-ASS say-PART-EVID be-DS.NSIM

Ha·csokonay-la ko·laws-ʔa··yʔik he-y-ke-kewʔa-t
Coyote-NOM.SG rump-DEF-ALL REFL-TH-RED-make-SS.CONS

ketay-ʔas nes-ya··kwa cʔelay-wa··yʔik
two-times CAUS-eat-when sky-OBV-ALL

neskaltey-ʔa··yʔik xa-yela-k-laknoʔo. ʔe··ta "weʔil,"
other.side-DEF-ALL AUG-sit-PART-EVID be-SS.NPURP all.right

no-k-laknoʔo. "weʔil-coʔ," no-k-laknoʔo. "na·kwa
say-PART-EVID all.right-RES say-PART-EVID Now

xa·-xa-w!" no-k-lakno?o. ?e·ta ?exwa-la
move.SG.AUG-AUG-IMP say-PART-EVID be-SS.NPURP buzzard-NOM.SG

ha-kla-ta-k-lakno?o.
move.SG-down-CIS-PART-EVID

(9) ?e·-kla Ha·cosokonay-la xa·-xa-k-lakno?o
be-DS.NSIM Coyote-NOM.SG move.SG.AUG-AUG-PART-EVID

kwa·-kwan-wa·-y?ik. ?e·-kla we·?is "tickan-pax
RED-woman-OBV-ALL be-DS.NSIM one person-just

toxwno·no?
toxwano·-no-we-?e," no-k-lakno?o. ?e·-kla "te·-la
smell-CONT-DECL-PRES say-PART-EVID be-DS.NSIM this-NOM.SG

toxwno·no?
toxwano·-no-we-?e," no-k-lakno?o we·?is. ?e·-kwa
smell-CONT-DECL-PRES say-PART-EVID one be-DS.SIM

kaltey-?a·-y?ik he-n-ti-txo?o-k-la
outside-DEF-ALL REFL-TH-RED-move.about-PART-NOM.SG

"ha-txil-na-t ya·ce-w," no-k-lakno?o.
move.SG-out-ABL-SS.CONS look-IMP say-PART-EVID

?e·-kla we·?is ha-txil-na-l?ok
be-DS.NSIM one move.SG-out-ABL-when

Ha·csokonay-la he-ylapela-k-lakno?o lak
Coyote-NOM.SG REFL-stand-PART-EVID 3SG

ta·-ta-kxo-na-k-lakno?o. ?e·-kla kwa·-kwan-wa·-k
COM-move.PL-in-ABL-PART-EVID be-DS.NSIM RED-woman-OBV-ACC

"?o·c!" no-no-n-lakno?o. "he-co-cxo·-k-la
oh! RED-say-CONT-EVID REFL-RED-fear-PART-NOM.SG

?o·s?ow
ke-w-sok-a·we," no-k-lakno?o. "na·kw ?e-wes?a-w!"
1.OBJ-OBJ.PL-own-PERF say-PART-EVID now prepare-IMP

no-k-lakno?o. "ta·-ta-kla-no-n,"
say-PART-EVID COM-move.PL-down-CONT-GER

no-k-lakno?o.
say-PART-EVID

(10) ?e·-kla ketay-ta ta?ance-nes?e-k-lakno?o he·tya·-?a·-ka-y.
be-DS.NSIM two-DET grasp-DU-PART-EVID arm-DEF-PL-INST

?e·-ta "c?o·ma-w!" no-k-lakno?o. "ya·cen-ape-w!"
be-SS.NPURP close.eyes-IMP say-PART-EVID look-NEG-IMP

no-k-lakno?o. ta-kla-na-k-lakno?o ?e·-t ketay-ta
say-PART-EVID move.DU-down-ABL-PART-EVID be-SS.CONS two-DET

he-koxa-nes?e-l-ka?ak ?a·xwa ketay-?a·-la
REFL-tire-DU-3-when 3PL.too two-DEF-NOM.SG

ta?an-ce-nes-no-k-lakno?o.
grasp-?-DU-CONT-PART-EVID

(11) ?e·-kwa caka-wa·-?a·-la-k ha·cin-tak nakwto·-k-lakno?o.
be-DS.SIM river-OBV-DEF-SG-ACC close-just approach-PART-EVID

?e·-kwa "ha·cin xasto-·kwa," no-k-lakno?o. "c?o·ma-w!"
be-DS.SIM near remain-MIR say-PART-EVID close.eyes-IMP

no-k-lakno?o. Ha·csokonay-la c?o·ma-k-lakno?o
say-PART-EVID Coyote-NOM.SG close.eyes-PART-EVID

?e·-t ?a·x-?a·-y?ik x-e·pac-a·to-·kwa Ha·csokonay-la-k
be-SS.CONS water-DEF-ALL AUG-glide-FUT-MIR Coyote-SG-ACC

"we·?il ya·cena-·-we," no-k-lakno?o. no-k-la
all.right look-2.OBJ-DECL say-PART-EVID say-PART-NOM.SG

Ha·csokonay-la ya·cena-·kwa ?a·x-?a·-y?ik
Coyote-NOM.SG look-MIR water-DEF-ALL

x-e·pace-k-lakno?o. ?e·-kla Ha·csokonay-la
AUG-glide-PART-EVID be-DS.NSIM Coyote-NOM.SG

ca·cxok-a·-yʔik [*sic*] so·yanʔ-an "Quack, quack,"
middle-DEF-ALL swim-GER quack-quack

no-no-k-laknoʔo. so·na he-koʔo-t so·na
say-CONT-PART-EVID duck REFL-transform-SS.CONS duck

kwa·-kwan-ka ʔe·-no-k-laknoʔo,
RED-woman-NOM.PL be-CONT-PART-EVID

he·panonoʔo
naʔa he·panewa-na-we-ʔe ʔo·ʔa-he·pano-n-e·-ka-k.
thus narrate-CONT-DECL-PRES night-narrate-GER-this-PL-ACC

Coyote and the Duck Women: Free English Translation

[1] Coyote was living with his mother's mother, and, as he was, he was wandering about along the river. While [he was] doing so, there were bunch of people laughing. Coyote was standing near a tree and peered down below—there were four women bathing with no clothes on at all! [2] Then Coyote stole those women's belt and went off back to the camp. Then Coyote arrived and asked his grandmother: "Put this away. If anyone comes here and asks for the belt, don't tell them." Then his grandmother said: "All right." And Coyote went off. [3] Just then, a woman arrived to the tipi and asked about the belt. The old woman said: "I haven't seen it," to which the woman responded: "You're lying! I can just smell it in there. Just show me it. I did away with it just like this." Then the old woman gave the belt to her, and grasping the belt, the woman disappeared. [4] Then while the old woman was sitting down, Coyote arrived and said: "Did anyone come by?!" The old woman replied: "A woman came by and took the belt and went away." Then Coyote said: "What direction did she go in?" Then the old lady said: "I don't know," and Coyote went off and lay himself down weeping for four days. [5] As he did, Buzzard arrived and said: "How come you're weeping so much? How will your weeping make you see her any more? She's on the other side of the sky." Then Coyote said: "Take me up [into the sky]." Buzzard replied: "That hole in the sky is on the other side. Prepare some meat and four bags—do this and you'd be able to come up with me." [6] Then Coyote killed a buffalo and filled four bags full of meat, and when Buzzard arrived he said: "All right, let's go." Then Buzzard got all packed up with meat and when Coyote mounted Buzzard, they rose up flying and flew up and away. "Whenever I fall in any direction, put the meat in my mouth. When you do, it will make me go straight up." [7] Then Coyote fed

Buzzard as the two were going off and up and finished off just one bag. Then three remained, and so he opened one more and fed him meat as he flew up and away. When he then finished that one, he opened one more and fed it to Buzzard for him to fly up and away. When he finished that one, he opened up the last one and fed it to Buzzard for him to fly up and away. When there remained just a very short distance to the hole in the sky, the meat was all gone. [8] Then Coyote said: "The meat is all gone." Buzzard said: "Oh, now what are you going to do?" Coyote then twice transformed himself into a rump of meat to feed Buzzard, and they sat down to rest on the other side of the sky. Then Coyote said: "All right, there they are! Now get a move on!" And then Buzzard came down. [9] Then Coyote got to the women, and one said: "[The belt] smells just like a human." Another one said: "It really smells." When they then [heard] someone moving about outside, one of them said: "Go out and look." When one of them went out [to check], Coyote was just standing there, so she brought him in, and the women kept on saying: "Oh, a monster owns us! Now get ready, bring him down." [10] Then two of them grabbed hold of him by the arms and said: "Close your eyes! Don't look!" They brought him down, and when those two got tired, the other two also grabbed hold of him. [11] When they got right up next to the river, they said: "There's still a little bit left, shut your eyes!" Coyote shut his eyes, and as they were about to glide down onto the water, they said to Coyote: "Now you can look." And Coyote gazed in astonishment at them as they glided down onto the water. Then with Coyote swimming in the middle of the water, they kept on saying: "Quack, quack!" They had transformed themselves into ducks—they were duck women! They've always told night stories like that.

9. Coyote, Quail, and Beaver

(1) Ha·csokonay-la silwe-no-k-lakno?o. ?e·-no-·-la
Coyote-NOM.SG wander-CONT-PART-EVID be-CONT-PART-NOM.SG

caka-wixwan-?a·-y?ik ha·-na-·kwa Tickan-yasxaw?a[·]-la[15]
river-small-DEF-ALL move.SG-ABL-DS.SIM people-frighten-NOM.SG

ta·-ha-ho·-k-lakno?o.
COM-move.SG-meet-PART-EVID

(2) ?e·-kla Ha·csokonay-la "hecu·-?a·-y?ik ha·-na-no-ka?"
be-DS.NSIM Coyote-NOM.SG what-DEF-ALL move.SG-ABL-CONT-2

no-k-lakno?o. ?e·-kla Tickan-yasxaw-la [*sic*] "to·na
say-PART-EVID be-DS.NSIM people-frighter-NOM.SG just

silweno?s
silwe-no-?e-s," no-k-lakno?o.
wander-CONT-PRES-1 say-PART-EVID

(3) ?e·-kla Ha·csokonay-la "hecu· he-sto·-ye·-ka?"
be-DS.NSIM Coyote-NOM.SG what REFL-call-INGR-2

no-k-lakno?o. ?e·-kla "'Tickan-yasxaw?a'
say-PART-EVID be-DS.NSIM people-frighten

kenesto·no?olok
ke-nes-[s]to·na-we-?e-lok," no-k-lakno?o. ?e·-kla
1.OBJ-CAUS-call[?]-DECL-PRES-3.PL say-PART-EVID be-DS.NSIM

Ha·cosokonay-la "na·kweta?an ke-yasxa-w,"
Coyote-NOM.SG very.well 1.OBJ-frighten-IMP

no-k-lakno?o. ?e·-kla "na·kw. he?e·-k
say-PART-EVID be-DS.NSIM all.right that-ACC

kilix-pax-e?e·-k ha·cin-e?e-k han-pil-na-w,"
river-high-that-ACC near-that-ACC move.SG-TH-other-ABL-IMP

15. The final segment -?a might be the remnants of a frozen definite suffix -?a·.

no-k-lakno?o   Tickan-yasxaw?a-la.
say-PART-EVID   people-frighten-NOM.SG

?e·-kla   Ha·csokonay-la   "hey?,"   no-k-lakno?o.
be-DS.NSIM   Coyote-NOM.SG   hey   say-PART-EVID

(4)   ?e·-ta   ha·-na-kwa   te·-w?an   yoxa-na-k-lakno?o.
be-when   move.SG-ABL-DS.SIM   this-ADESS   fly-ABL-PART-EVID

?e·-ta   yox-an-xa·-xa-t   kilix-pax-a·cin-wa·-y?ik
be-SS.NPURP   fly-GER-move.SG.AUG-AUG-SS.CONS   river-high-near-OBV-ALL

he-cne-k-lakno?o.   ?e·-kwa   Ha·csokonay-la
REFL-lie-PART-EVID   be-DS.SIM   Coyote-NOM.SG

we·-l?a-t   ?ey-ta-k-lakno?o.   kilix-pax-wa·-?a·-la-k
yonder-?-SS.CONS   do-move.PL-PART-EVID   river-high-OBV-DEF-SG-ACC

ha·cin-?a·-y?ik   ha·-na-·kwa   tickan-yasxaw?a-la
near-DEF-ALL   move.SG-ABL-DS.SIM   people-frighten-NOM.SG

yox-na-k-lakno?o.   ?e·-kla   Ha·csokonay-la
fly-ABL-PART-EVID   be-DS.NSIM   Coyote-NOM.SG

he-xsasa-ta   kilix-pax-wa·-[y]?ik [*sic*]
REFL-yelp-SS.NPURP   river-high-OBV-ALL

wa·-na-t   he-ylap-an-wa·-y?ik   yac-ya-txalka-t
fall-ABL-SS.CONS   REFL-stand-GER-OBV-ALL (='tree')   fasten-TH-hang-SS.CONS

ha·-ya-ta-txalka-no-k-lakno?o.   ?e·-kwa
move.SG-TH-RED-hang-CONT-PART-EVID   be-DS.SIM

Tickan-yasxaw?a-la   yox-na-k-lakno?o.
people-frighten-NOM.SG   fly-ABL-PART-EVID

(5)   ?e·-no-k-la-k   he-ylap-an-[n]e-kam-an
be-CONT-PART-SG-ACC   REFL-stand-GER-TH-gnaw-GER (='beaver')

we-wxa·-yo-n-la ketay-ta
RED-grow.up-INGR-PART-NOM.SG two-DET
(='children')

he-kta·we-nes-no-k-lakno?o. ?e·-no-la Ha·csokonay-wa·-?a·-la-k
REFL-count-DU-CONT-PART-EVID be-CONT-NOM.SG Coyote-OBV-DEF-SG-ACC
(='play')

ya·ce-k-lakno?o ?e·-t ye-yka?ay-?a·-la-k
see-PART-EVID be-SS.CONS RED-grow.big-DEF-SG-ACC
(='parents')

w-e·pake-k-lakno?o.
OBJ.PL-tell-PART-EVID

"?ekwan-wixwan-la he-wa-wak-a·-we. ya?aco-w!
dog-little-NOM.SG REFL-RED-die-ASS-DECL revive-IMP

he-kta·wa-nes?e-·s," no-k-lakno?o we-wxa·-yo·-n-wa·-?a·-la.
REFL-play-DU-1[16] say-PART-EVID RED-grow.big-INGR-GER-OBV-DEF-NOM.SG

?e·-kla "wa·xes ?ekwan ye·-l-kwa??"
be-DS.NSIM surely dog be-3-MIR

no-k-lakno?o. ?e·-kla "he·?," no-k-lakno?o.
say-PART-EVID be-DS.NSIM yes say-PART-EVID

(6) ?e·-kla ya?aco·-k-lakno?o ?e·-kla we-te·-kta·we-no-k-lakno?o.
be-DS.NSIM revive-PART-EVID be- DS.NSIM OBJ.PL-COM.REFL-play-CONT-PART-EVID

tana·to·nesno?s
?e·-no-k-la-k "te·-w?an ta-n-a·to·-nes-no-we-?e-s.
be-CONT-PART-SG-ACC this-ADESS move.PL-ABL-FUT-DU-CONT-DECL-PRES-1

16. Hoijer (1972, 37 [no. 5]) translates this word as 'we want to play with him' but in fact it is in the indicative present, not another modal form.

ya·c-we-xwel-p-aʔa. [*sic*] we-te·-kta·we-w," no-k-laknoʔo.
watch-OBJ.PL-miss-NEG-ASS OBJ.PL-COM.REFL-play-IMP say-PART-EVID

ʔe·-kla "hehe·ʔ," no-k-laknoʔo.
be-DS.NSIM all.right say-PART-EVID

(7) ta-na-nesʔe-k-laknoʔo ye-ykaʔay-wa·-ʔa·-la. ʔe·-kwa
move.PL-ABL-DU-PART-EVID RED-grow.big-OBV-DEF-NOM.SG be-DS.SIM

Ha·csokonay-la cikwa·tak we·-kla-xe-no-k-laknoʔo.
Coyote-NOM.SG violent fall-down-AUG-CONT-PART-EVID

ʔe·-no-[Ø]-la kwe·-la-k taʔane-t yaxwe-ncaka-k-laknoʔo.
be-CONT-PART-NOM.SG club-SG-ACC grasp-SS.CONS club-kill-PART-EVID

ʔe·-ta ha·-na-k-laknoʔo Ha·csokonay-la.
be-SS.NPURP move.SG-ABL-PART-EVID Coyote-NOM.SG

(8) ʔe·-kwa ye-ykaʔay-wa·-ʔa·-la ta-xka-nesʔe-k-laknoʔo
be-DS.SIM RED-grow.big-OBV-DEF-NOM.SG move.PL-back-DU-PART-EVID

ʔe·-t ya·ce-k-laknoʔo. "heheyʔ," no-k-laknoʔo.
be-SS.CONS see-PART-EVID all.right say-PART-EVID

"we·l-te·-la ʔa·x-e·-ka-k xan-ap-aʔa
DEM.ANIM-this-NOM.SG water-that-PL-ACC drink-NEG-ASS.3SG

silwe·-n-ʔok henox ʔ-a·to·-nʔei," no-k-laknoʔo.
wander -3-while good become-FUT-ASS-ASS2 say-PART-EVID

(9) ʔe·-k-la-k pas-ʔe-ta Ha·csokonay-la
be-PART-SG-ACC time-be-SS.NPURP Coyote-NOM.SG

ʔa·x-ʔey-nack-a·to-no-k-laknoʔo.
water-become-die-FUT-CONT-PART-EVID

ʔe·-no·-la waʔan-pax ʔawas-na·t-an-ʔa·-yʔik
be-CONT-PART-NOM.SG as.soon.as buffalo-step-GER-DEF-ALL

ʔa·x-la-k xan-a·to-·kwa
water-SG-ACC drink-FUT-when

he-ylap-an-[n]e-kam-an-wa·-ʔa·-la	pancal-ayco-ta-no-k-laknoʔo.
REFL-stand-GER-TH-gnaw-GER-OBV-DEF-NOM.SG	open.mouth-up-CIS-CONT-PART-EVID

ʔe·-l-kaʔak	Ha·csokonay-la	"he·ya!"	no·-ta
happen-3-when	Coyote-NOM.SG	hey	say-SS.NPURP

ya-lxil-na-no-k-laknoʔo.	ʔe·-no-la	waʔanpax	to·no
TH-run-ABL-CONT-PART-EVID	be-CONT-NOM.SG	just.as	just

xane·-kwa	ya-mʔacx-an-ʔa·-la-k
drink-when	TH-sneeze-GER-DEF-SG-ACC (='nose')

nac-kayce-k-laknoʔo.[17]	ʔe·-kla	Ha·csokonay-la
bite-off-PART-EVID	be-DS.NSIM	Coyote-NOM.SG

ya-mʔacx-an-ʔa·-la-k	ca·cxok-pax-ʔe·-ta	ha·-na-no-k-laknoʔo.
TH-sneeze-GER-DEF-SG-ACC	center-only-be-SS.NPURP	move.SG-ABL-CONT-PART-EVID

ʔe·-no-·-la	ha·c-la-k	ya-mʔacx-an
be-CONT-PART-NOM.SG	mud-SG-ACC	TH-sneeze-GER

he-ykoʔo-k-laknoʔo.	ʔe·ta	ha·-na-no-k-laknoʔo.
REFL-make-PART-EVID	be-SS.NPURP	move.SG-ABL-CONT-PART-EVID

(10)

cʔawʔal-ʔa·-yʔik	ha·-na-·kwa	ya-coxʔ-an-ʔa·-la
distance-DEF-ALL	move.SG-ABL-when	TH-camp-GER-DEF-NOM.SG

we·l-ʔat	he-yace-no-k-laknoʔo	we·ʔis-pax	ya-coxʔ-an-away-la.
DEM.ANIM-?	REFL-see-CONT-PART-EVID	one-just	TH-camp-GER-tall-NOM.SG

ʔe·-kla	Ha·csokonay-la	wa·-yʔik	ha·-na-no-k-laknoʔo.
be-DS.NSIM	Coyote-NOM.SG	OBV-ALL	move.SG-ABL-CONT-PART-EVID

ʔe·-no-·-la	xa·-xa-k-laknoʔo.	ʔe·-kwa
be-CONT-PART-EVID	move.SG.AUG-AUG-PART-EVID	be-DS.SIM

17. Hoijer (1972, 23 [no. 245]) treats this verb along with biting verbs *nac-*, but an alternative might be to group it with *nacaka-* 'kill.'

ʔa·yay-ʔa·-yʔik ya-coxʔ-an-wa·-ʔa·-la-k
inside-DEF-ALL TH-camp-GER-OBV-DEF-SG-ACC

he·-xʔaxʔayʔo·-no-k-laknoʔo.
REFL-laugh-CONT-PART-EVID

(11) ʔe·-kla Ha·csokonay-la ya-kwlax-an-ʔa·-la
be-DS.NSIM Coyote-NOM.SG TH-open-GER-DEF-NOM.SG

ya-kwlaxe-ta
TH-open-SS.NPURP

he-lʔeya-kxo-na-k-laknoʔo. ʔe·-l-ʔok kwa·-kwan-osaʔas-ka
REFL-look-in-ABL-PART-EVID be-3-when RED-woman-old-NOM.PL

sikiti-ta ʔe·-no-k-laknoʔo. ʔe·-t we·ʔis ya·ce-k-laknoʔo
four-DET be-CONT-PART-EVID be-SS.CONS one see-PART-EVID

Ha·csokonay-la-k ʔe·t "ha-kxo-ta-w," no-k-laknoʔo.
Coyote-SG-ACC be-SS.CONS move.SG-in-CIS-IMP say-PART-EVID

ʔe·-kla Ha·csokonay-la xʔaxʔayʔa-no-k-laknoʔo. ʔe·-kla
be-DS.NSIM Coyote-NOM.SG laugh-CONT-PART-EVID be-DS.NSIM

ʔecinʔe "ha-kxo-ta-w," no-k-laknoʔo. ʔe·-kla Ha·csokonay-la
then move.SG-in-CIS-IMP say-PART-EVID be-DS.NSIM Coyote-NOM.SG

xʔaxʔayʔa-no-k-laknoʔo. ʔe·-kla "holaw-ʔa·-la-k wa·-tel
laugh-CONT-PART-EVID be-DS.NSIM last-DEF-SG-ACC yonder-DIR

ya-mk-a·tewa·-nes," no-k-laknoʔo. ʔe·-ta
TH-call-FUT-2.OBJ-1.SBJ say-PART-EVID be-SS.NPURP

"ha-kxo-ta-w," no-k-laknoʔo.
move.SG-in-CIS-IMP say-PART-EVID

ʔe·-kla Ha·csokonay-la ha-kxo-na-k-laknoʔo.
be-DS.NSIM Coyote-NOM.SG move.SG-in-ABL-PART-EVID

(12) ʔe·-kla cʔa·px-an-ʔa·-yʔik nes-yela-ta
be-DS.NSIM prepare.bed-GER-DEF-ALL (='bed') CAUS-sit-SS.NPURP

ta·-he·-malo·-no-n-lakno?o.
COM-REFL-play.sexually-CONT-PART-EVID

?e·-no-k-la-k	we·?is	kwa·n-wa·-?a·-la
be-CONT-PART-SG-ACC	one	woman-OBV-DEF-NOM.SG

ya-m?acx-an-?a·-y?ik	?ey-netxno?o-k-lakno?o.
TH-sneeze-GER-DEF-ALL	do-poke-PART-EVID

?e·-kla	ha·c-ya-m?acx-an-wa·-?a·-la
be-DS.NSIM	mud-TH-sneeze-GER-OBV-DEF-NOM.SG

xa-wa-na-k-lakno?o.	?e·-kla	kwan-wa·-ka
AUG-fall-ABL-PART-EVID	be-DS.NSIM	woman-OBV-NOM.PL

he·-xe-xsa·yo·-ta	ha·-na-ci-cxile-xeyne-k-lakno?o.
REFL-RED-scream-SS.NPURP	move.SG-ABL-RED-run-far-PART-EVID

?e·-kla	Ha·csokonay-la	yan-ci-cxil-a·xeyne-k-lakno?o.
be-DS.NSIM	Coyote-NOM.SG	TH-RED-run-far-PART-EVID

we·-tic.
yonder-like

Coyote, Quail, and Beaver: Free English Translation

[1] Coyote was wandering about and, as he was doing so, happened upon a small river where Quail met him. [2] Coyote asked him: "Where are you headed?" Quail responded: "I'm just wandering about." [3] So Coyote asked him: "What are you called?" And [Quail] responded: "They call me 'One Who Frightens People.'" So Coyote said: "Okay then, frighten me!" Then Quail said: "All right. Go over near to that high riverbank." Coyote said: "All right." [4] Then as [Coyote] went off, [Quail] flew off and landed near the high riverbank and lay down. Then as Coyote got near the high riverbank, Quail flew off and Coyote yelped and fell from the bluff and got caught on a tree and was hanged there. Then Quail flew off. [5] After this, two beaver children were playing, and one of them saw Coyote and told their parents. "A little dog has been killed. Revive him, we're playing!" the children said. "Are you sure it's a dog?" [the parents] responded. "Yes," [the kids] said. [6] So they revived him, and he played with them, and the [parents] said: "We're heading off in this direction; keep an eye on them and play with them." So Coyote said: "All right." [7] As the two parents went off, Coyote violently fell down on

them, grabbed a club, and beat them to death. Then Coyote walked away. [8] Then the two grown-ups came home and saw [what had happened], and said: "All right, that guy isn't going to drink any of this water while he wanders about until you get better." [9] As such, after a while, Coyote was about to die of thirst, and right when he was about to drink water from a buffalo footprint, Beaver came up with his mouth open. As it happened, Coyote said: "Hey!" and ran off—just when he was drinking [Beaver] bit off his nose. Coyote only had half a nose and went off to make a nose out of mud and got on his way. [10] He went a distance to a camp a bit away and just one tall tipi could be seen. Coyote was going in that direction, and when he arrived someone was laughing inside the tipi. [11] Then Coyote opened it up and looked inside. When he did, there were four old women inside and one saw him and said: "Come in." Coyote started to laugh, and so they said: "Come on in!" Still Coyote was laughing. "For the last time, I'm calling you over here," she said. "Come inside!" Then Coyote went inside. [12] They sat him down on the bed and messed around with him.[18] Then one woman poked at his nose, and the mud-nose fell off! When this happened, the women screamed and screamed and ran right out [of the tipi], far far away. Then Coyote ran away too. So it goes.

18. That is, sexually. An act of indeterminate nature.

10. Coyote and the Turkeys

(1) Ha·csokonay-la silwe-no-k-lakno?o. ?e·-no-·-la
Coyote-NOM.SG wander-CONT-PART-EVID be-CONT-PART-NOM.SG

cakaw-kwa·low-?a·-y?ik xa·-xa-k-lakno?o. ?e·-ta
river-big-DEF-ALL move.SG-AUG-PART-EVID be-SS.NPURP

cakaw-a·cin-?a·-y?ik ha·-na-·kwa hemaxan-ka
river-near-DEF-ALL move.SG-ABL-when turkey-NOM.PL

ha·naxoka·-tak haho·-no-k-lakno?o.
great.number-very gather-CONT-PART-EVID

?e·-kla Ha·csokonayla "xa·-xa-t
be-DS.NSIM Coyote-NOM.SG move.SG.AUG-AUG-SS.CONS

ya·ce-s-a?a," no-k-lakno?o.
see-1-ASS say-PART-EVID

(2) ?e·-ta ha·-na-k-lakno?o. ?e·-t
be-SS.NPURP move.SG-ABL-PART-EVID be-SS.CONS

xa·-xa-k-lakno?o
move.SG.AUG-AUG-PART-EVID

hemaxan-a·naxok-wa·-y?ik ?e·-t "hecu·
turkey-many-OBV-ALL be-SS.CONS what

?o·snoka
?a-we·s-no-ka?" no-k-lakno?o. ?e·-kla
do-1/2.SBJ.PL-CONT-2 say-PART-EVID be-DS.NSIM

he·malewa·to·sno?s
"he·-malew-a·tewa-we·s-no-?e-s," no-k-lakno?o.
REFL-dance-FUT-1/2.SBJ.PL-CONT-PRES-1 say-PART-EVID

?e·-kla Ha·csokonay-la "hehe·?," no-k-lakno?o.
be-DS.NSIM Coyote-NOM.SG all.right say-PART-EVID

"he-y?acew-a·ha?a," no-k-lakno?o. ?e·-kla
REFL-see-INTENT say-PART-EVID be-DS.NSIM

hemaxan-la "henox ʔ-a·to-nʔey," no-k-laknoʔo.
turkey-NOM.SG good do-FUT-2POT say-PART-EVID

ʔe·-kwa "we·ʔil!" no-k-laknoʔo.
be-DS.S7IM all.right say-PART-EVID

(3) ʔe·-kla he·-malo·-k-laknoʔo hemaxan-wa·-ka.
be-DS.NSIM REFL-dance-PART-EVID turkey-OBV-NOM.PL

ʔe·kla Ha·csokonay-la he-ylapa-t
be-DS.NSIM Coyote-NOM.SG REFL-stand-SS.CONS

he-yʔaco·-no-k-laknoʔo. ʔe·-kwa losos-ʔita
REFL-see-CONT-PART-EVID be-DS.SIM all-DET

hemaxan-wa·-ʔa·-la he-y-ka-kawo·-k-laknoʔo.
turkey-OBV-DEF-NOM.SG REFL-TH-RED-dance.Kick.Dance-PART-EVID

ʔe·-kla Ha·csokonay-la he-skwace-no-k-laknoʔo. ʔe·-kwa
be-DS.NSIM Coyote-NOM.SG REFL-enjoy-CONT-PART-EVID be-DS.SIM

hemaxan-wa·-ka "ʔakeke· wilʔi wilʔi," no-·kwa
turkey-OBV-NOM.PL [meaningless words for dance] say-DS.SIM

he-ka-kawo·-no-k-laknoʔo.
REFL-RED-dance.Kick.Dance-CONT-PART-EVID

(4) ʔe·-kla Ha·csokonay-la nesexe-we-ta
be-DS.NSIM Coyote-NOM.SG frighten-INGR-SS.CONS

he-tay-ʔo·-he-y-ka-kawo·-k-laknoʔo.
REFL-join-do-REFL-TH-RED-dance.Kick.Dance-PART-EVID

ʔe·-t pas-ʔe-ta "wa·-tax he-kto·-l-kaʔak
be-SS.CONS time-be-SS.NPURP yonder-ANIM REFL-sing-3-while

cʔocʔomanoʔo
tamo·-tak cʔo-cʔoma-no-we-ʔe," no-k-laknoʔo Ha·csokonay-la.
tight-very RED-shut-CONT-DECL-PRES say-PART-EVID Coyote-NOM.SG

ʔe·-kla hemaxan-wa·-ka losos-ʔita tamo·-tak
be-DS.NSIM turkey-OBV-NOM.PL all-DET tight-very

cʔo-cʔoma-ta he-y-ka-kawo·-kwa Ha·csokonay-la
RED-shut-SS.NPURP REFL-TH-RED-dance.Kick.Dance-DS.SIM Coyote-NOM.SG

ya·ce-na-no-k-laknoʔo. hemaxan-kwa·lo·-ka-k
see-ABL-CONT-PART-EVID turkey-big-PL-ACC

nataya-no-k-laknoʔo.
select-CONT-PART-EVID

(5) ʔe·-no·-la kwa·lo·-la-k ya·ce-t kw·e-ʔa·-la-k
be-CONT-PART-EVID big-SG-ACC see-SS.CONS club-DEF-SG-ACC

taʔane-k-laknoʔo. ʔe·-ta hemaxan-kwa·lo·-wa·-ʔa·-la-k
grasp-PART-EVID be-SS.NPURP turkey-big-OBV-DEF-SG-ACC

yaxw-nacka-k-laknoʔo. ʔe·-ta ʔecinʔe ketay
by.club-kill-PART-EVID be-SS.NPURP then two

kala-ka-k yaxw-nacka-k-laknoʔo. ʔe·-ta
other-PL-ACC by.club-kill-PART-EVID be-SS.NPURP

ʔecinʔe ketay yaxwe-nca-k-laknoʔo. ʔe·-ta ʔecinʔe
then two by.club-kill-PART-EVID be-SS.NPURP then

yaxw-c-a·to·-kwa hemaxan-we·ʔis
by.club-strike-FUT-DS.SIM turkey-one

ke-w-ya·lo·n-to·x-a·to·no-t-aʔa
"ke-we-ya·lo·n-to·x-a·tewa-no-t-aʔa!"
1.OBJ-OBJ.PL-kill-finish-FUT-CONT-EP-3.ASS

no-k-laknoʔo.
say-PART-EVID

(6) ʔe·-kla hemaxan-wa·-ka losos-ʔita ya-yace-na-k-laknoʔo.
be-DS.NSIM turkey-OBV-NOM.PL all-DET RED-see-ABL-PART-EVID

ʔe·-kwa hemaxan-la "we·ʔil," no-k-laknoʔo. ʔe·-kla
be-DS.SIM turkey-NOM.SG all.right say-PART-EVID be-DS.NSIM

"hete-ca?" no-k-la "he-ylap-an-eʔe·-k!"
what-place say-PART-EVID REFL-stand-GER-THAT-ACC

no-k-lakno?o. ?e·-kla "?a·kay!"
say-PART-EVID be-DS.NSIM no

no-k-lakno?o. "we·-y?ik ?-a·pe-no-n!"
say-PART-EVID yonder-ALL do-NEG-CONT-3

no-k-lakno?o. "xe·s-e?e·-k!" no-k-lakno?o. ?e·-kla
say-PART-EVID sand-that-ACC say-PART-EVID be-DS.NSIM

"?a·kay!" no-k-lakno?o. "we·-y?ik ?-a·pe-no-n!"
no say-PART-EVID wonder-ALL do-NEG-CONT-3

no-k-lakno?o. ?e·-kwa "we·?il," no-k-lakno?o.
say-PART-EVID be-DS.SIM all.right say-PART-EVID

"c?el-te·-ca ?e·-no-n!" no-k-lakno?o. ?e·-kla
sky-this-place be-CONT-3 say-PART-EVID be-DS.NSIM

hemaxan-a·naxok-wa·-?a·-la losos-a·tak-ita
turkey-many-OBV-DEF-NOM.SG all-very-DET

yu-yuxa-na-co-coxo-k-lakno?o.
RED-fly-ABL-RED-afraid-PART-EVID

Coyote and the Turkeys: Free English Translation

[1] Coyote was wandering about and while doing so came to a big river. At the same time, a whole bunch of turkeys were gathering near the river. Then Coyote said: "I'm going to see [what's going on]." [2] So he went off and got to the place where all the turkeys were and said: "What are y'all doing?" Then they said: "We're going to dance." Then Coyote said: "All right, I'm going to watch." The turkey responded: "Good deal, all right." And [Coyote] replied: "Okay now!" [3] So the Turkeys began to dance, and Coyote was just standing there watching them. All the Turkeys began to do the Kick Dance, and Coyote was really enjoying it. When the Turkeys cried out *?akeke· wil?i wil?i,* they did the Kick Dance, over and over. [4] Then Coyote started to frighten them and joined in doing the Kick Dance with them. A while passed, and Coyote said: "While that one over there is singing, they all kept shutting[19] their eyes very tightly." Then all the turkeys closed their

19. Hoijer translates this as 'everyone should shut their eyes,' but the verb is actually a pluractional past continuous verb. It is thus an indirect, not a direct, suggestion.

eyes very tightly and danced while Coyote was watching them—he was taking his pick of the big turkeys. [5] Then, seeing a big one, he picked up club and clubbed the turkey to death, and then he killed two others with his club, and when he was about to club another turkey, it said: "He's going to finish us all off!" [6] Then all the turkeys kept looking around, and a turkey said: "Let's go!" Then another said: "Where to?" "That tree over there!" said the first. "No, let's not go there," another said. "All right, let's go up there in the air!" Then every single last one of all those turkeys flew up afraid into the sky.

11. Coyote and Mouse

(1) Hanilesʔaw-la we-ta-ya-coxʔa-no-k-laknoʔo. ʔe··no-··la
mouse-NOM.SG OBJ.PL-COM-TH-live-CONT-PART-EVID do-CONT-PART-EVID

ʔo·ca-ʔa··la-k he-kto·ʔo-n we-nes-yakwa-no-k-laknoʔo.
children-DEF-SG-ACC REFL-sing-GER OBJ.PL-CAUS-dance-CONT-PART-EVID

ʔe··kwa Ha·csokonay-la silwe-no-··la
be-DS.SIM Coyote-NOM.SG wander-CONT-PART-NOM.SG

so-sko··na-k-laknoʔo
RED-listen-ABL-PART-EVID

he-kto··k-wa··ʔa··la-k ʔe··t wa··yʔik
REFL-sing-PART-OBV-DEF-SG-ACC be-SS.CONS OBV-ALL

ya-coxʔ-an-ʔa··yʔik
TH-camp-GER-DEF-ALL

xa··xa-k-laknoʔo. ʔe··t he-lʔey-kxo-na-k-laknoʔo.
move.SG.AUG-AUG-PART-EVID be-SS.CONS REFL-look-in-ABL-PART-EVID

ʔe··l-ʔok hanilesʔa-wa··ʔa··la he-kto··no-k-laknoʔo.
be-3-when mouse-OBV-DEF-NOM.SG REFL-sing-CONT-PART-EVID

(2) ʔe··kla Ha·csokonay-la "he-kto··ne-k-eʔe··la-k,"
be-DS.NSIM Coyote-NOM.SG REFL-sing-2-PART-that-SG-ACC

no-k-laknoʔo. "k-e·ke-w!" no-k-laknoʔo.
say-PART-EVID 1.OBJ-give-IMP say-PART-EVID

ʔe··kla hanilesʔaw-la "wilʔa,"
be-DS.NSIM mouse-NOM.SG no

kexacno·noʔo
no-k-laknoʔo. "ke-xacno··no-we-ʔe," no-k-laknoʔo.
say-PART-EVID 1.OBJ-belong-CONT-DECL-PRES say-PART-EVID

ʔe··kla Ha·csokonay-la "ʔo·ko," no-k-laknoʔo.
be-DS.NSIM Coyote-NOM.SG No say-PART-EVID

"k-e·ke-w!" no-k-laknoʔo. ʔe·-kla hanilesʔaw-la
1.OBJ-give-IMP say-PART-EVID be-DS.NSIM mouse-NOM.SG

ʔekape·noʔo·ʔ
"tickan-e·-ka-k ʔek-ape-·-no-we ʔe·-ʔ," no-k-laknoʔo
person-this-PL-ACC give-NEG-2.OBJ-CONT-DECL-PAST-1.SBJ say-PART-EVID

hanilesʔaw-la. ʔe·-kla Ha·sokonay-la "ʔokay!"
mouse-NOM.SG be-DS.NSIM Coyote-NOM.SG no!

no-k-laknoʔo. "k-e·ke-w!" no-k-laknoʔo. ʔe·-kla
say-PART-EVID 1.OBJ-give-IMP say-PART-EVID be-DS.NSIM

hanilesʔaw-la "sa·ya o·ca-te-la we-nes-yakwa-l-ʔila
Mouse-NOM.SG 1.SG.NOM child-this-NOM.SG OBJ.PL-CAUS-dance-3-as

kexacno·noʔo
ke-xacno·-no-we-ʔe," no-k-laknoʔo hanilesʔaw-la.
1.OBJ-belong-CONT-DECL-PRES say-PART-EVID mouse-NOM.SG

(3) ʔe·-kla Ha·csokonay-la xaclo·-k-laknoʔo. "na·kw!"
be-DS.NSIM Coyote-NOM.SG get.angry-PART-EVID all.right

no-k-laknoʔo. "k-e·ke-w he-kto·-n
say-PART-EVID 1.OBJ-give-IMP REFL-sing-GER

na·xen te·-la-k!"
2.SG.GEN this-SG-ACC

no-k-laknoʔo. ʔe·-kla hanilesʔaw-la
say-PART-EVID be-DS.NSIM mouse-NOM.SG

"waʔan-a·lesok," no-·-ta ʔo·ca-ʔa·-la-k
just.as-wait? say-PART-SS.NPURP children-DEF-SG-ACC

hacip-kalak-a·-wʔan we-ta[·]-ta-kxo-na-k-laknoʔo.
hole-other-DEF-ADESS OBJ.PL-COM-move.PL-in-ABL-PART-EVID

ʔe·-t hacip-kalak-a·-yʔik
be-SS.CONS hole-other-DEF-ALL

we-ta[·]-ta-txil-na-k-laknoʔo
OBJ.PL-COM-RED-move.PL-ABL-PART-EVID

ʔe·-t we-ta[·]-saxwa-k-laknoʔo.
be-SS.CONS OBJ.PL-COM-run.away-PART-EVID

(4) ʔe·-kla Ha·csokonay-la ha-kxo-na-t
be-DS.NSIM Coyote-NOM.SG move.SG-in-ABL-SS.CONS

hacip-kalak-wa·-yʔik
hole-other-OBV-ALL

he-ylapa-ta "newey!" no-·-no-k-laknoʔo.
REFL-stand-SS.NPURP come.here say-PF-CONT-PART-EVID

ʔe·-kla to·nes ʔe·-no-k-laknoʔo.
be-DS.NSIM silence be-CONT-PART-EVID

e·-kla Ha·csokonay-la
be-DS.NSIM Coyote-NOM.SG

xaclo·-t ha-txil-na-k-laknoʔo.
get.angry-SS.CONS move.SG-out-ABL-PART-EVID

ʔe·-ta ha·-na-k-laknoʔo Ha·csokonay-la.
be-SS.NPURP move.SG-ABL-PART-EVID Coyote-NOM.SG

(5) no·noʔo he·pano·noʔo
no-·-no-we-ʔe. ʔa·ʔa he·pano-·-no-we-ʔe
say-PF-CONT-DECL-PRES so narrate-PF-CONT-DECL-PRES

ʔo·ʔo·-pano·-n-wa·-ka-k. we·-tic.
night-narrate-GER-OBV-PL-ACC that-like

Coyote and Mouse: Free English Translation

[1] Mouse was living with her children and by singing to them she made them dance. At just that time, Coyote was wandering by and began to listen in to the song and came up to the camp and looked in. When he did, Mouse was singing. [2] Then Coyote said: "That song you're singing, give it to me!" Then Mouse said: "No, it belongs to me." Then Coyote said: "Nope, give it to me!" Mouse replied: "I've never given it to you people." Then Coyote said: "No, give it to me!" Then Mouse said: "The thing that makes these children dance belongs to me!" [3] Then Coyote got angry and said: "Now look here, give me this song of yours!" Then Mouse

said: "Wait a minute," as she took her children with her from one hole and out another and ran away. [4] Then Coyote went into the [first] hole and said: "Come on out!" And there was silence. Then Coyote got angry and left [the hole] and went away. [5] They've always said that—they've always told such night stories. So it goes.

12. Coyote and Prairie Turtle

(1) Mayʔan-la | ha·-na-no-k-laknoʔo. | ʔe·-kwa
prairie.turtle-NOM.SG | move.SG-ABL-CONT-PART-EVID | be-DS.SIM

ʔawas-atak-la[20] | he-n-ce·la-k-laknoʔo
meat-much-NOM.SG (=‘buffalo’) | REFL-TH-lie-PART-EVID

lak. | mayʔan-wa·-ʔa·-la | ya·ce-t
3SGACC | prairie.turtle-OBV-DEF-NOM.SG | see-SS.CONS

ha·c-ʔa·-yʔik | ha-kxo-na-k-laknoʔo | ʔe·-t
ground-DEF-ALL | move.SG-in-ABL-PART-EVID | be-SS.CONS

ʔawas-la | he-cne-k-wa·-yʔik
meat-NOM.SG (=‘buffalo’) | REFL-lie.down-PART-OBV-ALL

xa·-xa-k-laknoʔo. | ʔe·-t
move.SG.AUG-AUG-PART-EVID | be-SS.CONS

ʔawas-wa·-ʔa·-la-k | ca·l-ʔa·-la-k | nace-k-laknoʔo.
meat-OBV-DEF-SG-ACC | testicle-DEF-ALL | bite-PART-EVID

ʔe·-kla | ʔawas-wa·-ʔa·-la | holkemʔacxe-tan-ʔan
be-DS.NSIM | meat-OBV-DEF-NOM.SG | buck-go.along-GER

ʔawas-wa·-ʔa·-la | he-wawa-t | xe·-cne-k-laknoʔo.
meat-OBV-DEF-NOM.SG | REFL-die-SS.CONS | AUG-lie.down-PART-EVID

(2) ʔe·-kla | mayʔan-wa·-ʔa·-la | xalʔo·-n-ka-k
be-DS.NSIM | prairie.turtle-OBV-DEF-NOM.SG | cut.with.knife-GER-PL-ACC

naʔa | he-kto·-no-k-laknoʔo·
thus | REFL-sing-CONT-PART-EVID

20. Probably a naming taboo related to this animal’s sacred character in Plains Indians culture. Compare the taboo against bears within Indo-European: Germanic (English) *bear* < PIE **bher-* ‘bright, brown,’ alongside Slavic (Russian) *medved* < PIE **medhu-* ‘honey” + **$h_1$ed-* ‘eat.’

saʔaxey cʔemes-la-k no-kxo-s no-kxo-s.
arrow ʔ-SG-ACC say-in-1 say-in-1

(3) ʔe·-kla Ha·csokonay-la so-sko·-na-t
be-DS.NSIM Coyote-NOM.SG RED-hear-ABL-SS.CONS

xa·-xa-k-laknoʔo.
move.SG.AUG-AUG-PART-EVID

ʔe·-t "hecu· no-·-no-ka ʔ," no-k-laknoʔo.
be-SS.CONS what say-PF-CONT-2 say-PART-EVID

ʔe·-kla mayʔan-la "saxʔay ya-kew-ʔ-a·to-l-ʔila
be-DS.NSIM prairie.turtle-NOM.SG arrow TH-make-do-FUT-3-DS.SIM

xalʔo·-n-ka-k k-e·-kpayo·-l-kaʔak
cut.with.knife-GER-PL-ACC 1OBJ-REFL-have.nothing-3-but

no·noʔs
no-·-no-ʔe-s," no-k-laknoʔo.
say-PF-CONT-PRES-1 say-PART-EVID

(4) ʔe·-kla Ha·csokonay-la "to·na no-·ka,"
be-DS.NSIM Coyote-NOM.SG false say-2

no-k-laknoʔo. "we·-c n-a·pe-no-·ka,"
say-PART-EVID that-manner say-NEG-CONT-2

no-k-laknoʔo. ʔe·-kla mayʔan-la "ʔalʔ,"
say-PART-EVID be-DS.NSIM prairie.turtle-NOM.SG all.right

no-k-laknoʔo. "ʔawas-la-k ya·lona-t
say-PART-EVID meat-SG-ACC kill-SS.CONS

no·nʔs [*sic*]
xalʔo·-n-a-k [*sic*] ʔe·-l-ʔila no-·-n[o]-ʔe-s,"
cut.with.knife-GER-DEF-ACC be-3-DS.SIM say-PF-CONT-PRES-1

no-k-laknoʔo.
say-PART-EVID

(5) ʔe·-kla Ha·csokonay-la
be-DS.NSIM Coyote-NOM.SG

"neykanak-xa·-xa-no-[Ø]-ʔa·-la[21]
first-move.SG.AUG-AUG-CONT-PART-DEF-NOM.SG

xa·-ʔa·-la-k losos to·x-a·to-nwa-ʔ," no-k-laknoʔo.
fat-DEF-SG-ACC all finish-FUT-DEON-DEON.3 say-PART-EVID

ʔe·-kla mayʔan-la "we·ʔil," no-k-laknoʔo.
be-DS.NSIM prairie.turtle-NOM.SG all.right say-PART-EVID

ʔe·-kla Ha·csokonay-la "we·ʔil," no-·-ta
be-DS.NSIM Coyote-NOM.SG all.right say-PART-SS.NPURP

he-kwa·-na-·kwa mayʔan-la ha·c-ʔa·-yʔik
REFL-run-ABL-as prairie.turtle-NOM.SG ground-DEF-ALL

ha-kxo-na-t neykanak xa·-xa-t
move.SG-in-ABL-SS.CONS first move.SG.AUG-AUG-SS.CONS

ʔawas-wa·-ʔa·-la-k xa·-ʔa·-la-k
meat-OBV-DEF-SG-ACC fat-DEF-SG-ACC

losos to·xa-k-laknoʔo ʔe·-ta
all finish-PART-EVID be-SS.NPURP

ʔasoy-ʔa·-yʔik he-cne-no-k-laknoʔo.
belly-DEF-ALL REFL-lie.down-CONT-PART-EVID

(6) ʔe·-kwa Ha·csokonay-la ya-n-ci-cxil-xa·-xa-t
be-DS.SIM Coyote-NOM.SG TH-TH-RED-run-move.SG.AUG-AUG-SS.CONS

ʔawas-wa·-ʔa·-la-k xa·-ʔa·-la-k losos
meat-OBV-DEF-SG-ACC fat-DEF-SG-ACC all

ta·kona-tola-na-k-laknoʔo. ʔe·-l-ʔok
seek-in.vain-ABL-PART-EVID be-3-if

mayʔan-la ʔasoy-ʔa·-yʔik he-cne-la-k
prairie.turtle-NOM.SG belly-DEF-ALL REFL-lie.down-SG-ACC

21. A fourth type of participial head, with null exponence, in addition to *-k*, *-n*, and vowel length.

Ha·csokonay-la	taʔane-t	yatexan-ʔa·-yʔik
Coyote-NOM.SG	grasp-SS.CONS	stone-DEF-ALL

mayʔan-wa·-ʔa·-la-k	yal-ta-tamʔaxe-k-laknoʔo.
prairie.turtle-OBV-DEF-SG-ACC	throw-RED-smash-PART-EVID

ʔe·-ta	ha·-nʔa-n	mʔe·tna-k-laknoʔo.	we·-tic.
be-SS.NPURP	move.SG-ABL-PART	lightning.strike-PART-EVID	that-like

Coyote and Prairie Turtle: Free English Translation

[1] Prairie Turtle was walking along as a big ol' buffalo was lying down. Seeing him on the ground, Prairie Turtle walked up to the buffalo lying down, and when he got up to the buffalo he bit him on the balls. The buffalo was bucking up and down and fell down and died. [2] That Prairie Turtle was singing along with his knives: *saʔaxey cʔemeslak nokxos, nokxos.* [3] Then Coyote came up to him and heard him singing: "What are you saying?" he said. So Prairie Turtle responded: "I'm going to make an arrow, [but] I don't have any knives." [4] Coyote said: "You're lying! You shouldn't speak that way." Then Prairie Turtle said: "All right. I was saying that if there are knives let's kill a buffalo." [5] Then Coyote said: "The first one to get there gets to finish off the fat." Prairie Turtle said: "All right." And Coyote agreed: "Okay." While Coyote was running off, Prairie Turtle dug into the ground, got there first, and finished off all the fat. Then he lay down on his belly. [6] When Coyote ran right up to the buffalo, he looked all over in vain for the fat. Then Coyote picked up Prairie Turtle lying down on his belly and bashed him over and over against a rock. Then as he was moving off, lightning struck him. So it goes.

13. Coyote Steals the Buffalo

(1)

ya-cox-ʔan-a·naxok-a·-yʔik	ha·ʔako·n-osaʔas-ka
TH-camp-GER-large-DEF-ALL	man-young-NOM.PL

he-ka·lwe-no-k-laknoʔo	saxʔay-ka-k.
REFL-gamble-CONT-PART-EVID	arrow-PL-ACC

ʔe·-kwa	we·ʔis	xa·-xa-k-laknoʔo
be-DS.SIM	one	move.SG.AUG-AUG-PART-EVID

he-sanko·-n-ʔa·-la	kaxaw-pax-la.	ʔe·-kla
REFL-dress-GER-DEF-NOM.SG (=‘clothing’)	black-just-NOM.SG	be-DS.NSIM

he·-nexʔey-o·-no-k-laknoʔo.	ya·cxwe·lpo·sʔew “ya·c-xwe·l-pe-we·sʔe-w,”
REFL-be.ignorant-INGR-CONT-PART-EVID	look-miss-NEG-1/2.SBJ.PL-IMP

no-·-no-k-laknoʔo.
say-PF-CONT-PART-EVID

(2)

ʔe·-kwa	taxas-ca·cxok-wa-k-la
be-DS.SIM	sun-middle-INGR-PART-NOM.SG

he-yax-yaxa-no-k-laknoʔo.
REFL-RED-eat-CONT-PART-EVID

ʔe-kla	he-sanko·-n-kaxaw-pax-wa·-ʔa·-la
be-DS.NSIM	REFL-dress-GER-black-just-OBV-DEF-NOM.SG

yakew-ʔan-kwa·low-la-k	yaxa-no-k-laknoʔo.	ʔe·-kla
make-GER-big-SG-ACC (=‘sausage’ [i.e., thing that is made])	eat-CONT-PART-EVID	be-DS.NSIM

ha·ʔako·n-osaʔas-wa·-ka	ya·cxwe·lpo·sʔew “ya·c-xwe·l-ape-we·sʔe-w,”
man-young-OBV-NOM.PL	look-miss-NEG-1/2.SBJ.PL-IMP

no-·-no-n-k-laknoʔo.
say-CONT-PART-PART-EVID

(3)
ʔe·-kwa he-sanko·-n-kaxaw-pax-wa·-ʔa·-la "ha·-n-a·haʔa,"
be-DS.SIM REFL-dress-GER-black-just-OBV-DEF-NOM.SG move.SG-ABL-INTENT

no-k-laknoʔo ʔe·-ta yox-na-k-laknoʔo. ʔe·-kla
say-PART-EVID be-SS.NPURP fly-ABL-PART-EVID be-DS.NSIM

ya·ce-no-n-laknoʔo. ya-yace-·kwa cʔawʔal
see-CONT-PART-EVID RED-look-while far.away

ʔe·-na-k-laknoʔo.
be-ABL-PART-EVID

(4)
ʔe·-kla "Yoxa·n-kamlew-la-k[22] yamko·sʔew ya-maka-we·sʔe-w,"
be-DS.NSIM fly-bat$^{?}$-SG-ACC TH-call-1/2.SBJ.PL-IMP
(='bat')

no-k-la ya-mka-k-laknoʔo. ʔe·-kla
say-PART-NOM.SG TH-call-PART-EVID be-DS.NSIM

yoxa·n-kamlew-la xa·-xa-k-laknoʔo
fly-bat-NOM.SG move.SG.AUG-AUG-PART-EVID

ʔe·-t "we·-lʔat ʔe·-n-e·l," no-k-laknoʔo.
be-SS.CONS yonder-DET be-CONT-JUSS say-PART-EVID

"we·-lʔat cakaw-ʔa·-la-k we·ʔis-pax
yonder-DET river-DEF-SG-ACC one-just

ha-yxe-na-kwa," no-k-laknoʔo.
move.SG-across-ABL-MIR say-PART-EVID

"ʔe·-ta ʔecinʔe ha-yxe-na-kwa," no-k-laknoʔo
be-SS.NPURP then move.SG-across-ABL-MIR say-PART-EVID

yoxa·n-kamle-wa·-ʔa·-la "we·-lʔat ʔe·-ta
fly-bat-OBV-DEF-NOM.SG yonder-ANIM.DEM be-SS.NPURP

kalak-la-k ha-yxe-na-kwa. we·-lʔat
other-SG-ACC move.SG-across-ABL-MIR yonder-ANIM.DEM

22. The root *-kamlew-* is a cranberry morph: it only exists in this word.

ʔecinʔe kalak-la-k ha-yxe-na-kwa,"
then other-SG-ACC move.SG-across-ABL-MIR

no-k-laknoʔo. ʔe·-ta "we·-lʔat
say-PART-EVID be-SS.NPURP yonder-ANIM.DEM

ya-coxʔ-an-ʔa·-yʔik xa·-xa-kwa,"
TH-camp-GER-DEF-ALL move.SG.AUG-AUG-MIR

no-k-laknoʔo yoxa·n-kamlew-ʔa·-la.
say-PART-EVID fly-bat-DEF-NOM.SG

(5) ʔe·-kla taxs-o·-k-la ha-wna-na-no-k-laknoʔo
be-DS.NSIM be.dawn-INGR-PART-EVID TH-move.camp-ABL-CONT-PART-EVID

ʔe·-t cakaw-ʔa·-la-k we·ʔis-pax
be-SS.CONS river-DEF-SG-ACC one-just

ha-wna-xaya-k-laknoʔo. ʔe·t taxs-o·-kwa
TH-move.camp-several-PART-EVID be-SS.CONS be.dawn-INGR-DS.SIM

ha-wna-na-no-k-laknoʔo. ʔecinʔe
TH-move.camp-ABL-CONT-PART-EVID then

cakaw-ʔa·-yʔik ha-wna-te-k-laknoʔo.
river-DEF-ALL TH-move.camp-CIS-PART-EVID

ʔe·-t taxs-o·-kwa
be-SS.CONS be.dawn-INGR-DS.SIM

ha-wna-na-no-k-laknoʔo. ʔe·-t cakaw-ʔa·-yʔik
TH-move.camp-ABL-CONT-PART-EVID be-SS.CONS river-DEF-ALL

ha-wna-xaya-k-laknoʔo. ʔe·-t taxs-o·-kwa
TH-move.camp-several-PART-EVID be-SS.CONS be.dawn-INGR-DS.SIM

ha-wna-na-k-laknoʔo ʔe·-t cakaw-ʔa·-yʔik
TH-move.camp-ABL-PART-EVID be-SS.CONS river-DEF-ALL

ha-wna-xaya-k-laknoʔo. ʔe·-t taxs-o·-kwa
TH-move.camp-several-PART-EVID be-SS.CONS be.dawn-INGR-DS.SIM

he-sanko·-n-kaxaw-pax-a·cin-ʔa·-yʔik
REFL-dress-GER-black-just-close-DEF-ALL

ha-wna-te-k-laknoʔo.
TH-move.camp-CIS-PART-EVID

(6) ʔe·-kwa h-e·pano·-k-la Ha·csokonay-la-k
be-DS.SIM REFL-narrate-PART-NOM.SG Coyote-SG-ACC

ya-mka-k-laknoʔo. ʔe·-kla "heheyʔ,"
TH-call-PART-EVID be-DS.NSIM all.right

no-k-laknoʔo ʔe·-ta xa·-xa-k-laknoʔo.
say-PART-EVID be-SS.NPURP move.SG.AUG-AUG-PART-EVID

ʔe·-kla kokon-ʔa·-la "na·ya losos
be-DS.NSIM chief-DEF-NOM.SG 2.SG.NOM all

hatxesenoʔoyno
ha-txese-no-we-ʔey-no hecu·-ʔaxey-ka-k. ʔawas-elʔa·t-la-k
TH-know-CONT-DECL-PAST-PAST.2.SG what-ever-PL-ACC meat-yonder-SG-ACC

na·ya kena ho·ʔoxaw-a·to-ne-k-coʔ," no-k-la
2.SG.NOM maybe steal-FUT-2.SG-PART-RES say-PART-EVID

Ha·csokonay-la "hehe·ʔ," no-k-laknoʔo.
Coyote-NOM.SG all.right say-PART-EVID

"taxs-o·-k-la he-ceco·-n
be.dawn-INGR-PART-NOM.SG REFL-turn.back-GER

keywʔeco·sʔow
ha-wna-ne·-ta ke-ywʔeca-we·sʔe-w,"
TH-move.camp-ABL-SS.NPURP 1.OBJ-look.out.for-1/2.SBJ.PL-IMP

no-k-laknoʔo Ha·csokonay-la.
say-PART-EVID Coyote-NOM.SG

(7) taxs-o·-kla ha-wna-na-k-laknoʔo. ʔe·-kla
be.dawn-INGR-DS.NSIM TH-move.camp-ABL-PART-EVID be-DS.NSIM

heykoʔot
Ha·csokonay-la ʔekwan-wixwan he-yakewa-we-ʔe-t
Coyote-NOM.SG dog-little REFL-make-DECL-PAST-SS.CONS

he-cne-no-k-laknoʔo ha-wn-an-can-an-ʔa·-yʔik
REFL-lie.down-CONT-PART-EVID TH-move.camp-GER-break-GER-DEF-ALL

ʔe·-kwa ʔawas-wa·-ʔa·-la-k sokano-ʔa·-lʔan ʔo·ca-ʔa[·]-la
be-DS.SIM meat-OBV-DEF-SG-ACC own-DEF-GEN children-DEF-NOM.SG

metis-ʔita ha-wn-an-can-an-wa·-yʔik
three-DET TH-move.camp-GER-break-GER-DEF-ALL

xaya-t to·kona-no-n-laknoʔo hecu·-ʔax-ka-k. ʔe·-t
go-SS.CONS search-CONT-PART-EVID what-any-PL-ACC be-SS.CONS

Ha·csokonay-wixwan-ayon-tak-la-k nen-xʔale-k-laknoʔo.
Coyote-little-itch-very-SG-ACC TH-find-PART-EVID
(= 'fleabitten Coyote')

ʔe·-t taʔane-ta ya-coxʔ-an-ʔa·-yʔik
be-SS.CONS grasp-SS.NPURP TH-camp-GER-DEF-ALL

xaya-k-laknoʔo.
go-PART-EVID

(8)
nenxʔalo·sʔoʔs
ʔe·-t "ʔekwan-wixwan-la-k nen-xʔale-we·sʔe-ʔs,"
be-SS.CONS dog-little-SG-ACC TH-find-1/2.SBJ.PL-1

no-k-laknoʔo ʔo·ca-wa·-ka.
say-PART-EVID children-OBV-NOM.PL

ʔe·-kla haʔako·n-ʔa·-la "taʔane-ta-w," no-k-laknoʔo
be-DS.NSIM man-DEF-NOM.SG grasp-CIS-IMP say-PART-EVID

ʔe·-kla ʔeke-k-laknoʔo. ʔe·-kla naxc-an-la-k
be-DS.NSIM give-PART-EVID be-DS.NSIM build.fire-GER-SG-ACC
(= 'a burning stick')

taʔane-ta nemt-an-ʔa·-yʔik ya-tsa-k-laknoʔo.
grasp-SS.NPURP close.eyes-GER-DEF-ALL TH-stab-PART-EVID

ʔe·-kla nemʔet-ape-k-laknoʔo. ʔe·-kla tan-ʔa·-yʔik
be-DS.NSIM close.eyes-NEG-PART-EVID be-DS.NSIM tail-DEF-ALL

yʔoco-k-laknoʔo. ʔe·-kla ʔekwan-wixwan-es
pinch-PART-EVID be-DS.NSIM dog-little-INST

he-xsasa-k-laknoʔo. ʔe·-kla haʔako·n-wa·-ʔa·-la "hehe·ʔ.
REFL-yelp-PART-EVID be-DS.NSIM man-OBV-DEF-NOM.SG all.right

hekta·wo·sʔow
ʔekwan-la," no-k-laknoʔo. "he-kta·wa-we·sʔe-w,"
dog-NOM.SG say-PART-EVID REFL-play-1/2.SBJ.PL-IMP

no-k-laknoʔo.
say-PART-EVID

(9) ʔe·-kla ʔo·ca-wa·-ka kotok-a·yay-ʔa·-yʔik
be-DS.NSIM children-OBV-NOM.PL room-inside-DEF-ALL

nes-e-cne-no-n-laknoʔo.
CAUS-REFL-lie.down-CONT-PART-EVID

ʔe·-no-k-la-k metis he-ne·-kwa "ʔawas-ka-k ya·lo·na-w
be-CONT-PART-SG-ACC three REFL-lie-when meat-PL-ACC kill-IMP

yaxa-no-n," no-k-laknoʔo. ʔe·-kla ya-txw-an-ʔa·-la-k
eat-CONT-PART say-PART-EVID be-DS.NSIM TH-fill.pipe-GER-DEF-SG-ACC

taʔane-ta
grasp-SS.NPURP

ʔawas-nes-kap-an-wa·-yʔik we-ta-xa-t-xa-ta
meat-CAUS-close-GER-OBV-ALL OBJ.PL-COM-AUG-move.PL-AUG-SS.NPURP

ya-kwlax-an-ʔa·-la-k nes-nepaxke-k-laknoʔo.
TH-open-GER-DEF-SG-ACC CAUS-smoke-PART-EVID

ʔe·-kla he-ya-kwlaxe-k-laknoʔo.
be-DS.NSIM REFL-TH-open-PART-EVID

ʔe·-kla ʔawas-maslak-la he-ylapa-·-la "hecu·-la-k
be-DS.NSIM meat-white-NOM.SG REFL-stand-PART-NOM.SG what-SG-ACC

ʔey-aʔaʔ" no-k-laknoʔo. ʔe·-kla "ʔawas-ka-k
be-ASS.3 say-PART-EVID be-DS.NSIM meat-PL-ACC

ya·lo·na·tonoʔos
ya·lo·n-a·tewa-no-we-ʔe-s," no-k-laknoʔo. ʔe·-kla
kill-FUT-CONT-DECL-PRES-1 say-PART-EVID be-DS.NSIM

"hehe·ʔ," no-·-ta we·ʔis-pax ʔey-kana-txil-na-k-laknoʔo.
all.right say-PART-SS.NPURP one-just CAUS-take-out-ABL-PART-EVID

ʔe·-kla ya·lo·na-k-laknoʔo ʔe·-t yaxa-no-n-laknoʔo.
be-DS.NSIM kill-PART-EVID be-SS.CONS eat-CONT-PART-EVID

(10) ʔe·-t ʔoʔo·-kwa Ha·csokonay-la losos
be-SS.CONS be.night-DS.SIM Coyote-NOM.SG all

he-cocxa·-yo·-no-k ya-txw-an-ʔa·-la-k
REFL-sleep-INGR-CONT-PART TH-fill.pipe-GER-DEF-SG-ACC

taʔane-ta xa·-xa-t ʔawas-nes-kap-an-wa·-yʔik
grasp-SS.NPURP move.SG.AUG-AUG-SS.CONS meat-CAUS-close-GER-OBV-ALL

nes-nepaxke-k-laknoʔo. ʔe·-kla ya-kwlax-an-wa·-ʔa·-la
CAUS-smoke-PART-EVID be-DS.NSIM TH-open-GER-OBV-DEF-NOM.SG

he-ya-kwlaxe-k-laknoʔo. ʔe·-l-ʔok ʔawas-maslak-la
REFL-TH-open-PART-EVID be-3-when meat-white-NOM.SG

he-ylapa-·-la "hecu·-ka-k ʔe·y-aʔaʔ" no-k-laknoʔo.
REFL-stand-PART-NOM.SG what-PL-ACC be-ASS.3 say-PART-EVID

ʔe·-kla Ha·csokonay-la "ʔawas-eʔe·-la-k losos
be-DS.NSIM Coyote-NOM.SG meat-that-SG-ACC all

ʔ-a·to-te·-se-k,"[23] no-k-laknoʔo. ʔe·-kla ʔawas-wa·-ʔa·-la
be-FUT-ʔ-1-PART say-PART-EVID be-DS.NSIM meat-OBV-DEF-NOM.SG

23. Possibly incorporation of *te·-* 'that' into the stem?

"hehe·ʔ," no-k-laknoʔo. "we·ʔil," no-·-kla
all.right say-PART-EVID all.right say-PART-DS.NSIM

ʔawas-atak-a·-la losos-a·tak heykewa-txil-na-k-laknoʔo.
meat-very-DEF-NOM.SG all-very move.as.group-out-ABL-PART-EVID

ʔe·-kla Ha·csokonay-la neykanak ya-cox-ʔan-a·naxok-wa·-yʔik
be-DS.NSIM Coyote-NOM.SG first TH-camp-GER-big-OBV-ALL

xa·-xa-t "ʔawas-ʔa·-la ha·naxok
move.SG.AUG-AUG-SS.CONS meat-DEF-NOM.SG many

heykew-ta-kwa!" no-·-kla
move.as.group-CIS-MIR say-PART-DS.NSIM

ʔekwan-esxaw-ʔa·-ka-k w-e·s-yacx-e·-kwa
dog-big-DEF-PL-ACC OBJ.PL-REFL.CAUS-mount-DS.SIM

ʔawas-wa·-ʔa·-la heykew-xa·-xa-k-la
meat-OBV-DEF-NOM.SG move.as.group-move.SG.AUG-AUG-PART-NOM.SG

ʔey-we-ncaka-no-n-laknoʔo.
CAUS-OBJ.PL-kill-CONT-PART-EVID

(11) he·pano·noʔo
naʔa he·pano·-no-we-ʔe ʔo·ʔo·-pano-n-wa·-ka-k
So narrate-CONT-DECL-PRES night-narrate-GER-OBV-PL-ACC

tinay-ʔa·-lʔas. holaw-ʔa·-la we·-lʔat-coʔ. we·-tic.
ancient-DEF-INST.SG end-DEF-NOM.SG yonder-DEM-RES yonder-like

Coyote Steals the Buffalo: Free English Translation

[1] There were many men in a large camp gambling for arrows. While this was going on, a man dressed completely in black arrived whom they didn't recognize: "Watch him closely," they kept saying. [2] As it became noon, they were eating. The one dressed all in black was eating a big sausage. The young men were saying: "Watch him closely." [3] Then the one dressed all in black said: "I'm going off," and he flew away. They watched him for a while, and while they watched him he went farther and farther away. [4] "Let's call him 'Bat,'" they said, and so they called him that. Then Bat arrived and said: "That one should go over there. That

one has really just crossed the river! Now another has crossed! Now he's crossed another one! And he's crossed another one! Now he's arrived at the camp." [5] Then at dawn they began to move camp, and they made camp at the first river. Then when the sun came up again, they moved again and settled down at the next river. Then at daybreak they moved camp again and settled down at the next river. Then when day came they moved camp and settled down at a river. Then at daybreak they moved camp close to the one all clothed in black. [6] Around this time, they held council and called Coyote over. "All right," he said and came over. The chief said: "You have always known about everything. Maybe you can steal us some meat from the buffalo over there?" Coyote said: "All right. After sunrise, move the camp back and watch out for me." [7] Then day came and they moved camp. Coyote changed himself into a little dog and was lying down. Three of the buffalo-owner's children came to the abandoned camp and were looking around for anything left behind. There they found flea-bitten Coyote, picked him up, and left. [8] Then the children said: "We've found a little dog!" Then a man said: "Bring it here," and they gave it to him. Then he picked up a burning stick and stabbed it into [Coyote's] eyes, but he didn't blink. Then [the man] pinched him on the tail and the little dog yelped. So the man said: "Okay, it's a dog. Go and play." [9] Then the children made him lie down inside their room. As such, when he had lain down for three days, one of them said: "Kill some buffalo to eat." Then he grabbed his pipe and went off to the buffalo enclosure, and smoked at the gate, whereupon it opened up on its own. Then a white buffalo standing there said: "What are you doing?" So Coyote said: "I'm going to kill some buffalo." [The white buffalo] responded: "All right." And he took out and killed just one of the buffalo and ate it. [10] Then at night when everyone was asleep, Coyote took his pipe and went to the buffalo enclosure and smoked there at the gate, which opened by itself. A white buffalo was standing there and said: "What is it?" Coyote responded: "I'm going to need all these buffalo." Then the [white] buffalo said: "All right, let's go," and every last one of them stampeded out together. Then Coyote got to the camp first and said: "A whole bunch of buffalo are coming!" and while they were mounting their horses the buffalo stampeded right over them, killing them. [11] That's how they told night stories in the old days. That's the end. So it goes.

14. Coyote Steals Fire

(1) ya-cox-ʔan-a·xok ya-cox-ʔo-no-k-laknoʔo.
TH-camp-GER-many TH-camp-INGR-CONT-PART-EVID

ʔe·-no-k-la-k h-e·pano·-no-k-laknoʔo
be-CONT-PART-SG-ACC REFL-narrate-CONT-PART-EVID

tickan-a·ʔas naxc-an-la-k
people-many build.fire-GER-SG-ACC

ho·ʔoxaw-a·to-l-ʔila. ʔe·-l-ʔok ʔecas
steal-FUT-3-while be-3-when some

he-tlo·-no-n-laknoʔo.
REFL-refuse-CONT-PART-EVID

(2) ʔe·-no-k-la-k Ha·csokonay-la silwe-no-k-laknoʔo
be-CONT-PART-SG-ACC Coyote-NOM.SG wander-CONT-PART-EVID

ʔe·-no-·-la ya-cox-ʔan-a·ʔas-wa·-yʔik
be-CONT-PART-NOM.SG TH-camp-GER-many-OBV-ALL

ha·-na-k-laknoʔo ʔe·-t xa·-xa-k-laknoʔo
move.SG-ABL-PART-EVID be-SS.CONS move.SG.AUG-AUG-PART-EVID

h-e·pano·-k-wa·-yʔik.
REFL-narrate-PART-OBV-ALL

(3) ʔe·-kla "yela-w," no-k-laknoʔo kokon-ʔa·-la.
be-DS.NSIM sit-IMP say-PART-EVID chief-DEF-NOM.SG

ʔe·-kla Ha·csokonay-la yela-k-laknoʔo.
be-DS.NSIM Coyote-NOM.SG sit-PART-EVID

kokon-wa·-ʔa·-la ha-cxo-t he-ylapa-ta
chief-OBV-DEF-NOM.SG move.SG-up-SS.CONS REFL-stand-SS.NPURP

"wa·-tel h-e·panew-o·s-no-s-uk [*sic*]
OBV-manner REFL-narrate-1/2.SBJ.PL-CONT-1-when

naxc-an-la-k ho·ʔoxaw-a·to-l-ʔila," no-k-laknoʔo
build.fire-GER-SG-ACC steal-FUT-3-while say-PART-EVID

kokon-wa·-ʔa·-la. “ʔe·-ta ʔ-a·n-ʔok
chief-OBV-DEF-NOM.SG be-SS.NPURP do-?-since

kewanoxo·noʔ
ke-w-anoxo·-no-we-ʔe,” no-k-laknoʔo.
1.OBJ-OBJ.PL-know-CONT-DECL say-PART-EVID

(4) ʔe·-kla kalak-la “Ha·csokonay-la losos
be-DS.NSIM other-NOM.SG Coyote-NOM.SG All

ʔe·noʔo
hecu·-ʔaxe·-ka-k henox-pax ʔe·-no-we-ʔe.
what-ever-PL-ACC good-just do-CONT-DECL-PRES

newo·sʔew
we·-lʔat-la-k newe-we·sʔe-w,” no-k-laknoʔo. ʔe·-kla
that-DET-SG-ACC tell-1/2.SBJ.PL-IMP say-PART-EVID be-DS.NSIM

kokon-wa·-ʔa·-la “he-tec ʔ-a·to-ne-k-yelkwaʔ”
chief-OBV-DEF-NOM.SG this-like do-FUT-2-PART-Q

no-k-laknoʔo Ha·csokonay-la-k. ʔe·-kla
say-PART-EVID Coyote-SG-ACC be-DS.NSIM

yela-no-k-laknoʔo Ha·csokonay-la. ʔe·-no-·-la
sit-CONT-PART-EVID Coyote-NOM.SG do-CONT-PART-NOM.SG

“hehe·ʔ,” no-k-laknoʔo. “to·no ʔe·-t
all.right say-PART-EVID perhaps be-SS.CONS

ya·c-a·haʔa,” no-k-laknoʔo. ʔe·-kla
see-INTENT say-PART-EVID be-DS.NSIM

waʔan-pax h-e·pano-k-laknoʔo.
exactly-just REFL-narrate-PART-EVID

(5) ʔe·-kla Ha·csokonay-la ha·-na-k-laknoʔo
be-DS.NSIM Coyote-NOM.SG move.SG-ABL-PART-EVID

naxc-an-wa·-yʔik. naʔas-ʔo·ʔo·t-la
build.fire-GER-OBV-ALL light-night-NOM.SG

soke·la-k-lakno?o   naxc-an-wa·-?a·-la-k.
own-PART-EVID   build.fire-GER-OBV-DEF-SG-ACC

Ha·csokonay-la   xa·-xa-k-lakno?o   naxc-an-wa·-y?ik
Coyote-NOM.SG   move.SG.AUG-AUG-PART-EVID   build.fire-GER-OBV-ALL

?e·-l-?ok   ha·?ako·n-la   yele·la-k-lakno?o
be-3-when   man-NOM.SG   sit-RED$^?$-PART-EVID

naxc-an-a·cin-?a·-y?ik   ?e·-ta   ya·co-xwel-pe·-no-k-lakno?o
build.fire-GER-NEAR-DEF-ALL   be-SS.NPURP   see-miss-NEG-CONT-PART-EVID

naxc-an-wa·-?a·-la-k.   ?e·-kla   Ha·csokonay-la
build.fire-GER-OBV-DEF-SG-ACC   be-DS.NSIM   Coyote-NOM.SG

yela-k-lakno?o   ?e·ta   ya·ce-no-k-lakno?o
sit-PART-EVID   be-SS.NPURP   see-CONT-PART-EVID

ha·?ako·n-wa·-?a·-la-k.   ?o·?a-?a·-la-k   metis
man-OBV-DEF-SG-ACC   night-DEF-SG-ACC   three

coxn-ape-no-k-lakno?o.
sleep-NEG-PART-EVID

(6)   ?e·-no-k-la   Ha·csokonay-la   "hecu·   ?e·-l-?ila
be-CONT-PART-NOM.SG   Coyote-NOM.SG   what   be-3-while

coxn-ape-no·-ka?"   no-k-lakno?o.   ?e·-kla
sleep-NEG-CONT-2   say-PART-EVID   be-DS.NSIM

coxnapeno?o·?
ha·?ako·n-wa·-?a·-la   "coxn-ape-no-we-?e·-?,"   no-k-lakno?o.
man-OBV-DEF-NOM.SG   sleep-NEG-CONT-DECL-PAST-1   say-PART-EVID

nenx?aleno?o·?
"naxc-an-te·-la-k   nenx?ale-no-we-?e·-?,"   no-k-lakno?o.
build.fire-GER-this-SG-ACC   guard-CONT-DECL-PAST-1   say-PART-EVID

(7)   ?e·-kla   Ha·csokonay-la   nemt-an-?a·-y?ik
be-DS.NSIM   Coyote-NOM.SG   close.eyes-GER-DEF-ALL

ya·ce-no-k-lakno?o.   ?e·-ta   Ha·csokonay-la
watch-CONT-PART-EVID   be-SS.NPURP   Coyote-NOM.SG

ke·wan-la-k   noko-k-lakno?o   ?e·-ta
fine.white.ash-SG-ACC   gather-PART-EVID   be-SS.NPURP

ha·?ako·n-wa·-?a·-la-k   nemt-an-?a·-y?ik
man-OBV-DEF-SG-ACC   close.eyes-DEF-ALL

yale-k-lakno?o.   ?e·-kla   ha·?ako·n-wa·-?a·-la
throw-PART-EVID   be-DS.NSIM   man-OBV-DEF-NOM.SG

ya·cen-ape-k-lakno?o.
see-NEG-PART-EVID

(8) ?e·-kwa   Ha·csokonay-la   naxc-an-wa·-?a·-la-k
be-DS.SIM   Coyote-NOM.SG   build.fire-GER-OBV-DEF-SG-ACC

ha-wses-an-?a·-la-k   s?a·c-?a·-ka-y   ?oyoko·-k-lakno?o
TH-glow-GER-DEF-SG-ACC   finger.nail-DEF-PL-INST   tuck-PART-EVID

?e·-ta   tan-?a·-y?ik   ?oyoko·-k-lakno?o.
be-SS.NPURP   tail-DEF-ALL   tuck-PART-EVID

?e·-ta   ya-lxil-n-a·to-·kwa   ha·?ako·n-wa·-?a·-la
be-SS.NPURP   TH-run.off-ABL-FUT-when   man-OBV-DEF-NOM.SG

kwe·-?a·-la-k   ta·kona-no-k-lakno?o.   ?e·-no-·-la
club-DEF-SG-ACC   search-CONT-PART-EVID   be-CONT-PART-NOM.SG

nen-x?ale-k-lakno?o   ?e·-t   ta?ane-k-lakno?o   ?e·-t
TH-find-PART-EVID   be-SS.CONS   grasp-PART-EVID   be-SS.CONS

Ha·csokonay-wa·-?a·-la-k   ya-xw-ce-k-lakno?o
Coyote-OBV-DEF-SG-ACC   TH-beat-?-PART-EVID

?e·-t   ya-xw-nacka-k-lakno?o   ?a·x-?a·-y?ik.
be-SS.CONS   TH-beat-die-PART-EVID   water-DEF-ALL

(9) ?e·-kla   Ha·csokonay-la   he-wawa-t   he-cne-no-·-la
be-DS.NSIM   Coyote-NOM.SG   REFL-die-SS.CONS   REFL-lie-CONT-PART-EVID

?aco·-k-lakno?o   ?e·t   "?o·c!"   no-k-lakno?o.
revive-PART-EVID   be-SS.CONS   oh!   say-PART-EVID

"ke-cxwa-na-k-yeʔ!" no-k-laknoʔo. ʔe·-t
1OBJ-sleep-ABL-PART-Q say-PART-EVID be-SS.CONS

no-noto·-n-ʔa·-yʔik napoxa-no-k-laknoʔo. ʔe·-l-ʔok
RED-touch-GER-DEF-ALL blow-CONT-PART-EVID be-3-when

naxc-an-ʔa·-ka kape·-laknoʔo lok
build.fire-GER-DEF-NOM.PL be.nothing-EVID 3SG.ACC

no-noto·-n we·ʔis-pax
RED-touch-GER one-just

naxc-an-ʔa·-la wixwan-tak ye·la-k-laknoʔo.
build.fire-GER-DEF-NOM.SG small-very sit-PART-EVID

(10) ʔe·-kla Ha·csokonay-la ʔekwan-esxaw-yax-an-ka-k
be-DS.NSIM Coyote-NOM.SG dog-big-eat-GER-PL-ACC

noko-ta naxc-an-wa·-ʔa·-la-k
gather-SS.NPURP build.fire-GER-OBV-DEF-SG-ACC

ʔekwan-esxaw-yax-an-ʔa·-yʔik
dog-big-eat-GER-DEF-ALL

cane-ta napoxa-k-la mʔelne-k-laknoʔo.
leave-SS.NPURP blow-PART-NOM.SG flame-PART-EVID

ʔe·-kla Ha·csokonay-la ʔekwan-esxaw-yax-an-a·ʔas-ʔa·-yʔik
be-DS.NSIM Coyote-NOM.SG dog-big-eat-GER-MUCH-DEF-ALL

mʔayʔe-k-laknoʔo. ʔe·-ta neskaltey-ʔa·-yʔik
set.fire-PART-EVID be-SS.NPURP outside-DEF-ALL

mʔayʔe-k-laknoʔo ʔecinʔe ʔe·-ta
set.fire-PART-EVID then be-SS.NPURP

ya-cox-ʔan-a·ʔas-wa·-yʔik he-nkwa·-na-k-laknoʔo.
TH-camp-GER-much-OBV-ALL REFL-run-ABL-PART-EVID

(11) ʔe·t ya-cox-ʔan-a·ʔas-wa·-yʔik ha·cin-ʔa·-yʔik
be-SS.CONS TH-camp-GER-much-OBV-ALL near-DEF-ALL

yaxoxona-no-k-laknoʔo. ʔe·-kla tickan-ʔa·-la
pant-CONT-PART-EVID be-DS.NSIM people-DEF-NOM.SG

so-sko·no-t   Ha·csokonay-la-k   ta·-haho·-n-lakno?o
RED-hear-SS.CONS   Coyote-SG-ACC   COM-run-PART-EVID

?e·-t   ?a·x-ka-k   nes-xane-no-n-lakno?o
be-SS.CONS   water-PL-ACC   CAUS-drink.water-CONT-PART-EVID

Ha·csokonay-la-k.
Coyote-SG-ACC

?e·-kla   Ha·csokonay-la   "naxc-an-wa·-?a·-la-k
be-DS.NSIM   Coyote-NOM.SG   build.fire-GER-OBV-DEF-SG-ACC

ho·?oxawe·-kwa-?a-s!"[24]   no-k-lakno?o.   "we·-l?at   naw-t-e·l!"
steal-MIR-PAST-1   say-PART-EVID   that-DET   burn-CIS-JUSS

no-k-lakno?o   Ha·csokonay-la.
say-PART-EVID   Coyote-NOM.SG

(12)   ?e·-kla   ha·-wane-no-k-lakno?o
be-DS.NSIM   move.SG-decamp-CONT-PART-EVID

?e·-t   kalak-a·-y?ik
be-SS.CONS   other-DEF-ALL

hawna-xaya-k-lakno?o.   ?e·-kwa   Ha·csokonay-la-k
encamp-go-PART-EVID   be-DS.SIM   Coyote-SG-ACC

kwa·n-enox-a·tak-la   nes-ta·?e·-k-lakno?o.
woman-pretty-very-NOM.SG   CAUS-grasp-PART-EVID

(13)   ?e·-kla   we·-l?at   naxc-an   kan-we-k-lakno?o.   na?a
be-DS.NSIM   that-DEM   build.fire-GER   possess-INGR-PART-EVID   So

he·panono?o
h-e·pano-no-we-?e   ?o·?-o·pano·-n-wa·-ka-k.   we·-tic.
REFL-narrate-CONT-DECL-PRES   night-narrate-GER-OBV-PL-ACC   that-like

24. The only extant example of a mirative in the first person singular.

Coyote Steals Fire: Free English Translation

[1] Many tipis were getting set up, and while that was going on, many people were taking part in a great council about when fire was going to be stolen—some people had been refusing to do it. [2] At the same time, Coyote was wandering about and went walking along toward the camp where he came upon the council. [3] "Sit down," said the chief, so Coyote sat down. Then the chief got up and stood: "We've made a decision like this to steal fire," he said, "but having done so we don't know what to do." [4] Then another said: "Everything Coyote has ever done has always been quite good. Let's tell him to do it." Then the chief said to Coyote: "Do you think you can do it?" Then Coyote was sitting down, and, as he was, he said: "All right. Perhaps I'll do it and see." They deliberated just like that. [5] Then Coyote went off to the fire. The moon owned the fire, so Coyote went to the fire. As he did, a man had been sitting by the fire for a long time and had been watching it closely. Coyote sat down and kept on looking at the man—for three nights he didn't sleep. [6] Then Coyote asked him: "How come you're not sleeping?" So the man said: "I have never slept—I've always guarded this fire." [7] So Coyote kept looking at his eyes, gathered together some fine white ash, and threw it in the man's eyes. Then the man couldn't see. [8] While he did this, Coyote tucked some glowing embers from the fire under his fingernails and to his tail, and when Coyote was about to run away, the man looked for his club and found it. Then he beat Coyote with it—he beat him to death right into the water. [9] Then Coyote (who had just been lying there dead) revived, and Coyote said: "Oh! Have I been sleeping for a long time?" and was blowing on his fingers. When he did, there were no sparks there, but on one finger there lay a tiny little spark. [10] Then Coyote gathered some dry grass,[25] and set the spark into it and began to blow it into a flame. Then Coyote set fire to a lot of grass and then set fire to a place outside and then ran off to the big camp. [11] Then at a place near the big camp, Coyote was panting, and when people heard him they came running up to him and gave Coyote water to drink. Then Coyote said: "I have stolen the fire for you! Let it burn in this direction." [12] Then they moved camp and made camp elsewhere. Then they gave him a very pretty woman to marry. [13] So that's how people came to have fire. They've always told night stories like that. So it goes.

25. Literally 'horse-food.'

15. The Prairie Turtle

(1)

mayʔan-la	ha·-na-no-k-laknoʔo.	ha·-na-la
prairie.turtle-NOM.SG	move.SG-ABL-CONT-PART-EVID	move.SG-ABL-NOM.SG

ha·-na-la	na·to·n-ʔa·-yʔik	ha-yco-na-k-laknoʔo
move.SG-ABL-NOM.SG	mountain-DEF-ALL	move.SG-up-ABL-PART-EVID

ʔe·-t	ʔa·wʔay	he-ylapa-no-k-laknoʔo.
be-SS.CONS	thither	REFL-stand-CONT-PART-EVID

ʔe·-no-·-la	xa·way-ta-k-laknoʔo	ʔe·-t
be-CONT-PART-NOM.SG	turn-CIS-PART-EVID	be-SS.CONS

ya·ce-na-k-laknoʔo	ʔe·-ta-k-a·-yʔik.	ʔe·ta
look-ABL-PART-EVID	be-CIS-PART-DEF-ALL	be-SS.NPURP

"we·-lʔat	ʔe·-ta-k-a·-yʔik	cʔapol-is	ta·l-ʔa!"
that-DEM	be-CIS-PART-DEF-ALL	gray-mist-INST	be.lost-ASS.3

no-·-ta	xa-ytic-ne-k-laknoʔo	ʔe·t
say-PART-SS.NPURP	AUG-fall-ABL-PART-EVID	be-SS.CONS

he-wawa-k-laknoʔo.	we·-tic.
REFL-die-PART-EVID	that-like

The Prairie Turtle: Free English Translation

[1] A prairie turtle was walking along, and he walked and walked and hiked up a mountain. Then he stood off in that direction and turned around in this direction and looked back in the direction of the way he had come. "The way I've come is lost in gray mist!" Then he fell, tumbled downward, and was killed. So it goes.

16. The Man Who Married a Buffalo Woman

(1)

Ha·ʔako·n-osas-la	ʔekaka·-la-k
man-young-NOM.SG	maternal.grandmother-SG-ACC

ta·-ya-coxʔa-no-k-laknoʔo.
COM-TH-camp-CONT-PART-EVID

ʔe·-no-k-la-k	he-pay-xwet-an-la
be-CONT-PART-SG-ACC (='female, woman')	REFL-bead-wear-GER-NOM.SG

xa·-xa-k-laknoʔo	ʔe·t
move.SG.AUG-AUG-PART-EVID	be-SS.CONS

ta·ʔe·-n-aʔa	ʔe·-no-k-laknoʔo	ha·ʔako·n-osas-la
grasp-CONT-ASS.3 (='marry')	be-CONT-PART-EVID	man-young-NOM.SG

wa·-ʔa·-la-k.	ʔe·-l-ʔok	he-tlo·-no-k-laknoʔo.
OBV-DEF-SG-ACC	do-3-when	REFL-refuse-CONT-PART-EVID

(2)

ʔe·-no-·-la	hetwan-ʔax	he-nce-·kwa	ta·ʔe·-k-laknoʔo.
be-CONT-PART-EVID	several-?	REFL-days. pass-when	grasp-PART-EVID (='marry')

yax-an-e·-ka-k	ta·-yaxa-l-kaʔak	he-tlo·-no-k-laknoʔo.
eat-GER-that-PL-ACC	COM-eat-3-when	REFL-refuse-CONT-PART-EVID

he-pay-xwet-an-wa·-ʔa·-la	"ʔekwan-e·-ka-k-pax
REFL-bead-wear-GER-OBV-DEF-NOM.SG (='female, woman')	dog-that-PL-ACC-just

yaxanoʔo·ʔ

yaxa-no-we-ʔe·-ʔ,"	no·-no-k-laknoʔo.
eat-CONT-DECL-PAST-1	say-CONT-PART-EVID

(3)

ʔe·-kla	ha·ʔako·n-osas-wa·-ʔa·-la	kwa·n-ko·sʔa-tic-wa·-ʔa·-la-k
be-DS.NSIM	man-young-OBV-DEF-NOM.SG	woman-old-little-OBV-DEF-SG-ACC

he-pake-k-laknoʔo. ʔe··kla "hecu· ʔ-a·to·-l-ʔa,"
REFL-tell-PART-EVID be-DS.NSIM what do-FUT-3-ASS.3

no-k-laknoʔo. "ya·lo·na-w we·ʔis-pax," no-k-laknoʔo.
say-PART-EVID kill-IMP one-just say-PART-EVID

(4) ʔe··kla ya·lo·na-k-laknoʔo. ʔe··kla
be-DS.NSIM kill-PART-EVID be-DS.NSIM

he-pay-xwet-an-wa··ʔa··la yax-to·xa-k-laknoʔo
REFL-bead-wear-GER-OBV-DEF-NOM.SG eat-finish-PART-EVID
(='woman')

ʔekwan-wa··ʔa··la-k ʔe··kla ʔecinʔeya· lo·na-k-laknoʔo.
dog-OBV-DEF-SG-ACC be-DS.NSIM then kill-PART-EVID

ʔe··kla he-pay-xwet-an-wa··ʔa··la yax-to·xa-k-laknoʔo.
be-DS.NSIM REFL-bead-wear-GER-OBV-DEF-NOM.SG eat-finish-PART-EVID
(='woman')

ʔecinʔe. ʔe··kla ʔecinʔe ya·lo·na-k-laknoʔo.
then be-DS.NSIM then kill-PART-EVID

ʔe··kla he-pay-xwet-an-wa··ʔa··la yax-to·xa-k-laknoʔo.
be-DS.NSIM REFl-bead-wear-GER-OBV-DEF-NOM.SG eat-finish-PART-EVID

ʔe··kla ʔecinʔeho law-ʔa··la-k ya·lo·na-k-laknoʔo.
be-DS.NSIM then last-DEF-SG-ACC kill-PART-EVID

ʔe··kla he-pay-xwet-an-wa··ʔa··la yax-to·xa-k-laknoʔo.
be-DS.NSIM REFL-bead-wear-GER-OBV-DEF-NOM.SG eat-finish-PART-EVID

(5) tanasike
ʔe··ta "we·ʔil," no-k-laknoʔo. "ta-na-s-k-ye,"
be-SS.NPURP all.right say-PART-EVID move.PL-ABL-1-PART-Q

no-k-laknoʔo. ʔe··kla ha·ʔako·n-osas-wa··ʔa··la
say-PART-EVID be-DS.NSIM man-young-OBV-DEF-NOM.SG

"waʔan-a·lesok," no-k-laknoʔo.
just.as-wait? say-PART-EVID

(6) "ya·ce-w," no-k-lakno?o he-pay-xwet-an-ko·s?a-tic-wa·-?a·-la-k.
look-IMP say-PART-EVID REFL-bead-wear-GER-old-little-OBV-DEF-SG-ACC
(='woman')

"ha·-na-·kwa-nes ne-kam-an-e?e·-la-k ?a·x-e?e·-k
move.SG-ABL-when-1 TH-gnaw-GER-that-SG-ACC water-that-ACC
(='bone')

yacela-kla-na-w," no-k-lakno?o.
throw-down-ABL-IMP say-PART-EVID

?e·yo?ok
"?e·y(a?)-?ok losos-?ita ta-yco-t-a·to-nwa-?,"
do-when all-DET move.PL-up-CIS-FUT-DEON-DEON3

no-k-lakno?o. "ya-n?a·nw-an-el-?a·t-as nes-kwit-we-yce-w,"
say-PART-EVID TH-chain-GER-that-DEF-INST CAUS-tie-OBJ.PL-tie-IMP

no-k-lakno?o. "?e·-la nes-exewe·-s-?ok ma·tan
say-PART-EVID be-NOM.SG CAUS-shout-1-when quickly

we-cxe-w," no-k-lakno?o
OBJ.PL-loosen-IMP say-PART-EVID

(7) ?e·-ta ta-na-nes?e-k-lakno?o. ?awas-a·naxok-a·-y?ik
be-SS.NPURP move.PL-ABL-DU-PART-EVID meat-large-DEF-ALL
(='buffalo')

ta·-xa-t-xa-k-lakno?o.
COM-AUG-move.PL-AUG-PART-EVID

(8) ta-na-nes?e-·kwa he-pay-xwet-an-wa·-?a·-la "he-tec
move.PL-ABL-DU-when REFL-bead-wear-GER-OBV-DEF-NOM.SG this-manner

?-a·to-ne-k-ye hecu·-?axey-ka nen-koxo-·-l-?ok?"
do-FUT-2-PART-Q what-ever-NOM.PL TH-go.PL-2.OBJ-3.SBJ-when

no-k-lakno?o. ?e·-kla ha·?ako·n-osas-wa·-?a·-la "te·c
say-PART-EVID be-DS.NSIM man-young-OBV-DEF-NOM.SG thus

ʔ-a·to-se-k-coʔ,"	no-k-laknoʔo	ʔe·-ta
do-FUT-1-PART-RES	say-PART-EVID	be-SS.NPURP

he-nkwa·-na-k-laknoʔo	cakaw-tic-la-k.
REFL-run-ABL-PART-EVID	river-little-SG-ACC

wa·-yʔik	he-nkwaya-kla-na-k-laknoʔo.
OBV-ALL	REFL-run-down-ABL-PART-EVID

(9)

ʔe·-kwa	he-pay-xwet-an-wa·-ʔa·-la	ha-kla-na-t
be-DS.SIM	REFL-bead-wear-GER-OBV-DEF-NOM.SG	move.SG-down-ABL-SS.CONS

ta·kona-no-k-laknoʔo.	"hete-k	ʔey-aʔa?"
seek-CONT-PART-EVID	where-ACC	be-ASS.2

no-no-k-laknoʔo.	ʔe·-kwa	ʔekwan-esxaw-yax-an
say-CONT-PART-EVID	be-DS.SIM	dog-big-eat-GER

xʔaton-tak	ye·la-k-laknoʔo	lak.
green/blue-very	lie-PART-EVID	3SGACC

wa·-yʔik-ita	ha·ʔako·n-osas-wa·-ʔa·-la
OBV-ALL-DET	man-young-OBV-DEF-NOM.SG

he-yl[a]pa-cxo-k-laknoʔo.
REFL-stand-rise-PART-EVID

(10)

ʔe·-kla	he-pay-xwet-an-wa·-ʔa·-la	"ʔecinʔe,"
be-DS.NSIM	REFL-bead-wear-GER-OBV-DEF-NOM.SG	then

no-k-laknoʔo.	ʔe·-kla	ha·ʔako·n-osas-wa·-ʔa·-la
say-PART-EVID	be-DS.NSIM	man-young-OBV-DEF-NOM.SG

caka-wixwan-ʔa·-yʔik	he-nkwaya-k-laknoʔo.
river-small-DEF-ALL	REFL-run-PART-EVID

ʔe·-kla	he-pay-xwet-an-wa·-ʔa·-la	ha-kla-na-t
be-DS.NSIM	REFL-bead-wear-GER-OBV-DEF-NOM.SG	move.SG-down-ABL-SS.CONS

ta·kona-no-k-laknoʔo.	ʔe·-l-ʔok	ʔa·x-ʔa·-la
seek-CONT-PART-EVID	be-3-when	water-DEF-NOM.SG

xʔaton-tak yeˑla-k-laknoʔo lak. waˑ-yʔik-ta
green/blue-very lie-PART-EVID obv-ALL-SS.NPURP

haˑʔakoˑn-osas-waˑ-ʔaˑ-la ha-cxo-k-laknoʔo.
man-young-OBV-DEF-NOM.SG move.SG-rise-PART-EVID

(11) ʔeˑ-kla he-pay-xwet-an-waˑ-ʔaˑ-la "ʔecinʔe,"
be-DS.NSIM REFL-bead-wear-GER-OBV-DEF-NOM.SG then

no-k-laknoʔo. ʔeˑ-kla haˑʔakoˑn-osas-waˑ-ʔaˑ-la
say-PART-EVID be-DS.NSIM man-young-OBV-DEF-NOM.SG

ʔoʔs
"waʔan-pax ʔe-we-ʔe-s," no-k-laknoʔo.
just.as-just do-DECL-PAST-1 say-PART-EVID

(12) ʔeˑ-ta ta-na-nesʔe-kwa ʔawas-ʔaˑ-la
be-SS.NPURP move.PL-ABL-DU-when meat-DEF-NOM.SG

haˑnaxok-aˑ-tak heykew-ta-no-k-laknoʔo.
large-DEF-very move.as.group-CIS-PART-EVID

ʔeˑ-kwa he-pay-xwet-an-waˑ-ʔaˑ-la
be-DS.SIM REFL-bead-wear-GER-OBV-DEF-NOM.SG

taˑ-xa-t-xa-k-laknoʔo ʔawas-waˑ-yʔik. ʔeˑ-ta "weˑʔil!"
COM-AUG-move.PL-AUG-PART-EVID meat-OBV-ALL be-SS.NPURP all.right

nenkoxoˑsʔow!
no-k-laknoʔo. "nen-koxa-weˑsʔa-w," no-k-laknoʔo.
say-PART-EVID TH-chase-1/2.SBJ.PL-IMP say-PART-EVID

(13) ʔeˑ-kla ʔawas-waˑ-ka nen-koxo-k-laknoʔo.
be-DS.NSIM meat-OBV-NOM.PL TH-chase-PART-EVID

ʔeˑ-kla ya-lxil-na-k-laknoʔo haˑʔakoˑn-osas-waˑ-ʔaˑ-la.
be-DS.NSIM TH-run-ABL-PART-EVID man-young-OBV-DEF-NOM.SG

ʔeˑ-t ʔawas-waˑ-ka he-wl-aˑto-ˑkwa
be-SS.CONS meat-OBV-NOM.PL REFL-catch-FUT-when

caka-wixwan-ʔa·-yʔik he-nkwaya-k-laknoʔo.
river-small-DEF-ALL REFL-run-PART-EVID

ʔe·-kla ʔawas-wa·-ka he·-nexʔeyo·-no-klaknoʔo.
be-DS.NSIM meat-OBV-NOM.PL REFL-be.ignorant-CONT-PART-EVID

(14) yamko·ʔow
"he-pay-xwet-an-elʔa·t-la-k ya-makawa-we·sʔa-w," no-k-laknoʔo.
REFL-bead-wear-GER-yonder-SG-ACC TH-call-1/2.SBJ.PL-IMP say-PART-EVID

ʔe·-kwa he-pay-xwet-an-wa·-ʔa·-la "te·l
be-DS.SIM REFL-bead-wear-GER-OBV-DEF-NOM.SG here

ʔe·-n-aʔa!" no-k-laknoʔo.
be-CONT-ASS.3SG say-PART-EVID

"ʔekwan-esxaw-yax-an-xʔaton-wa·-ʔa·-la-k!" ʔe·-kla
dog-big-eat-GER-green/blue-OBV-DEF-SG-ACC be-DS.NSIM
(='green fodder')

ʔawas-ʔa·-la yax-to·xa-k-la ha-cxo-t
meat-DEF-NOM.SG eat-finish-PART-NOM.SG move.SG-rise-SS.CONS

ya-lxil-na-k-laknoʔo.
TH-run-ABL-PART-EVID

(15) ʔe·-kwa ʔecinʔe he-wl-a·to-·kwa caka-wixwan-ʔa·-yʔik
be-DS.SIM then REFL-catch-FUT-when river-small-DEF-ALL

he-nkwaya-kla-na-k-laknoʔo. ʔe·-kla ʔawas-ʔa·-la
REFL-run-down-ABL-PART-EVID be-DS.NSIM meat-DEF-NOM.SG

he·-nexʔe-yo·-k-la he-pay-xwet-an-wa·-ʔa·-la
REFL-know-INGR-PART-NOM.SG REFL-bead-wear-GER-OBV-DEF-NOM.SG
(='be ignorant')

"te·l ʔe·-n-aʔa!" no-k-laknoʔo. "ʔa·x-wa·-ʔa·-la-k!"
here be-CONT-3.ASS say-PART-EVID water-OBV-DEF-SG-ACC

ʔe·-kla ʔawas-ʔa·-la he-xa-xano·-t
be-DS.NSIM meat-DEF-NOM.SG REFL-RED-drink-SS.CONS

xan-to·x-a·to-·kwa ha-cxo-t ya-lxil-na-k-lakno?o.
drink-finish-FUT-when move.SG-rise-SS.CONS TH-run-ABL-PART-EVID

(16) ?e·-t sax?ay-la-k yalpa-ta
be-SS.CONS arrow-SG-ACC stand-SS.NPURP

c?el-?a·-y?ik yela-k-la
top-DEF-ALL sit-PART-NOM.SG

he-ylap-an-awa·-tak he-yko?o-k-lakno?o.
REFL-stand-GER-tall-very REFL-become-PART-EVID

?e·-kla tickan-wa·-?a·-la c?el-?a·-y?ik yela-no-k-lakno?o.
be-DS.NSIM people-OBV-DEF-NOM.SG top-DEF-ALL sit-CONT-PART-EVID

he·-nes?eyo·-no-k-lakno?o. ?e·-kla
REFL-be.ignorant-CONT-PART-EVID be-DS.NSIM

he-pay-xwet-an-wa·-?a·-la-k ya-mka-k-la
REFL-bead-wear-GER-OBV-DEF-SG-ACC TH-call-PART-NOM.SG

"ke-nex?e·-kwa," no-k-lakno?o. ?e·-kla
1.OBJ-know-MIR say-PART-EVID be-DS.NSIM

?awas-wa·-ka heykew-na-no-k-lakno?o.
meat-OBV-NOM.PL move.as.group-ABL-CONT-PART-EVID

(17) ?e·-kwa ?awas-ayon-tak-la he-ylap-an-?a·yay-wa·-y?ik
be-DS.SIM meat-itch-very-NOM.SG REFL-stand-GER-under-OBV-ALL

he-cne-no-k-lakno?o. ?e·-kwa tickan-wa·-?a·-la
REFL-lie-CONT-PART-EVID be-DS.SIM person-OBV-DEF-NOM.SG

m?e·yca-k-lakno?o. ?e·-kla so·la-t ?awas-wa·-?a·-la-k
urinate-PART-EVID be-DS.NSIM drip-SS.CONS meat-OBV-DEF-SG-ACC

ya-m?acx-an-?a·-y?ik so·l-to·xa-k-lakno?o.
TH-sneeze-GER-DEF-ALL drip-finish-PART-EVID (='drop onto')

?e·-kla ?awas-wa·-?a·-la hawa·-tak nexale-k-lakno?o.
be-DS.NSIM meat-OBV-DEF-NOM.SG loud-very bellow-PART-EVID

ʔe·-kla ʔawas-a·naxok-wa·-ʔa·-la he-ce-co·-n
be-DS.NSIM meat-many-OBV-DEF-NOM.SG REFL-RED-go.back-GER

he-ylap-an-wa·-yʔik xaya-k-laknoʔo.
REFL-stand-GER-OBV-ALL arrive-PART-EVID

(18) ʔe·-kla ʔawas-ayon-wa·-ʔa·-la "ya-mʔacx-an te·l
be-DS.NSIM meat-itch-OBV-DEF-NOM.SG TH-sneeze-GER here

so·l-ke-to·xa-kwa!" no-k-laknoʔo.
drip-1.OBJ-finish-MIR say-PART-EVID

ʔe·-kla ʔawas-wa·-ka ya·c-ayco-na-l-ʔok
be-DS.NSIM meat-OBV-NOM.PL look-up-ABL-3-when

he-ylap-an-cʔel-ʔa·-yʔik yele·la-k-laknoʔo.
REFL-stand-GER-top-DEF-ALL sit-PART-EVID

ʔe·-kla ʔawas-a·ʔakon-la ketay-ta
be-DS.NSIM meat-male-NOM.SG two-DET

he-ylap-an-wa·-ʔa·-la-k kan-xa-yco-n-ʔa·-lʔas
REFL-stand-GER-OBV-DEF-SG-ACC throw-AUG-up-GER-DEF-INST (='horn')

he-wle-nesʔe-k-laknoʔo he-ylap-an-wa·-ʔa·-la-k.
REFL-catch-DU-PART-EVID REFL-stand-GER-OBV-DEF-SG-ACC

ʔe·-t ʔey-xamc-a·to-t ʔe·-ta
be-SS.CONS do-break-FUT-SS.CONS be-SS.NPURP

ha-koxanec-no-k-laknoʔo.
TH-be.tired-CONT-PART-EVID

(19) ʔe·-kwa tickan-wa·-ʔa·-la nes-exewe-no-k-laknoʔo.
be-DS.SIM person-OBV-DEF-NOM.SG CAUS-shout-CONT-PART-EVID

ʔe·-l-kaʔak ʔekwan-wa·-ka he-ya-yle-no-n-laknoʔo.
be-3-when dog-OBV-NOM.PL REFL-RED-struggle-CONT-PART-EVID

we·ʔis ʔey-xespe-k-laknoʔo. ʔe·-kla we·ʔis
one do-loose-PART-EVID be-DS.NSIM one

ʔey-xespe-k-laknoʔo. ʔe·-kla ʔecinʔe weʔis
CAUS-loose-PART-EVID be-DS.NSIM then one

ʔey-xespe-k-laknoʔo. ʔe·-kla ʔecinʔeho law-ʔa·-la
CAUS-loose-PART-EVID be-DS.NSIM then last-DEF-NOM.SG

ʔey-xespe-k-laknoʔo.
CAUS-loose-PART-EVID

(20) ʔe·kla ʔekwan-wa·-ka losos-ʔita
be-DS.NSIM dog-OBV-NOM.PL all-DET

ha·-na-ci-cxil-xaya-t
move.SG-ABL-RED-run-arrive-SS.CONS

ʔawas-wa·-ʔa·-la-k we-nen-koxo-k-laknoʔo ʔe·-t
meat-OBV-DEF-SG-ACC OBJ.PL-TH-chase-PART-EVID be-SS.CONS

salk-an-ʔa·-ka-k nac-we-xe-xesʔape-no-k-laknoʔo.
pull.sinew-GER-DEF-PL-ACC bite-OBJ.PL-RED-cut.sinewy.matter-CONT-PART-EVID

ʔe·-l-kaʔak ʔawas-wa·-ka yela-kla-na-k-laknoʔo.
be-3-when meat-OBV-NOM.PL sit-down-ABL-PART-EVID

ʔe·-kwa tickan-wa·-ʔa·-la ʔey-we-ncaka-no-k-laknoʔo
be-DS.SIM person-OBV-DEF-NOM.SG CAUS-OBJ.PL-kill-CONT-PART-EVID

ʔawas-wa·-ka-k.
meat-OBV-PL-ACC

(21) ʔe·-kwa ʔawase-pay-xwet-an-wa·-ʔa·-la "sa·ya ʔe·-n-a·-nʔe-s!
be-DS.SIM meat-bead-wear-GER-OBV-DEF-NOM.SG 1.SG.NOM be-CONT-ASS-1/2.ASS-1

ke-cn-o·sʔe-w!" no-no-k-laknoʔo. ʔe·-kla
1.OBJ-leave-1/2.SBJ.PL-IMP say-CONT-PART-EVID be-DS.NSIM

tickan-wa·-ʔa·-la "to·na-n-aʔa! he-wl-o·sʔe-w!"
person-OBV-DEF-NOM.SG lie-CONT-ASS.3 REFL-catch-1/2.SBJ.PL-IMP

no-k-laknoʔo. ʔe·-kla ʔekwan-wa·-ka
say-PART-EVID be-DS.NSIM dog-OBV-NOM.PL

ya·lo·na-k-laknoʔo	ʔawas-ta·ʔe·-k-wa·-ʔa·-la-k.
kill-PART-EVID	meat-grasp-PART-OBV-DEF-SG-ACC

(22)

	he·pano·noʔo	
Naʔa	h-e·pano·-no-we-ʔe.	we·-tic.
So	REFL-narrate-CONT-DECL-PAST	that-like

The Man Who Married a Buffalo Woman: Free English Translation

[1] A young man was living with his mother's mother, and a woman came to them with the intention of marrying him. He kept on refusing, though. [2] Now, after several days passed by, he married her. When they ate together, the woman always refused the different types of food. "I have always eaten only dogs," she said. [3] Then the young man told the old woman about it. She said: "What'll the difference be? Kill just one [dog]." [4] So he killed one, and the woman ate the entire dog up. Then he killed another one, and she ate that one up too. Then he killed another dog, and the woman ate that one too. [5] Then she said: "All right, are we going now?" The young man responded: "Wait just a minute." [6] He [turned to] the old woman and said: "Look, when I go off, throw that bone down into the water. When you do so, they'll all come up. Tie them up with that chain, and when I make a shout, quickly loosen them." [7] Then they went off to large herd of buffalo, arriving together. [8] When they went, the woman said: "How will you behave if someone goes after you?" So the young man said: "I would do this," and then he ran off to a little creek, right down to that place. [9] As he did, the woman also went down and was looking for him. "Where are you?" she kept on saying. A lot of very green fodder was lying there, and the young man stood up from his position there. [10] Then the woman said: "Do it again!" and the young man ran down to the small creek. The woman went down after him to look for him, and when she got down there, the water was very dark blue. Right the young man rose up. [11] The woman said: "One more time," and the young man replied: "I'm doing just that." [12] And then as the two went on a very large herd of buffalo was stampeding this way, and the woman went along with him toward the buffalo and then said: "All right! Chase after him!" [13] Then the buffalo chased him and the young man ran off, and when the buffalo were about to catch him, he ran to the small creek and the buffalo didn't know where he was. [14] "Call over the woman," they said. Then the woman said: "Here he is—in the green grass!" Then the buffalo finished eating, got up, and ran off. [15] Just when they were about to catch him, he ran into the small creek, and the buffalo didn't know where he was,

so the woman said: "Here he is, in the water!" Then the buffalo kept drinking and drinking, and when they finished drinking, they got up and ran away. [16] Then an arrow with its head sticking into the ground turned into a very tall tree, with a person sitting at its top. They didn't know what to do, and the woman whom they had called said: "I really don't know." Then the buffalo stampeded away. [17] Then while a very itchy buffalo was lying down beneath a tree, a person came up to him and pissed all over him! Then it started to drip on his nose, and the buffalo bellowed very loudly, and all the buffalo went back to that tree. [18] Then the itchy buffalo said: "Something has dripped onto my nose!" Then when all the buffalo looked up, there he was sitting on top of the tree. So two bulls caught hold of the tree with their horns and were about to break it up, but they got very tired. [19] Then while a person was shouting, the dogs kept on struggling: one got loose, then another got loose, then another got loose, and finally the last one got loose. [20] Then all the dogs got there at a running pace and were chasing the buffalo, biting their sinews off as they did. The buffalo sat down as the man was killing them. [21] Meanwhile, the buffalo woman was saying: "It's me! Spare me!" But the man said: "She's lying! Catch her!" So the dogs killed her, that buffalo wife. [22] They've always told it like that. So it goes.

17. The Four Young Men and Little One

(1) ha·ʔako·n-osaʔas-ka sikit-ita ya-coxʔo-no-n-laknoʔo.
man-young-NOM.PL four-DET TH-camp-CONT-PART-EVID

ʔe·-no-n-la-k we·ʔis no-noto·-n-e·san-an-ʔa·-yʔik
be-CONT-PART-SG-ACC one RED-touch-GER-point-GER-DEF-ALL

natokay-we-k-laknoʔo ʔe·-t kwa·low heykoʔo·kwa he-yakewa-we-ʔe·-kwa
boil-INGR-PART-EVID be-SS.CONS big REFL-make-when

natokay-wa-n-wa·-ʔa·-la ʔey-tisʔapxe-ta nasʔoka-k-la
boil-INGR-GER-OBV-DEF-NOM.SG do-puncture-SS.NPURP squeeze-PART-NOM.SG

wixwan-la wan-atxil-na-k-laknoʔo natokay-wa-n-wa·-yʔik-ita.
small-NOM.SG fall-forward-ABL-PART-EVID boil-INGR-GER-OBV-ALL-DET

(2) ʔe·-kla "ha·ʔako·n-osaʔas-wa·-ka taʔane-no-n," no-k-laknoʔo.
be-DS.NSIM man-young-OBV-NOM.PL grasp-CONT-GER say-PART-EVID

ʔe·-t taʔane-k-la ʔoʔayo·-n-wa·-ʔa·-la
be-SS.CONS grasp-PART-NOM.SG be.little-GER-OBV-DEF-NOM.SG

wexwa-no-k-laknoʔo.
grow-CONT-PART-EVID

kwa·lo·-nʔa he-ykoʔo-k-laknoʔo. ʔe·-kwa ʔekwan-la-k
big-COMP REFL-make-PART-EVID be-DS.SIM dog-SG-ACC

nes-ta·-he-kta[·]we-no-k-laknoʔo.
CAUS-COM-REFL-count-CONT-PART-EVID

(3) ʔe·-kwa wixwan-wa·-ʔa·-la kwa·low he-ykoʔo-k-laknoʔo.
be-DS.SIM small-OBV-DEF-NOM.SG big REFL-make-PART-EVID

ʔe·-kwa ha·ʔako·n-osaʔas-wa·-ka nes-a-yace-ta
be-DS.SIM man-young-OBV-NOM.PL CAUS-TH-stay.at.home-SS.NPURP

silayo·-no-k-laknoʔo. ʔe·-l-ʔila ʔo·ʔo·-kwa yate-no-k-laknoʔo.
wander-CONT-PART-EVID be-3-when be.night-when return-CONT-PART-EVID

(4) ʔe·-no-k-la-k wa·-taʔas "taxso·-l-ʔok te-wʔan
be-CONT-PART-SG-ACC this-time be.dawn-3-when this-ADESS

ha·-n-ape-w," no-k-laknoʔo. "we·-yʔik
move.SG-CONT-NEG-IMP say-PART-EVID that-ALL

ko·sʔaʔas-la ketay-ta ya-cox-ʔan-esawe·-la-k."
old.folks-NOM.SG two-SS.NPURP TH-camp-GER-3.PL.GEN?-SG-ACC

ʔe·-kla wixwan-wa·-ʔa·-la "hehe·ʔ," no-k-laknoʔo.
be-DS.NSIM small-OBV-DEF-NOM.SG all.right say-PART-EVID

(5) ʔe·-kwa ha·ʔako·n-osaʔas-wa·-ʔa·-la na·ʔe·-k-laknoʔo.
be-DS.SIM man-young-OBV-DEF-NOM.SG go.off-PART-EVID

ʔe·-kwa wixwan-wa·-ʔa·-la "xa·-xa-t ya·ce-s-aʔa
be-DS.SIM small-OBV-DEF-NOM.SG move.SG.AUG-AUG-SS.CONS see-1-ASS

ho·sʔaʔas-wa·-yʔik," no-k-laknoʔo. ʔe·-ta ha·-na-k-laknoʔo.
old.folks-OBV-ALL say-PART-EVID be-SS.NPURP move.SG-ABL-PART-EVID

(6) ya-cox-ʔan-ʔa·-yʔik xa·-xa-t nes-kap-an-ʔa·-yʔik
TH-camp-GER-DEF-ALL move.SG.AUG-AUG-SS.CONS CAUS-shut-GER-DEF-ALL

helʔeya-kxo-na-no-k-laknoʔo. ʔe·-l-ʔok ko·sʔaʔas-wa·-ʔa·-la
peer-in-ABL-CONT-PART-EVID be-3-when old.folks-OBV-DEF-NOM.SG

he-cne-nes[ʔe-k]-laknoʔo lak. wixwan-wa·-ʔa·-la kwe·-la-k
REFL-lie-DU-[PART]-EVID 3SGACC small-OBV-DEF-NOM.SG stick-SG-ACC

taʔane-ta naxc-an-ʔa·-yʔik nes-amʔamʔa-ta
grasp-SS.NPURP make.fire-GER-DEF-ALL CAUS-start.burning-SS.NPURP

kalak-a·-la-k nen-xile-k-laknoʔo. ʔe·-kla
other-DEF-SG-ACC TH-poke-PART-EVID be-DS.NSIM

hew-ʔa·-tan[a]	cʔetxan-ayxe-na-t
that-DEF-toward	jump-across-ABL-SS.CONS

ta·-he·-sokyo·-no-k-laknoʔo.	ʔe·-kla	wixwan-wa·-ʔa·-la
COM-REFL-fight-CONT-PART-EVID	be-DS.NSIM	small-OBV-DEF-NOM.SG

xʔaxaʔayʔa-no-k-laknoʔo.
laugh-CONT-PART-EVID

(7)

ʔe·-no-la	ha-kxo-na-k-laknoʔo.	ʔe·-t	"ʔo·c,"
be-CONT-NOM.SG	move.SG-in-ABL-PART-EVID	be-SS.CONS	oh

		yaxanesnoyno
no-no-k-laknoʔo.	"hecu·-ka-k	yaxa-nes-no-ey-noʔ"
say-CONT-PART-EVID	what-PL-ACC	eat-DU-CONT-PAST-2

no-k-laknoʔo.	ʔe·-kla	ho·sʔaʔas-wa·-ʔa·-la
say-PART-EVID	be-when	old.folks-OBV-DEF-NOM.SG

kewyaxʔe·noʔo	
"ke-we-yaxʔe·-no-we-ʔe,"	no-k-laknoʔo.
1.OBJ-OBJ.PL-be.hungry-CONT-DECL-PAST	say-PART-EVID

ʔe·-kla	wixwan-wa·-ʔa·-la	"na·kw	ʔe-nesʔe-w,"	no-k-laknoʔo.
be-when	small-OBV-DEF-NOM.SG	well	be-DU-IMP	say-PART-EVID

"we-ta[·]-xa-t-xa-·-s-ʔok	yaxa-nesʔe-w,"
OBJ.PL-COM-AUG-move.PL-AUG-2.OBJ-1-when	eat-DU-IMP

no-k-laknoʔo.	ʔe·-kla	ko·sʔaʔas-wa·-ʔa·-la
say-PART-EVID	be-DS.NSIM	old.folks-OBV-DEF-NOM.SG

"he-tec	ʔe·-ta	ke-w-ta·-tan-a·to-ʔaʔ"
this-way	be-SS.NPURP	1.OBJ-OBJ.PL-COM-grasp-FUT-ASS

no-k-laknoʔo.	ʔe·-kla	wixwan-wa·-ʔa·-la
say-PART-EVID	be-DS.NSIM	small-OBV-DEF-NOM.SG

"we-mam-a·tewa-·-nwa-sʔ,"	no-k-laknoʔo.	ʔe·-kla
OBJ.PL-carry-FUT-2.OBJ-DEON-1	say-PART-EVID	be-DS.NSIM

"we·ʔil,"	no-k-laknoʔo.
all.right	say-PART-EVID

(8) ʔe··kla wixwan-wa··ʔa··la we-mama-ta
be-DS.NSIM small-OBV-DEF-NOM.SG OBJ.PL-carry-SS.NPURP

ha··na-k-laknoʔo ya-cox-ʔan hosaʔas-wa··lʔan.
move.SG-ABL-PART-EVID TH-camp-GER young-OBV-GEN

ya-cox-ʔan-ʔa··yʔik we-ta[·]-xa-t-xa-ta
TH-camp-GER-DEF-ALL OBJ.PL-COM-AUG-move.PL-AUG-SS.NPURP

"we·ʔil," no-k-laknoʔo. "na·kw xa-ta-kla-na-nesʔe-w,"[26]
all.right say-PART-EVID well AUG-move.PL-down-ABL-DU-IMP

no-k-laknoʔo. no-l-ʔok xa-ta-kla-n-ape-nes-no-k-laknoʔo.
say-PART-EVID say-3-when AUG-move.PL-down-ABL-NEG-DU-PART-EVID

(9) ʔe··kwa ʔo·ʔo··k-laknoʔo. ʔe··kwa ha·ʔako·n-osaʔas-wa··ka
be-DS.SIM be.night-PART-EVID be-DS.SIM man-young-OBV-NOM.PL

yate-k-laknoʔo ʔe··t "hecu· ʔe··no-ka?" no-k-laknoʔo.
return-PART-EVID be-SS.CONS what be-CONT-NOM.PL say-PART-EVID

ʔe··kla "heʔe··k ho·sʔaʔas-wa··yʔik xa·xoʔs xa··xa-we-ʔs,"
be-DS.NSIM yonder-ACC old.folks-OBV-ALL move.SG.AUG-AUG-DECL-1

no-k-laknoʔo. "ʔe··t we-mama-ta-xkoʔ-s yaxa-nesʔe-w
say-PART-EVID be-SS.CONS OBJ.PL-carry-move.PL-back-1 eat-DU-IMP

no-t," no-k-laknoʔo. "ʔe-s-i-k-la
say-SS.CONS say-PART-EVID do-1-EP-PART-NOM.SG

xataklanapenesnoʔ
xa-ta-kla-na-ape-nesʔe-no-we-ʔe," no-k-laknoʔo.
AUG-move.PL-down-ABL-NEG-DU-CONT-DECL-PRES say-PART-EVID

26. This form illustrates well how verbs of motion that subcategorize for the number of their arguments are not in fact subcategorizing for the same thing. The lexical root *ha-* semantically selects for a single individual argument, while the root *ta-* selects for a two or more individual arguments, and *-nesʔe-* selects for a cardinality of precisely two.

(10)

ʔe·-kla	ha·ʔako·n-osaʔas-wa·-ʔa·-la	"ʔawas-ka-k	noko-ta
be-DS.NSIM	man-young-OBV-DEF-NOM.SG	meat-PL-ACC	fetch-SS.NPURP

we-ta-xa-t-xa-ta	'na·kw	xa-ta-kla-na-ta
OBJ.PL-COM-AUG-move.PL-AUG-SS.NPURP	well	AUG-move.PL-down-ABL-SS.NPRUP

yaxa-nesʔe-w,'	no-w,"	no-k-laknoʔo.	ʔe·-kla
eat-DU-IMP	say-IMP	say-PART-EVID	be-DS.NSIM

wixwan-wa·-ʔa·-la	we-ta-ta-na-k-laknoʔo.
small-OBV-DEF-NOM.SG	OBJ.PL-COM-move.PL-ABL-PART-EVID

we-ta-xa-t-xa-ta	"we·ʔil,"	no-k-laknoʔo.
OBJ.PL-COM-AUG-move.PL-AUG-SS.NPURP	all.right	say-PART-EVID

"xa-ta-kla-na-ta	yaxa-nesʔe-w,"
AUG-move.PL-down-ABL-SS.NPURP	eat-DU-IMP

no-k-laknoʔo.	ʔe·-kla	xa-ta-kla-na-nesʔe-k-laknoʔo.
say-PART-EVID	be-DS.NSIM	AUG-move.PL-down-ABL-DU-PART-EVID

ʔe·-kwa	ha·-na-k-laknoʔo.
be-DS.SIM	move.SG-ABL-PART-EVID

(11)

wixwan-wa·-ʔa·-la	xa·-xa-k-la	"ha-kla-na-t
small-OBV-DEF-NOM.SG	move.SG.AUG-AUG-PART-NOM.SG	move.SG-down-ABL-SS.CONS

panxo-w,"	no-k-laknoʔo.	ʔe·-kla	wixwan-wa·-ʔa·-la
bathe-IMP	say-PART-EVID	be-DS.NSIM	small-OBV-DEF-NOM.SG

ha-kla-na-t	cakaw-ʔa·-yʔik	panxo-no-k-laknoʔo
move.SG-down-ABL-SS.CONS	river-DEF-ALL	bathe-CONT-PART-EVID

ʔe·-t	ha-yco-ta-·kwa
be-SS.CONS	move.SG-up-CIS-when

"taxso·-l-ʔok	te-wʔan	ha·-n-ape-w,"
be.dawn-3-when	this-ADESS	move.SG-ABL-NEG-IMP

no-k-laknoʔo.	"we·-yʔik	kwa·n-la	he-co-cxo·-k-la
say-PART-EVID	that-ALL	woman-NOM.SG	REFL-RED-fear-PART-NOM.SG

ʔey-we-ncaka-no-k-noʔo.”	ʔe·-kla	wixwan-wa·-ʔa·-la
do-OBJ.PL-kill-CONT-PART-EVID	be-DS.NSIM	small-OBV-DEF-NOM.SG

“hehe·ʔ,”	no-k-laknoʔo.
all.right	say-PART-EVID

(12)

taxso·-k-la	ha·ʔako·n-osaʔas-wa·-ka	na·ʔe·-kwa
be.dawn-PART-NOM.SG	man-young-OBV-NOM.PL	go-DS.SIM

wixwan-wa·-ʔa·-la	ha·-na-k-laknoʔo
small-OBV-DEF-NOM.SG	move.SG-ABL-PART-EVID

kwa·n-e-co-cxo·-k-wa·-yʔik.
woman-EP-RED-FEAR-PART-OBV-ALL

ʔe·-t	waʔan	ha·-na-·kwa	kwa·n-wa·-ʔa·-la
be-SS.CONS	just.as	move.SG-ABL-when	woman-OBV-DEF-NOM.SG

ta·-haho-k-laknoʔo.
COM-meet-PART-EVID

ʔe·-l-ʔok	yakelʔ-an-ʔa·-ka	yanʔanwan-cikak-a·-tak
be-3-when	poke-GER-DEF-NOM.PL	iron-sharp-DEF-very

wixwan-wa·-ʔa·-la-k	ya·ce-t	yakelʔ-a·to·-kwa
small-OBV-DEF-SG-ACC	see-SS.CONS	jab-FUT-DS.SIM

wixwan-wa·-ʔa·-la	“waʔana·lesok!”	no-k-laknoʔo.
small-OBV-DEF-NOM.SG	wait	say-PART-EVID

(13)

ʔe·ta	cakaw-ʔa·-yʔik	ha-kla-na-t	yatexan-ka-k
be-SS.NPURP	river-DEF-ALL	move.SG-down-ABL-SS.CONS	stone-PL-ACC

yacax-ʔa·-ka-y	he-nes-anankapa-ta	ha-yco-na-k-laknoʔo.
chest-DEF-PL-INST	REFL-CAUS-stick-SS.NPURP	move.SG-up-ABL-PART-EVID

ʔe·-kwa	kwa·n-e-co-cxo·-k-wa·-ʔa·-la
be-DS.SIM	woman-EP-RED-fear-PART-OBV-DEF-NOM.SG

ta·-haho-k-la	wixwan-wa·-ʔa·-la	“we·ʔil,”
COM-meet-PART-NOM.SG	small-OBV-DEF-NOM.SG	all.right

no-k-laknoʔo yacax-ʔa·-yʔik t-ec
say-PART-EVID chest-DEF-ALL this-way

ʔe·-k-laknoʔo. ʔe·-kla kwa·n-wa·-ʔa·-la
do-PART-EVID be-DS.NSIM woman-OBV-DEF-NOM.SG

yakelʔe-k-laknoʔo wixwan-wa·-ʔa·-la-k ʔe·-t
jab-PART-EVID small-OBV-DEF-SG-ACC be-SS.CONS

ha-yticne-k-laknoʔo he-wawa-t.
TH-fall.ABL-PART-EVID REFL-die-SS.CONS

(14) ʔe·-kla wixwan-wa·-ʔa·-la ha·-na-k-laknoʔo.
be-DS.NSIM small-OBV-DEF-NOM.SG move.SG-ABL-PART-EVID

ya-coxʔ-an-ʔa·-yʔik xa·-xa-·kwa haʔako·n-osaʔas-wa·-ka
TH-camp-GER-DEF-ALL move.SG-AUG-DS.SIM man-young-OBV-NOM.PL

yate-k-laknoʔo. ʔe·-t "he-teca ʔe·-no-kaʔ" no-k-laknoʔo.
return-PART-EVID be-SS.CONS what-place be-cont-2 say-PART-EVID

ʔe·-kla wixwan-wa·-ʔa·-la "he·-wʔan
be-DS.NSIM small-OBV-DEF-NOM.SG that-ADESS

ya·lo·noʔs
kwa·n-e-co-cxo·-k-wa·-ʔa·-la-k ya·lo·na-we-ʔe-s," no-k-laknoʔo.
woman-EP-RED-fear-PART-OBV-DEF-SG-ACC kill-DECL-PAST-1 say-PART-EVID

(15) ʔe·-kla "taxso·-l-ʔok heʔe·-l na·to·n-eʔe·-la-k,"
be-DS.NSIM be.dawn-3-when that-dir mountain-that-SG-ACC

no-k-laknoʔo. "yan-cacayʔ-ape-w," no-k-laknoʔo.
say-PART-EVID TH-meddle-NEG-IMP say-PART-EVID

(16) ʔe·-t taxso-·kwa na·ʔe·-k-la wixwan-wa·-ʔa·-la
be-SS.CONS be.dawn-when go-PART-NOM.SG small-OBV-DEF-NOM.SG

na·to·n-wa·-yʔik xa·-xa-t ha-wa-wne-ta-xka-t
mountain-OBV-ALL move.SG.AUG-AUG-SS.CONS TH-RED-carry-move.PL-back-SS.CONS

ya-coxʔ-an-a·cin-ʔa·-yʔik nes-yela-k-laknoʔo.
TH-camp-GER-near-DEF-ALL CAUS-sit-PART-EVID

ʔe·-kwa ʔo·ʔoʔ-k-la haʔako·n-osaʔas-k-wa·-ka
be-DS.SIM be.night-PART-NOM.SG man-young-PART-OBV-NOM.PL

he·nexʔe-yo·-k-laknoʔo. ʔe·-t ʔo·ʔa-ʔa·-la-k pas-ʔita
lost-INGR-PART-EVID be-SS.CONS night-DEF-SG-ACC late-DET

yate-k-laknoʔo.
return-PART-EVID

(17) ʔe·-t "hecu· e·-no-kaʔ," no-k-laknoʔo wixwan-wa·-ʔa·-la-k.
be-SS.CONS what do-CONT-2 say-PART-EVID small-OBV-DEF-SG-ACC

ʔe·-kla na·to·n-eʔe·-la-k xa·-xa-t
be-DS.NSIM mountain-that-SG-ACC move.SG.AUG-AUG-SS.CONS

"ha-wa-wne-ta-xko-ʔs," no-k-laknoʔo.
TH-RED-carry-move.PL-back-1 say-PART-EVID

ʔe·kla "na·kw he-ce-co·-n ha-wa-wne-xa-t-[x]a-w,"
be-DS.NSIM all.right REFL-RED-back-GER TH-RED-carry-AUG-move.PL-AUG-IMP

no-k-laknoʔo. ʔe·-kla wixwan-wa·-ʔa·-la
say-PART-EVID be-DS.NSIM small-OBV-DEF-NOM.SG

ha-wane-ta-na-k-laknoʔo[27] he-ce-co·-n na·to·n-wa·-ʔa·-la-k.
TH-carry-move.PL-ABL-PART-EVID REFL-RED-back-GER mountain-OBV-DEF-SG-ACC

(18) ʔe·-ta ha·-xey-ta-·kwa "ya·ce-w," no-k-laknoʔo.
be-SS.NPURP move.SG-LOC-CIS-when look-IMP say-PART-EVID

27. Another example of how the distinction between *ha-* 'move.SG' and *ta-* 'move.PL' is not strictly the number of arguments but rather more a schematic representation of events. Here Little One and one other thing are both going somewhere, with Little One carrying it.

"nes-wal-ʔan-ʔok   kwa·lo·-tak-[k]a   na·ce-w!"
CAUS-catch.fish-GER-when   big-very-NOM.PL   bite-IMP

"n-a·p-a·to·-ne-k-coʔ,"[28]   no-k-laknoʔo.
say-NEG.2.OBJ-FUT-2-PART-RES   say-PART-EVID

(19) taxso·-k-la   na·ʔe·-kwa   wixwan-wa·-ʔa·-la
be.dawn-PART-NOM.SG   go-when   small-OBV-DEF-NOM.SG

cakaw-ʔa·-yʔik   ha-kla-na-t   nes-walʔe-no-k-laknoʔo
river-DEF-ALL   move.SG-down-ABL-SS.CONS   CAUS-catch.fish-CONT-PART-EVID

ʔi·s-ʔa[·]-ka-k.   ʔe·-no·-la   kana-kla-na-ta
minnow-DEF-PL-ACC   be-CONT-PART-NOM.SG   throw-down-ABL-SS.NPURP

"we·-lʔat   kwa·lo·-tak-[k]a
that-DEM   big-very-NOM.PL

na·ce-w!"   no-k-laknoʔo.   ʔe·-kla
bite-IMP   say-PART-EVID   be-DS.NSIM

ʔa·x-wa·ʔal-sokano-[Ø]-ʔa·-la   na·ce-k-laknoʔo.
water-time[?]-own-PART-DEF-NOM.SG   bite-PART-EVID

ʔe·-kla   wixwan-wa·-ʔa·-la   ʔa·x-a·cin-ʔa·-yʔik
be-DS.NSIM   small-OBV-DEF-NOM.SG   water-near-DEF-ALL

nexelco·-kana-yco-ta·-kwa   kwa·ko·-tak
drag-throw-up-CIS-when   wide-very

pancale-k-laknoʔo   ʔa·x-wa·ʔal-sokona-·-la
open.mouth-PART-EVID   water-time-own-PART-NOM.SG

ʔe·-t   wixwan-wa·-ʔa·-la-k   wa-wana-ta
be-SS.CONS   small-OBV-DEF-SG-ACC   RED-swallow-SS.NPURP

ha-kla-na-k-laknoʔo   ʔa·x-wa·-yʔik.
move.SG-down-ABL-PART-EVID   water-OBV-ALL

28. The negative suffix *-ape-* has a short vowel, not a long one. This might possibly be a marking of a second-person object, which only manifests as vowel length.

(20) ʔe·-kla wixwan-wa·-ʔa·-la ʔa·yay-ʔa·-yʔik
be-DS.NSIM small-OBV-DEF-NOM.SG inside-DEF-ALL

yela-ta "te·-la hecu·-yeʔ," no-no-k-laknoʔo.
sit-SS.NPURP this-NOM.SG what-Q say-CONT-PART-EVID

ʔe·-l-kaʔak he-co-cxo·-k-wa·-ʔa·-la "we·-tec-a·we,"
be-3-when REFL-RED-fear-PART-OBV-DEF-NOM.SG that-like-EMPH

no-no-k-laknoʔo. "e[·]-n te·-laʔ" no-k-laknoʔo
say-CONT-PART-EVID be-GER this-NOM.SG say-PART-EVID

yacan-an-ʔa·-la-k. ʔe·-kla "we·-lʔat-la yacan-an-a·we,"
beat$^{?}$-GER-DEF-SG-ACC (='heart') be-DS.NSIM that-DEM-NOM.SG beat-GER-EMPH

no-k-laknoʔo. ʔe·-kla wixwan-wa·-ʔa·-la
say-PART-EVID be-DS.NSIM small-OBV-DEF-NOM.SG

"he-tec ʔ-a·to-k-ye sʔe·ta-l-ʔok?" ʔe·-kla
what-way do-FUT-PART-Q cut-3-if be-DS.NSIM

he-co-cxo·-k-wa·-ʔa·-la "we·-yʔik ke-sʔe·ta-l-ʔok
REFL-RED-fear-PART-OBV-DEF-NOM.SG that-ALL 1.OBJ-cut-3-if

henkway-silw-an ʔa·x-kapay-eʔe·-k xaka·-tak
run-wander-GER water-nothing-that-ACC wide-very

ke-pancale-ta k-e·-waw-a·to-k-coʔ," no-k-laknoʔo.
1.OBJ-open.mouth-SS.NPURP 1.OBJ-REFL-die-FUT-PART-RES say-PART-EVID

(21) ʔe·-kla wixwan-wa·-ʔa·-la yacan-an-wa·-yʔik
be-DS.NSIM small-OBV-DEF-NOM.SG beat-GER-OBV-ALL

sʔe·ta-k-laknoʔo. ʔe·-kla he-co-cxo·-k-wa·-ʔa·-la
cut-PART-EVID be-DS.NSIM REFL-RED-fear-PART-OBV-DEF-NOM.SG

x-e·nkwa·-ta-no-k-laknoʔo. ʔe·t ʔa·x-cʔel-ʔa·-yʔik
AUG-run-CIS-CONT-PART-EVID be-SS.CONS water-surface-DEF-ALL

xaka·-tak pancele-ta he-wawa-k-laknoʔo. ʔe·-kla
wide-very open.mouth-SS.NPURP REFL-die-PART-EVID be-DS.NSIM

wixwan-wa·-ʔa·-la ha-txil-na-k-laknoʔo. ʔe·-t
small-OBV-DEF-NOM.SG move.SG-back-ABL-EVID be-SS.CONS

ya-cox-ʔan-ʔa·-yʔik xa·-xa·-kwa ʔo·ʔo·-k-laknoʔo.
TH-camp-GER-DEF-ALL move.SG.AUG-AUG-when be.night-PART-EVID

(22) ʔe·-kwa ha·ʔako·n-osaʔas-wa·-ka yate-k-laknoʔo
be-DS.SIM man-young-OBV-NOM.PL return-PART-EVID

kewʔa·xʔe·yoʔ
ʔe·-t "ke-we-ʔa·x-ʔe·ye-we-ʔe," no-k-laknoʔo
be-SS.CONS 1.OBJ-OBJ.PL-water-need-DECL-PRES say-PART-EVID

"ha-kla-na-t ʔa·x-ka-k yako-w,"
move.SG-down-ABL-SS.CONS water-PL-ACC make-IMP

no-k-laknoʔo. ʔe·-kla wixwan-wa·-ʔa·-la
say-PART-EVID be-DS.NSIM small-OBV-DEF-NOM.SG

yakw-an-ʔa·-la-k[29] taʔane-ta ha-kla-na-k-laknoʔo.
kick-GER-DEF-SG-ACC grasp-SS.NPURP move.SG-down-ABL-PART-EVID
(='bucket')

(23) ʔe·-ta ha-yco-ta-t ma·ka-no-k-laknoʔo
be-SS.NPURP move.SG-up-CIS-SS.CONS cry-CONT-PART-EVID

wixwan-wa·-ʔa·-la. ʔe·-kla ha·ʔako·n-osaʔas-·a [*sic*][30]
small-OBV-DEF-NOM.SG be-DS.NSIM man-young-NOM.SG

"hecu ʔe·-kwa?" no-k-laknoʔo.
what be-MIR say-PART-EVID

ʔe·-kla "ʔa·x-ke-la," no-k-laknoʔo. "hakne-k-a·we,"
be-DS.NSIM water-1.POSS-NOM.SG say-PART-EVID be.dry-PART-EMPH

no-k-laknoʔo. ʔe·-kla ha·ʔako·n-osaʔas-wa·-ka
say-PART-EVID be-DS.NSIM man-young-OBV-NOM.PL

"hecu ʔe·-t?" no-k-laknoʔo. ʔe·-kla
what do-SS.CONS say-PART-EVID be-DS.NSIM

29. Etymologically, this word originally referred to buckskins that were used as leggings but could also be used to retrieve water.

30. Possibly a typographical error on Hoijer's part. If his ⟨:⟩ = ⟨l⟩, then the noun ends in a bare case ending *-la*.

"kwa·lo·-tak-la   na·ce-w,"   no-so-k-la   na·ce-k-la
big-SUP-NOM.SG   bite-IMP   say-1-PART-NOM.SG   hit-PART-NOM.SG

ʔeykanayconoʔs
"ʔey-kana-yco-no-we-ʔe-s,"   no-k-laknoʔo.
do-pull-up-CONT-DECL-PAST-1   say-PART-EVID

(24) ʔe·-kla   ha·ʔako·n-osaʔas-wa·-ka   "na·kw.
be-DS.NSIM   man-young-OBV-NOM.PL   all.right

ʔe·[y]-ta-kla-na-w!"   no-k-laknoʔo.   ʔe·-kla
CAUS-move.PL-down-ABL-IMP   say-PART-EVID   be-DS.NSIM

ha-txil-na-k-laknoʔo   ʔe·-t   he-co-cxo·-k-wa·-ʔa·-la-k
move.SG-out-ABL-PART-EVID   be-SS.CONS   REFL-RED-fear-PART-OBV-DEF-SG-ACC

nexel-ci-cxwa-no-k-laknoʔo.   "ʔih, ʔih, ʔih,"
$drag_1$-RED-$drag_2$-CONT-PART-EVID   ee, ee ee

no-no-k-laknoʔo.   ʔe·[y]-ta-kla-na-k-laknoʔo
say-CONT-PART-EVID   CAUS-move.PL-down-ABL-PART-EVID

ʔe·-t   cane-k-laknoʔo.   ʔe·-ta   ʔa·x-ʔa·-la-k
be-SS.CONS   leave-PART-EVID   be-SS.NPURP   water-DEF-SG-ACC

yakotaycotaklaknoʔo
yakw-ta-yco-ta-k-laknoʔo.   he-xa-xano·-k-laknoʔo.
water-move.PL-up-CIS-PART-EVID   REFL-RED-drink-PART-EVID

(25) ʔe·-ta   "ya·ce-w!"   no-k-laknoʔo.   "taxso·-l-ʔok   heʔe-l
be-SS.NPURP   look-IMP   say-PART-EVID   be.dawn-3-when   that-direction

na·to·n-eʔe·-k   ha-yco-n-ape-w,"   no-k-laknoʔo.
mountain-that-ACC   move.SG-up-ABL-NEG-IMP   say-PART-EVID

ʔe·noʔo·lʔok
"we·-yʔik   kwa·-kwan-osaʔas-ka   sikit-ita   ʔe·-no-we-ʔe·-l-ʔok,"
that-ALL   RED-woman-young-NOM.PL   four-DET   be-CONT-DECL-PAST-3-when

no-k-laknoʔo.   ʔe·-kla   wixwan-wa·-ʔa·-la   "hehe·ʔ,"
say-PART-EVID   be-DS.NSIM   small-OBV-DEF-NOM.SG   all.right

no·k-laknoʔo.
say-PART-EVID

(26) ʔe·-t   taxso·-kwa   ha·ʔakon-osaʔas-wa·-ʔa·-la
be-SS.CONS   be.dawn-DS.SIM   man-young-OBV-DEF-NOM.SG

na·ʔe·-kwa   na·to·n-wa·-yʔik   ha·-na-k-laknoʔo
go-DS.SIM   mountain-OBV-ALL   move.SG-ABL-PART-EVID

ʔe·-t   ha-yco-na-k-laknoʔo.   ʔe·-l-ʔok
be-SS.CONS   move.SG-up-ABL-PART-EVID   be-3-when

he-n-pa-pasxa-yo·-no-k-laknoʔo.   ʔe·-kla
RECIP-TH-RED-play.ball-RECIP-CONT-PART-EVID   be-DS.NSIM

wixwan-wa·-ʔa·-la   "hehe·ʔ,"   no-k-laknoʔo.
small-OBV-DEF-NOM.SG   all.right   say-PART-EVID

ʔe·-kla   wixwan-wa·-ʔa·-la   saxʔay-ʔa·-lʔas   yake-t
be-DS.NSIM   small-OBV-DEF-NOM.SG   arrow-DEF-INST   shoot-SS.CONS

na-pasx-an-ʔa·-la-k   yake-k-laknoʔo.   ʔe·-kla
TH-play.ball-GER-DEF-SG-ACC   shoot-PART-EVID   be-DS.NSIM

kwa·-kwan-wa·-ka   "ʔo·c!"   no-no-n-laknoʔo.
RED-woman-OBV-NOM.PL   all.right   say-CONT-PART-EVID

"wa·-tel   sokano-ʔa·-la,"   no-k-laknoʔo.
obv-that.DIR   own-DEF-NOM.SG   say-PART-EVID

"he-xa-mk-apa-yʔe·-k-laknoʔo,"   no-k-laknoʔo.
REFL-AUG-cry-NEG-INGR-PART-EVID   say-PART-EVID
(='cannot be defeated')

(27) ʔe·-kwa   wixwan-wa·-ʔa·-la   ha-yco-na-k-laknoʔo
be-DS.SIM   small-OBV-DEF-NOM.SG   move.SG-up-ABL-PART-EVID

ʔe·-t   na-pasxan-wa·-ʔa·-la-k   saxʔay-ʔa·-la-k
be-SS.CONS   TH-play.ball-OBV-DEF-SG-ACC   arrow-DEF-SG-ACC

xʔe·pa-k-laknoʔo.   ʔe·-ta   "we·ʔil,"   no-k-laknoʔo.
pull-PART-EVID   be-SS.NPURP   all.right   say-PART-EVID

“we-ta-ta-na·-s,” no-k-laknoʔo. ʔe·-kla
OBJ.PL-COM-move.PL-ABL-2.OBJ-1 say-PART-EVID be-DS.NSIM

he-pay-xwet-an-osaʔas-wa·-ka
REFL-bead-wear-GER-young-OBV-NOM.PL

“wilʔa,” no-k-laknoʔo. ʔe·-kla wixwan-wa·-ʔa·-la
no say-PART-EVID be-DS.NSIM small-OBV-DEF-NOM.SG

ma·ka-no-k-laknoʔo. ʔe·-kla kwa·-kwan-wa·-ka
cry-CONT-PART-EVID be-DS.NSIM RED-woman-OBV-NOM.PL

ta-sa-ta-na-n-laknoʔo [*sic*][31] ya-cox-ʔan-ʔa·-yʔik.
COM-RED-move.PL-ABL-PART-EVID TH-camp-GER-DEF-ALL

(28) ʔe·-kwa ʔo·ʔo·-kla ha·ʔako·n-osaʔas-wa·-ka yate-k-laknoʔo
be-DS.SIM be.night-DS.NSIM man-young-OBV-NOM.PL return-PART-EVID

ʔe·-t “hecu· ʔe·-ka?” no-k-laknoʔo. ʔe·-kla
be-SS.CONS what do-2 say-PART-EVID be-DS.NSIM

wixwan-wa·-ʔa·-la “kwa·-kwan-wa·-ʔa·-la-k”[32] no-k-laknoʔo.
small-OBV-DEF-NOM.SG RED-woman-OBV-DEF-SG-ACC say-PART-EVID

wetataxkoʔs
“we-ta-ta-xka-we-ʔe-s,” no-k-laknoʔo. ʔe·-kla “ʔix
OBJ.PL-COM-move.PL-back-DECL-PAST-1 say-PART-EVID be-when bad

ʔe·-ne-k-a·we,” no-k-laknoʔo. ʔe·-kla
do-2-PART-EMPH say-PART-EVID be-DS.NSIM

wixwan-wa·-ʔa·-la ma·ka-no-k-laknoʔo.
small-OBV-DEF-NOM.SG cry-CONT-PART-EVID

ʔe·-kla kox-na-k-laknoʔo. ʔe·-kla we-nes-e·soko·-k-laknoʔo.
be-DS.NSIM enter-ABL-PART-EVID be-DS.NSIM OBJ.PL-get.married-PART-EVID

31. If this is not a typographic error, this might be evidence for dissimilation in a sequence of three distinct *ta*-morphs: the comitative prefix, pluractional reduplication, and the root ta- ‘move.PL.’

32 The conflict between the pluralizing reduplication and the singular suffix might be only apparent. The reduplication of this noun actually indicates a group of women (a lexical plural), in which case the number morphology would naturally usually be plural as well (cf. *kwa·kwanwa·ka* just four sets of lines above in [27], line 7).

(29) ʔe·-kla “ya·ce-w!” no-k-laknoʔo. “taxso·-l-ʔok
be-DS.NSIM look-imp say-PART-EVID be.dawn-3-when

te·-wʔan ha·-n-ape-w!” no-k-laknoʔo. “we·-yʔik
this-ADESS move.SG-ABL-NEG-IMP say-PART-EVID that-ALL

ʔawas-e-co-cxo·-k-la ʔey-we-yce-no-k-laknoʔo,”
meat-REFL-RED-fear-PART-NOM.SG do-OBJ.PL-catch-CONT-PART-EVID

no-k-laknoʔo. ʔe·-kla wixwan-wa·-ʔa·-la
say-PART-EVID be-DS.NSIM small-OBV-DEF-NOM.SG

“hehe·ʔ,” no-k-laknoʔo.
all.right say-PART-EVID

(30) taxso·-kla ha·ʔako·n-osaʔas-wa·-ʔa·-la na·ʔe·-kwa
be.dawn-DS.NSIM man-young-OBV-DEF-NOM.PL go-when

ʔawas-wa·-wʔan ha·-na-k-laknoʔo. ʔe·-kwa
meat-OBV-ADESS move.SG-ABL-PART-EVID be-DS.SIM

ʔawas-wa·-ʔa·-la ta·-ha·ho·-k-laknoʔo ʔe·-t
meat-OBV-DEF-NOM.SG COM-move.SG-PART-EVID be-SS.CONS

wixwan-wa·-ʔa·-la-k taʔane-t kalat-a·-yʔik
small-OBV-DEF-SG-ACC grasp-SS.CONS back-DEF-ALL

he-caka-ta ha·-na-no-k-laknoʔo.
REFL-putˀ - SS.NPURP move.SG-ABL-CONT-PART-EVID

ʔe·-kwa wixwan-wa·-ʔa·-la ha·-na·-kwa
be-DS.SIM small-OBV-DEF-NOM.SG move.SG-ABL-when

“ya·-yasʔey! ʔawas-la k-a·ya,[33] k-a·ya!” no-k-laknoʔo.
RED-friend meat-NOM.SG 1OBJ-haveˀ 1OBJ-haveˀ say-PART-EVID

(31) ʔe·-kla ha·ʔako·n-osaʔas-wa·-ʔa·-la soko·na-t “we·ʔil!”
be-DS.NSIM man-young-OBV-DEF-NOM.SG hearˀ-SS.CONS all.right

no-k-laknoʔo. ʔe·-ta ha·-na-ci-cxil-na·-kwa
say-PART-EVID be-SS.NPURP move.SG-ABL-RED-run-ABL-when

33. Possibly an otherwise unattested stative verb paradigm.

we·ʔl ha-wa-wne-ta xa·-na-k-laknoʔo
over.yonder TH-RED-carry-SS.NPURP AUG.move.SG.AUG-ABL-PART-EVID

ʔawas-a·ʔako·n-e-co-cxo·-k-la. ʔe·-kla
meat-young-RED-fear-PART-NOM.SG be-DS.NSIM

ha·ʔako·n-osaʔas-wa·-ʔa·-la ʔawas-wa·-ʔa·-la-k
man-man-OBV-DEF-NOM.SG meat-OBV-DEF-SG-ACC

he-ya-yako·-ta-na-k-laknoʔo. ʔe·-l-ʔok he-waw-ape-ta
REFL-RED-hit?-move.PL-ABL-PART-EVID be-3-when REFL-die-NEG-SS.NPURP

ha·-na-no-k-laknoʔo. ʔe·-kwa saxʔay-ʔa·-la-k
move.SG-ABL-CONT-PART-EVID be-DS.SIM arrow-DEF-SG-ACC

yak-to·xa-ta nexʔewa·-ka-k kanxayo-n-ʔa·-ka-y
hit-finish-SS.NPURP bow-PL-ACC horn-GER?-DEF-PL-INST

ka[·]-na-yo-yoxa-ta he-ma-ma·ko·-ta-na-k-laknoʔo
throw-ABL-RED-fly-SS.NPURP REFL-RED-cry-move.PL-ABL-PART-EVID

yacoxʔ-an-ʔa·-wʔan.
camp-GER-DEF-ADESS

(32) ʔe·-t xa·ya-t lasas-a·tak he-pcana-n-laknoʔo.
be-SS.CONS move.SG.AUG-SS.CONS bald-very REFL-sheer -PART-EVID

ʔe·-ta he-sko-no-n-laknoʔo.
be-SS.NPURP REFL-sit.down.PL-CONT-PART-EVID

(33) ʔe·-kwa ʔawas-wa·-ʔa·-la wixwan-wa·-ʔa·-la-k
be-DS.SIM meat-OBV-DEF-NOM.SG small-OBV-DEF-SG-ACC

ʔey-kana-kxo-n-a·to-k-a·-la samox-a·tak
CAUS-throw-in-ABL-FUT-PART-DEF-NOM.SG red-very

he-yace-no-k-laknoʔo. ha·cin
REFL-look-CONT-PART-EVID near

ʔe·-xa-t-xa-l-ʔok naxc-an
CAUS-AUG-move.PL-AUG-3-when build.fire-GER

ye·la-k-laknoʔo   lak.
sit-PART-EVID   3SGACC

(34) ʔey-kana-kxo-n-a·to·-k-w[a]   wixwan-wa·-ʔa·-la
CAUS-throw-down-ABL-FUT-PART-OBV   small-OBV-DEF-NOM.SG

"waʔana·lesox!"   no-k-laknoʔo   ʔe·-ta   kalat   cʔel-ʔa·-yʔik
wait.a.moment   say-PART-EVID   be-SS.NPURP   back   top-DEF-ALL

yocacxe-k-laknoʔo.[34]   ʔe·-ta   "we·ʔil,"   no-k-laknoʔo.
squat-PART-EVID   be-SS.NPURP   all.right   say-PART-EVID

heklax-kana-kxo-n-a·to·-k-w[a]   ʔawas-wa·-ʔa·-la-k
buck-throw-down-ABL-FUT-PART-OBV   meat-OBV-DEF-SG-ACC

wixwan-wa·-ʔa·-la   yakaw-kana-kxo-na-ta   cʔel-eʔe-ca
small-OBV-DEF-NOM.SG   kick-throw-down-ABL-SS.NPURP   sky-this-place

wa·n-ayco-na-k-laknoʔo.   xasʔok   heykoʔot he-yakewa-ʔa-t
jump-up-ABL-PART-EVID   grassy.plant   make-CAUS-SS.CONS

xa-wana-k-laknoʔo   cʔawʔal-ʔa·-yʔik
AUG-jump-PART-EVID   far.off-DEF-ALL

wixwan-wa·-ʔa·-la.   ʔe·-ta   ha·-na-k-laknoʔo
small-OBV-DEF-NOM.SG   be-SS.NPURP   move.SG-ABL-PART-EVID

yacox ʔan ʔa· wʔan.
camp-GER-DEF-ADESS

(35) ʔe·-t   ʔo·ʔo·-kwa   yacox-ʔan-a·cin-ʔa·-yʔik   xa·xa-ta
be-SS.CONS   be.night-DS.SIM   camp-GER-near-DEF-ALL   arrive-SS.NPURP

ʔekwan-wixwan-wa·-ʔa·-la-k   [a whistling sound]
dog-small-OBV-DEF-SG-ACC

no-k-laknoʔo.   ʔe·-kla   ʔekwan-wa·-ʔa·-la
say-PART-EVID   be-DS.NSIM   dog-OBV-DEF-NOM.SG

34. Possibly a lexicalized derivative of *ya-* 'CAUS' + *cacx-* 'center, middle part.'

x-e·nkwa·-ta-no-k-laknoʔo. ʔe·-l-kaʔak
AUG-run-CIS-CONT-PART-EVID be-3-when

"hemaya-ʔila no-no-kwa," no-k-laknoʔo.
be.ghost-when say-CONT-MIR say-PART-EVID

ʔe·-l-kaʔak ʔekwan-wa·-ʔa·-la [a whining sound]
be-3-when dog-OBV-DEF-NOM.SG

no-no-k-laknoʔo. ʔe·-kla we·ʔis "cane-w,"
say-CONT-PART-EVID be-DS.NSIM one leave-IMP

no-k-laknoʔo. ʔe·-kla ʔekwan-wa·-ʔa·-la-k
say-PART-EVID be-DS.NSIM dog-OBV-DEF-SG-ACC

cane-k-laknoʔo. ʔe[·]-kla cʔetxa-na-txil-na-k-laknoʔo.
leave-PART-EVID be-DS.NSIM jump-ABL-out-ABL-PART-EVID

(36) ʔe·-t pasʔe·-kwa wa·-tel kwete-ta
be-SS.CONS be.short.time-DS.SIM that-direction carry.in.arms-SS.NPURP

ha-kxo-ta-k-laknoʔo.
move.SG-in-CIS-PART-EVID

ʔe·-t xʔaxʔayʔa-no-k-laknoʔo. we-yace-l-ʔila
be-SS.CONS laugh-CONT-PART-EVID OBJ.PL-look-3-when

ha·ʔako·n-osaʔas-wa·-ʔa·-la-k. ʔe·-ta "losos-ʔita
man-young-OBV-DEF-SG-ACC be-SS.NPURP all-DET

panxo·sʔew
ta-kla-na-t panxo-we·sʔe-w," no-k-laknoʔo.
move.PL-down-ABL-SS.CONS bathe-1/2-SBJ.PL-IMP say-PART-EVID

ʔe·-kla losos-ʔita ta-kla-na-t he-pnonoxo·-t[35]
be-DS.NSIM all-DET move.PL-down-ABL-SS.CONS REFL-bathe.PLUR-SS.CONS

waʔan-wa·ʔal he-ykoʔo-n-laknoʔo.
just.as.before REFL-make-PART-EVID

35. Stem-internal reduplication of an underlying form /panoxo/. Whether this results from an earlier morphological complex form combining /pa-/ + /RED/ + /noxo/ is unclear but synchronically implausible.

(37)	we··tic.	xelik	ha·ʔako·n-osaʔas-ka	ʔe··no-k-laknoʔo.
	this-like	goose	man-young-NOM.PL	be-CONT-PART-EVID

The Four Young Men and Little One: Free English Translation

[1] So there were four young men living together, and one of the four got a boil on his index finger. When it grew big enough, he burst it and, as he squeezed it, out fell Little One from the boil. [2] The young men said: "Let's keep him,' and then while [they were] keeping the little baby, he got bigger. He got a little bigger, and when he did, they gave him a dog to play with. [3] When Little One got big, the young men made him stay at home while they wandered about; they usually returned at night. [4] Then this time they said: "Tomorrow don't go in this direction; over that way there are two old guys in their tipi." Then Little One said: "All right." [5] So the young man went off, and Little One said: "I'm going to go over and look at the old folks." So he went off. [6] So he went off to the camp and when he peered into the tent-flaps, the two old guys were lying down. Little One picked up a stick, set it alight in the fire, and poked him with it. Then he jumped all the way over there, and the one old guy was fighting with the other. So Little One was laughing. [7] Then he went in and said: "Oh, what are y'all eating?" and the old guys replied: "We have [always] been hungry." So Little One said: "Well, be [ready]: when I get home to y'all, you two can eat." Then the old guys said: "How do you think you're going to take us?" So Little One said: "I'll carry y'all on my back." So they said: "All right." [8] Then Little One carried them and went off [to] the camp of the young guys. He arrived at the camp with them and said: "All right, now, you two go on down," and when he said that the two wouldn't go down. [9] When night fell, the young men returned and said: "What are you doing?" So [Little One] said: "I went over there to the old guys and carried them on my back and told them to eat. After I did that, those two would not get down." [10] Then the young man said: "Go get meat, bring it back, and tell them: 'Now, get down and eat.'" Little One took them back and after he brought them back said: "All right, get down and eat." So the two got down as he went off. [11] Little One, who arrived, said: "Go down and bathe." Then he went down to the river and was bathing. When he came back up, they told him: "Tomorrow don't go this way. Over there lives a monster woman who is said to kill people." Then Little One said: "All right." [12] At dawn, after the young men had left, Little One went off to the monster woman and just as he went off, the woman met him. Right when she was about to stab Little One with her pointy iron elbows, he said: "Wait just a second!" [13] And then he went down to the river and stuck stones to his chest and

came back up, and when he did, the monster woman was there to meet him. He pointed at his chest and said: "All right!" The monster woman stabbed Little One, but she fell down dead. [14] Then Little One went off and when he got to the camp, the young men had returned. They asked him: "Where have you been?" So Little One said: "Over that way I killed the monster woman." [15] Then they said: "Tomorrow don't meddle with that mountain over that way." [16] So when it was dawn, Little One left and got to the mountain and brought it back with him to the camp and set it down. When it got dark, the young men got lost and returned only late at night. [17] Then they asked Little One: "What have you been doing?" He said: "I got to the mountain and brought it back." So they said: "Well, you better carry it back then!" Then Little One carried the mountain back where it had been. [18] Then when he came back, they said: "Look, when you catch fish, you won't have said: "Gimme a bite, Big Ones!" [19] So the next day, when Little One left, he went down to the river and was fishing for minnows. Then he threw his line down into the water and said: "Come on, bite, Big Ones!" Then the One Who Owns All the Water took the bait, and as Little One dragged him up close to the edge of the water, the One Who Owns All the Water opened up his mouth real wide, swallowed up Little One, and went back down into the water. [20] Then Little One sat down inside and kept on saying: "What the hell is this?" and the monster kept on saying it's such and such. [Little One] said: "And this?" pointing to the heart. [The monster] replied: "That's my heart." Then Little One said: "How would you act if it were cut out?" Then the monster said: "If someone cut out my heart, I'd be flopping about all over the place where there is no water; it'd make me open my mouth and would be the death of me." [21] Then Little One cut at the heart, and the monster ran about in circles and opened his mouth real wide at the water's surface and died. Then Little One went back to camp; when he arrived, it was already dark. [22] When the young men returned, they said: "We're real thirsty, go down and get some water." So Little One grabbed the bucket and went on down. [23] Then Little One came back up and was crying. The young men said: "What's the matter?" So Little One replied: "Our water has dried up." So the young men said: "What do you mean?" So [Little One] said: "I said: "Gimme a bite, Big One," and when he bit I pulled him up. [24] Then the young men said: "All right. Throw him in!" So he went out and the monster kept dragging him along: "Eeh, eeh, eeh!" he kept saying. He threw him in and left, and water came bubbling up: they drank. [25] Then they said: "Don't climb that mountain over there tomorrow. Four young women are living there." So Little One said: "All right." [26] Then at daybreak when the young man left, [Little One] went off to the mountain and hiked up it. As he did, [the women] were playing ball with each other and Little

One said: "All right." Then Little One shot the ball with one of his arrows, and the women said: "Oh no, the one who shot the arrow supposedly can't be beaten!" [27] As it happened, Little One went up and pulled the arrow from the ball and said: "All right, I'll go off with y'all." But the women said: "No!" and Little One cried. Then the women went off with him to the camp. [28] As night fell, the young men returned and said: "What are you doing?" So Little One said: "I brought those women here." They replied: "You've done wrong." Then Little One was crying and they made him go inside and get married to them. [29] Then they said: "Look, tomorrow don't go off in this direction! There's a monster buffalo over there that always captures people." So Little One said: "All right." [30] When morning came, as the young men went off in search of buffalo, [Little One] went off, and the buffalo met him and grabbed Little One and put him on his back and was going off. While Little One was going off, he said: "Friends! The buffalo has me, he has me!" [31] So the young men heard him and said: "All right!" and as they ran a good way off, the monstrous buffalo bull was carrying [Little One] and going far away. So the young men were constantly running and striking the buffalo [with arrows]. When he didn't die, he kept on going and when they'd used up all their arrows, he bucked their bows up with his horns, and they left crying and crying back toward the camp. [32] Then they arrived and they shaved themselves very bald and sat down together. [33] So, as the buffalo was about to throw Little One in, it looked very red, and in fact when he got closer it was a fire. [34] Right when the buffalo was about to throw him in, Little One said: "Wait just a second!" and he squatted on the buffalo's back and said: "All right." The buffalo was about to buck him off into the fire, Little One kicked down and jumped up into the sky. Little One turned himself into a plant and leaped away far off, and then he went off toward the camp. [35] Then at night, he arrived at the camp and made a whistling sound to the little dog. The dog was running around in circles, and he said: "It's a ghost that's speaking to him!" After that, the dog started to whine, and one [of the young men] said: "Leave him be." He let go of him and [the dog] jumped away. [36] Then, after a little while had passed, he carried [the dog] in his arms and came inside and was laughing. When he saw the young men [who had cut off their hair], he said: "All of you should go down and bathe." So they all went down and bathed and were turned back into what they were before. [37] So it goes: the young men were geese.

18. The Fearsome One and His Wife

(1) Tickan-la kwa·n-ʔa·-la-k ta·-yacox-ʔo·-no-k-laknoʔo.
person-NOM.SG woman-DEF-SG-ACC COM-camp-CAUS?-CONT-PART-EVID

ʔe·-no-k-la-k ʔaw-ka-k ta·kona-no-k-laknoʔo
be-CONT-PART-SG-ACC deer-PL-ACC seek-CONT-PART-EVID

ʔa·nʔok ya·lo·n-ape-no-k-laknoʔo ʔa·ʔa
but kill-NEG-CONT-PART-EVID and/so

ta·-yax-ʔe·-no-k-laknoʔo.
COM-eat-CAUS-CONT-PART-EVID
(='be hungry')

(2) ʔe·-no·-la ʔecinʔe ʔaw-ka-k
be-CONT-PART-NOM.SG then deer-PL-ACC

ta·kona-ha·-na-k-laknoʔo. ʔe[:]-la[36]
seek-move.SG-ABL-PART-EVID be.PART-NOM.SG

ke·sxa-ya-·kwa ha·-hey-ta-k-laknoʔo ʔe·-t
evening-INGR-when move.SG-LOC-CIS-PART-EVID be-SS.CONS

cʔetxane-ta-k[x]o-na-k-laknoʔo kotok-a·-yʔik.
jump-move.PL-in-ABL-PART-EVID room-DEF-ALL

ʔe·-kla kwa·n-wa·-ʔa·-la ya·ce-no-k-laknoʔo. ʔe·-l-ʔok
be-DS.NSIM woman-OBV-DEF-NOM.SG look-CONT-PART-EVID be-3-if

ha·ʔako·n-wa·-ʔa·-la yakw-an-waʔasay-ʔa·-la kap-e[:]-laknoʔo
man-OBV-DEF-NOM.SG kick-GER-half-DEF-NOM.SG nothing-be.PART-EVID
(='half leg')

lak. he-yces-o·-no-k-laknoʔo.
3SGACC REFL-be.frightened-INGR-CONT-PART-EVID

36. Hoijer (1933) recognizes a distinction between heavy and superheavy syllables, but his 1972 selection of texts did not. Based on his translation of this passage and on the use of added morae as a marker of participles elsewhere (cf. the previous line), this could probably be read as a trimoraic rather than bimoraic.

(3) ʔe·-kwa ha·ʔako·n-wa·-ʔa-la “na·kw ʔe-ʔe-yo-w!
be-DS.SIM man-OBV-DEF-NOM.SG all.right RED-do-INGR-IMP

ke-yax-ʔe·-no-·kwa!” no-k-lakno?o. ʔe·-kla
1.OBJ-eat-CAUS-CONT-MIR say-PART-EVID be-DS.NSIM

kwa·n-wa·-ʔa·-la “hecu·-ka-k ʔe-ʔe-yo·-sʔ?” no-k-laknoʔo.
woman-OBV-DEF-NOM.SG what-PL-ACC RED-do-INGR-1 say-PART-EVID

ʔe·-kla “ʔalʔ te·-la-k,” no-k-laknoʔo yakw-an-ʔa·xen-ʔa·-la-k.
be-DS.NSIM well this-SG-ACC say-PART-EVID kick-GER-3.SG.GEN-DEF-SG-ACC

ʔe·-kla “hehe·sʔ,” no-k-laknoʔo kwa·n-wa·-ʔa·-la.
be-DS.NSIM all.right say-PART-EVID woman-OBV-DEF-NOM.SG

“ʔa·x-ka-k yako-ta-ʔa·haʔa,” no-k-laknoʔo.
water-PL-ACC prepare-CIS-INTENT say-PART-EVID

(4) ʔe·-ta yakw-an-ʔa·-la-k taʔane-ta
be-SS.NPURP be.water-GER-DEF-SG-ACC grasp-SS.NPURP

ʔa·x-enca·n-ʔa·-yʔik ha-kla-na-k-laknoʔo.
water-pond-DEF-ALL move.SG-down-ABL-PART-EVID

ʔe·-l-ʔok kaw-la ʔa·x-ʔa·-yʔik
be-3-when crane-NOM.SG water-DEF-ALL

he-ylapa-t yaxa-no-k-laknoʔo. ʔe·-kla kwa·n-wa·-ʔa·-la
REFL-stand-SS.CONS eat-CONT-PART-EVID be-DS.NSIM woman-OBV-DEF-NOM.SG

“ʔe·-ta-w,” no-k-laknoʔo. ʔe·-kla kaw-a·-ʔa·-la
move$^{?}$-CIS-IMP say-PART-EVID be-DS.NSIM crane-OBV-DEF-NOM.SG

xa·xa-k-laknoʔo. “hecu ʔe·-kwaʔ,” no-k-laknoʔo.
move.SG.AUG-AUG-PART-EVID what be-MIR say-PART-EVID

ʔe·-kla “ha·ʔako·n-sa·ken-ʔa·-la
be-DS.NSIM man-1.SG.GEN-DEF-NOM.SG

heykoʔokwa
he-co-cxo·-k he-yake-we-ʔe-kwa ʔe·-t kena
REFL-RED-fear-PART REFL-make-DECL-PRES-MIR be-SS.CONS perhaps

keta·plew
ke-yx-a·to-no-kwa. ke-ta·-ha-ple-w ʔe·-t
1.OBJ-eat-FUT-CONT-MIR 1.OBJ-COM-TH-help-IMP be-SS.CONS

ke-ta[·]-ta-yxe-na-w kanaʔay-eʔe·-k.
1.OBJ-COM-move.PL-across-ABL-IMP other.side-that-ACC

ʔe·yoʔok
ʔe·ya-we-ʔe-k[a] yalxiln-a·haʔa," no-k-laknoʔo.
do-DECL-PRES-2 run-INTENT say-PART-EVID

(5) ʔe·-kla kaw-a·-ʔa·-la "ʔokxayʔoc-ka-k noko-t
be-DS.NSIM crane-OBV-DEF-NOM.SG shell.fish-PL-ACC gather-SS.CONS

ʔe·yoʔok
k-e·ke-w. ʔe·-yo-we-ʔe-k[a] yaxa-ta
1.OBJ-give-IMP do-INGR-DECL-PRES-2 eat-SS.CONS

ʔ-a·haʔa," no-k-laknoʔo. ʔe·-kla
do-INTENT say-PART-EVID be-DS.NSIM

kwa·n-wa·-ʔa·-la noko-t ʔeke-k-laknoʔo.
woman-OBV-DEF-NOM.SG gather-SS.CONS give-PART-EVID

ʔe·-kla yaxa-no-k-laknoʔo ʔe·-t to·xa-ta
be-DS.NSIM eat-CONT-PART-EVID be-SS.CONS finish-SS.NPURP

"we·ʔil," no-k-laknoʔo.
all.right say-PART-EVID

(6) he-kaya-kla-na-k-laknoʔo. ʔe·-kla kwa·n-wa·-ʔa·-la
REFL-bend-down-ABL-PART-EVID be-DS.NSIM woman-OBV-DEF-NOM.SG

ya-klʔax-an-ca·cxo[k]-a·-yʔik[37] ha-yxo-k-laknoʔo
TH-break-GER-center-DEF-ALL move.SG-across-PART-EVID
(='the center of the neck')

37. Probably a typo. Hoijer lists this root as *ca·cxok-*, so the /1/ is unlikely. Also, stem-final /k/ alone, with no other phonemes, optionally allows realization of the definite suffix without the glottal stop, as here.

ʔenik kanaʔakay-ʔa·-yʔik he-sʔekena-yxe-na-k-laknoʔo
and other.side-DEF-ALL REFL-stretch.neck-across-ABL-PART-EVID

ʔe·-ta "we·ʔil," no-k-laknoʔo. ʔe·-kla
be-SS.CONS all.right say-PART-EVID be-DS.NSIM

kwa·n-wa·-ʔa·-la yalxil-na-k-laknoʔo.
woman-OBV-DEF-NOM.SG run-ABL-PART-EVID

(7) ʔe·-t cʔawʔal henkwa·-na-·kwa haʔako·n-wa·-ʔa·-la
be-SS.CONS far.away run-ABL-when man-OBV-DEF-NOM.SG

"newey!" no-no-k-laknoʔo. ʔe·-l-ʔok kapay-ʔe·-no-k-la
hurry say-CONT-PART-EVID be-3-when nothing-be-CONT-PART-NOM.SG

ha-kla-na-k-laknoʔo. ʔe·-l-ʔok kwa·n-wa·-ʔa·-la
move.SG-down-ABL-PART-EVID be-3-when woman-OBV-DEF-NOM.SG

kape·la-k-laknoʔo lak.
nothing-PART-EVID 3SGACC

(8) kaw-a·-ʔa·-la-k "ʔe·-ta-w!" no-k-laknoʔo. ʔe·-kla
crane-OBV-DEF-SG-ACC move-CIS-IMP say-PART-EVID be-DS.NSIM

xa·-xa-k-laknoʔo. "hecu ʔe·-kwaʔ,"
move.SG.AUG-AUG-PART-EVID what be-MIR

no-k-laknoʔo. ʔe·-kla no-k-laknoʔo.
say-PART-EVID be-DS.NSIM say-PART-EVID

ʔe·-kla "kwa·n-la wa·-teca ha-kla-ta-k-e·-la-k
be-DS.NSIM woman-NOM.SG this-place move.SG-down-CIS-PART-this-SG-ACC

ya·c-ape-[ʔ]ka-ʔ?" no-k-laknoʔo. ʔe·-kla "he·ʔ," no-k-laknoʔo.
see-NEG-INTER-2.SG-INTER say-PART-EVID be-DS.NSIM yes say-PART-EVID

(9) ʔe·-kla haʔako·n-wa·-ʔa·-la "to·na-no-·-ka," no-k-laknoʔo.
be-DS.NSIM man-OBV-DEF-NOM.SG lie-CONT-?-2 say-PART-EVID

“na·ya	ta·-haple-ne-k-a·we,”	no-k-laknoʔo.	ʔe·-kla
2.SG.NOM	COM-help-2-PART-PERF	say-PART-EVID	be-DS.NSIM

kaw-la	“ʔa·kay,”	no-k-laknoʔo.	“sa·-pax
crane-NOM.SG	no	say-PART-EVID	1.SG-only

ʔe·noʔs ʔe·-no-ʔe-s,”	no-k-laknoʔo.	ʔe·-kla
be-CONT-PRES-1.SG	say-PART-EVID	be-DS.NSIM

“to·na-no-nwa-nʔey!”	no-k-laknoʔo.
lie-CONT-DEON-DEON2	say-PART-EVID

(10)

“ya·ce-w,”	no-k-laknoʔo	ha·ʔako·n-wa·-ʔa·-la.	keta·plew “ke-ta·-ha-ple-w,”
look-IMP	say-PART-EVID	man-OBV-DEF-NOM.SG	1.OBJ-COM-TH-help-IMP

no-k-laknoʔo.	“ke-ta-ta-yxe-na-w,”	no-k-laknoʔo.
say-PART-EVID	1.OBJ-COM-move.PL-cross-ABL-IMP	say-PART-EVID

ʔe·-kla	“hehe·ʔ,”	no-k-laknoʔo.	“ʔokxayʔoc-ka-k
be-DS.NSIM	all.right	say-PART-EVID	shell.fish-PL-ACC

noko-t	k-e·ke-w,”	no-k-laknoʔo.
gather-SS.CONS	1.OBJ-give-IMP	say-PART-EVID

(11)

ʔe·-kla	noko-t	ʔeke-k-la	yaxa-no-k-la
be-DS.NSIM	gather-SS.CONS	give-PART-NOM.SG	eat-CONT-PART-NOM.SG

to·xa-ta	“we·ʔil,”	no-k-laknoʔo.
finish-SS.NPURP	all.right	say-PART-EVID

ʔe·-kla	ya-klʔax-an-ʔa·-yʔik	ha-yxo-k-laknoʔo
be-DS.NSIM	TH-break-GER-DEF-ALL	move.SG-across-PART-EVID

ʔenik	kaw-a·-ʔa·-la	he-sʔeke-na-t
and	crane-OBV-DEF-NOM.SG	REFL-stretch.neck-ABL-SS.CONS

ʔa·x-ca·cxok-a·-yʔik	ʔe·-ta	“ʔaye!”	no-k-laknoʔo.
water-middle-DEF-ALL	be-SS.NPURP	ouch!	say-PART-EVID

"hecu· ʔe·-kwaʔ?" no-k-laknoʔo ha·ʔako·n-wa·-ʔa·-la.
what be-MIR say-PART-EVID man-OBV-DEF-NOM.SG

ʔe·noʔ
ʔe·-kla "cikew ʔe·-no-ʔe," no-k-laknoʔo kaw-a·-ʔa·-la.
be-DS.NSIM painful be-CONT-PRES say-PART-EVID crane-OBV-DEF-NOM.SG

ʔe·-ta ya-klʔax-an-ʔa·-la-k he-ce-co·-n te·-c
be-SS.NPURP TH-break-GER-DEF-SG-ACC REFL-RED-back-PART this-manner

ʔey-akxo-na-k-laknoʔo.
CAUS-in-ABL-PART-EVID

ʔe·-kwa ha·ʔako·n-wa·-ʔa·-la xa-wana-k-laknoʔo. ʔa·x-ʔa·-yʔik.
be-DS.SIM man-OBV-DEF-NOM.SG AUG-fall-PART-EVID water-DEF-ALL

ʔe·-kla kaw-la yox-na-k-laknoʔo.
be-DS.NSIM crane-NOM.SG fly-ABL-PART-EVID

(12) ʔe·-kla ha·ʔako·n-wa·-ʔa·-la ha-yxe-na-t
be-DS.NSIM man-OBV-DEF-NOM.SG move.SG-across-ABL-SS.CONS

cʔel-ʔe·-k-laknoʔo.
top-do-PART-EVID
(='follow after')

(13) cʔawʔal he-nkwa·-na·-kwa yane·yo·-k-laknoʔo
far.away REFL-run-ABL-when approach-ing-PART-EVID

ke·sxa-ya·-kwa.
be.evening-INGR-when

ʔe·-kwa heka·new-la cʔetxana-no·lka-no-k-laknoʔo.
be-DS.SIM skunk-NOM.SG jump-here.and.there-CONT-PART-EVID

ʔe·-kla kwa·n-wa·-ʔa·-la he-nkway-xa·xa-t
be-DS.NSIM woman-OBV-DEF-NOM.SG REFL-run-arrive-SS.CONS

keta·plew
"ke-ta·-ha-ple-w," no-k-laknoʔo. "he-co-cxo·-k-la
1.OBJ-COM-TH-help-IMP say-PART-EVID REFL-RED-fear-PART-NOM.SG

ke-ne-nkoxo-kwa," no-k-laknoʔo. ʔe·-kwa ha·cin
1.OBJ-TH-chase-MIR say-PART-EVID be-DS.SIM near

he-nkwa·-ta-k-laknoʔo. ʔe·-kla kwa·n-wa·-ʔa·-la
REFL-run-CIS-PART-EVID be-DS.NSIM woman-OBV-DEF-NOM.SG

"ma·tan ʔe-w!" no-k-laknoʔo.
quick be-IMP say-PART-EVID

(14) ʔe·-kla heka·new-la "yake·-na-kaxaw-ka-k ʔey-we-yce-w,"
be-DS.NSIM skunk-NOM.SG swing.leg-ABL-black-PL-ACC CAUS-OBJ.PL-catch-IMP

no-k-laknoʔo. "yaxa-taʔe·-s," no-k-laknoʔo. ʔe·-kla
say-PART-EVID eat-grasp-1 say-PART-EVID be-DS.NSIM

kwa·n-wa·-ʔa·-la ʔey-we-yce-t ʔeke-k-laknoʔo.
woman-OBV-DEF-NOM.SG CAUS-OBJ.PL-catch-SS.CONS give-PART-EVID

(15) ʔe·-kla heka·new-la yaxa-ta "we·ʔil," no-k-laknoʔo.
be-DS.NSIM skunk-NOM.SG eat-SS.NPURP all.right say-PART-EVID

ʔe·-ta holopa-k-laknoʔo ʔe·-ta no·s-ʔa·-la-k te·-c
be-SS.NPURP eat-PART-EVID be-SS.NPURP anus-DEF-SG-ACC this-manner

heykoʔoklaknoʔo
he-yakewa-ʔa-k-laknoʔo xakay. ʔe·-kla kwa·n-wa·-ʔa·-la
REFL-make-INGR?-PART-EVID wide be-DS.NSIM woman-OBV-DEF-NOM.SG

ha-kxo-na-k-laknoʔo no·s-ʔa·-yʔik ʔe·-t yela-no-k-laknoʔo.
move.SG-in-ABL-PART-EVID anus-DEF-ALL be-SS.CONS sit-CONT-PART-EVID

(16) ʔe·-kwa ha·ʔako·n-wa·-ʔa·-la xa·-xa-k-laknoʔo.
be-DS.SIM man-OBV-DEF-NOM.SG move.SG.AUG-AUG-PART-EVID

ʔe·-t "kwa·n-la wa·-teca he-nkw-a·to-ʔ. ya·c-ape-[ʔ]-ka-ʔ?"
be-SS.CONS woman-NOM.SG this-place REFL-run-FUT-EP see-NEG-INTER-2-INTER

no-k-laknoʔo. ʔe·-kla "he·ʔ," no-k-laknoʔo. "sa·-pax
say-PART-EVID be-when yes say-PART-EVID 1.SG-only

ʔe·-n[o]-ʔs," no-k-laknoʔo. ʔe·-kla ha·-k-la
be-cont-1 say-PART-EVID be-when move.SG-PART-NOM.SG

haʔako·n-wa·-ʔa·-la "to·na-no-nwa-nʔey!" no-k-laknoʔo.
man-OBV-DEF-NOM.SG lie-CONT-DEON-DEON2 say-PART-EVID

"na·kwetaʔan holopa-w!" no-k-laknoʔo.
come.now bend.over-IMP say-PART-EVID

"no·s-eʔe·-k ya·ce·-s!" no-k-laknoʔo.
anus-this-ACC see-1 say-PART-EVID

ʔe·-kla "ʔeyew," no-k-laknoʔo.
be-DS.NSIM all.right say-PART-EVID

ʔe·-ta holopa-k-laknoʔo. ʔe·-kla ha·ʔako·n-wa·-ʔa·-la
be-SS.NPURP bend.over-PART-EVID be-DS.NSIM man-OBV-DEF-NOM.SG

no·s-a·cin-ʔa·-yʔik yela-kxo-na-ta he-n-xilsa-ta ya·ce·-kwa
anus-near-DEF-ALL sit-in-ABL-SS.NPURP REFL-TH-peer-SS.NPURP see-when

xʔop-co-cow-nacka-k-laknoʔo.[38] ʔe·-ta "we·ʔil!"
fart$_1$-RED-fart$_2$-kill-PART-EVID be-SS.NPURP all.right

no-k-laknoʔo. ʔe·-kla kwa·n-wa·-ʔa·-la yalxil-na-k-laknoʔo.
say-PART-EVID be-when woman-OBV-DEF-NOM.SG run-ABL-PART-EVID

(17) cʔawʔal koxota-·kwa yane·-yo·-k-laknoʔo ʔaco·-t.
far.away run.from.fear-when close-INGR-PART-EVID revive-SS.CONS

ke·sxa-ya·-kwa cakaw-kwa·low-ʔa·-yʔik he-nkwaya-kla-na-·kwa
be.evening-INGR-when river-big-DEF-ALL REFL-run-down-ABL-when

38. Hoijer (1972, 82) defines *xʔopcocwa-* as 'discharge wind, gas, fetid fluid (as a skunk).' The initial element *xʔop-* is probably a fossilized incorporated noun.

cakaw-ʔa·-yʔik yake-no-k-laknoʔo.
river-DEF-ALL shoot-CONT-PART-EVID

ʔe·-kwa he-nkwaya-kla-na-l-ʔok ha·ʔa·ko·n-la
be-DS.SIM REFL-run-down-ABL-3-when man-NOM.SG

kwa·lo·-tak-la hemaxan-ka-k we-yke-no-k-laknoʔo.
big-very-NOM.SG turkey-PL-ACC OBJ.PL-shoot-CONT-PART-EVID

keta·plew
ʔe·-kla kwa·n-wa·-ʔa·-la "ke-ta·-ha-ple-w!" no-k-laknoʔo.
be-DS.NSIM woman-OBV-DEF-NOM.SG 1.OBJ-COM-TH-help-IMP say-PART-EVID

"he-co-cxo·-k-la ke-nen-koxo-no-kwa," no-k-laknoʔo.
REFL-RED-fear-PART-NOM.SG 1.OBJ-TH-chase-CONT-MIR say-PART-EVID

xa·nat
ʔe·-kla "na·kw. te·-wʔan xa-ha·-na-t
be-DS.NSIM all.right this-ADESS AUG-move.SG-ABL-SS.CONS

he-ylape-w," no-k-laknoʔo.
REFL-stand-IMP say-PART-EVID

(18) ʔe·-kwa ha·ʔako·n-wa·-ʔa·la he-nkwaya-kla-na-k-laknoʔo
be-DS.SIM man-OBV-DEF-NOM.SG REFL-run-down-ABL-PART-EVID

ʔe·-t "kwa·n-la wa·-teca he-nkwaya-kla-ta-k-e-la-k
be-SS.CONS woman-NOM.SG this-place REFL-run-down-CIS-PART-EP-SG-ACC

ya·c-ape-kaʔ?" no-k-laknoʔo. ʔe·-kla "he·ʔ," no-k-laknoʔo.
see-NEG-2 say-PART-EVID be-DS.NSIM yes say-PART-EVID

(19) ʔe·-kwa ʔo·ʔo·-k-laknoʔo. ʔe·-kla naxce-k-laknoʔo kwa·low
be-DS.SIM be.night-PART-EVID be-DS.NSIM build.fire-PART-EVID big

ʔe·-ta hemaxan-ʔa·-la-k ketay we-nwele-k-laknoʔo. ʔe·-ta
be-SS.NPURP turkey-DEF-SG-ACC two OBJ.PL-roast-PART-EVID be-SS.NPURP

“na·-xwa	te·-la-k	nawle-t	yaxa-w,”
2.SG-also	this-SG-ACC	roast	eat-IMP

no-k-lakno?o	?e·-ta	we·?is-pax
say-PART-EVID	be-SS.NPURP	one-only

?eke-k-lakno?o.	?e·-kla	metis	ne-lte-ta	to·xa-k-lakno?o.
give-PART-EVID	be-DS.NSIM	three	TH-pluck-SS.NPURP	finish-PART-EVID

?e·-kla	?ecin?e	?eke-k-la	?ecin?e	to·xa-k-lakno?o.
be-DS.NSIM	then	give-PART-EVID	then	finish-PART-EVID

(20)

?e·-kwa	tickan-kwa·low-?a·-la	yaxa-no-k-lakno?o.
be-DS.SIM	person-big-DEF-NOM.SG	eat-CONT-PART-EVID

hemaxan-ka-k	kwa·n-wa·-?a·-la-k	nes-yaxa-no-k-lakno?o.
turkey-PL-ACC	woman-OBV-DEF-SG-ACC	CAUS-eat-CONT-PART-EVID

?e·-l-ka?ak	he-co-cxo·-k-wa·-?a·-la	“hecu	?e·-no-ka?”
be-3-but	REFL-RED-fear-PART-OBV-DEF-NOM.SG	what	do-CONT-2

no-k-lakno?o.	“hecu·-?ax	?a·-pe-no-?-s,”	no-k-lakno?o.
say-PART-EVID	what-INDEF	do-NEG-CONT-PRES-1	say-PART-EVID

“wa?anpax	yax?a·-n-?ok	wa?an	we·-y?ik	he-cne-w,”
as.soon.as	eat-GER-when	exactly	that-ALL	REFL-lie.down-IMP

no-k-lakno?o.	“?e·-ye·-n	sa·-xwa	wa?an-wa·-ca
say-PART-EVID	be-INGR-GER	1.SG-also	exactly-this-place

he-cn-a·?,”	no-k-lakno?o.
REFL-lie.down-INTENT.1	say-PART-EVID

(21)

he-co-cxo·-k-wa·-?a·-la	he-cne-k-lakno?o.
REFL-RED-fear-PART-OBV-DEF-NOM.SG	REFL-lie.down-PART-EVID

tickan-kwa·lo-wa·-?a·-la	he-cne-k-lakno?o.	?e·-kla
person-big-OBV-DEF-NOM.SG	REFL-lie.down-PART-EVID	be-DS.NSIM

he-co-cxo·-k-wa·-?a·-la	“he-tec
REFL-RED-fear-PART-OBV-DEF-NOM.SG	what-manner

ʔeye·-no-k-ye," no-k-laknoʔo. "coxn-a·tak-we-l-ʔila?"
behave-CONT-PART-Q say-PART-EVID sleep-very-INGR-3-if

ʔe·-kla "na·t-an-kwa·low-sa·ken-elʔa·t-la-k te·-c
be-DS.NSIM step-GER-big-1.SG.GEN-yonder-SG-ACC this-like

ʔenoʔo·ʔ
ʔe-no-ʔe·-ʔ," no-k-laknoʔo. ʔe·-ta "ʔen na·ya?"
be-CONT-PAST-1 say-PART-EVID be-SS.NPURP and 2.SG.NOM

no-k-laknoʔo ʔe·-kla he-co-cxo·-k-wa·-ʔa·-la
say-PART-EVID be-DS.NSIM REFL-RED-fear-PART-OBV-DEF-NOM.SG

kexʔopcocwanoʔo
"sa·-sik naʔas ke-cxwa-na-l-ʔila ke-xʔop-co-cwa-no-we-ʔe,"
1.SG.ACC when 1.OBJ-sleep-ABL-3-if 1.OBJ-fart$_1$-RED-fart$_2$-CONT-DECL-PRES

no-k-laknoʔo. ʔe·-kla "heyʔ," no-k-laknoʔo.
say-PART-EVID be-when all.right say-PART-EVID

(22) ha·ʔako·n-wa·-ʔa·-la na·t-an-ʔa·-la-k te·-c ʔe·-no-k-laknoʔo.
man-OBV-DEF-NOM.SG step-GER-DEF-SG-ACC this-like be-CONT-PART-EVID

ʔe·-kla he-co-cxo·-k-wa·-ʔa·-la
be-when REFL-RED-fear-PART-OBV-DEF-NOM.SG

xʔop-co-cwa-no-k-laknoʔo. ʔe·-kwa
fart$_1$-RED-fart$_2$-CONT-PART-EVID be-DS.SIM

he-co-cxo·-k-wa·-ʔa·-la yela-cxo-k-laknoʔo.
REFL-RED-fear-PART-OBV-DEF-NOM.SG sit-rise-PART-EVID

ʔe·-kla tickan-kwa·low-a·-ʔa·-la "nes-kaltey-eʔe·-k[39] x-e·-cne-w.
be-DS.NSIM person-big-OBV-DEF-NOM.SG other.side-that-ACC AUG-REFL-lie-IMP

cʔetxa-t-a·to-no-kwa," no-k-laknoʔo.
jump-CIS-FUT-CONT-MIR say-PART-EVID

39. This looks like a combination of *nes-* 'CAUS-' and *kaltey-* 'outside,' but if that was its historic origin it is no longer compositionally reconstructible.

(23) ʔe··kwa cʔetxa-na-k-laknoʔo he-co-cxo··k-wa··ʔa··la
be-DS.SIM jump-ABL-PART-EVID REFL-RED-fear-PART-OBV-DEF-NOM.SG

ʔe·t tickan-kwa·lo-wa··ʔa··la-k he-wle-k-laknoʔo. ʔe··kla
be-SS.CONS person-big-OBV-DEF-SG-ACC REFL-catch-PART-EVID be-DS.NSIM

kanaʔakay-ʔa··yʔik kan-ayxe-na-k-laknoʔo ʔe··ta
other.side-DEF-ALL throw-across-ABL-PART-EVID be-SS.NPURP

cʔetxan-ayxe-na-t ta··he··sokyo··k-laknoʔo. ʔe··kla
jump-across-ABL-SS.CONS COM-REFL-fight-PART-EVID be-DS.NSIM

tickan-kwa·lo-wa··ʔa··la he-co-cxo··k-wa··ʔa··la-k.
person-big-OBV-DEF-NOM.SG REFL-RED-fear-PART-OBV-DEF-SG-ACC

to-top-to·xa-k-laknoʔo ʔe··t ya·lo·na-k-laknoʔo.
RED-cut.up-finish-PART-EVID be-SS.CONS kill-PART-EVID

(24) ʔe··kla kwa·n-wa··ʔa··la "ta·ʔe-ye···s," no-no-k-laknoʔo.
be-DS.NSIM woman-OBV-DEF-NOM.SG grasp-INGR-1 say-CONT-PART-EVID

ʔe··kla "kwa·n-e··ka-k ke·skwacape·noʔo
ke-heskwac-ape···no-we-ʔe,"
be-DS.NSIM woman-that-PL-ACC 1.OBJ-want-NEG-2.OBJ-CONT-DECL-PRES

no-k-laknoʔo. "k-e·xtawa-k-la ya·lo·noʔs
ya·lo·na-we-ʔe-s,"
say-PART-EVID 1.OBJ-pity-PART-NOM.SG kill-DECL-PAST-1

no-k-laknoʔo. "na·kwa ha··na-w," no-k-laknoʔo.
say-PART-EVID well move.SG-ABL-IMP say-PART-EVID

ʔe··kla kwa·n-wa··ʔa··la ha··na-k-laknoʔo.
be-DS.NSIM woman-OBV-DEF-NOM.SG move.SG-ABL-PART-EVID

he·saxew-la ʔe··no-k-laknoʔo.
giant-NOM.SG be-CONT-PART-EVID

The Fearsome One and His Wife: Free English Translation

[1] So a man was living with his wife. He was searching for deer but not killing any and so they were both hungry. [2] So he again went off looking for deer, and when it became evening he got back and went hobbling into the room. The woman was looking at him, as the man was missing half his leg—she was frightened! [3] Right then the man said: "Okay, cook something! I'm hungry!" So the woman said: "What kinds of things should I start cooking?" And he said: "How about this?" [and he pointed to] his own leg. Then she said: "All right. I'll prepare it in some water." [4] Then she grabbed the bucket and went down to the pond, and when she got there, Crane was standing in the water eating. So the woman said: "Come here!" and Crane came to her. "What is it?" he said. "My husband has really become a monster and might eat me! Help me and take me across to the other side [of the pond]. When you do that, I'm going to run away." [5] So Crane said: "Gather together some shellfish and give them to me; when you do, after I eat them I'll take you across." Then the woman gathered together [the shellfish] and handed them over. After he had eaten them all up, he said: "All right." [6] He bent down and the woman straddled the back of his neck, he stretched his neck across the pond, and he said: "All right." Then the woman ran away. [7] Then when she had run away, the man kept on saying: "Hurry!" but when he did no one was there, and when he went down, the woman was not there. [8] So he said [to Crane]: "Come here!" and Crane came to him and said: "What is it?" So [the man] said: "Did you not see a woman coming down this way?" And Crane said: "Yes [I did not see her]." [9] Then the man said: "You're lying! You have been helping her." So Crane said: "No, it was just me here." But the man kept on saying: "You've got to be lying!" [10] "See here, help me out, take me across." So [Crane] said: "All right. Gather together some shellfish and give them to me." [11] So, after gathering them together, he gave [Crane] some to eat, who finished it off and said: "Let's go." Then [the man] mounted [Crane's] neck and Crane stretched it out across the middle of the water and said: "Ouch!" The man responded: "What is it?" "It's painful," Crane said and pulled his neck back in. So the man fell into the water, and Crane flew off. [12] So the man crossed the water and went after [the woman]. [13] As he ran far off, he got closer to her when it was getting dark. Now, a skunk was jumping around here and there, and the woman ran up to him [and said]: "Help me! A monster is chasing me." So he was running up her near here, and the woman said: "Be quick!" [14] So Skunk said: "Catch grasshoppers [for me]. I'm hungry!" So the woman caught some [grasshoppers] and gave them to him. [15] Then Skunk ate them and said: "Okay." He bent over and opened his butt *this* wide, and the

woman went in and sat inside it. [16] The man arrived and said: "A woman is about to run this way. Did you not see her?" Then [Skunk] said: "Yeah, I've been here by myself." So the man who had come there said: "You're lying! Come on, bend over, I want to see your butt." Skunk said: "Okay," and bent over. Then man sat in close to the skunk's butt and looked at it, and as he looked, Skunk killed him with a big ol' fart. Skunk said: "All right," and the woman ran off. [17] Although the woman took flight far, far away, [the man] got close to her after he came back to life. When it got dark, she ran down to the big river and there was someone shooting by the river. As she ran down, a very big man was shooting turkeys, and the woman said: "Help me! A monster is chasing me!" So he said: "Okay, move over this way and stand still." [18] So the man ran down and said: "A woman just came running down this way, did you not see her?" So [the big man] replied: "Yeah." [19] When night fell, [the big man] built a big fire, roasted two turkeys, and said [to the first man]: "You too should roast and eat one." So he gave just one [to the man]. He plucked three [feathers] and finished it off [raw]. Then [the big man] gave him some more, and again he finished it off [raw]. [20] While the big man was eating the turkeys, he was feeding the woman some too, but the monster [grew suspicious and] said: "What are you doing?" So [the big man] said: "I haven't been doing anything. As soon as you have eaten, lie down right there. I also am going to lie down right here." [21] So the monster lay down, and the big man lay down. Then the monster asked: "How do you behave when you're sleeping deeply?" So [the big man] said: "I do this with that big toe of mine. And you?" Then the monster said: "When I go to sleep, I fart a lot." So [the big man] said: "All right." [22] The man was fiddling with his toe like this, and the monster was farting, and as he did, he sat up and the big man said [to the woman]: "Lie over to that side; he's about to jump over this way." [23] Then the monster jumped over there and the big man caught him and threw him across to the other side [of the river]. He jumped over to the other side and fought with him—he cut up into pieces and killed him. [24] Then the woman kept on saying: "I'm going to marry you!" but he said: "I never wanted to marry those kinds of women. I pitied you and so I killed him. Now get out of here!" Then the woman went off. He was a giant.

19. A Poor Mexican and His Chief

(1) ka·nos-kokon-la ʔahan-ʔa·-la-k ta·-ʔe·-no-k-laknoʔo.
Mexican-chief-NOM.SG daughter-DEF-SG-ACC COM-be-CONT-PART-EVID

ka·nos-e·xatok-la-k nes-ʔe·-no-k-laknoʔo.
Mexican-poor-SG-ACC CAUS-do-CONT-PART-EVID

(2) ʔe·-no-k-la-k "taxso·-l-ʔok he-wʔan
be-CONT-PART-SG-ACC be.dawn-3-when that-ADESS

ha·csokonay-eykaʔay-ʔok-e·-ka samox ʔe·noʔo ʔe·-no-we-ʔe.
wolf-big-fur-this-NOM.PL red be-CONT-DECL-PRES

wa·-ʔa·-la-k xa·-xa-t ʔey-we-yce-t
OBV-DEF-SG-ACC move.SG.AUG-AUG-SS.CONS CAUS-OBJ.PL-catch-SS.CONS

ʔok-a·-la-k we-pcen-ʔe·-ta-w," no-k-laknoʔo
fur/hide-DEF-SG-ACC OBJ.PL-shear-?-CIS-IMP say-PART-EVID

ka·nos-kokon-wa·-ʔa·-la. ʔe·-kla he·xatok-wa·-ʔa·-la
Mexican-chief-OBV-DEF-NOM.SG be-DS.NSIM poor.one-OBV-DEF-NOM.SG

"hehe·ʔ," no-k-laknoʔo.
all.right say-PART-EVID

(3) taxso·-k-la kokon-wa·-ʔa·-la ʔekwan-esxaw-aycepan-tak-la-k
be.dawn-PART-EVID chief-OBV-DEF-NOM.SG dog-big-lean-very-SG-ACC

ʔe·-ta he-ywaxk-an-la-k nes-ayxo-k-laknoʔo.
be-SS.NPURP REFL-lame-GER-SG-ACC CAUS-across-PART-EVID

xalʔo·-n-ʔa·-la-k ʔeke-k-laknoʔo. ʔe·-kla
cut.with.knife-GER-DEF-SG-ACC give-PART-EVID be-DS.NSIM

taʔane-ta ʔekwan-esxaw-ʔa·-la-k ha-yxo-ta
grasp-SS.NPURP dog-big-DEF-SG-ACC TH-across-SS.NPURP

cakaw-ʔa·-yʔik	ha-kla-na-t	yela-ta	ʔa·x-a·cin-ʔa·-yʔik
river-DEF-ALL	TH-down-ABL-SS.CONS	sit-SS.NPURP	water-near-DEF-ALL

ma·ka-no-k-laknoʔo.
cry-CONT-PART-EVID

(4)

ʔe-no-n-la-k	ʔa·x-wa·-yʔik-ita	ʔekwan-esxaw-la
be-CONT-PART-SG-ACC	water-OBV-ALL-DET	dog-big-NOM.SG

maslak-pax-la	ha-yco-ta-k-laknoʔo	ʔe·-t
white-quite-NOM.SG	move.SG-up-CIS-PART-EVID	be-SS.CONS

"hecu	ʔe·-t	ma·ka-no-kaʔ"
what	be-SS.CONS	cry-CONT-2

no-k-laknoʔo.	ʔe·-kla	"kokon-ke-la
say-PART-EVID	be-DS.NSIM	chief-1.POSS-NOM.SG

ha·csokonay-eykaʔay-samox-ka-k	[k]e-nes-ʔe-y-wey-coʔ,"
wolf-big-red-PL-ACC	1.OBJ-CAUS-CAUS-TH-bind-RES

no-k-laknoʔo.	ʔe·-kla	ʔekwan-esxaw-maslak-pax-wa·-ʔa·-la
say-PART-EVID	be-DS.NSIM	dog-big-white-only-OBV-DEF-NOM.SG

"na·kw	sa·sik	k-a·-yoxo-w,"	no-k-laknkoʔo.
all.right	1.SG.ACC	1.OBJ-TH-ride-IMP	say-PART-EVID

(5)

ʔe·-kla	ʔekwan-esxaw-maslak-pax-wa·-ʔa·-la	ha-yxo-ta
be-DS.NSIM	dog-big-white-only-OBV-DEF-NOM.SG	move.SG-across-SS.NPURP

ha·-na-k-laknoʔo.	ʔe·-t	ha·csokonay-ka	yeykaʔay-ka
move.SG-ABL-PART-EVID	be-SS.CONS	wolf-NOM.PL	big-NOM.PL

ʔe·-no-wa·-yʔik	ha-na·-kwa	ha·csokonay-samox-wa·-ka
be-CONT-that-ALL	move.SG-ABL-DS.SIM	wolf-red-OBV-NOM.PL

nen-koxo-k-laknoʔo.	ʔe·-kla	ya-lxil-na-k-laknoʔo
TH-chase-PART-EVID	be-DS.NSIM	TH-run-abl-PART-EVID

ʔe·-t	xamʔal-ʔa·-yʔik	nes-enkwa·n-an
be-SS.CONS	prairie-DEF-ALL	CAUS-run-GER

no·henemʔa·-n-la-k xa-ka-na-k-laknoʔo. ʔe·-kla
see.reflection-GER-SG-ACC AUG-throw-ABL-PART-EVID be-DS.NSIM

ha·csokonay-wa·-ka xa-ytice-no-k-laknoʔo.
wolf-OBV-NOM.PL AUG-fall-CONT-PART-EVID

ʔe·-kla ka·nos-e·xatok-wa·-ʔa·-la ha·csokonay-wa·-ʔa·-la-k
be-DS.NSIM Mexican-poor-OBV-DEF-NOM.SG wolf-OBV-DEF-SG-ACC

we-pcena-no-k-laknoʔo ʔoka·-la-k ʔe·-ta noko-ta
OBJ.PL-cut.off-CONT-PART-EVID fur-SG-ACC be-SS.NPURP gather-SS.NPURP

ha·-na-k-laknoʔo.
move.SG-ABL-PART-EVID

(6) ʔe·-t ʔekwan-esxaw-ʔa·-la-k cane-k-wa·-yʔik
be-SS.CONS dog-big-DEF-SG-ACC leave-PART-OBV-ALL

xa·-xa-t he-wle-k-laknoʔo
AUG.move.SG-AUG-SS.CONS REFL-catch-PART-EVID

ʔekwan-esxaw-aycap-an-wa·-ʔa·-la-k.
dog-big-lean-GER-OBV-DEF-SG-ACC

ʔe·-kla ʔekwan-esxaw-maslak-pax-we·-ʔa·-la ʔa·x-wa·-yʔik
be-DS.NSIM dog-big-white-just-OBV-DEF-NOM.SG water-OBV-ALL

ha-kla-na-k-laknoʔo. ʔe·-kwa ka·nos-e·xatok-wa·-ʔa·-la
move.SG-down-ABL-PART-EVID be-DS.SIM Mexican-poor-OBV-DEF-NOM.SG

ha·-na-k-laknoʔo.
move.SG-ABL-PART-EVID

(7) ʔe·-t xa·-xa-k-laknoʔo ʔe·-t ʔeke-k-laknoʔo.
be-SS.CONS AUG.move.SG-AUG-PART-EVID be-SS.CONS give-PART-EVID

ʔe·-kla "he-tec ʔe·-t wa·-til we-pce-no-kaʔ"
be-DS.NSIM what-manner be-SS.CONS this-way OBJ.PL-shear-CONT-2

no-k-laknoʔo. ʔe·-kla ka·nos-e·xatok-wa·-ʔa·-la
say-PART-EVID be-DS.NSIM Mexican-poor-OBV-DEF-NOM.SG

"ha·csokonay-wa·-ka-k ʔey-we-yce-ta
wolf-OBV-PL-ACC CAUS-OBJ.PL-catch-SS.NPURP

wepcenoʔs
we-pce-no-we-ʔe-s," no-k-laknoʔo.
OBJ.PL-shear-DECL-PRES-1 say-PART-EVID

(8) ʔe·-kla ka·nos-kokon-wa·-ʔa·-la "hehe·ʔ," no-k-laknoʔo.
be-DS.NSIM Mexican-chief-OBV-DEF-NOM.SG all.right say-PART-EVID

"ʔekwan-esxaw-yax-an haklanan he-co-cxo·-k
dog-big-eat-GER sharp REFL-RED-fear-PART

ʔe·noʔo
ʔe·-no-we-ʔe," no-k-laknoʔo. "taxso·-l-ʔok sikt-as
be-CONT-DECL-PRES say-PART-EVID be.dawn-3-when four-fold

yaxw-ka-kayʔac-a-txil-na-no-[Ø]-ʔa·-la
club-RED-cut.off.at.joint-TH-out-ABL-CONT-PART-DEF-NOM.SG

ʔahan-wesik-te·-la-k ta·ʔ-a·to-nwa-ʔ," no-k-laknoʔo.
daughter-1.SG.GEN-this-SG-ACC grasp-FUT-DEON-DEON.3 say-PART-EVID

(9) ʔe·-k-la-k taxso·-k-la ka·nos-kokon-wa·-ʔa·-la
be-PART-SG-ACC be.dawn-PART-NOM.SG Mexican-chief-OBV-DEF-NOM.SG

ʔekwan-esxaw-e·xatok-wa·-ʔa·-la-k nes-ayxo-k-laknoʔo
dog-big-poor-OBV-DEF-SG-ACC CAUS-across-PART-EVID

ka·nos-e·xatok-wa·-ʔa·-la-k
Mexican-poor-OBV-DEF-SG-ACC

ʔe·-ta xalʔo·-n-away-ʔa·-la-k nes-taʔane-k-laknoʔo.
be-SS.NPURP cut.with.knife-GER-long-DEF-SG-ACC CAUS-take-PART-EVID

taʔane-ta caka-wa·-yʔik ha-kla-na-t
take-SS.NPURP river-OBV-ALL move.SG-down-ABL-SS.CONS

yela-ta ma·ka-no-k-lakno?o.
sit-SS.NPURP cry-CONT-PART-EVID

(10) ʔe·-kwa ʔekwan-esxaw-maslak-pax-wa·-ʔa·-la ha-yco-ta-k-laknoʔo.
be-DS.SIM dog-big-white-only-OBV-DEF-NOM.SG move.SG-up-CIS-PART-EVID

"hecu ʔe-kwa?" no-k-laknoʔo. ʔe·-kla
what do-MIR say-PART-EVID be-DS.NSIM

"ʔekwan-esxaw-yax-an-aklanan-e-co-cxo·-k-la-k
dog-big-eat-GER-sharp-REFL-RED-fear-PART-SG-ACC

ʔey-ka-kayc-a·to-k-noʔo," no-k-laknoʔo. ʔe·-kla
CAUS-RED-cut.off.at.joint-FUT-PART-EVID say-PART-EVID be-DS.NSIM

"hehe·ʔ k-a·-yaxo-w," no-k-laknoʔo. ʔe·-kla
all.right 1.OBJ-TH-ride-IMP say-PART-EVID be-DS.NSIM

ha-yxo-k-laknoʔo maslak-pax-wa·-ʔa·-la-k.
move.SG-across-PART-EVID white-just-obv-DEF-SG-ACC

(11) ka·nos-ʔa·-la ha·ʔas ha-ho·-k-laknoʔo ʔenik sikit-ita
Mexican-DEF-NOM.SG many TH-gather-PART-EVID and four-DET

ka·nos-ka ʔekwan-esxaw-enox-ka-k
Mexican-NOM.PL dog-big-good-PL-ACC

w-e·s-yacx-e[·]-ta
OBJ.PL-REFL.CAUS-mount-INGR-SS.NPURP

ʔekwan-esxaw-yax-an-wa·-ʔa·-la-k nes-a·-na-ci-cxilʔ-an
dog-big-eat-GER-OBV-DEF-SG-ACC CAUS-move.SG-ABL-RED-run-GER

ʔey-ka-kayceta-na-k-laknoʔo. ʔe·-l-ʔila ke·spax
CAUS-RED-cut.off.at.joint-ABL-PART-EVID be-3-when almost

ʔe·-kwa ʔekwan-esxaw-ʔa·-ka-k
be-DS.SIM dog-big-DEF-PL-ACC

yasʔe-n-we-ncaka-no-k-laknoʔo.
be.lacerated-GER-OBJ.PL-die-CONT-PART-EVID

ʔekwan-esxaw-yax-an-wa·-ʔa·-la.
dog-big-eat-GER-OBV-DEF-NOM.SG

(12) ʔe·-no-k-la ka·nos-e·xatok-wa·-ʔa·-la ʔa·-xwa
be-CONT-PART-NOM.SG Mexican-poor-OBV-DEF-NOM.SG 3SG-also

nes-enkwa·nʔ-an ʔey-ka-kayce-ta-na-k-laknoʔo
CAUS-run-GER CAUS-RED-cut.off.at.joint-move.PL-ABL-PART-EVID

ʔe·-t siktas ʔey-ka-kayce-xa-txil-na-k-laknoʔo
be-SS.CONS four CAUS-RED-cut.off.at.joint-AUG.move.SG-out-ABL-PART-EVID

ʔe·-t ha·-na-k-laknoʔo.
be-SS.CONS move.SG-ABL-PART-EVID

(13) xa·-xa-t "hecu·-la we-yno-·kwa?" no-k-laknoʔo
AUG.move.SG-AUG-SS.CONS what-NOM.SG OBJ.PL-win-MIR say-PART-EVID

kokon-wa·-ʔa·-la. ʔe·-kla ka·nos-e·xatok-wa·-ʔa·-la
chief-OBV-DEF-NOM.SG be-DS.NSIM Mexican-poor-OBV-DEF-NOM.SG

ʔoʔs
"sa·ya ʔe-we-ʔe-s," no-k-laknoʔo. ʔe·-kla
1.SG.NOM do-DECL-PAST-1 say-PART-EVID be-DS.NSIM

"hehe·ʔ," no-k-laknoʔo.
all.right say-PART-EVID

(14) ʔe·-kwa ʔahan-wa·-ʔa·-la
be-DS.SIM daughter-OBV-DEF-NOM.SG

"he-ykwec-an-sa·ken-ʔa·-la-k
REFL-put.on.round.object-GER-1.SG.GEN-DEF-SG-ACC

ʔeykana·xeynoʔs
ʔey-kan-a·xey-na-we-ʔe-s," no-k-laknoʔo. ʔe·-kla
CAUS-throw-across-ABL-DECL-PAST-1 say-PART-EVID be-DS.NSIM

"ta·kona-w,"	no-k-laknoʔo.	"hehe·ʔ,"	no-k-laknoʔo.
seek-IMP	say-PART-EVID	all.right	say-PART-EVID

(15)

ʔok-maʔek-la=ʔen	ʔekwan-la=ʔan	we-nes-ta·kona-k-laknoʔo.
hide/skin-cat-SG=and	dog-SG=and	OBJ.PL-CAUS-look.for-PART-EVID

ʔe[·]-kla	ta-na-nesʔe-k-laknoʔo.	cakaw-kwa·low-ʔa·-yʔik
be-DS.NSIM	move.PL-ABL-DU-PART-EVID	river-big-DEF-ALL

xa-t-xa-ta	"ta-yxe-na-si-k-[y]e,"	no-k-laknoʔo.
AUG-move.PL-AUG-SS.NPURP	move.PL-across-ABL-1-PART-Q	say-PART-EVID

"wa·te-wʔan	ʔ-a·pe-k-a·we,"	no-k-laknoʔo
this.side-ADESS	be-NEG-PART-PERF	say-PART-EVID

ʔekwan-wa·-ʔa·-la.	ha·c-ʔita	so-soya-na-nesʔe-k-laknoʔo
dog-OBV-DEF-NOM.SG	both-DET	RED-swim-ABL-DU-PART-EVID

kanaʔakay-ʔa·-yʔik.	so-syaw-ta-yxe-na-ta
other.side-DEF-ALL	RED-swim-move.PL-across-ABL-SS.NPURP

ta-na-nesʔe-k-laknoʔo.
move.PL-ABL-DU-PART-EVID

(16)

ʔe·-kwa	hanil-esʔaw-ʔa·-la	ha·naxok-ita
be-DS.SIM	wood.rat-worthless-DEF-NOM.SG	many-DET

we-ta·-ho·-k-laknoʔo	ʔekwan-wa·-ʔa-la-k.
OBJ.PL-COM-meet-PART-EVID	dog-OBV-DEF-SG-ACC

ʔe·-t	"hecu	ʔe·-t
be-SS.CONS	what	be-SS.CONS

ta-slo·-nes-no-ka?"	no-k-laknoʔo.	ʔe·-kla
move.PL-wander-DU-CONT-2	say-PART-EVID	be-DS.NSIM

ʔekwan-wa·-ʔa·-la	"he-ykwec-an-la-k
dog-OBV-DEF-NOM.SG	REFL-put.on.round.object-GER-SG-ACC

ta·konanesnoʔs

ta·kona-nesʔe-no-we-ʔe-s,"	no-k-laknoʔo.	ʔe·kla
look.for-DU-CONT-DECL-PRES-1	say-PART-EVID	be-DS.NSIM

"ʔo·ʔo·-kwa	ta·kono·-s-ʔa·haʔa,"	no-k-laknoʔo.
be.night-DS.SIM	look.for-1-INTENT	say-PART-EVID

	ya·coʔo
"he-ykwec-an-wa·-ʔa·-la-k	ya·ca-we-ʔe,"
REFL-put.on.round.object-GER-OBV-DEF-SG-ACC	see-DECL-PAST

		ta·kono·sʔew	
no-k-laknoʔo.	ʔe·-kla	"ta·kona-we·sʔe-w	ʔo·ʔo·-kwa,"
say-PART-EVID	be-DS.NSIM	look.for-1/2.SBJ.PL-IMP	be.night-DS.SIM

no-k-laknoʔo.
say-PART-EVID

(17)

ʔo·ʔo·-k-la	weʔis	he-pay-xwet-an-la
be.night-PART-NOM.SG	one	REFL-bead-wear-GER-NOM.SG

he-ykwec-an-wa·-ʔa·-la-k	he-ykwece-ta
REFL-put.on.round.object-GER-OBV-DEF-SG-ACC	REFL-put.on.round.object-SS.NPURP

coxna-no-k-laknoʔo.	ʔe·-kwa	hanil-esʔa-wa·-ka
sleep-CONT-PART-EVID	be-DS.SIM	wood.rat-worthless-OBV-NOM.PL

he-pay-xwet-an-wa·-ʔa·-la-k	nes-coxn-ape-no-n-laknoʔo.[40]
REFL-bead-wear-GER-OBV-DEF-SG-ACC	CAUS-sleep-NEG-CONT-PART-EVID

ʔe·-no-k-la-k	we-ykon-a·to-t	we-ykona-k-la
be-CONT-PART-SG-ACC	OBJ.PL-strike-FUT-SS.CONS	OBJ.PL-strike-PART-NOM.SG

he-ykwec-an-wa·-ʔa·-la	he-xʔepa-t
REFL-put.on.round.object-OBV-DEF-NOM.SG	REFL-slip.off-SS.CONS

wa·-na-k-laknoʔo	cʔa·px-an-ʔa·yay-ʔa·-yʔik.
fall-ABL-PART-EVID	prepare.bed-GER-under-DEF-ALL

ʔe·-kwa	tax-ko-kos-ʔe-k-laknoʔo
be-DS.SIM	be.quiet$_1$-RED-be.quiet$_2$-INGR-PART-EVID

40. Note the ambiguity in the negation here. In context, the meaning is 'they supposedly didn't cause her to sleep,' not 'they supposedly caused her not to sleep.'

ʔe·-ta xeyne-k-laknoʔo.
be-SS.NPURP move.away-PART-EVID

(18) hanil-wa·-ka ʔekwan-wa·=lʔen ʔok-maʔek-wa·=lʔen
wood.rat-OBV-NOM.PL dog-OBV=and hide-cat-OBV=and

nenxʔalo·sʔoʔs
we-y-maka-t "nen-xʔal-we·sʔa-we-ʔe-s," no-k-laknoʔo.
OBJ.PL-TH-cry-SS.CONS TH-find-1/2.SBJ.PL-DECL-PRES-1 say-PART-EVID

ʔeke-k-laknoʔo.
give-PART-EVID

(19) taʔane-ta ta-na-nesʔe-k-laknoʔo. cakaw-a·-yʔik
grasp-SS.NPURP move.PL-ABL-DU-PART-EVID river-DEF-ALL

xa-t-xa-nesʔe-k-laknoʔo. ʔe·-kla ʔekwan-wa·-ʔa-la
AUG-move.PL-AUG-DU-PART-EVID be-DS.NSIM dog-OBV-DEF-NOM.SG

he-ykwec-an-wa·-ʔa·-la-k komo-k-laknoʔo.
REFL-put.on.round.object-GER-OBV-DEF-SG-ACC put.in.mouth-PART-EVID

so-soya-na-nesʔe-k-laknoʔo ca·csok-a·-yʔik.
RED-swim-ABL-DU-PART-EVID middle-DEF-ALL

ʔe·-kwa ʔekwan-wa·-ʔa·-la
be-DS.SIM dog-OBV-DEF-NOM.SG

nes-laxke-t he-ykwec-an-wa·-ʔa·-la
CAUS-clear.throat-SS.CONS REFL-put.on.round.object-GER-OBV-DEF-NOM.SG

ne-lʔaya-k-laknoʔo. ʔe·-ta ta-yxe-na-nesʔe-k-laknoʔo
TH-spit.out-PART-EVID be-SS.NPURP move.PL-across-ABL-DU-PART-EVID

ʔe·-ta he·-sok-yo·-nesʔe-k-laknoʔo.
be-SS.NPURP REFL-quarrel-INGR-DU-PART-EVID

(20) ʔe·-kwa ka·nos-la nes-walʔ-an-la-k
be-DS.SIM Mexican-NOM.SG CAUS-fish-GER-SG-ACC

ʔey-kan-ayco-na-k-laknoʔo.　ʔe·-kla　"xa-t-xa-t
CAUS-throw-across-ABL-PART-EVID　be-DS.NSIM　AUG-move.PL-AUG-SS.CONS

yakew-ʔan-ʔa·-la-k　hesʔeke-t　yaxa-ta
make-GER-DEF-SG-ACC (='guts')　ask-SS.CONS　eat-SS.NPURP

ta-na-ce-k-ce,"　no-k-laknoʔo.　ʔe·-kla　"ʔey-e-w,"
move.PL-ABL-1-PART-RES　say-PART-EVID　be-DS.NSIM　be-EP-IMP

no-k-laknoʔo.　ʔekwan-wa·-ʔa·-la　xile-k-laknoʔo.
say-PART-EVID　dog-OBV-DEF-NOM.SG　cut.open-PART-EVID

ʔe·-l-ʔok　he-ykwec-an-wa·-ʔa·-la　ʔasoy-ʔa·-yʔik
be-3-when　REFL-put.on.round.object-GER-OBV-DEF-NOM.SG　belly-DEF-ALL

he-cne·la-k-laknoʔo　lak.　taʔane-ta　ta-na-[n]esʔe-k-laknoʔo.
REFL-lie-PART-EVID　3SGACC　grasp-SS.NPURP　move.PL-ABL-DU-PART-EVID

xa-t-xa-nesʔe-k-laknoʔo　ʔe·-t　ʔeke-nesʔe-k-laknoʔo.
AUG-move.PL-AUG-DU-PART-EVID　be-SS.CONS　give-DU-PART-EVID

(21)　ʔe·-kla　ka·nos-kokon-wa·-ʔa·-la　"taxso·-l-ʔok
be-DS.NSIM　Mexican-chief-OBV-DEF-NOM.SG　be.dawn-3-when

na·hewo·sʔew
yanʔa·nwan-pax　na·hewa-we·sʔe-w　ʔe·-ta　samox-a·tak
iron-just　build.house-1/2.SBJ.PL-IMP　be-SS.NPURP　red-very

neska·lo·sʔew
nes-ka·la-we·sʔe-w,"　no-k-laknoʔo.　ʔe·-kla
CAUS-be.hot-1/2.SBJ.PL-IMP　say-PART-EVID　be-DS.NSIM

taxso-·kwa　yanʔa·nwan-pax　na·ho·-ta
be.dawn-when　iron-just　build.house-SS.NPURP

ke·sxaya-·kwa　samox-a·tak　nes-ka·le-k-laknoʔo.
be.evening-when　red-very　CAUS-be.hot-PART-EVID

ʔe·-ta “ka·nos-e·xatok-eʔe·-la-k ʔe·-xa-t-xa-t
be-SS.NPURP Mexican-poor-that-SG-ACC CAUS-AUG-move.PL-AUG-SS.CONS

kan-akxo-n-o·sʔe-w. ha-mʔam-to·x-a·tew-e·l,”
throw-across-CONT-1/2.SBJ.PL-IMP TH-burn-finish-FUT-JUSS

no-k-laknoʔo. ʔe·-kla ka·nos-wa·-ʔa·-la-k
say-PART-EVID be-DS.NSIM Mexican-OBV-DEF-SG-ACC

he·xatok-wa·-ʔa·-la-k ʔe·-xa-t-xa-t
poor-OBV-DEF-SG-ACC CAUS-AUG-move.PL-AUG-SS.CONS

kan-akxo-na-k-laknoʔo. ʔe·-ta na·ʔe·-k-laknoʔo.
throw-across-ABL-PART-EVID be-SS.NPURP leave-PART-EVID

(22) taxso·-l-ʔok na·ho·-n-yanʔa·nwan-pax-wa·-ʔa·-la
be.dawn-3-when build.house-GER-iron-just-OBV-DEF-NOM.SG

na·ho·-n-enoxa·-tak. taxso·-k-laknoʔo. ʔe·-kla
build.house-GER-beautiful-very be.dawn-PART-EVID be-DS.NSIM

kokon-wa·-ʔa·-la xa·-xa-t
chief-OBV-DEF-NOM.SG AUG.move.SG-AUG-SS.CONS

ya-kwlax-an-ʔa·-yʔik
TH-open.door-GER-DEF-ALL

ya-kwlaxe-ta helʔeya-kxo-na-·-l-ʔok yela-t
TH-open.door-SS.NPURP peer-inside-ABL-?-3-when sit-SS.CONS

nes-coto-na-k-laknoʔo. ka·nos-e·xatok-wa·-ʔa·-la
CAUS-draw-ABL-PART-EVID Mexican-poor-OBV-DEF-NOM.SG

kokon-kwa·low he-ykoʔo-k-laknoʔo.
chief-big REFL-become-PART-EVID

(23) “na·hew-o·sʔe-w,” no-k-laknoʔo he·xatok-wa·-ʔa·-la.
build.house-1/2.SBJ.PL-IMP say-PART-EVID poor-OBV-DEF-NOM.SG

“yanʔa·nwan-pax,” no-k-laknoʔo. na·ho·-ta
iron-just say-PART-EVID build.house-SS.NPURP

naxce-k-laknoʔo. “samox-a·tak ka·la-·kwa
build.fire-PART-EVID red-very be.hot-when

ka·nos-kokon-wa·-ʔa·-la-k	kana-kxo-n-o·sʔe-w,"	no-k-laknoʔo.
Mexican-chief-OBV-DEF-SG-ACC	throw-in-CONT-1/2.SBJ.PL-IMP	say-PART-EVID

kana-kxo-na-n-laknoʔo.	ʔe·-kla	kokon-kwa·lo-wa·-ʔa·-la
throw-in-ABL-PART-EVID	be-DS.NSIM	chief-big-OBV-DEF-NOM.SG

ha-mʔam-to·xa-k-laknoʔo.	ʔe·kla	ka·nos-e·xatok-wa·-ʔa·-la
TH-burn-finish-PART-EVID	be-DS.NSIM	Mexican-poor-OBV-DEF-NOM.SG

ka·nos-kokon-kwa·lo-wa·-lʔan	ʔahan-ʔa·-la-k	ta·ʔe·-k-laknoʔo.
Mexican-chief-big-OBV-GEN	daughter-DEF-SG-ACC	grasp-PART-EVID (='marry')

A Poor Mexican and His Chief: Free English Translation

[1] A Mexican chief was living with his daughter. He was making a poor Mexican do all kinds of things. [2] The Mexican chief said to him: "Tomorrow off in that direction there will be big wolves with red fur. Go off that way, catch them, and shear off their fur." So the poor guy said: "All right." [3] In the morning, the chief made him get on a very poor and lame horse. He gave him a knife and then took the horse and mounted it and went down to the river, sat next to the river, and was weeping. [4] Then an all-white horse came up and said: "Why are you crying?" So he said: "My chief has made me catch big red wolves." Then the horse that was white all over said: "All right, ride me." [5] So he mounted the horse that was white all over and went off. There were big wolves near where they were and as he left the wolves chased him. He made [the horse] run to the prairie and threw away a mirror, [making] the wolves fall down. So the poor Mexican cut off the pelts of the wolves, gathered them together, and went off. [6] Then he got back to where he had left the horse and caught the lean horse. So the horse that was white all over went down to the water and the poor Mexican went away. [7] Then he got back [home] and gave [the pelts to the chief], and [the chief] said: "How exactly did you shear [the pelts from the wolves]?" So the poor Mexican said: "I just caught the wolves and was shearing them." [8] Then the Mexican chief said: "All right, there's [a field of] grass that's been frighteningly sharp. Tomorrow anyone cutting a swath through it four times would be able to marry this daughter of mine." [9] So, when dawn broke, the Mexican chief made the poor Mexican mount the poor horse; he also made him take his sword. He grabbed it and went down to the river where he sat down and wept. [10] So the horse that was white all over came up and said: "What is it?" So he said: "That frighteningly sharp grass is

supposed to be cut down." So [the horse] said: "All right, ride me." So he mounted the one who was all white. [11] Many Mexicans had gathered together and the Mexicans had mounted good horses and were making the horses run and chopping down [the grass] over and over, but when they did it, the grass was slashing their horses to death. [12] So the poor Mexican also made his horse run and the two of them went along chopping [the grass], and four times he cut a swath right through it and then he went away. [13] So he went back, and the chief said: "Which one won?!" The poor Mexican said: "I did it!" and [the chief] said: "All right." [14] At that point, the daughter said: "I've lost my ring!" and he said: "Go look for it." So she said: "All right." [15] She made a cat and a dog go look for it and so the two of them left. They arrived at the big river and the dog said: "Are we going across? It's not on this side." Both of them swam and swam off to the other side—they swam and swam going along and the two went off. [16] A bunch of mice met the dog and said: "What are you two doing wandering around?" So the dog said: "We two are looking for a ring." Then [a mouse] said: "I'm going to look for it at night—I've seen that ring." [17] So night fell and one girl was wearing that very ring while she was sleeping. But the mice would not let her sleep, and, as such, she was about to hit them, but in hitting them the ring slipped off [her finger] and fell under the bed. When it did, they all hushed and went away. [18] The mice cried out to the dog and cat: "We've found it!" and they gave it to [the dog and cat]. [19] They grabbed it and both left. They went to the river, and the dog put the ring in his mouth. They swam and swam to the middle [of the river], and the dog coughed and spit out the ring [from his mouth]. So they went across and got into a fight. [20] As they did, a Mexican caught a fish, and they said: "Let's go over there and ask for some guts to eat." "Sure thing," he said. The dog cut [the fish's] belly open, and the ring was lying inside there. He grabbed it, and they both went off back [to the poor Mexican] and gave it to him. [21] So the Mexican chief said: "Tomorrow y'all build a house made of iron and make it so hot it's red." So the next day, they built a house made of iron and when evening came they made it so hot it was red. [The Mexican chief] said: "Take that poor Mexican and throw him in and burn him right up." So they took the poor Mexican and threw him in and left him there. [22] In the morning, the house made all of iron was a very beautiful house. The sun rose and so the chief went to the door, opened it, and when he looked inside, the poor Mexican was sitting there writing! He had become a big chief. [23] "Build a house," the poor guy said, "one all of iron." So they built a house and lit a fire. "When it gets red hot, throw the Mexican chief inside." They threw him in, and the Mexican chief burned right up, and the poor Mexican married the Mexican chief's daughter.*

Part III

Tonkawa Texts

Old Stories

20. The Man Who Married a Bear

(1)

Tickanwa·tic-ka	ʔaw-ka-k	ta·kona-na·ʔe·-k-laknoʔo.
Tonkawa-NOM.PL	deer-PL-ACC	look.for-move.en.masse-PART-EVID

hetwan-ʔax[1]	ʔe·-ta	kokon-ʔa·-la	we·ʔis-pax
several-DEF	be-SS.NPURP	chief-DEF-NOM.SG	one-just

ye·la-k-laknoʔo.	hetwan-pax	he-cne-no-n-laknoʔo.
sit-PART-EVID	several-just	REFL-lie-CONT-PART-EVID

ʔe·-kwa	kokon-ʔa·-la	no-k-laknoʔo.
be-DS.SIM	chief-DEF-NOM.SG	say-PART-EVID

		ya·lo·no·sʔew	
"ʔaw-ka-k	ha·ʔas	ya·lo·na-we·sʔe-w	ʔa·ʔa
deer-PL-ACC	many	kill-1/2.SBJ.PL-IMP	and

yakewʔo·sʔew		
yakewʔa-we·sʔe-w.	ʔ-o·sʔe·-yen	na·ʔe·-no-n
make.ready-1/2.SBJ.PL-IMP	do-1/2.SBJ.PL-2.PL	move.en.masse-CONT-PART

he-ce-co·-n	yacox-ʔan-eʔe·-k."
REFL-RED-back-PART	camp-GER-this-ACC

(2)

ʔaw-e·-ka-k	ha·ʔas	ya·lo·na-no-n-laknoʔo.	ʔe·-l-ʔok
deer-that-PL-ACC	many	kill-CONT-PART-EVID	do-3-though

we·ʔis-pax-la	ya·lo·n-ape-no-k-laknoʔo	hecu·-ʔax-e·-ka-k.
one-just-NOM.SG	kill-NEG-CONT-PART-EVID	what-ever-that-PL-ACC

ʔe·-no-k-la	kokon-ʔa·-la	no-k-laknoʔo	"holaw-ʔa·-la-k
be-CONT-PART-NOM.SG	chief-DEF-NOM.SG	say-PART-EVID	last-DEF-SG-ACC

ta·kona-no-n	ʔaw-ka-k	taxas-wa·-tak."	ʔe·-kla	we·ʔis
look.for-CONT-PART	deer-PL-ACC	be.dawn-OBV-very	be-DS.NSIM	one

1. *hetwanʔax* and *hetwanpax* both derive from *hetwan* 'how many?' with the added definite suffix eliminating the question interpretation.

ha·ʔako·n-osas-la man-young-NOM.SG he-ta-txan-ape-no-k-laknoʔo REFL-RED-speak-NEG-CONT-PART-EVID ʔe·-ta be-SS.NPURP

ta·key-ʔa·-la-k head-DEF-SG-ACC he-kaya-k-laknoʔo REFL-bend-PART-EVID ʔe·-ta be-SS.NPURP yela-no-k-laknoʔo. sit-CONT-PART-EVID

(3) ʔe·-kla be-DS.NSIM kokona-wa·-ʔa·-la chief-OBV-DEF-NOM.SG "hecu· what ʔe-ye·[l]kwaʔ" be-Q

no-k-laknoʔo. say-PART-EVID ʔe·kla be-DS.NSIM ha·ʔako·n-osas-wa·-ʔa·-la man-young-OBV-DEF-NOM.SG "sa·ya 1.SG.NOM

k-e·sa-n-ap-a·to-k-coʔ," 1.OBJ-point-ABL-NEG-FUT-PART-RES (='be able to go off that way') no-k-laknoʔo. say-PART-EVID ʔe·kla be-DS.NSIM

kokon-wa·-ʔa·-la chief-OBV-DEF-NOM.SG "hecu· what ʔe·-tʔ" be-SS.CONS

no-k-laknoʔo. say-PART-EVID ʔe·kla be-DS.NSIM ha·ʔako·n-osas-wa·-ʔa·-la man-young-OBV-DEF-NOM.SG

naxackanwoʔo·ʔ
"naxac-kan-we-we-ʔe·-ʔ," visit.friend-ASSOC-INGR-DECL-PAST-1 no-k-laknoʔo. say-PART-EVID ʔe·-kla be-DS.NSIM

kokon-wa·-ʔa·-la chief-OBV-DEF-NOM.SG (='marry') "hecu·-la-k what-SG-ACC ta·ʔe·noʔ
ta·ʔe·-no-we-ʔeʔ" grasp-CONT-DECL-PAST

no-k-laknoʔo. say-PART-EVID ʔe·-kla be-DS.NSIM

ha·ʔako·n-osas-wa·-ʔa·-la man-young-OBV-DEF-NOM.SG "ne-ncop-an-la-k TH-be.hurt-GER-SG-ACC (='bear') ta·ʔoʔo·ʔ
ta·ʔe-we-ʔe·-ʔ," grasp-INGR-PAST-1

no-k-laknoʔo. say-PART-EVID

(4) ʔe·-kla | kokon-wa·-ʔa·-la | "heheyʔ," | no-k-laknoʔo
be-DS.NSIM | chief-OBV-DEF-NOM.SG | okay | say-PART-EVID

"na·ʔe·-no-k | yacox-ʔan-e·ʔe·-k | xa-yan-ʔok | we-pako·-s-a·haʔa
go-CONT-PART | camp-GER-that-ACC | AUG-go-when | OBJ.PL-tell-1-INTENT

wenkewaneka·lak | ʔo·sʔe·sʔok
we-nekewa-ne-k-a·-la-k. | ʔe-we·sʔe·-s-ʔok | losos
OBJ.PL-be.kin-2-PART-DEF-SG-ACC | do-1/2.SBJ.PL-1-when | all

ha-txes-a·to-nwaʔa-ne-k," | no-k-laknoʔo.
TH-know-FUT-DEON-2-PART | say-PART-EVID

ʔe·-kla | kokon-wa·-ʔa·-la | "holawʔ-a·-la-k | ta·kona-no-n
be-DS.NSIM | chief-OBV-DEF-NOM.SG | last-DEF-SG-ACC | look.for-CONT-GER

ʔaw-ka-k | ʔe·-ta | ho·s-taxso·-n | na·ʔe·-no-n,"
deer-PL-ACC | be-SS.NPURP | early-be.dawn-GER | leave-CONT-GER

no-k-laknoʔo. | ʔe·-ta | ha·ʔako·n-osas-wa·-ʔa·-la
say-PART-EVID | be-SS.NPURP | man-young-OBV-DEF-NOM.SG

ma·ka-no-k-laknoʔo.
weep-CONT-PART-EVID

(5) ʔe·-kwa | o·ʔa-ʔa·-la-k | he-co-cxa·-yo·-k-laknoʔo.
be-DS.SIM | night-DEF-SG-ACC | REFL-RED-sleep-INGR-PART-EVID

ho·s-taxso-n | ha-co-cxo-k-laknoʔo | ʔe·-t
early-be.dawn-GER | TH-RED-wake.up-PART-EVID | be-SS.CONS

he-yax-yaxa-ta | ʔaw-ka-k
REFL-RED-eat-SS.NPURP | deer-PL-ACC

ta·kona-na·ʔe·-k-laknoʔo. | ʔe·-t
look.for-leave-PART-EVID | be-SS.CONS

ke·sxa-ya-·kwa | yate-k-laknoʔo | hawna·-ta-n-ʔa·-yʔik.
be.evening-INGR-when | return.PL-PART-EVID | move.camp-CIS-GER-DEF-ADDESS

ʔe·-k-latoy | ha·ʔako·n-osas-wa·-ʔa·-la | xwe·yʔik-a·tak
be-PART-but | man-young-OBV-DEF-NOM.SG | last-very

ha·-xey-ta-k-laknoʔo.
move.SG-LOC-CIS-PART-EVID

(6) ʔe·-kla kokon-wa·-ʔa·-la "yaxa-kaʔʔ" no-k-laknoʔo.
be-DS.NSIM chief-OBV-DEF-NOM.SG eat-2 say-PART-EVID

ʔe·-kla "he·ʔ," no-k-laknoʔo. ʔe·-kla kokon-wa·-ʔa·-la
be-DS.NSIM yes say-PART-EVID be-DS.NSIM chief-OBV-DEF-NOM.SG

"taxso·-kwa naʔe·-no-n," no-k-laknoʔo. ʔe·-kla
be.dawn-DS.SIM go.away-CONT-GER say-PART-EVID be-DS.NSIM

ha·ʔako·n-osas-wa·-ʔa·-la ma·ka-no-k-laknoʔo ʔe·-ta
man-young-OBV-DEF-NOM.SG weep-CONT-PART-EVID be-SS.NPURP

"sa·ya k-e·sa-n-ap-a·to-nwa-ʔ," no-k-laknoʔo.
1.SG.NOM 1.OBJ-point-ABL-NEG-FUT-DEON-DEON3 say-PART-EVID

ʔe·kla kokon-wa·-ʔa·-la "hehe·ʔ henox-coʔ,"
be-DS.NSIM chief-OBV-DEF-NOM.SG yes good-RES

no-k-laknoʔo. ʔe·-ta cane-ta naʔe·-k-laknoʔo
say-PART-EVID be-SS.NPURP leave-SS.NPURP go.away-PART-EVID

yacox-ʔan-ʔa·-yʔik ʔe·-t w-e·-pake-k-laknoʔo
camp-GER-DEF-ALL be-SS.CONS OBJ.PL-REFL-tell-PART-EVID

we-nekewa-k-a·-la-k.
OBJ.PL-be.kin-PART-DEF-SG-ACC

(7) ʔe·-k-la-k ne-ncop-an-yaxoy-sila-yo·-n-ka
be-PART-SG-ACC TH-fearsome-GER-hunt-wander-INGR-GER-NOM.PL

ha·cin-ʔa·-yʔik tickan-wa·-ʔa·-la ʔe·-k-a·-yʔik
near-DEF-ALL person-OBV-DEF-NOM.SG be-PART-DEF-ALL

yaʔa-·kwa ʔekwan-ʔa·-la tekek-a·-yʔik
move.along.PL-when dog-DEF-NOM.SG bush-DEF-ALL

kox-na-ta he-n-ko-kxa-no-k-laknoʔo.
move.in-ABL-SS.NPURP REFL-TH-RED-move.in-CONT-PART-EVID

ʔe·-kla ketay-ta ta-kxo-na-nesʔe-k-laknoʔo tekek-wa·-yʔik.
be-DS.NSIM two-SS.NPURP move.PL-in-ABL-DU-PART-EVID bush-OBV-ALL

ʔe·-l-ʔok tickan-la he-ylapa-ta ʔe·kwan-ʔa·-la-k
be-3-when person-NOM.SG REFL-stand-SS.NPURP dog-DEF-SG-ACC

we-yle-no-k-laknoʔo kwe·h-es. ʔe·-l-ʔok kesʔacan-ʔa·-wʔan
OBJ.PL-throw-CONT-PART-EVID stick-INST be-3-when below.waist-DEF-ADESS

ne-ncop-an ye·la-k-laknoʔo ʔenik xokos-ʔa-wʔan tickan
TH-fearsome-GER sit-PART-EVID and waist.up-DEF-ADESS person

ye·la-k-laknoʔo lak. hecu·-ʔax ʔ-a·pe-ta
sit-PART-EVID 3SGACC what-ever do-NEG-SS.NPURP

saxwa-k-laknoʔo. ʔe·-t yacox-ʔan-ʔa·-yʔik xaya-ta
run.away-PART-EVID be-SS.CONS camp-GER-DEF-ALL arrive-SS.NPURP

h-e·-pano·-no-k-laknoʔo.
REFL-TH-tell-CONT-PART-EVID

(8) ʔe·-no-k-la-k kalak-a·-ka ne-ncop-an
be-CONT-PART-SG-ACC other-DEF-NOM.PL TH-fearsome-GER

yaxo·-k-laknoʔo. ʔe·-t ha·cin-ʔa·-yʔik
hunt-PART-EVID be-SS.CONS near-DEF-ALL

yaʔa·-kwa we·ʔis hacip-la-k
move.along.PL-when one cave-SG-ACC

nen-xʔale-k-laknoʔo. ʔe·-kla ketay-ta
TH-find-PART-EVID be-DS.NSIM two-DET

ta-kxo-na-nesʔe-k-laknoʔo hacip-wa·-yʔik.
move.PL-in-ABL-PL-PART-EVID cave-OBV-ALL

ʔe·-l-ʔok we-wxa·-yo·-n-la ketay-ta
be-3-when PL-grow.up-INGR-GER-NOM.SG two-DET

h-e·-malo·-nes-no-k-laknoʔo ʔa·yay-ʔa·-yʔik. ʔe·-kla
REFL-TH-play-DU-PART-EVID inside-DEF-ALL be-DS.NSIM

kalak-a·-la	saxʔay-la-k=wa·-lʔas	ʔey-we-ncaka-k-laknoʔo
other-DEF-NOM.SG	arrow-SG-ACC=OBV-INST	CAUS-OBJ.PL-die-PART-EVID

ne-ncop-an-we-wxa·-yo·-n-wa·-ʔa·-la-k	ʔe·-ta
TH-fearsome-GER-PL-grow.up-INGR-GER-OBV-DEF-SG-ACC	be-SS.NPURP

ne-xel-ci-cwa-ta-txil-na-k-laknoʔo.
TH-$drag_1$-RED-$drag_2$-RED-move.out-ABL-PART-EVID

(9)

ʔe·-kwa	kalak-a·-ka	"kwa·low-ʔa·-la	ye·la-k-a·we,"
be-DS.SIM	other-DEF-NOM.PL	big-DEF-NOM.SG	sit-PART-PERF

no-k-laknoʔo.	ʔe·-kla	he-ce-co·-n	ta-kxo-na-nesʔe-k-laknoʔo.
say-PART-EVID	be-DS.NSIM	REFL-RED-back-GER	move.PL-in-ABL-DU-PAR-EVID

ʔe·-l-ʔok	kaxo·-tak-a·-yʔik	ha·ʔako·n-la	yele·la-k-laknoʔo.
be-3-when	black-very-DEF-ALL	man-NOM.SG	sit.INGR-PART-EVID

ʔe·-t	ha·ʔako·n-wa·-ʔa·-la	"sa·-xwa	ke-yalo·na-nesʔe-w.
be-SS.CONS	man-OBV-DEF-NOM.SG	1.SG-also	1.OBJ-kill-DU-IMP

		ʔeywencakanesʔo·ka
tinay	ʔo·ca-sa·ken-ʔa·-la-k	ʔey-we-nacaka-nesʔe-we·-ka,"
already	child-1.SG.GEN-DEF-SG-ACC	CAUS-OBJ.PL-die-DU-DECL.PAST-2

no-k-laknoʔo.	ʔe·-kla	ketay-wa·-ʔa·-la
say-PART-EVID	be-DS.NSIM	two-OBV-DEF-NOM.SG

ya-la-lxil-na-nesʔe-k-laknoʔo.
TH-RED-scurry-ABL-DU-PART-EVID

(10)

	he·pano·noʔo		
naʔa	h-e·-pano·-no-we-ʔe	tinay-wa·-lʔas	we·ʔil
So	REFL-TH-tell-CONT-DECL-PAST	long.ago-OBV-INST	just.as

		sosko·nanoʔo·ʔ
ʔe·-no-k-laknoʔo.	no-·kwa	so-sko·na-no-we-ʔe·-ʔ
happen-CONT-PART-EVID	say-when	RED-listen-CONT-DECL-PAST-1

waʔan	wixwan-ta.	we·-tic.
just.as	small-SS.NPURP	this-like

The Man Who Married a Bear: Free English Translation

[1] Some Tonkawas went off in search of some deer. There were a few of them, and there was just one chief. Several days [had] passed when the chief announced: "Go off and kill a bunch of deer and dress them, and when y'all have done so, let's go back to the camp over there." [2] Although they were killing many deer, one of them wasn't killing anything at all. The chief said to him: "The last day for killing deer is today." But the one young man was not talking, and he hung his head low and was sitting there. [3] So the chief said: "What is going on?" The young man replied: "I won't be able to head off that way." So the chief said: "What is it?" The young man said: "I've gotten married." The chief said: "Whom did you marry?" The young man replied: "I got married to a bear." [4] So the chief said: "Okay, when we go to the camp over that way, we're going to tell your family about it. When we do, you would all know about it."[2] So the chief said: "Let's go look for the last deer and leave early in the morning." [He said that] and the young man was crying. [5] When night fell, they all fell asleep, and woke up early the next morning. They each ate and left to look for deer. Then around dusk, they came back to the camp, but the young man was the very last to return. [6] So the chief said: "Are you eating?" and [the young man] said: "Yes." So the chief said: "Let's go back in the morning." And again the young man was crying and said: "I won't be able to head off that way." So the chief said: "Yes, that's fine." Then he left and went away to the camp and told his family about it. [7] Then there were bear hunters near where the man lived; when they moved along, their dog was going in and out of the bushes. Both [of the hunters] went into those bushes, and when they did, there was a man standing there [in the bushes] throwing things at them with a stick. From the waist down, he was a bear and from the waist up he was a human. They didn't do anything and ran away and got back to the camp where they told people about it. [8] After that other people hunted bear, and as they went along they found a cave. Then both [of the bear hunters] went inside the cave and [saw that] there were two children playing in the cave. Then one of them killed them with his arrow and dragged and dragged the bear child off as he went out.[3] [9] At that moment, the other one said: "The big one's been in there!" Then when they went back in, a man was sitting in the deep dark [of the cave], and he said: "Kill me too—you've already killed my child." Then the two scurried off. [10] They've always told it like that, in the olden days just as it happened. When they spoke, I was listening as a little kid. So it goes.

2. Hoijer (1972, 76) translates this as 'they will know about it,' but the morphology of the verb is clearly second person.

3. Although there were apparently two bear-children, only one of them was dragged off and killed.

21. The Tonkawa and the Bear

(1) Tickan-wa·-ka ha·ʔako·n-osaʔas-ka na·ʔe·-k-laknoʔo.
Tonkawa-OBV-NOM.PL man-young-NOM.PL travel-PART-EVID

ʔe·-t hetwan-ʔax he-cne-no-n-laknoʔo. ʔe·-kwa
be-SS.CONS several-DEF REFL-lie-CONT-PART-EVID be-DS.SIM

hawna·te-n-laknoʔo ʔo·ʔo·-k-la. taxso·-kla
make.camp-PART-EVID be.night-PART-NOM.SG be.dawn-DS.NSIM

yaxa-ta na·ʔe·-k-laknoʔo xamʔal-ʔa·-yʔik.
eat-SS.NPURP travel-PART-EVID plain-DEF-ALL

(2) ʔe·-kwa we·ʔis ha·ʔako·n-osas-la "ʔawas-la
be-DS.SIM one man-young-NOM.SG meat-NOM.SG (='buffalo')

x-a·-na-no-kwa," no-k-laknoʔo. "ya·lo·na-t yaxa-n,"
AUG-move.SG-ABL-CONT-MIR say-PART-EVID kill-SS.CONS eat-GER

no-k-laknoʔo. ʔe·-kla losos-ʔita "we·ʔil," no-k-laknoʔo.
say-PART-EVID be-DS.NSIM all-DEM all.right say-PART-EVID

(3) ʔe·-ta ha·-na-ci-cxil-na-k-laknoʔo na·to·n-ʔa·-yʔik.
be-SS.NPURP move.SG-ABL-RED-run-ABL-PART-EVID mountain-DEF-ALL

"wa·-teca ʔe·-no-n," no-k-laknoʔo.
this-place be-CONT-PART say-PART-EVID

"ʔ-o·se·-kwa-nes ʔawas-elʔa·t-la ha-yco-ta-l-ʔok
do-1/2.SBJ.PL-when-1 meat-yonder-NOM.SG move.SG-up-CIS-3-when

ya·lo·na-no-n," no-k-laknoʔo.
kill-CONT-GER say-PART-EVID

(4) ʔe·-kwa wa·-tel ha-yco-ta-l-ʔok
be-DS.SIM this-manner move.SG-up-CIS-3-when

ne-ncop-an-e-co-cxo·-k-la ʔe·-no-k-laknoʔo.
TH-fearsome-GER-REFL-RED-fear-PART-NOM.SG be-CONT-PART-EVID

ne-ncop-an-wa·-ʔa·-la we-panʔoxo-t
TH-fearsome-GER-OBV-DEF-NOM.SG OBJ.PL-smell-SS.CONS

he-ylapa-cxo-k-laknoʔo ʔe·-ta sʔo·yxok-no-no-k-laknoʔo
REFL-stand-rise-PART-EVID be-SS.NPURP fearsome.noise-say-CONT-PART-EVID

ʔa·ʔa kala-ʔa·-yʔik ʔo·n-ʔa·-la he-ycile-no-k-laknoʔo.
and mouth-DEF-ALL blood-DEF-NOM.SG REFL-pour-CONT-PART-EVID

ʔe·-kla "he-co-cxo·-k-la ʔe·-no-ta-ʔa!"
be-DS.NSIM REFL-RED-fear-PART-NOM.SG be-CONT-CIS-INTENT

no-k-laknoʔo.
say-PART-EVID

ʔe·-kla ha·ʔako·n-osas-la he-ya-yl-an-ʔa·-la
be-DS.NSIM man-young-NOM.SG REFL-RED-move.about-GER-DEF-NOM.SG

he-toxa-k-laknoʔo.
REFL-finish-PART-EVID

(5) ʔe·-kla "taʔan-c-o·sʔe-w," no-k-laknoʔo.
be-DS.NSIM take.hold-up-1/2.SBJ.PL-IMP say-PART-EVID

ʔe·-kla ha·ʔako·n-osaʔas-ʔa·-la
be-DS.NSIM man-young-DEF-NOM.SG

sikit-ita taʔan-ce-ta saxwa-k-laknoʔo
four-DET grasp-up-SS.NPURP run.away.PL-PART-EVID

ʔe·-l-ʔok ne-ncop-an-wa·-ʔa·-la we-cn-apa-no-k-laknoʔo.
be-3-when TH-fearsome-GER-OBV-DEF-NOM.SG OBJ.PL-leave-NEG-CONT-PART-EVID

cʔawʔal nen-koxo-tana-no-k-laknoʔo.
long.way TH-pursue-run-CONT-PART-EVID

(6) ʔe·-kwa we·ʔis "cakaw-tic-eʔe·-k ta-kla-na-ta hewʔis
be-DS.SIM one river-little-that-ACC move.PL-down-ABL-SS.NPURP little.while

nots-o·sʔe-w,"	no-k-laknoʔo.
stop-1/2.SBJ.PL-IMP	say-PART-EVID

ʔe·-kla	cakaw-atic-wa·-yʔik
be-DS.NSIM	river-little-OBV-ALL

ta-kla-na-ta	notso-k-laknoʔo.	ʔe·-kwa	we·ʔis
move.PL-down-ABL-SS.NPURP	stop-PART-EVID	be-DS.SIM	one

"he-ykwec-an=ʔen	he-yxaxal-an=ʔen
REFL-put.on.round.object-GER=and	REFL-put.on.earring-GER=and

he-nenw-an=ʔen	xʔaton=ʔen	makik=en
REFL-paint.red-GER=and	blue/green=and	yellow=and

he-pay-ʔan=ʔen	hakoxw-ʔen	k-e·k-o·sʔe-w.
REFL-string.together-GER=and	short=and	1.OBJ-give-1/2.SBJ.PL-IMP

ʔe·-ta	heʔe·-k	na·to·n-eʔe·-k
be-SS.NPURP	that-ACC	mountain-that-ACC

ʔe·-ta	nots-o·sʔe-w,"	no-k-laknoʔo.
be-SS.NPURP	stop-1/2.SBJ.PL-IMP	say-PART-EVID

(7)

ʔe·-kla	na·ʔe·-kwa	ha·ʔako·n-osas-wa·-ʔa·-la
be-DS.NSIM	go.away-when	man-young-OBV-DEF-NOM.SG

ya-txw-an-samox-ʔa·-la-k	ya-txo-k-laknoʔo	ʔe·-t
TH-fill.pipe-GER-red-DEF-SG-ACC (='red pipe')	TH-fill-PART-EVID	be-SS.CONS

nepaxke-ta	nes-nepaxke-k-laknoʔo	ne-ncop-an-wa·-ʔa·-la-k.
smoke-SS.NPURP	CAUS-smoke-PART-EVID	TH-fearsome-GER-OBV-DEF-SG-ACC

ʔe·-ta	"waʔan-pax	ʔe·-ta	ke-w-cane-w
be-SS.NPURP	just.now-just	be-SS.NPURP	1.OBJ-OBJ.PL-leave-IMP

he·xatok	ʔ-o·s-no-so-k,"
poor	be-1/2.SBJ.PL-CONT-1-PART

no-k-laknoʔo.	"ʔecinʔe	we·-tic	ʔ-a·pe-w,"	no-k-laknoʔo.
say-PART-EVID	then	that-like	do-NEG-IMP	say-PART-EVID

ʔe·-ta ha-yco-na-k-laknoʔo na·to·n-wa·-yʔik.
be-SS.NPURP move.SG-up-ABL-PART-EVID mountain-OBV-ALL

(8) ʔe·-t haʔako·n-osaʔas-wa·-ʔa·-la-k "saxw-ap-o·sʔe-w,"
be-SS.CONS man-young-OBV-DEF-SG-ACC run.away-NEG-1/2.SBJ.PL-IMP

no-k-laknoʔo. ʔe·-kwa ne-ncop-an-wa·-ʔa·-la
say-PART-EVID be-DS.SIM TH-fearsome-GER-OBV-DEF-NOM.SG

cakaw-a·-yʔik ha-kla-ta-k-laknoʔo ʔe·-ta kapay
river-OBV-ALL move.SG-down-CIS-PART-EVID be-SS.NPURP nothing

ʔe·-no-k-laknoʔo. pas ʔe·-ta he-ce-co·-n
do-CONT-PART-EVID later be-SS.NPURP REFL-RED-back-GER

ha-yco-na-k-laknoʔo. ʔe·-t ha·-na-k-laknoʔo.
move.SG-up-ABL-PART-EVID be-SS.CONS move.SG-ABL-PART-EVID

ʔe·-kwa haʔako·n-osas-la
be-DS.SIM man-young-NOM.SG

he-ya-yl-ape-no-ʔ-wa·-ʔa·-la
REFL-RED-move.about-NEG-CONT-PART-OBV-DEF-NOM.SG

he-ho·-k-laknoʔo. ʔe[·]-kla haʔako·n-osas-we·ʔis
REFL-recover-PART-EVID be-DS.NSIM man-young-one

"ke-w-cane-t-aʔa," no-k-laknoʔo.
1.OBJ-OBJ.PL-leave-CIS-ASS say-PART-EVID

(9) ʔe·-ta yacox-ʔan-ʔa·-yʔik na·ʔe·-k-laknoʔo. ʔe·-t
be-SS.NPURP camp-GER-DEF-ALL go.away-PART-EVID be-SS.CONS

xaya-t h-e·-pano·-no-k-laknoʔo. we·-tic.
arrive-SS.CONS REFL-TH-recount-CONT-PART-EVID that-like

The Tonkawa and the Bear: Free English Translation

[1] Some young Tonkawa men were traveling and several days had gone by, so they made camp one night. In the morning, they ate and traveled to the plain. [2] One young man said: "A lot of buffalo are stampeding off away! Let's kill some and eat them." So they all said: "All right." [3] Then they ran off to the mountain

and [one of them] said: "Let's stay here. When we do so, when that buffalo over there comes up, let's go about killing him." [4] So when they came up that way, there was a scary bear. The bear smelled them and got up on his haunches and gave a terrible growl—blood was pouring from his mouth. So they said: "A monster is coming!" And the young man stood completely still. [5] So they said: "Grab hold of him!" Four young men grabbed hold of him and ran away, but the bear wouldn't let them go—he kept pursuing them for a long way. [6] As he did, they said: "Let's go down to the the creek and stop there for a while." So they went down to the creek and stopped there. One of them said: "Give me your rings, earrings, red paint, blue paint, yellow paint, and short beads. Then go back over that way to the mountain over there and stay put." [7] Then when they left, the young man filled his red pipe, smoked it, and then made the bear smoke it. Then he said: "Leave us poor people alone right now. Don't act like that again." Then he went up the mountain. [8] And he said to the young men: "Don't run away." As he said this, the bear came down to the river and wasn't doing anything. Later he went back up and was going off when the young man who could not move recovered. So the young man said: "He is about to leave us." [9] So they went to the camp and when they got there they told everyone about it. So it goes.

22. Two Young Men

(1) tinay-ʔa·-la-k | tickan-wa·c-e·-ka | h-e·-pano·-no-ʔ.
long.ago-DEF-SG-ACC | person-real?-this-NOM.PL (='Tonkawas') | REFL-TH-narrate-CONT-PRES

ʔe·-l-kaʔak | sosko·nanoʔo·ʔ sosko·na-no-we-ʔe·-ʔ. | tickan-a·ʔas
be-3-but | hear-CONT-DECL-PAST-1 | person-many

ʔe·-no-k-a·-lʔas.
do-CONT-PART-DEF-INST

(2) ha·ʔako·n-osaʔas-la | ketay-ta | h-e·-cʔeyʔo-nes-no-k-laknoʔo
man-young-NOM.SG | two-DET | REFL-TH-be.jealous-DU-CONT-PART-EVID

kwa·n-la-k | ʔe·-l-ʔila. | hawna-n-ʔila
woman-SG-ACC | be-3-since | move.camp-GER-while

hawna-xaya-l-ʔila | kalak-a·-la
move.camp-arrive.PL-3-while | other-DEF-NOM.SG

ya·c-xwe·l-ape-no-k-laknoʔo. | ʔe·-l-ʔok
see-fail-NEG-CONT-PART-EVID | be-3-when

hatxe[s]e-no-k-laknoʔo | kalak-wa·-ʔa·-la.
know-CONT-PART-EVID | other-OBV-DEF-NOM.SG

(3) ʔe·-no-k-la-k | kalak-a·-la | ʔekwan-esxaw
be-CONT-PART-SG-ACC | other-DEF-NOM.SG | dog-big

yaxwya·-na-k-laknoʔo. | ʔe·-kla | kalak-a·-la
move.to.fight-ABL-PART-EVID | be-DS.NSIM | other-DEF-NOM.SG

ya·ce-t | ne-ykanak-w-an | x-e·-nkwa·-na-t
see-SS.CONS | TH-in.front-be-GER | AUG-TH-run-ABL-SS.CONS

na·to·n-ʔayay-ʔa·-yʔik | he-cne-no-k-laknoʔo
mountain-foot-DEF-ALL | REFL-lie-CONT-PART-EVID

	he-ykoʔo-t
ʔawas	he-yakewa-we-ʔe-t.
meat	REFL-transform-DECL-PAST-SS.CONS
(='buffalo')	

(4)

ʔe·-kwa	ha·ʔako·n-osas-kalak-wa·-ʔa·-la	ha-yco-na-k-laknoʔo
be-DS.SIM	man-young-other-OBV-DEF-NOM.SG	move.SG-up-ABL-PART-EVID

na·to·n-cʔel-ʔa·-yʔik.	ʔe·-l-ʔok	na·to·n-ʔayay-wa·-yʔik
mountain-top-DEF-ALL	be-3-when	mountain-bottom-OBV-ALL

ʔawas-la	he-cne·la-k-laknoʔo	lak.	hewʔa·tan
meat-NOM.SG	REFL-lie-PART-EVID	3SGACC	other.side

x-e·-nkwa·-na-k-laknoʔo	ʔawas-la	he-cne-k-wa·-yʔik
AUG-REFL-run-ABL-PART-EVID	meat-NOM.SG	REFL-lie-PART-OBV-ALL

yak-a·to-t	saxʔay-la-k=wa·-ʔa·-lʔas[4]	ha·cin-ʔa·-yʔik
shoot-FUT-SS.CONS	arrow-SG-ACC-OBV-DEF-INST	near-DEF-ALL

caka-wixwan	ye·la-k-laknoʔo	lak	cʔel-ʔa·-yʔik
river-small	sit-PART-EVID	3SG	top-DEF-ALL

he-cne·la-k-laknoʔo	ʔawas-wa·-ʔa·-la	lak-a·-la-k.
REFL-lie-PART-EVID	meat-OBV-DEF-NOM.SG	3SG-DEF-SG-ACC

(5)

ha·ʔako·n-osas-wa·-ʔa·-la	yak-a·to-·kwa	cʔetxa-na-k-laknoʔo
man-young-OBV-DEF-NOM.SG	shoot-FUT-when	jump-ABL-PART-EVID

ʔe·-t	ne-nkoxo-k-laknoʔo.	ʔe·-t	he-wl-a·to-·kwa
be-SS.CONS	TH-chase-PART-EVID	be-SS.CONS	REFL-catch-FUT-when

yox-na-k-laknoʔo	ʔe·-t	he-ylap-an-ʔa·-yʔik
fly-ABL-PART-EVID	be-SS.CONS	REFL-stand-GER-DEF-ALL

xa-yela-k-laknoʔo.
AUG-stand-PART-EVID

4. Postposition indicating means or instrumentality, which governs the accusative: *saxʔay-la-**k**=wa·-ʔa·-lʔas* (arrow-SG-ACC-OBV-DEF-INST).

(6) ʔe·-kla ʔawas-wa·-ʔa·-la ʔa·yay-ʔa·-yʔik
be-DS.NSIM meat-OBV-DEF-NOM.SG under-DEF-ALL

he-kwa·a-na-ta he-ylapa-k-laknoʔo ʔe·-ta ya·ce-k-laknoʔo.
REFL-run-ABL-SS.NPURP REFL-stand-PART-EVID be-SS.NPURP see-PART-EVID

heyceso·nok
ʔe·-t "hecu·-ʔa·x-ʔa·-la-k he-yacesawa-ne-k,"[5]
be-SS.CONS what-ever-DEF-SG-ACC REFL-fear-2-PART

no-k-laknoʔo
say-PART-EVID

ʔawas-wa·-ʔa·-la. ʔe·-kla kalak-wa·-ʔa·-la "he-tec
meat-OBV-DEF-NOM.SG be-DS.NSIM other-OBV-DEF-NOM.SG what-manner

ʔ-a·n-ʔok ke-yalmet-a·to-ne-k-yeʔ?" no-k-laknoʔo.
do-ʔ-if 1.OBJ-deceive-FUT-2-PART-Q say-PART-EVID

cʔel-ʔa·-yʔik yela-no-ʔ-wa·-ʔa·-la tansa·le
top-DEF-ALL sit-CONT-PART-OBV-DEF-NOM.SG chicken.hawk

yela-k-laknoʔo.
sit-PART-EVID

(7) ʔe·-kla ʔawas-wa·-ʔa·-la ha·-n-ʔan tickan
be-DS.NSIM meat-OBV-DEF-NOM.SG move.SG-ABL-GER person

heykoʔot
he-ykewa-ʔe-t we·-lʔat ha·-na-k-laknoʔo
REFL-make-PRES-SS.CONS that-DEM move.SG-ABL-PART-EVID

ʔe·-kla kalak-wa·-ʔa·-la ha-kla-na-k-laknoʔo
be-DS.NSIM other-OBV-DEF-NOM.SG move.SG-down-ABL-PART-EVID

ʔe·ta ha·-na-k-laknoʔo tickan
be-SS.NPURP move.SG-ABL-PART-EVID person

5. The participial agreement suffix is possibly a result of vowel harmony: *ne-* is expected.

heykoʔot
he-yakewa-ʔe-t hawna·-ta-n-ʔa·-yʔik
REFL-make-PAST-SS.CONS move.camp-CIS-GER-DEF-ALL

ʔe·-t he-pa-pane-k-laknoʔo.
be-SS.CONS REFL-RED-tell-PART-EVID

(8) ʔe·-no-k-la-k hawna-no-k-laknoʔo ʔe·-t
be-CONT-PART-SG-ACC move.camp-CONT-PART-EVID be-SS.CONS

kalak-a·-yʔik hawna-xaya-k-laknoʔo cakaw-a·cin-ʔa·-yʔik.
other-DEF-ALL move.camp-arrive.PL-PART-EVID river-near-DEF-ALL

ʔe·-kla kalak-a·-la ʔawas-wa·-ʔa·-la
be-DS.NSIM other-DEF-NOM.SG meat-OBV-DEF-NOM.SG

ya·ce-no-k-laknoʔo.
look-CONT-PART-EVID

(9) ʔe·-kwa kalak tansa·le-wa·-ʔa·-la
be-DS.SIM other chicken.hawk-OBV-DEF-NOM.SG

ne-nxas-ʔan-kakn-aʔa
TH-ignite-GER-go.off.for-ASS

ha·-n-a·to-·kwa ʔawas-wa·-ʔa·-la neykanak
move.SG-ABL-FUT-when meat-OBV-DEF-NOM.SG ahead

caka-wa·-yʔik ha-kla-na-t ma·lo[l]-atak
river-OBV-ALL move.SG-down-ABL-SS.CONS plum-much (=‘persimmon’)

heykoʔoklaknoʔo
he-yakewa-ʔe-k-laknoʔo. ʔe·-kwa tansa·le-wa·-ʔa·-la
REFL-make-PAST-PART-EVID be-DS.SIM chicken.hawk-OBV-DEF-NOM.SG

ha-kla-ta-k-laknoʔo ʔe·-t ya·ce-k-laknoʔo
move.SG-down-CIS-PART-EVID be-SS.CONS see-PART-EVID

ma·lol-wa·-ʔa·-la-k ʔe·t yaxa-k-laknoʔo we·ʔis-pax.
plum-OBV-DEF-SG-ACC be-SS.CONS eat-PART-EVID one-just

(10)

ʔe·-ta	ha-yco-na-k-laknoʔo	hawna·-ta-ʔa·-yʔik
be-SS.NPURP	move.SG-up-ABL-PART-EVID	move.camp-CIS-DEF-ALL

ʔ-a·ʔa	ʔace-k-laknoʔo	cikew.
be-intent	be.sick-PART-EVID	extremely

ʔe·-t	"ʔawas-elʔa·t-la-k	xa·-xa-t	he-pake-w,"
be-SS.CONS	meat-yonder-SG-ACC	AUG.move.SG-AUG-SS.CONS	refl-TELL-IMP

no-k-laknoʔo	tansa·le-wa·-ʔa·-la.
say-PART-EVID	chicken.hawk-OBV-DEF-NOM.SG

"ʔe·-yo-ʔok	ma·tan	ʔe·-ta-h-a·tew-e·l	ʔe·t
do-2-when	quick	CAUS-CIS-move.SG-FUT-JUSS	be-SS.CONS

kayxoy-a·tew-e·l,"	no-k-laknoʔo.
cure-FUT-JUSS	say-PART-EVID

(11)

ʔe·-kla	he-pay-xwet-an-la	xa·-xa-t
be-DS.NSIM	REFL-bead-wear-GER-NOM.SG	AUG.move.SG-AUG-SS.CONS

he-pake-k-laknoʔo	ʔawas-wa·-ʔa·-la-k.	ʔe·-kla
REFL-tell-PART-EVID	meat-OBV-DEF-SG-ACC	be-DS.NSIM

ʔawas-wa·-ʔa·-la	he-tlo·-k-laknoʔo.
meat-OBV-DEF-NOM.SG	REFL-refuse-PART-EVID

"cane-n.	ʔa·cos[6]	he-hew-a·to-nwa-ʔ,"
leave-GER	be.sick.INST	RED-recover-FUT-DEON-DEON3

no-k-laknoʔo	ʔawas-wa·-ʔa·-la.	ʔe·-kla
say-PART-EVID	meat-OBV-DEF-NOM.SG	be-DS.NSIM

kwa·n-wa·-ʔa·-la
woman-OBV-DEF-NOM.SG

he-ce-co·-n	xa·-xa-k-laknoʔo	ʔe·-t
REFL-RED-back-GER	AUG.move.SG-AUG-PART-EVID	be-SS.CONS

6. An irregular form. The stem is *ʔa·ce-wa-* 'be sick'; here there is null derivation of a noun plus the instrumental *-(a)s*. By regular sound law this results in *ʔa·cos*.

hetlo·noʔ
"he-talo·-no-we-ʔe," no-k-laknoʔo.
REFL-refuse-CONT-DECL-PAST say-PART-EVID

ʔe·-kla tansa·le-wa·-ʔa·-la "hehe·ʔ," no-k-laknoʔo.
be-DS.NSIM chicken.hawk-OBV-DEF-NOM.SG all.right say-PART-EVID

"henox-coʔ," no-k-laknoʔo.
well-RES say-PART-EVID

(12) ʔe·-t ʔo·ʔo·-kwa ʔawas-wa·-ʔa·-la cikew
be-SS.CONS be.night-when meat-OBV-DEF-NOM.SG violently

ʔace-k-laknoʔo ʔe·-kwa tansa·le-wa·-ʔa·-la neykanak
be.sick-PART-EVID be-DS.SIM chicken.hawk-OBV-DEF-NOM.SG ahead

he-toxa-k-laknoʔo. ʔenik ʔawas-wa·-ʔa·-la ʔa·-xwa
REFL-finish-PART-EVID be meat-OBV-DEF-NOM.SG 3SG-also

he-toxa-k-laknoʔo. ha·c-ʔita he-toxa-nesʔe-k-laknoʔo.
REFL-finish-PART-EVID both-DET REFL-finish-DU-PART-EVID

(13) he·pano·noʔo
naʔa h-e·-pano·-no-we-ʔe tickan-wa·-ce·-ka.
SO REFL-TH-tell-CONT-DECL-PAST person-OBV-DIST-NOM.PL

sosko·nanoʔo·ʔ
ʔe·-l-kaʔak so-sko·na-no-we-ʔe·-ʔ. we·-tic.
do-3-when RED-listen-CONT-DECL-PAST.1-1 this-like

Two Young Men: Free English Translation

[1] Tonkawas have always talked about the past long ago. Whenever they did, I was listening to what many people were doing. [2] Two young men were jealous of each other because of a woman. As the camp moved about here and there and came to places far and wide, one [of the young men] kept a close eye on the other, and when he did, the other [young man] knew about it. [3] Then one of them went off to contend for horses. The other [young man] saw him go on ahead and run far off to the foot of the mountain and stay there—he had turned himself into a buffalo. [4] So the other young man went up to the top of the mountain, and, as he

did, a buffalo was lying at the foot of the mountain. He ran to the other side of the mountain to where a buffalo lay and shot at it with an arrow close to a small river. At the top that buffalo was lying there. [5] When the young man shot at him, [the buffalo] jumped up and chased him, but right as he was about to catch him, [the other young man] flew away and set down in a tree. [6] So the buffalo ran under [its branches] and stood there and looked at him. He said: "You're [someone who is] afraid of everything." So the other young man replied: "How do you think you're going to fool me?" The one sitting at the top [of the tree] was a chicken hawk. [7] So the buffalo went away and turned himself [back] into a man and went off. Then the other young man came down and, going off, turned himself into a man again and went back to the camp and told everyone about it. [8] After that, they were moving camp and came to pitch tents somewhere else near a river. Then [the man who had been a chicken hawk] was looking for buffalo. [9] So while the one who'd been a chicken hawk [really] was off looking for firewood, the [one who had been a] buffalo went down to the river and turned himself into a persimmon fruit. When he did that, the chicken hawk came down, saw the persimmon, and ate just that very one. [10] Then he went up to the camp and got violently sick. So the chicken hawk said: "Go over to that buffalo over there and tell him. When you do, let him bring him over real quick and cure him." [11] Then a young woman went over and told the buffalo, but the buffalo refused [to do it]. "Leave him; he'll get better on his own," the buffalo said. So the woman went back and said: "He refuses." So the chicken hawk said: "All right. It's okay." [12] Then at night the buffalo grew violently sick, and when this happened the chicken hawk died first, and then the buffalo also died. Both were finished off. [13] Tonkawas have always told it like that. When they did, I listened carefully. So it goes.

23. The Man Who Became a Fish

(1)

Ha·ʔako·n-osaʔas-ka	na·ʔe-k-laknoʔo	ʔe·-t	hetwan-ʔax
man-young-NOM.PL	travel-PART-EVID	be-SS.CONS	how.many-DET

he-cne-ta-na-no-laknoʔo.	ʔe·-no-k-la-k
REFL-lie.down-move.PL-ABL-CONT-PART-EVID	be-CONT-PART-SG-ACC

ke·sxaya-·kwa	hawna·-ta-k-laknoʔo
be.evening-DS.SIM	make.camp-CIS-PART-EVID

ʔe·t	he-cne-k-laknoʔo	yax-ape-ta.
be-SS.CONS	REFL-lie.down-PART-EVID	eat-NEG-SS.NPURP

ʔe·-la	taxso·-k-la	na·ʔe-k-laknoʔo
do-NOM.SG	be.dawn-PART-NOM.SG	travel-PART-EVID

ʔe·-t	ʔaw-ka-k	ya·lo·n-a·to-n-ʔok
be-SS.CONS	deer-PL-ACC	kill-FUT-CONT-if

ya·c-ape-no-n-laknoʔo.
see-NEG-CONT-PART-EVID

(2)

ʔe·-no-k-la-k	we·ʔis	tanmaslak-la-k	ya·lo·na-k-laknoʔo
be-CONT-PART-SG-ACC	one	rabbit-SG-ACC	kill-PART-EVID

ʔe·nik	kalak-la	se·nan-la-k	ya·lo·na-k-laknoʔo.	ʔe·-ta
and	other-NOM.SG	snake-SG-ACC	kill-PART-EVID	be-SS.NPURP

tanmaslak-wa·-ʔa·-la-k	ʔo·ʔo·-k-la	yaxa-no-n-laknoʔo
rabbit-OBV-DEF-SG-ACC	be.night-part-NOM.SG	eat-CONT-PART-EVID

ʔe·-t	taxso-·kwa	na·ʔe·-k-laknoʔo.	ʔe·-t
be-SS.CONS	be.dawn-when	travel-PART-EVID	be-SS.CONS

hecu·-ʔax-ʔa·-ka-k	ya·lo·n-ape-no-n-laknoʔo.
what-DET-DEF-PL-ACC	kill-NEG-CONT-PART-EVID

(3)

ʔe·-no-k-la-k	ʔecinʔe	we·ʔis	tanmaslak-la-k	ya·lo·na-k-laknoʔo
be-CONT-PART-SG-ACC	then	one	rabbit-SG-ACC	kill-PART-EVID

ʔenik we·ʔis neswalʔan-la-k ya·lo·na-k-laknoʔo. ʔe·-ta
and one fish-SG-ACC kill-PART-EVID be-SS.NPURP

ʔo·ʔo·-kwa tanmaslak-wa·-ʔa·-la-k yaxa-no-n-laknoʔo.
be.night-DS.SIM rabbit-OBV-DEF-SG-ACC eat-CONT-PART-EVID

ʔe·-kla ha·ʔako·n-osas-la tanmaslak-te·-la-k yaxa-ta
be-DS.NSIM man-young-NOM.SG rabbit-this-SG-ACC eat-SS.NPURP

"neswalʔan-eʔe·-la-k yaxa-·s-ʔok neswalʔan
fish-DIST-SG-ACC eat-1-if fish

he-ykewʔ-a·to-nwa-ʔ," no-no-k-laknoʔo. ʔe·-ta
REFL-make-FUT-DEON-DEON3 say-CONT-PART-EVID be-SS.NPURP

neswalʔan-wa·-ʔa·-la-k yaxa-ta tanmaslak-wa·-ʔa·-la-k
fish-OBV-DEF-SG-ACC eat-SS.NPURP rabbit-OBV-DEF-SG-ACC

yaxa-k-laknoʔo.
eat-PART-EVID

(4) ʔe·-ta ʔo·ʔo·-k-la naxc-an-ʔa·-yʔik
be-SS.NPURP be.night-PART-NOM.SG build.fire-GER-DEF-ALL

xa-ykac-ta-t h-e·-pano-·kwa
AUG-sit.down.PL-CIS-SS.CONS REFL-TH-narrate-DS.SIM
(='sit down in a circle')

ha·ʔako·n-osas-neswalʔan-[k-e-ykewʔ-a·to-nwaʔ]-no-no-wa·-ʔa·-la
man-young-fish-[1.OBJ-REFL-make-FUT-COND]-say-CONT-OBV-DEF-NOM.SG

"ʔa·x-ka-k xane-taʔe·-s," no-no-k-laknoʔo. ʔe·-ta
water-PL-ACC drink-grasp-1 say-CONT-PART-EVID be-SS.NPURP

caka-wixwan-ʔa·-yʔik ha-kla-na-t xane-ta
river-small-DEF-ALL move.SG-down-ABL-SS.CONS drink-SS.NPURP

ha-yco-ta-no-k-laknoʔo. ʔe·-l-kaʔak "hecu·-ʔax
move.SG-up-CIS-CONT-PART-EVID be-3-but what-DET

keʔeyapenoʔ
ke-ʔey-ape-no-we-ʔe," no-no-k-laknoʔo.
1.OBJ-be-NEG-CONT-DECL-PRES say-CONT-PART-EVID

(5)

ʔe·-ta	papasanʔe	yel-an	"ʔa·x-ka-k
be-SS.NPURP	after.a.while	sit-GER	water-PL-ACC

xane-taʔe·-s,"	no-no-k-laknoʔo	ʔe·-ta
drink-grasp-1	say-CONT-PART-EVID	be-SS.NPURP

ha-kla-no-k-laknoʔo.	cakaw-ʔa·-yʔik	ʔe·-t
move.SG-down-CONT-PART-EVID	river-DEF-ALL	be-SS.CONS

xane-ta	ha-yco-ta-no-k-laknoʔo.	ʔe·-l-kaʔak
drink-SS	move.SG-up-CIS-CONT-PART-EVID	be-3-but

ha·ʔako·n-osaʔas-wa·-ka	"to·na-mo·-ka.	hecu·-ʔax
man-young-OBV-NOM.PL	false-speak?-2	what-DET

ʔey-e·-no-k-aw,"	no-no-n-laknoʔo.
CAUS-be-PART-PERF	say-CONT-PART-EVID

		keʔeyapenoʔ	
ʔe·-l-ʔok	"hecu·-ʔax	ke-ʔey-ape-no-ʔe,"	no-no-k-laknoʔo.
be-3-when	what-DET	1.OBJ-CAUS-NEG-CONT-PAST	say-CONT-PART-EVID

(6)

ʔe·-no·-la	ʔecinʔe	"a·x-ka-k	xane-taʔe·-s,"
be-CONT-PART-NOM.SG	then	water-PL-ACC	drink-grasp-1

no·-ta	ha-kla-na-k-laknoʔo.	ʔe·-t	pas
say-PART-SS.NPURP	move.SG-down-ABL-PART-EVID	be-SS.CONS	later

kapay-ʔe·-no-k-laknoʔo.	ʔe·-l-kaʔak	ha·ʔako·n-osaʔas-wa·-ka
nothing-be-CONT-PART-EVID	be-3-but	man-young-OBV-NOM.PL

"newey!"	no-no-k-laknoʔo.	ʔe·-l-ʔok	kapay-ʔe·-no-k-laknoʔo.
come	say-CONT-PART-EVID	be-3-if	nothing-be-CONT-PART-EVID

ʔe·-no-k-la	"h-e·-cocxa·-yo·-no-n,"	no-k-laknoʔo.
be-CONT-PART-NOM.SG	REFL-TH-sleep-INGR-CONT-GER (='several go to sleep')	say-PART-EVID

ʔe·-kla	he-n-pake-k-laknoʔo.
be-DS.NSIM	REFL-TH-lie.down-PART-EVID

(7) ʔe··t taxso··k-la he-cocxo··k-la we·ʔis
be-SS.CONS be.dawn-PART-NOM.SG REFL-sleep-PART-NOM.SG one

cakaw-ʔa··yʔik ha-kla-na-k-laknoʔo. ʔe··l-ʔok
river-DEF-ALL move.SG-down-ABL-PART-EVID be-3-if

ʔa·x-naʔas-ʔa··yʔik neswalʔan-kwa·lo··tak-la he-ylapa-t
water-clear-DEF-ALL fish-big-very-NOM.SG REFL-stand-SS.CONS

taʔa··la-k te··c ʔe··no-k-laknoʔo.
tail-SG-ACC this-manner be-CONT-PART-EVID

ʔe··kla ya·ce-ta ha-yco-ta-k-laknoʔo.
be-DS.NSIM look-SS.NPURP move.SG-up-CIS-PART-EVID

ʔe··t "ya·c-o·sʔe-w. w-e··pak-a·tewa-··nʔes.
be-SS.CONS look-1/2.PL-IMP OBJ.PL-TH-tell-FUT-2.OBJ-1

cakaw-e·ʔl ha-kla-nes-ʔok
river-yon move.SG-down-DU-if

neswalʔan-kwa·lo··tak-la he-ylapa-t
fish-big-very-NOM.SG REFL-stand-SS.CONS

ʔe·noʔo
tan-ʔa··la-k te··c ʔe··no-we-ʔe," no-k-laknoʔo.
tail-DEF-NOM.SG this-manner be-CONT-DECL-PAST say-PART-EVID

(8) ʔe··kla haʔako·n-osaʔas-wa··ka ta-kla-n[a]-t [*sic*]
be-DS.NSIM man-young-OBV-NOM.PL move.PL-down-ABL-SS.CONS

ya·ce-no-n-laknoʔo neswalʔan-kwa·lo-ʔa··la-k [*sic*].
look-CONT-PART-EVID fish-big-DEF-SG-ACC

ʔe··kla neswalʔan-wa··ʔa··la "sa·ya ʔe·t neswalʔan
be-DS.NSIM fish-OBV-DEF-NOM.SG 1.SG.NOM be-SS.CONS fish

keykewoʔ
ke-yakewa-we-ʔe," no-k-laknoʔo. "hecu· ʔ-a·to··lʔa,"
1.OBJ-make-DECL-PAST say-PART-EVID what be-FUT-POT.3SG

no-k-laknoʔo. "ya-cox-ʔan-eʔe··k na·ʔe··no-k
say-PART-EVID TH-camp-GER-this-ACC travel-CONT-PART

xaya·-n-ʔok w-e·-pak-o·sʔe-w we-nkewa-se-k-a·-la-k.
arrive-3-if OBJ.PL-TH-tell-1/2.PL-IMP OBJ.PL-be.related-1.SG-DEF-SG-ΛCC

ʔ-o·sʔe-yo-ʔok sosko·n-a·to-nwaʔa-nik," no-k-laknoʔo.
do-1/2.PL-?-if hear-FUT-DEON-DEON.3.PL say-PART-EVID

(9) "k-e·-wa-wap-a·to-k-coʔ," no-k-laknoʔo neswalʔan-wa·-ʔa·-la.
1.OBJ-REFL.TH-RED-die-FUT-PART-RES say-PART-EVID fish-OBV-DEF-NOM.SG

"to·na he-tec-ʔax ʔe·-kwa ke-ya[·]c-an-tica-n-ʔok
perhaps what-manner-ever be-DS.SIM 1.OBJ-see-GER-want-3-if

yate-t ke-yac-a·to·-sʔe-ni-k-coʔ," no-k-laknoʔo.
come.PL-SS.CONS 1.OBJ-see-FUT-1/2.PL-2-PART-RES say-PART-EVID

ʔe·-kla "he·ʔ," no-no-n-laknoʔo.
be-DS.NSIM all.right say-CONT-PART-EVID

ʔe·-ta "taxas-wa·-taʔas
be-SS.NPURP sun-this

na·ʔe·ya·tewo·s-noʔs
na·ʔe·-yo-a·tewa-we·se-no-we-ʔe-s," no-no-n-laknoʔo. ʔe·-kla
go.off-INGR-FUT-1/2.PL-CONT-DECL-PRES-1 say-CONT-PART-EVID be-DS.NSIM

neswalʔan-wa·-ʔa·-la "hehe·ʔ," no-k-laknoʔo.
fish-OBV-DEF-NOM.SG all.right say-PART-EVID

(10) ʔe·-kla ya-cox-ʔan-ʔa·-yʔik na·ʔe·-k-laknoʔo.
be-DS.NSIM TH-camp-GER-DEF-ALL go.off-PART-EVID

ʔe·-t h-e·-pano-no-k-laknoʔo.
be-SS.CONS REFL-TH-narrate-CONT-PART-EVID

(11) ʔe·-no-k-la-k pas-ʔita ʔecinʔe na·xsok-na-t [*sic*]
be-CONT-PART-SG-ACC later-quite then reconnoiter-ABL-SS.CONS

neswalʔan-wa·-yʔik xaya-l-ʔok waʔan-wa·ʔal
fish-OBV-ALL come-3-if just-as.before

he-ylape·la-k-lakno?o neswal?an-wa·-?a·-la lak.
REFL-stand-PART-EVID fish-OBV-DEF-SG-NOM.SG 3SG

he-tal?o·-ta na·?e·-k-lakno?o ?e·-t
REFL-pray-SS.NPURP go.off-PART-EVID be-SS.CONS

tickan-kalak-a·-ka-k ha·?as
person-other-DEF-PL-ACC many

?ey-we-ncaka-ta ?ekwan-esxaw ?a·-l-?ok
CAUS-OBJ.PL-kill-SS.NPURP dog-big do-3-if

ha·?as we-tanxo·-k-lakno?o. ?e·-t ya-cox-?an-?a·-w?an
many OBJ.PL-capture-PART-EVID be-SS.CONS TH-camp-GER-DEF-ADESS

na·?e·-t xaya-t h-e·-pano·-no-k-lakno?o.
go.off-SS.CONS come-SS.CONS REFL-TH-narrate-CONT-PART-EVID

tickan-wa·-ce·-ka na·xsok-na-?ila neswal?an-wa·-y?ik
person-OBV-DIST-NOM.PL reconnoiter-ABL-WHEN fish-OBV-ALL

xaya-t he-tal?o·-no-n-lakno?o. ?e·-l-ka
come-SS.CONS REFL-pray-CONT-PART-EVID be-3-NOM.PL

tickan-kalak-e·-ka-k ha·?as ya·lo·na-ta
person-other-this-NOM.PL-ACC many kill-SS.NPURP

?ekwan-esxaw-e·-ka-k ha·?as we-taxo·-no-n-lakno?o.
dog-big-this-PL-ACC many OBJ.PL-capture-CONT-PART-EVID

he·pano·no?o
na?a h-e·-pano·-no-we-?e.
SO REFL-TH-narrate-CONT-DECL-PAST

The Man Who Became a Fish: Free English Translation

[1] Some young men were traveling and several days had gone by. At nightfall, they made camp and lay down and didn't eat. Then at dawn they went out, but when they were going to kill some deer, they didn't see any. [2] After that, one of them killed a rabbit and another killed a snake. Then at night they were eating the rabbit and when the sun rose they went off and killed whatever things they could. [3] After that, one of them again killed a rabbit and one of them killed a

fish. Then at night they were eating the rabbit. A young man ate the rabbit and was saying: "If I ate that fish, I would turn into a fish." So he ate the fish and also ate the rabbit. [4] Then at night they sat down around the fire and, while they talked, the young man who said he'd be turned into a fish was saying: "I feel like I need to drink water." So he went down to the small river and drank and then was coming back up. But they were saying: "What's going on with you?" [5] So after a while sitting there, he kept on saying: "I feel like I need a drink." So he went down to the river, had a drink, and was coming back up, but the young men were saying: "You're not telling the truth. What's wrong with you?" But he said: "Nothing's wrong with me." [6] He also said: "I need to drink," and he went on down. Later he still wasn't [back]. So the young men kept calling out: "Come on!" But he wasn't there. After that, they said: "Let's go to sleep," and they lay down. [7] So at dawn one of the ones who had been sleeping went down to the river, and in clear water a very big fish stood and was [flapping] his tail like this. Then he saw it and came [back] up and said: "Look, I'll tell you this, when I went down to that river over there, a huge fish stood there and was [flapping] his tail like this." [8] So the young men went down and were looking at the big fish. The fish said: "I was turned into a fish. What could it be? Go over to that camp and when you get there tell my relatives. If you do, they would hear about it." [9] So the fish said: "I am about to die. Maybe if somehow they want to see me, [tell them:] come and you may see me." So, they all said: "All right. We'll go right away." And the fish replied: "Okay." [10] So they went off to the camp, and told [his relatives] about it. [11] After that, they went to scout around [near] the fish, and when they came he was standing there just as before. They prayed, went off, and killed many other people and captured a lot of horses as they did. So they went off back toward the camp and coming into it they told all about it. When Tonkawas go out scouting, they come and pray to that fish. Those who do kill many enemies and capture a lot of horses. They've always told it like that.

24. The Young Man Who Became a Shaman

(1)

ya-cox-ʔan-a·ʔas-ita	tickan-wa·c-ka	ya-cox-ʔo·-no-k-laknoʔo.
TH-camp-GER-many-DEM	person-real?-NOM.PL	TH-camp-INGR-CONT-PART-EVID

ʔe·-no-k-la-k	ha·ʔako·n-osas-kesam-kapay-la
be-CONT-PART-SG-ACC	man-young-sense-nothing-NOM.SG

	hecocxo·penoʔo	
"hecu·-ʔax-ey-ka-k	he-co-cxo·-pe-no-we-ʔe,"	no-no-k-laknoʔo.
what-ever-?-PL-ACC	REFL-RED-fear-NEG-DECL-PAST	say-CONT-PART-EVID

ʔe·-kla	we·ʔis	ha·ʔako·n-kwa·low-la	"wa·xesʔ"
be-DS.NSIM	one	man-big-NOM.SG	truly?

no-no-k-laknoʔo.	ʔe·-kla	"heyʔ,"	no-k-laknoʔo.
say-CONT-PART-EVID	be-DS.NSIM	all.right	say-PART-EVID

(2)

ʔe·-kla	"ʔo·ʔo·-l-ʔok	cakaw-kwa·low-eʔe·-k
be-DS.NSIM	be.night-3-if	river-big-yonder-ACC

ta·-ta-kla-na·-s-ʔok	naxc-an-kwa·low
COM-move.PL-down-ABL-1-if	build.fire-GER-big

ʔe·-ta	naxc-an-a·cin-ʔa·-yʔik
make-SS.NPURP	build.fire-GER-near-DEF-ALL

he-ylap-an-ʔan	hetew-ʔanʔax	nesexwe·-l-ʔok	na·-xwa
REFL-stand-GER-GER	where-ever	shout-3-if	2.SG-also

nesexwe-w,"	no-k-laknoʔo	ha·ʔako·n-kwa·lo·-ʔa·-la.
shout-IMP	say-PART-EVID	man-big-DEF-NOM.SG

ʔe·-kla	"heyʔ,"	no-k-laknoʔo.
be-DS.NSIM	all.right	say-PART-EVID

(3)

ʔe·-ta	cakaw-ʔa·-yʔik	ta·-ta-kla-na-k-laknoʔo.
be-SS.NPURP	river-DEF-ALL	COM-move.PL-down-ABL-PART-EVID

ʔe·-kla	ha·ʔako·n-osas-wa·-ʔa·-la	kwa·lo·-tak
be-DS.NSIM	man-young-OBV-DEF-NOM.SG	big-very

naxce-ta ha·cin-ʔa·-yʔik he-ylapa-k-laknoʔo.
build.fire-SS.NPURP near-DEF-ALL REFL-stand-PART-EVID

ʔe·-kla cakawa-kla-na-ʔa·-wʔan nesexwe-k-laknoʔo.
be-DS.NSIM river-down-ABL-DEF-ADESS shout-PART-EVID

ʔe·-kla ha·ʔako·n-osas-wa·-ʔa·-la ʔa·-xwa nesexwe-k-laknoʔo.
be-DS.NSIM man-young-OBV-DEF-NOM.SG 3SG-also shout-PART-EVID

(4) ʔe·-t papasanʔe ʔe·-kwa naxc-an-ʔa·-yʔik
be-SS.CONS little.while be-DS.SIM build.fire-GER-DEF-ALL

we·-lʔat ha-txil-ta-k-laknoʔo. ʔe·-l-ʔok xalʔo·-n-ʔa·-la-k
yonder-DEM move.SG-out-CIS-PART-EVID be-3-if sharpen-GER-DEF-SG-ACC

ketay noko-ta ʔa·ʔa xalʔo·-n-wa·-ʔa·-la-k
two gather-SS.NPURP and sharpen-GER-OBV-DEF-SG-ACC

xʔelʔe-no-k-laknoʔo. ʔe·-ta ha·ʔako·n-osas-wa·-ʔa·-la-k
sharpen-CONT-PART-EVID be-SS.NPURP man-young-OBV-DEF-SG-ACC

taʔance-k-laknoʔo. ʔe·-t to-topo-k-laknoʔo. ʔe·-kla
grasp-PART-EVID be-SS.CONS RED-cut-PART-EVID be-DS.NSIM

ha·ʔako·n-kwa·lo·-wa·-ʔa·-la ya·ce-ta ha·-na-k-laknoʔo
man-big-OBV-DEF-NOM.SG look-SS.NPURP move.SG-ABL-PART-EVID

ya-cox-ʔan-ʔa·-yʔik.
TH-camp-GER-DEF-ALL

(5) taxso·-kwa ha·ʔako·n-osas-wa·-ʔa·-la xa·-xa-k-laknoʔo
be.dawn-DS.SIM man-young-OBV-DEF-NOM.SG AUG.move.SG-AUG-PART-EVID

ʔe·-t xʔaxʔayʔa-no-k-laknoʔo. ʔe·-kla
be-SS.CONS laugh-CONT-PART-EVID be-DS.NSIM

ha·ʔako·n-kwa·lo·-ʔa·-la "wa·xes co-cxo·-pe-no-ne-k-awe," [*sic*]
man-big-DEF-NOM.SG truly RED-fear-NEG-CONT-2-PART-PERF

no-k-laknoʔo.
say-PART-EVID

(6)	ʔe·-k-la-k	we·-tic	he·saxew-la-k	coxnan-we-k-laknoʔo
	be-PART-SG-ACC	that-like	giant-SG-ACC	shaman-INGR-PART-EVID

		he·pano·noʔo
ha·ʔako·n-osas-wa·-ʔa·-la.[7]	naʔa	h-e·-pano·-no-we-ʔe.
man-young-OBV-DEF-NOM.SG	SO	REFL-TH-narrate-CONT-DECL-PAST

The Young Man Who Became a Shaman: Free English Translation

[1] Tonkawas were camping out in many different tipis, and a reckless young man was going around saying: "I've never been afraid of anything." So one of the elders kept on replying: "Really?" and the [young man] said: "Yep." [2] So the elder said: "When I take you to that big river over there at night, make a big fire and stand close to the fire; if anyone shouts, you shout too." [3] So they took him down to the river and the young man built a big fire and stood next to it. Then someone shouted down toward the river, and the young man shouted likewise. [4] After a little while, he came out to the fire. He'd gathered two knives and was sharpening them. Then the young man grabbed him and cut him into little bits. The elder saw what had happened and went away. [5] At daybreak, the young man arrived and was laughing. "You're really not afraid of anything," the elder said. [6] Anyway, the young man had become a giant shaman like that. It's always been told like that.

7. Hoijer's text has *ha:ʔako:nosasw**ea**:ʔa:la*, which is probably a typographical error.

25. The Old Blind Man

(1) ha·ʔako·n-ko·sʔa-tic-la ka·x-la ta·-h-e·-pano·-n-ʔa·-la-k
man-old-aged-like-NOM.SG blind-NOM.SG COM-REFL-TH-narrate-GER-DEF-SG-ACC (='friend')

ta·-ya-cox-ʔa-no-k-laknoʔo. ʔe·-no-k-la-k tickan-a·naxok
COM-TH-camp-GER-CONT-PART-EVID be-CONT-PART-SG-ACC person-many

hawn-a·te-k-laknoʔo. ʔe·-kla tickan-a·naxok-wa·-yʔik
move.camp-there?-PART-EVID be-DS.NSIM person-many-OBV-ALL

ta·-he-tayʔo·-no-k-laknoʔo.
COM-REFL-mix.together-CONT-PART-EVID

(2) ʔe·-no-la "taxso·-l-ʔok xamʔale·-wʔan ke-ta[·]-ta-na-w,"
be-CONT-NOM.SG be.dawn-3-when plains-ADESS 1.OBJ-COM-move.PL-ABL-IMP

no-k-laknoʔo. "ta-slo·-si-k-[y]e," no-k-laknoʔo.
say-PART-EVID move.PL-wander-1-PART-Q say-PART-EVID

ʔe·-kla "heyʔ," no-k-laknoʔo.
be-DS.NSIM all.right say-PART-EVID

(3) ʔe·-t taxso·-kwa ta-na-nesʔe-k-laknoʔo xamʔal-ʔa·-yʔik.
be-SS.CONS be.dawn-when move.PL-ABL-DU-PART-EVID plains-DEF-ALL

ʔe·-kwa ka·x-wa·-ʔa·-la "xamʔal-eʔe-la cʔawʔal-yeʔ?"
be-DS.SIM blind-OBV-DEF-NOM.SG plain-that-NOM.SG far.off-Q

no-k-laknoʔo. ʔe·-kla "he·ʔ," no-k-laknoʔo.
say-PART-EVID be-DS.NSIM all.right say-PART-EVID

ʔe·-kla ka·x-wa·-ʔa·-la "cikew yancicxilenoʔo·ʔ yan-ci-cxile-no-we-ʔe·-ʔ,"
be-DS.NSIM blind-OBV-DEF-NOM.SG fast TH-RED-run-CONT-DECL-PAST.1-1

	yancicxile·sʔok		
no-k-laknoʔo.	"yan-ci-cxile·-s-ʔok	ke-yace-w,"	no-k-laknoʔo
say-PART-EVID	TH-RED-run-1-when	1.OBJ-look-IMP	say-PART-EVID

ka·x-wa·-ʔa·-la.	ʔe·-kla	"he·ʔ,"	no-k-laknoʔo
blind-OBV-DEF-NOM.SG	be-DS.NSIM	all.right	say-PART-EVID

ha·ʔako·n-osas-wa·-ʔa·-la.
man-young-OBV-DEF-NOM.SG

(4)

ʔe·-kla	ka·x-wa·-ʔa·-la	he-sanko·-n-ʔa·-la-k
be-DS.NSIM	blind-OBV-DEF-NOM.SG	REFL-dress-GER-DEF-SG-ACC

he-xʔe-xʔepa-k-laknoʔo	ʔe·ta	"we·ʔil	yan-ci-cxil-a·haʔa,"
REFL-RED-pull.out-PART-EVID	be-SS.NPURP	all.right	TH-RED-run-INTENT

no-k-laknoʔo.	ʔe·-kla	"heyʔ,"	no-k-laknoʔo
say-PART-EVID	be-DS.NSIM	all.right	say-PART-EVID

ha·ʔako·n-osas-wa·-ʔa·-la	ʔe·-ta	"we·ʔil,"	no-k-laknoʔo.
man-young-OBV-DEF-NOM.SG	be-SS.NPURP	all.right	say-PART-EVID

(5)

ʔe·-kla ka·x-wa·-ʔa·-la	yan-ci-cxile-k-laknoʔo	ʔe·-t
be-DS.NSIM blind-OBV-DEF-NOM.SG	TH-RED-run-PART-EVID	be-SS.CONS

cʔawʔal	henkwa·-na-k-laknoʔo.	ʔe·-kwa
far.off	run.off-ABL-PART-EVID	be-DS.SIM

ha·ʔako·n-osas-wa·-ʔa·-la	ne-sexwe-ta	"he-ylapa-w!"
man-young-OBV-DEF-NOM.SG	TH-shout-SS.NPURP	REFL-stand-IMP

no-no-k-laknoʔo.	"cakaw-ʔa·-yʔik	ha·cin
say-CONT-PART-EVID	river-DEF-ALL	near

ya-xasto·-ka!"	no-k-laknoʔo.	ʔe·-l-ʔok
TH-remain-2	say-PART-EVID	be-3-though

ka·x-wa·-ʔa·-la	he-ylap-ape-no-k-laknoʔo.
blind-OBV-DEF-NOM.SG	REFL-stand-NEG-CONT-PART-EVID

waʔanes-kaltey cikwo·-tak yan-ci-cxile-no-k-laknoʔo.
as.soon.as-outside (='instead of') fast-very TH-RED-run-CONT-PART-EVID

ʔe·-l-kaʔak ha·ʔako·n-osas-wa·-ʔa·-la
be-3-but man-young-OBV-DEF-NOM.SG

ne-sexwe-no-k-laknoʔo. "he-ylapa-w!" no-no-k-laknoʔo.
TH-shout-CONT-PART-EVID REFL-stand-IMP say-CONT-PART-EVID

ʔe·-kwa cakaw-ʔa·-yʔik wa·-na-k-laknoʔo.
be-DS.SIM river-DEF-ALL fall-ABL-PART-EVID

(6) ʔe·-kla ha·ʔako·n-osas-wa·-ʔa·-la ha·-na-no-k-laknoʔo.
be-DS.NSIM man-young-OBV-DEF-NOM.SG move.SG-ABL-CONT-PART-EVID

ʔe·-no-·-la cakaw-a·-yʔik xa·-xa-l-ʔok
be-CONT-PART-NOM.SG river-OBV-ALL AUG.move.SG-AUG-3-when

kilix-pax-la-k ʔa·yay-ʔa·-yʔik he-cne-t
river.bank-high-SG-ACC under-DEF-ALL REFL-lie-SS.CONS

ma·ka-no-k-laknoʔo ka·x-wa·-ʔa·-la.
weep-CONT-PART-EVID blind-OBV-DEF-NOM.SG

ʔe·-kla ha·ʔako·n-osas-wa·-ʔa·-la ha-kla-na-t
be-DS.NSIM man-young-OBV-DEF-NOM.SG move.SG-down-ABL-SS.CONS

"hecu ʔe·-kwa," no-k-laknoʔo. ʔe·-kla ka·x-wa·-ʔa·-la
what be-MIR say-PART-EVID be-when blind-OBV-DEF-NOM.SG

"waʔanes-kaltey cikwo·-tak yan-ci-cxile-w
as.soon.as-outside fast-very TH-RED-run-IMP

ke-nwe-no-·ka," no-k-laknoʔo. ʔe·-kla haʔako·n-osas-wa·-ʔa·-la
1.OBJ-tell-cont-2 say-PART-EVID be-DS.NSIM man-young-OBV-DEF-NOM.SG

"to·na-no·-n-ʔey! ne-sexwe-ta 'he-[y]lape-w!'
false-say-POT1/2-POT2 TH-shout-SS.NPURP REFL-stand-IMP

newe·noʔs
newe-·-no-we-ʔe-s," no-k-laknoʔo. "ʔe-·s-ʔok
tell-2.OBJ-CONT-DECL-PAST-1 say-PART-EVID do-1-when

waʔanes-kaltey cikwo-·tak yan-ci-cxile-no-·ka,"
as.soon.as-outside fast-very TH-RED-run-CONT-2

no-k-laknoʔo. "he-hewa-w," no-k-laknoʔo.
say-PART-EVID REFL-stop-IMP say-PART-EVID

ʔe-·kla ka·x-wa-·ʔa-·la waʔan-pax
be-DS.NSIM blind-OBV-DEF-NOM.SG as.soon.as-quite

ma·ka-k-laknoʔo. "we·ʔil," no-k-laknoʔo.
weep-PART-EVID all.right say-PART-EVID

(7) ta-·ta-yco-na-k-laknoʔo. kilix-pax-wa-·yʔik. ʔe-·ta
COM-move.PL-up-ABL-PART-EVID river.bank-high-OBV-ALL be-SS.NPURP

ta-na-nes-no-k-laknoʔo ʔe-·t ya-cox-ʔan-ʔa-·yʔik
move.PL-ABL-DU-CONT-PART-EVID be-SS.CONS TH-camp-GER-DEF-ALL

xa-t-xa-nesʔ[e]-k-laknoʔo. ta-kxo-na-t
AUG-move.PL-AUG-DU-PART-EVID move.PL-in-ABL-SS.CONS

kotok-a-·yʔik he-cne-nes-no-k-laknoʔo.
room-DEF-ALL REFL-lie-DU-CONT-PART-EVID

(8) ʔe-·kwa ha·ʔako·n-osas-wa-·lʔan mʔacxan-an-ʔa-·la
be-DS.SIM man-young-OBV-GEN like-GER-DEF-NOM.SG

sa·xal-ʔa-·yʔik he-ylapa-no-k-laknoʔo. ʔe-·kwa
opening-DEF-ALL REFL-stand-CONT-PART-EVID be-DS.SIM

ko·sʔa-tic-wa-·ʔa-·la ʔey-ne-txoʔo-no-k-laknoʔo.
aged-like-OBV-DEF-NOM.SG CAUS-TH-poke-CONT-PART-EVID

ʔe-·kla ha·ʔako·n-osas-wa-·ʔa-·la "hecu
be-DS.NSIM man-young-OBV-DEF-NOM.SG what

ʔo-·kwaʔ?" no-k-laknoʔo. ʔe-·kla
happen-MIR say-PART-EVID be-DS.NSIM

ka·x-wa·-ʔa·-la	"we·l[ʔ]a!	kwa·n-ke-la	ʔok-a·-la
blind-OBV-DEF-NOM.SG	oh.my!	woman-2.POSS-NOM.SG	hair-DEF-NOM.SG

ha·ʔas	ha·we-·-la-k!"	no-k-laknoʔo.	ʔe·-kla
much	exist.3SG-PART-SG-ACC	say-PART-EVID	be-DS.NSIM

ha·ʔako·n-osasa-wa·-ʔa·-la [*sic*]	"o·c	he-co-co·-k!"
man-young-OBV-DEF-NOM.SG	oh	REFL-RED-be.quiet-PART

no-k-laknoʔo.	"te·-l	he-ylap-a·we,"	no-k-laknoʔo.
say-PART-EVID	this-place	REFL-stand-EMPH	say-PART-EVID

(9)

			noʔs
ʔe·-kla	ko·sʔa-tic-wa·-ʔa·-la	"wa·xes	no-we-ʔe-s,"
be-DS.NSIM	aged-like-OBV-DEF-NOM.SG	truly	say-DECL-PRES-1

no-k-laknoʔo.	"ʔok-aw	hawe-·-la-k!"	no-k-laknoʔo.
say-PART-EVID	hair-EMPH	exist.3SG-PART-SG-ACC	say-PART-EVID

ʔe·-kwa	kwa·n-wa·-ʔa·-la	so-sko·na-t	xaclo·-k-laknoʔo
be-DS.SIM	woman-OBV-DEF-NOM.SG	RED-hear-SS.CONS	be.angry-PART-EVID

ʔe·-t	nes-kapa-ta	ha·-xeyne-k-laknoʔo.
be-SS.CONS	CAUS-be.closed-SS.NPURP	move.SG-far-PART-EVID

		sosko·nanoʔ
ʔe·-kla	ha·ʔako·n-osas-wa·-ʔa·-la	"so-sko·na-no-we-ʔe,"
be-DS.NSIM	man-young-OBV-DEF-NOM.SG	RED-hear-CONT-DECL-PRES

		xaclewoʔ
no-k-laknoʔo.	"ʔe·-t	xacle-wa-we-ʔe
say-PART-EVID	be-SS.CONS	be.angry-INGR-DECL-PRES

	ha·xeynoʔ	
ʔe·-t	ha·-xeyno-we-ʔe,"	no-k-laknoʔo.
be-SS.CONS	move.SG-far-DECL-PRES	say-PART-EVID

(10)

ʔe·-t	metis	he-cne-·kwa	ha·ʔako·n-la
be-SS.CONS	three	REFL-lie-when	man-NOM.SG

xa··xa-k-laknoʔo	ka·x-wa··yʔik	ʔe··t
AUG.move.SG-AUG-PART-EVID	blind-OBV-ALL	be-SS.CONS

kwa·nwenxenekela	naxackanwoʔ
"kwa·n-we-n-xen-eke-la	naxac-kan-we-ʔe,"
woman-OBJ.PL-2-2.POSS-that-NOM.SG	as.friend-possessed-INGR-PAST

		ta·ʔoʔ	
no-k-laknoʔo.	"ha·ʔako·n-kalak-la-k	ta·ʔe-we-ʔe	ʔo·ʔa-tak,"
say-PART-EVID	man-other-SG-ACC	grasp-DECL-PAST	be.night-last

no-k-laknoʔo.	ʔe··kla	ha·ʔako·n-osas-wa··ʔa··la
say-PART-EVID	be-DS.NSIM	man-young-OBV-DEF-NOM.SG

xaclo··k-laknoʔo.	"heheyʔ,"	no-k-laknoʔo.
be.angry-PART-EVID	all.right	say-PART-EVID

"ʔo·ʔo··kwa	ya·lo·n-a·haʔa	kwa·n-wa··ʔa··la-k,"	no-k-laknoʔo.
be.night-DS.SIM	kill-INTENT	woman-OBV-DEF-SG-ACC	say-PART-EVID

(11)

ʔe··t	ʔo·ʔo··k-la	xalʔo·n-ʔa··la-k
be-SS.CONS	be.night-PART-NOM.SG	knife-DEF-SG-ACC

xʔelʔe-no-k-laknoʔo	ha-kla-na-n.	ʔe··ta
sharpen-CONT-PART-EVID	move.SG-down-ABL-GER	be-SS.NPURP

ka·x-wa··ʔa··la	"na·ya	yela-ʔe-w	wa··teca,"
blind-OBV-DEF-NOM.SG	2.SG.NOM	sit.down-be-IMP	this-place

no-k-laknoʔo.	"xa··xa-t	ya·lo·n-a·haʔa
say-PART-EVID	AUG.move.SG-AUG-SS.CONS	kill-INTENT

kwa·n-wa··ʔa··la-k,"	no-k-laknoʔo.	ʔe··kla
woman-OBV-DEF-SG-ACC	say-PART-EVID	be-DS.NSIM

		tasaʔeye·s [*sic*]
ka·x-wa··ʔa··la	ma·ka-no-k-laknoʔo.	"ta-taʔey-e-··s,"[8]
blind-OBV-DEF-NOM.SG	weep-CONT-PART-EVID	COM-join-2.OBJ-1

8. This form either is a mishearing on Hoijer's part for *tayʔewa-* 'be mixed together, be a group, join' or is a historically related root related to the same.

no-k-lakno?o. ?e·-kla "we·?il," no-k-lakno?o
say-PART-EVID be-DS.NSIM okay say-PART-EVID

?e·-ta ta·-ta-na-k-lakno?o.
be-SS.CONS COM-move.PL-ABL-PART-EVID

ya-cox-?an-away-kwa·low-?a·-y?ik xa-t-xa-nes?e-k-lakno?o.
TH-camp-GER-tall-big-DEF-ALL AUG-move.PL-AUG-DU-PART-EVID

(12) ?e·-kla ha·?ako·n-osas-wa·-?a·-la he-l?eya-kxo-na-k-lakno?o.
be-DS.NSIM man-young-OBV-DEF-NOM.SG REFL-peer-in-ABL-PART-EVID

?e·-l-?ok ha·?ako·n-kalak-la-k ta·-yela-no-k-lakno?o.
be-3-when man-other-SG-ACC COM-sit-CONT-PART-EVID

?e·-kla ha·?ako·n-osas-wa·-?a·-la "wa?an-wa·ca
be-DS.NSIM man-young-OBV-DEF-NOM.SG right-there

he-ylapa-w," no-k-lakno?o. "ha-kxo-na-t
REFL-stand-IMP say-PART-EVID move.SG-in-ABL-SS.CONS

ya·lo·n-a·ha?a," no-k-lakno?o. ?e·-kla
kill-INTENT say-PART-EVID be-DS.NSIM

ka·x-wa·-?a·-la "c?ame-w," no-k-lakno?o.
blind-OBV-DEF-NOM.SG let.go-IMP say-PART-EVID

"sa·ya ya·lo·n-a·?," no-k-lakno?o. ?e·-kla
1.SG.NOM kill-INT.1 say-PART-EVID be-DS.NSIM

ha·?ako·n-osas-wa·-?a·-la "he-tec ?-a·-n-?ok
man-young-OBV-DEF-NOM.SG what-way be-POT-POT1/2-when

henox ya·ce-t ya·lo·n-a·to-y-a?a?" no-k-lakno?o.
good look-SS.CONS kill-FUT-EP-INTENT say-PART-EVID

?e·-kla ka·x-wa·-?a·-la "kwa·n-wa·-?a·-la
be-DS.NSIM blind-OBV-DEF-NOM.SG woman-OBV-DEF-NOM.SG

yela-?e·-k-a·-y?ik k-e·-pake-w. ?e·-yo-?ok ya·lo·na-·?,"
sit-do-PART-DEF-ALL 1.OBJ-REFL-tell-IMP do-2-when kill-INT.1

no-k-lakno?o. ?e·-kla ha·?ako·n-osas-wa·-?a·-la "na·kwe·?il,"
say-PART-EVID be-DS.NSIM man-young-OBV-DEF-NOM.SG go.ahead

no-k-laknoʔo. "ha-kxo-na-n-ʔok hetewʔan-ʔax
say-PART-EVID move.SG-in-ABL-PART-when how.much-ever

ʔ-a·pe-ta kotok-ca·cxok-eʔe·-k ha-kxo-na-w,"
do-NEG-SS.NPURP room-center-that-ACC move.SG-in-ABL-IMP

no-k-laknoʔo haʔako·n-osas-wa·-ʔa·-la ʔe·-kla
say-PART-EVID man-young-OBV-DEF-NOM.SG do-DS.NSIM

"heyʔ," no-k-laknoʔo.
all.right say-PART-EVID

(13) xalʔo·n-ʔa·-la-k taʔane-ta ha-kxo-na-k-laknoʔo.
knife-DEF-SG-ACC grasp-SS.NPURP move.SG-in-ABL-PART-EVID

ʔe·-t maslak-asoy-ka ʔa·x-ka-k yako-t
be-SS.CONS cow-paunch-NOM.PL water-PL-ACC fetch-SS.CONS

yatxalkanoʔowe·ticlak
ya-txalka-no-we-ʔe-we·-tic-la-k ya-pasxa-t
TH-hang-CONT-DECL-PAST-that-like-SG-ACC TH-bump-SS.CONS

ya-tsa-k-laknoʔo. ʔe·-kwa kwa·n-wa·-ʔa·-la
TH-stab-PART-EVID be-DS.SIM woman-OBV-DEF-NOM.SG

ya-cox-ʔan-xwe·yʔik-a·-wʔan yan-ci-cxila·-xeyne-k-laknoʔo.
TH-camp-GER-rear-DEF-ADESS TH-RED-run-far-PART-EVID

(14) ʔe·-kla haʔako·n-osas-wa·-ʔa·-la he-ylapa-t
be-DS.NSIM man-young-OBV-DEF-NOM.SG REFL-stand-SS.CONS

xʔaxʔayʔe-no-k-laknoʔo. ʔe·-kla ka·x-wa·-ʔa·-la "hecu·
laugh-CONT-PART-EVID be-DS.NSIM blind-OBV-DEF-NOM.SG what

ʔo·-kwaʔ," no-k-laknoʔo. ʔe·-kla "tina·-tak
be-MIR say-PART-EVID be-DS.NSIM long.ago-very

yalxilnoʔ
waʔanes ha-kxo-na·-k=en ya-laxil-na-we-ʔe,"
as.soon.as move.SG-in-ABL-PART=and TH-run-ABL-DECL-PAST

no-k-laknoʔo. ʔe·-kla ka·x-wa·-ʔa·-la "hu!
say-PART-EVID be-when blind-OBV-DEF-NOM.SG Huh,

ya·lo·noʔs
to·na-now-a·-n-ʔey ya·lo·na-we-ʔe-s," no-k-laknoʔo.
false-say-POT-POT1/2-POT2 kill-DECL-PAST-1 say-PART-EVID

ʔe·-ta xalʔo·n-ʔa·-la-k
be-SS.NPURP knife-DEF-SG-ACC

taʔane-ta "ya·ce-w! xalʔo·n-te·-la kwa·n-ʔan
grasp-SS.NPURP look-IMP knife-this-NOM.SG woman-GEN

ʔo·n-pax-coʔ," no-k-laknoʔo. ʔe·-kla
blood-quite-RES say-PART-EVID be-DS.NSIM

ha·ʔako·n-osas-wa·-ʔa·-la "to·na-no-nw-a·-n-ʔey,"
man-young-OBV-DEF-NOM.SG false-RED-say-POT-POT1/2-POT2

yalxilenoʔ
no-k-laknoʔo. "tina·-tak ya-laxile-na-we-ʔe," no-k-laknoʔo.
say-PART-EVID long.ago-very TH-run-ABL-DECL-PAST say-PART-EVID

ʔe·-ta "na·kw ʔe·-ta-w," no-k-laknoʔo. ʔe·-ta
be-SS.NPURP all.right be-CIS-IMP say-PART-EVID be-SS.NPURP

ya-cox-ʔan-ʔa·-wʔan ta·-ta-na-k-laknoʔo.
TH-camp-GER-DEF-ADESS COM-move.PL-ABL-PART-EVID

(15) ta·-xa-t-xa-k-laknoʔo ya-cox-ʔan-ʔa·-yʔik. ʔe·-kwa
COM-AUG-move.PL-AUG-PART-EVID TH-camp-GER-DEF-ALL be-DS.SIM

"taxso-·kwa yaxoya-xey-ta-k no-·kwa," no-k-laknoʔo.
be.dawn-when hunt-move.to-CIS-PART say-when say-PART-EVID

ʔe·-kla ha·ʔako·n-osas-wa·-ʔa·-la "he-tayʔo·-he·-sokyaw-a·haʔa,"
be-DS.NSIM man-young-OBV-DEF-NOM.SG REFL-mix-REFL-fight-INTENT

ʔe·-kwa h-e·-[s]okyo·-no-k-laknoʔo[9] ʔe·-kwa
be-DS.SIM REFL-TH-fight-CONT-PART-EVID be-DS.SIM

ha·ʔako·n-osas-wa·-ʔa·-la ya·lo·na-k-laknoʔo.
man-young-OBV-DEF-NOM.SG kill-PART-EVID

9. The initial consonant of the root was probably a transcription error: Hoijer's old orthography used <c> for /s/.

(16) ʔe·-kla kalak-la xa·-xa-t
be-DS.NSIM other-NOM.SG AUG.move.SG-AUG-SS.CONS

ka·x-wa·-ʔa·-la-k
blind-OBV-DEF-SG-ACC

"ta·-h-e·-pano·-na·xen-ke-la-k ya·lo·na-kwa,"
COM-REFL-TH-narrate-2.SG.GEN-2.SG-ACC kill-MIR

no-k-laknoʔo. ʔe·-kla ka·x-wa·-ʔa·-la
say-PART-EVID be-DS.NSIM blind-OBV-DEF-NOM.SG

xe-xwe-ta ha-cxo-k-laknoʔo.
RED-wail-SS.NPURP move.SG-rise-PART-EVID

"ke-ta[·]-xa-t-xa-w," no-k-laknoʔo.
1.OBJ-COM-AUG-move.PL-AUG-IMP say-PART-EVID

(17) ʔe·-kla ta·-ta-na-k-laknoʔo. h-e·-sokyo·-k-wa·-yʔik
be-DS.NSIM COM-move.PL-ABL-PART-EVID REFL-TH-fight-PART-OBV-ALL

ta·-xa-t-xa-l-ʔok haʔako·n-osas-wa·-ʔa·-la
COM-AUG-move.PL-AUG-3-when man-young-OBV-DEF-NOM.SG

he-cne·la-k-laknoʔo. ko·sʔa-tic-wa·-ʔa·-la "he-telʔ"
REFL-be.lying-PART-EVID aged-like-OBV-DEF-NOM.SG that-place

no-k-laknoʔo. ʔe·-kla "te·[l]," no-k-laknoʔo. ʔe·-kla
say-PART-EVID be-DS.NSIM there say-PART-EVID be-DS.NSIM

ko·sʔa-tic-wa·-ʔa·-la xa·-xa-t yacax-ʔa·-yʔik
aged-like-OBV-DEF-NOM.SG AUG.move.SG-AUG-SS.CONS chest-DEF-ALL

he-cn-ayco-na·-kwa ya·lo·na-k-laknoʔo. ʔe·-kwa
REFL-lie-up-ABL-when kill-PART-EVID be-DS.SIM

nonoʔo
waʔan-pax h-e·-so-sokyo·-k-laknoʔo no-no-we-ʔe.
just.as-quite REFL-TH-RED-fight-PART-EVID say-CONT-DECL-PAST

he·pano·noʔo
ʔ-a·ʔa h-e·-pano·-no-we-ʔe.
do-ASS REFL-TH-narrate-CONT-DECL-PAST

The Old Blind Man: Free English Translation

[1] An old blind man was living with his friend, and many people were encamped around there. So they went to live with all the people there. [2] Then he said: "Tomorrow take me to the plains there. Aren't we going to wander about some?" So [his friend] said: "Okay." [3] Then in the morning the two of them went off to the plains and the blind man said: "Is the plain far off?" [His friend] said: "Yep." So the blind man said: "You ran real fast. When I run, watch me." So the young man said: "Okay." [4] So the blind man took his clothes off and said: "All right, I'm going to run." [His friend] said: "Okay." [5] So the blind man broke into a run and sprinted far off, while the young man was shouting: "Stand [still]! You're close to the river." Instead, the blind man didn't stand still but was running faster. The young man kept on shouting: "Stand still!" he said. Right then [the blind man] fell into the river. [6] So the young man went off, and when he arrived at the river, the blind man was lying under a high riverbank, crying. So the young man went down and said: "What's wrong?" The blind man said: "You told me to run very fast instead." But the young man said: "That's not at all true! I told you to stand where you are, but instead you kept running faster. Cut it out." So the blind man stopped crying and said: "Let's go." [7] He took him up to the high riverbank and the two went off and arrived at their tipi. They went into the room and lay down. [8] Just then, the young man's sweetheart was standing at the entrance [to the tipi], while the old man was poking him. So the young man said: "What is it?" The blind man responded: "Oh wow, your woman has a lot of [pubic] hair!" So the young man said: "Oh shut up! She's standing right there!" [9] Then the old one said: "I'm telling the truth. She has hair there!" When the woman heard this, she got angry and closed the tent flap and left. Then the young man said: "She heard you! She's angry and left." [10] So three days went by and a man came up to the blind man and said: "That woman of yours has gotten married. She married another man last night." So the young man got angry and said: "All right, tonight I'm going to kill that woman." [11] Then at night he sharpened his knife and went down. The blind man said: "You stay seated here. I'm going to go and kill that woman." So the blind man was crying: "Let me join you." And [the young man] said: "All right." And they both went off and arrived at the big tall tipi. [12] Then the young man looked inside, and she was sitting with another man, so the young man said: "Stay right there. I'm going in to kill her." But the blind man said: "Let it go—I'll kill her." So the young man said: "How do you think you're going to see well enough to kill her?" The blind man replied: "Tell me where the woman is sitting. When you do, I'll kill her." So the young man said: "Okay. When you go in, don't

do anything [but] go straight to the center of the room." The blind man said: "Okay." [13] He grabbed a knife and went in and bumped into some cow-paunches for fetching water and stabbed them, and right then the woman ran from the back of the tipi. [14] So the young man stood there and was laughing. The blind man said: "What is it?" So [the young man] said: "She's long gone—as soon as you went in she ran away." So the blind man said: "Hah, you're lying, I killed her!" Then he took the knife and said: "Look, this knife [is covered in] the woman's blood." So the young man said: "No, *you*'re lying—she ran away long ago. Come now." And they went together toward the tipi. [15] So they arrived at the camp and someone said: "Tomorrow they say a bunch of people are coming to fight." So the young man said: "I'm going to join in the fight," and so he joined in the fight, but when he did that young man got killed. [16] So someone else came up to the blind man and said: "They killed your friend." The blind man cried and got up and said: "Take me over there." [17] So they took him over there to where the fight had taken place, and when they arrived the young man['s body] was lying there. The old man said: "Where is he?" Someone said: "Over there." So the old man went over and as he lay on top of [the young man's] chest they killed him. Right then all the fighting stopped, they have always been saying. It's always been told like that.

26. The Two Young Tonkawas and the Osage

(1) Tickan-wa·c-ka ya-cox-ʔan-a·xok-a·-yʔik ya-coxʔa-no-k-laknoʔo.
person-real-NOM.PL TH-camp-GER-large-DEF-ALL TH-camp-CONT-PART-EVID

ʔe·-no-k-la-k tickan-wa·c-a·ʔako·n-osas-la=ʔen
be-CONT-PAR-SG-ACC person-real-man-young-NOM.SG=and

he-pay-xwet-an-osas-la=ʔen h-aʔatna-yo·-nes-no-k-laknoʔo.
REFL-bead-wear-GER-young-NOM.SG=and RECIP-love-RECIP-DU-CONT-PART-EVID

ta·xa-n ʔenik ʔe·-no-·-la nantoʔon-ʔa·-wʔan
be.hot-GER and be-CONT-PART-NOM.SG mountain-DEF-ADESS

ta·-ta-na-k-laknoʔo he-pay-xwet-an-osas-wa·-ʔa·-la-k.
COM-move.PL-ABL-PART-EVID REFL-bead-wear-GER-young-OBV-DEF-SG-ACC

ʔe·-t cʔawʔal ta·-ta-na-k-laknoʔo
be-SS.CONS far.away COM-move.PL-ABL-PART-EVID

ʔe·-t na·to·n-cʔel-ʔa·-yʔik yela-nes-no-k-laknoʔo ʔe·-ta
be-SS.CONS mountain-top-DEF-ALL sit-DU-CONT-PART-EVID be-SS.NPURP

h-e·malo·-nes-no-k-laknoʔo. ʔe·-no-·-la
REFL-fool.around-DU-CONT-PART-EVID do-CONT-PART-NOM.SG

he-cne-nes-no-k-laknoʔo ʔe·-no-·-la
REFL-lie-DU-CONT-PART-EVID be-CONT-PART-NOM.SG

cocxa·-yo·-nesʔe-k-laknoʔo.
sleep-INGR-DU-PART-EVID

(2) ʔe·-t pas ʔe·-kwa ha·ʔako·n-osas-wa·-ʔa·-la-k
be-SS.CONS little.time be-DS.SIM man-young-OBV-DEF-SG-ACC

yakw-an-ʔa·-yʔik ʔey-ne-txoʔo-no-k-laknoʔo. ʔe·-kla
kick-GER-DEF-ALL (='legs') CAUS-TH-prod-CONT-PART-EVID be-DS.NSIM

ha·ʔko·n-osas-wa·-ʔa·-la	ʔanco·-k-laknoʔo.
man-young-OBV-DEF-NOM.SG	be.awake-PART-EVID

ʔe·-t	ya·ce-na-l-ʔok	tickan-kalak-a
be-SS.CONS	look-ABL-3-when	person-other-DEF

he-ntose·la-k-laknoʔo	he-cne-nesʔe-k-wa·-yʔik	kwa·n-wa·-ʔa·-la-k
REFL-stand-PART-EVID	REFL-lie-DU-PART-OBV-ALL	woman-OBV-DEF-SG-ACC

"ʔanco-w,"	no-k-laknoʔo.	"tickan-kalak-a
be.awake-IMP	say-PART-EVID	person-other-DEF

ke-w-ʔey-we-yce-k-a·we,"	no-k-laknoʔo.
1.OBJ-OBJ.PL-CAUS-OBJ.PL-capture-PART-RES	say-PART-EVID

(3)

ʔe·-kla	he-pay-xwet-an-osas-wa·-ʔa·-la	ʔanco·-kwa
be-DS.NSIM	REFL-bead-wear-GER-young-OBV-DEF-NOM.SG	be.awake-DS.SIM

he·topow-a·-ka	ha·ʔako·n-osas-wa·-ʔa·-la-k	he-wle-k-laknoʔo
Osage-DEF-NOM.PL	man-young-OBV-DEF-SG-ACC	REFL-grasp-PART-EVID

ʔe·-t	ya-wye-k-laknoʔo	he·tya·-n-ʔa·-l=ʔen
be-SS.CONS	TH-bind-PART-EVID	reach-GER-DEF-EP=and

yakw-an-ʔa·-l=ʔen.	ʔe·-ta	ʔe·-we-ta-na-k-laknoʔo.
kick-GER-DEF-EP=and	be-SS.NPURP	CAUS-OBJ.PL-move.PL-ABL-PART-EVID

(4)

ʔe·-t	caka-wixw-an-ʔa·-yʔik	hawna·te-k-laknoʔo.
be-SS.CONS	river-small-GER-DEF-ALL	make.camp-PART-EVID

ʔe·-t	he-cne-ta	taxso·-kwa
be-SS.CONS	REFL-lie-SS.NPURP	be.dawn-DS.SIM

tickan-wa·c-a·ʔako·n-osas-wa·-ʔa·-la-k	he·topow-es
person-real-man-young-OBV-DEF-SG-ACC	Osage-INST

picne-k-laknoʔo	takey-ʔa·-la-k.	ʔe·-ta	na·ʔe·-t
cut-PART-EVID	head-DEF-SG-ACC	be-SS.NPURP	go.away-SS.CONS

neskaltey-ʔa·-yʔik hawnate-t he-cne-ta taxso·-kwa
other.side-DEF-ALL make.camp-SS.CONS REFL-lie-SS.NPURP be.dawn-DS.SIM

he-pay-xwet-an-osas-wa·-ʔa·-la
REFL-bead-wear-GER-young-OBV-DEF-NOM.SG

ha·ʔako·n-osas-wa·-ʔa·-la-k "hecu·-ʔax-e·-ka-k
man-young-OBV-DEF-SG-ACC what-ever-this?-PL-ACC

hatxesapenoynoʔ
ha-txes-ape-no-we-ʔei-noʔ?" no-k-laknoʔo. ʔe·-kla
TH-know-NEG-CONT-DECL-PAST.2-PAST2 say-PART-EVID be-DS.NSIM

"ha·ʔako·n-osas-tickan-wa·c-e·-ka
man-young-person-real-that-NOM.PL

ʔe·noʔo
ha-txes-an-pax ʔe·-no-we-ʔe, hecu·-ʔax-e·-ka-k," no-k-laknoʔo.
TH-know-GER-quite do-CONT-DECL-PAST what-ever-that-PL-ACC say-PART-EVID

(5) ʔe·-kla ha·ʔako·n-osas-wa·-ʔa·-la "hehe·ʔ," no-k-laknoʔo.
be-DS.NSIM man-young-OBV-DEF-NOM.SG all.right say-PART-EVID

"w-e·-pake-w," no-k-laknoʔo. "ʻʔawas-a·ʔako·n-saxʔo·-n-ka-k
OBJ.PL-REFL-tell-IMP say-PART-EVID meat-man-be.young-GER-PL-ACC

ta·kono·sʔew
ta·kona-we·sʔe-w' no-w," no-k-laknoʔo.
look.for-1/2.SBJ.PL-IMP say-IMP say-PART-EVID

(6) ʔe·-kla he-pay-xwet-an-osas-wa·-ʔa·-la he·topow-kokon-ʔa·-la-k
be-DS.NSIM REFL-bead-wear-GER-young-OBV-DEF-NOM.SG Osage-chief-DEF-SG-ACC

ta·kono·sʔew
he-pake-k-laknoʔo. "ʻawas-a·ʔako·n-saxʔo·-n-ka-k ta·kon-we·sʔe-w,'
REFL-tell-PART-EVID meat-man-be.young-GER-PL-ACC look.for-1/2.SBJ.PL-IMP

nonaʔa
no-no-aʔa," no-k-laknoʔo. ʔe·-kla he·topow-ʔa·-la
say-CONT-ASS say-PART-EVID be-DS.NSIM Osage-DEF-NOM.SG

ʔekwan-esxaw-ʔa·-la-k w-e·s-yacxe-ta na·ʔe·-k-laknoʔo
dog-big-DEF-SG-ACC OBJ.PL-CAUS-be.mounted-SS.NPURP go.away-PART-EVID

ta·kon-a·to-t ʔawas-wa·-ʔa·-la-k. ʔe·-t
look.for-FUT-SS.CONS meat-OBV-DEF-SG-ACC be-SS.CONS

ʔawas-a·ʔako·n-saxʔo·-n-la-k ya·lo·na-k-laknoʔo he·topow-ʔa·-ka
meat-man-be.young-GER-SG-ACC kill-PART-EVID Osage-DEF-NOM.PL

ʔe·-t haʔene-k-laknoʔo hawna·t-an-wa·-yʔik.
be-SS.CONS bring.back-PART-EVID make.camp-GER-OBV-ALL

(7) ʔe·-kla he-pay-xwet-an-osas-wa·-ʔa·-la
be-DS.NSIM REFL-bead-wear-GER-young-OBV-DEF-NOM.SG

ʔeʔeyo·-no-k-laknoʔo. ʔawas-wa·-ʔa·-la-k
prepare-CONT-PART-EVID meat-OBV-DEF-SG-ACC

ʔey-pake-no-k-laknoʔo ʔe·-ta
CAUS-be.sliced-CONT-PART-EVID be-SS.NPURP

nawle-no-k-laknoʔo hawses-an-ʔa·-yʔik. ʔe·-ta
broil-CONT-PART-EVID burn.thoroughly-GER-DEF-ALL be-SS.NPURP

xa·-ʔa·-la-k xwe·yʔik nawl-a·to-·kwa
fat-DEF-SG-ACC last broil-FUT-when

ha·ʔako·n-osas-wa·-ʔa·-la "waʔanes xa·-h-elʔa·t-la
man-young-OBV-DEF-NOM.SG as.soon.as fat-EP-yonder-NOM.SG

ha-mʔamʔa-t xa·-ʔa·-la ha·ʔas so·la-·kwa losos
TH-become.warm-SS.CONS fat-DEF-NOM.SG much drip-when all

taʔane-ta he-ykaca-k-eʔe·-k xa-ka-ta-w. ʔe·-yo-ʔok
take-SS.NPURP REFL-sit-PART-that-ACC AUG-throw-CIS-IMP (='swing in circle') do-2-when

he·topow-ʔa·-la	x-e·pac-a·to-nwaʔ.	ʔe·-kwa	matnokon
Osage-DEF-NOM.SG	AUG-fall.down. PL-FUT-DEON.3	be-DS.SIM	quickly

to-topo-w	ke-y-we-weye-k-te·-la-k,"	no-k-laknoʔo.
RED-cut-IMP	1.OBJ-TH-RED-bind-PART-this-SG-ACC	say-PART-EVID

(8)

ʔe·-kla	he-pay-xwet-an-osas-wa·-ʔa·-la	xa·-wa·-ʔa·-la-k
be-DS.NSIM	REFL-bead-wear-GER-young-OBV-DEF-NOM.SG	fat-OBV-DEF-SG-ACC

losos	taʔane-ta	yakca-k-a·-yʔik	xa-ka-ta-k-laknoʔo.
all	take-SS.NPURP	sit.PL-PART-DEF-ALL	AUG-throw-CIS-PART-EVID

ʔe·-kla	he·topow-ʔa·-la	x-e·pace-t
be-DS.NSIM	Osage-DEF-NOM.SG	AUG-fall.down-SS.CONS

ha-co-cox-ape-no-k-laknoʔo.	ʔe·kwa
TH-RED-stand.up-NEG-CONT-PART-EVID	be-DS.SIM

he-pay-xwet-an-osas-wa·-ʔa·-la
REFL-bead-wear-GER-young-OBV-DEF-NOM.SG

xalʔo·-n-ʔa·-la-k	taʔane-t	to-topa-k-laknoʔo
cut.with.knife-GER-DEF-SG-ACC	take-SS.CONS	RED-cut-PART-EVID

ya-wye-no-[Ø]-ʔa·-la-k	ha·ʔako·n-osas-wa·-ʔa·-la-k.	ʔe·-kla
TH-bind-CONT-PART-DEF-SG-ACC	man-young-OBV-DEF-SG-ACC	be-DS.NSIM

nexʔew-ʔa·-la-k	nok-an	ʔey-we-ncaka-no-k-laknoʔo
bow/gun-DEF-SG-ACC	pick-GER	CAUS-OBJ.PL-kill-CONT-PART-EVID

ʔe·t	losos	ʔey-we-ncaka-nesʔe-k-laknoʔo.	ʔe·-ta
be-SS.CONS	all	CAUS-OBJ.PL-kill-DU-PART-EVID	be-SS.NPURP

ta-na-nesʔe-k-laknoʔo	ya-cox-ʔan-ʔa·-wʔan.
move.PL-ABL-DU-PART-EVID	TH-camp-GER-DEF-ADESS

(9)

ʔe·-t	ta-na-nesʔe-·kwa	he·topow-kalak-la
be-SS.CONS	move.PL-ABL-DU-when	Osage-other-NOM.SG

na·to·n-ʔa·-yʔik	helʔey-ayco-ta-no-k-laknoʔo.	ʔe·-kla
mountain-DEF-ALL	peer-up-CIS-CONT-PART-EVID	be-DS.NSIM

kalak-a·-wʔan he·sa-na-no-k-laknoʔo. ʔe·-kla
other-DEF-ADESS point-ABL-CONT-PART-EVID be-when

tickan-wa·c-a·ʔako·n-wa·-ʔa·-la "hewl-a·haʔa,"
person-real-man-OBV-DEF-NOM.SG capture-INTENT

no-k-laknoʔo. "ʔe·-s-ʔok ke-taple-w. ma·tan
say-PART-EVID be-1-if 1.OBJ-help-IMP quickly

ya·lo·na-se-k-e," no-k-laknoʔo.
kill-1-PART-HORT say-PART-EVID

(10) ʔe·-ta henkwa·-na-k-laknoʔo ʔe·-t ha·cin-ʔa·-yʔik
be-SS.NPURP run-ABL-PART-EVID be-SS.CONS near-DEF-ALL

henkway-xa·-xa-k-laknoʔo. ʔe·-kwa he·topow-ʔa·-la
run-AUG.move.SG-AUG-PART-EVID be-DS.SIM Osage-DEF-NOM.SG

ya·ce-·kwa hewle-k-laknoʔo. ʔe·-kla
look-when capture-PART-EVID be-DS.NSIM

he·topow-ʔa·-la ta·-he·-wiwil-yo-·kwa
Osage-DEF-NOM.SG COM-RECIP$_1$-wrestle-RECIP$_2$-DS.SIM

he-pay-xwet-an-osas-wa·-ʔa·-la yan-ci-cxil-xa·-xa-k-laknoʔo
REFL-bead-wear-GER-young-OBV-DEF-NOM.SG TH-RED-run-AUG.move.SG-AUG-PART-EVID

ʔe·-t ta·-haple-k-laknoʔo. he·topow-ʔa·-la-k
be-SS.CONS COM-help-PART-EVID Osage-DEF-SG-ACC

taʔane-t yale-ta ya-wey-nesʔe-k-laknoʔo.
take-SS.CONS throw.a.missile-SS.NPURP TH-bind-DU-PART-EVID

ʔe·-ta "we·ʔil," no-k-laknoʔo ʔe·ta
be-SS.CONS all.right say-PART-EVID be-SS.NPURP

ta·-ta-na-k-laknoʔo ya-cox-ʔan-ʔa·-yʔik.
COM-move.PL-ABL-PART-EVID TH-camp-GER-DEF-ALL

(11) ʔo·ʔo·-kwa xa-t-xa-nesʔe-k-laknoʔo. ʔe·-t
be.night-DS.SIM AUG-move.PL-AUG-DU-PART-EVID be-SS.CONS

ʔeywencakanesʔoʔo·ʔ
"he·topow-ʔa·-la-k ha·ʔas ʔey-we-ncaka-nesʔe-we-ʔe·-ʔ,"
Osage-DEF-SG-ACC many CAUS-OBJ.PL-kill-DU-DECL-PAST-PAST.1

no-k-laknoʔo. "ʔe·-t we·ʔis-pax ya-wye-t
say-PART-EVID be-SS.CONS once-just TH-bind-SS.CONS

cana-nesʔoʔo·ʔ
cana-nesʔe-we-ʔe·-ʔ," no-k-laknoʔo. "taxso·-kwa
leave-DU-DECL-PAST.1-PAST.1 say-PART-EVID be.dawn-DS.SIM

hemʔas-ʔa·-la ya·lo·n-a-to-nwaʔ," no-k-laknoʔo.
mother.in.law-DEF-NOM.SG kill-FUT-DEON.3 say-PART-EVID

(12) ʔe·-k-la-k taxso·-kwa ha·naxok-ita na·ʔe·-k-laknoʔo
be-PART-SG-ACC be.dawn-DS.SIM great.many-quite go-PART-EVID

ha·n[a]xok-ʔey-we-ncaka-k-wa·-yʔik. xa·ya-t nexʔew-ʔa·-la-k
great.many-CAUS-OBJ.PL-kill-PART-OBV-ALL arrive-SS.CONS gun-DEF-SG-ACC

losos noko-ta hakay-ta-ʔa·-yʔik
all pick-SS.NPURP side.of-CIS-DEF-ALL

he·topow-la-k hewle-k-a·-yʔik yate-l-ʔok
Osage-SG-ACC capture-PART-DEF-ALL come-3-when

he-cne·la-k-laknoʔo lak. he-pay-xwet-an-osas-wa·-lʔan
REFL-be.lying-PART-EVID there REFL-bead-wear-GER-young-OBV-GEN

xʔay-ʔa·-la ʔey-kayc-an-la-k=wa·-lʔas ta·key-ʔa·-yʔik
mother-DEF-NOM CAUS-chop-GER-SG-ACC-=OBV-INST head-DEF-ALL

ʔey-kayca-k-laknoʔo ʔe·-t ya·lo·na-k-laknoʔo.
CAUS-chop-PART-EVID be-SS.CONS kill-PART-EVID

(13) ʔe·-ta ya-cox-ʔan-a·naxok-wa·-yʔik xa·ya-t
be-SS.NPURP TH-camp-GER-many-OBV-ALL arrive-SS.CONS

he·malo·-no-k-laknoʔo taxac-e·kin ʔo·ʔa-h-e·kin.
dance-CONT-PART-EVID be.day-ALL be.night-EP-ALL

The Two Young Tonkawas and the Osage: Free English Translation

[1] Some Tonkawas were living in a camp, and one young Tonkawa man and a young woman were in love with each other. It was summer, and he was moving off to the mountains with her. He went far away with her, and they were sitting on a mountain top and were fooling around with each other. They both lay down and fell asleep. [2] After a while, [he noticed] that someone was prodding him in the legs, and the young man woke up. When he looked, there were enemy tribesmen standing around where he was lying with the woman. "Wake up," he said, "enemies have captured us." [3] So the woman woke up and the Osages grabbed the young man and they bound his arms and legs and took them away. [4] They made camp by a small river and lay down, and when dawn broke the young Tonkawa man cut his hair as the Osages do. Then they moved to the other side of the river and and lay down. In the morning, the woman said: "Didn't you ever learn anything? Those young Tonkawa men usually know everything." [5] So the young man said: "Tell them this: go hunt for young buffalo bulls." [6] So the woman told the Osage chief: "Go hunt for young buffalo bulls," and the Osages mounted their horses and went off looking for buffalo. The Osages killed some young buffalo bulls and brought them back to the camp. [7] So the woman was preparing the meat, slicing it and broiling in the fire's embers. When she was about to broil the fatty meat last, the young man said: "As soon as that fatty meat gets warm, when the fat drips take all of it over to where they are sitting and swing it around in a circle—when you do, the Osages will all fall right over. Right then quickly cut this thing they bound me with." [8] So the woman took all the fatty meat to where they were sitting and and threw it around in a circle. The Osages fell right over and weren't able to stand up. At the same time, the woman took the knife and cut what they were binding the young man with. Then he picked up his gun and was killing them—they both killed them—and they left for the camp. [9] Then, as they both left, the other Osage looked up at the mountain, though he was facing the other direction. The young Tonkawa man said: "I'm going to capture him. If I do, help me. Quick, let's kill him." [10] So they ran real fast and sprinted up close to him, and when he saw the Osage, he grabbed him and captured him. As the Osage wrestled with him, the woman ran right up to him [the Tonkawa man] and helped him. He grabbed hold of [the Osage] and threw him [down on the ground] and tied him up and said: "All right." Then they went off to the camp together. [11] At night they arrived and [the young man] said: "We two have killed many Osages. We left just one tied up. In the morning, mother-in-law can go kill him." [12] So at dawn a bunch of them went off to where

they had killed all those Osages. They arrived and, picking up their guns, went right up next to the Osage who had been captured—when they came, he was still lying there. The woman's mother chopped his head off with an ax and killed him. [13] So they they went back to the big camp and danced and danced all day and all night.

27. The Man and the Cat

(1) yacoxʔanoklak
ya-cox-ʔan-a·xok-a·-yʔik ya-coxʔa-no-k-la-k
TH-camp-GER-large-DEF-ALL TH-camp-CONT-PART-SG-ACC

tickan-wa·c-la ha·ʔako·n-osas-la
person-real-NOM.SG man-young-NOM.SG

saxʔay-ka-k ʔe[y]-ʔe-yo·-no-k-laknoʔo.
arrow-PL-ACC CAUS-do-INGR-CONT-PART-EVID

ʔe·-no-k-la-k saxʔay yacka-ka-nan
be-CONT-PART-SG-ACC arrow spike-PL-ABL

xʔelʔe-no-k-laknoʔo yela-ta.
sharpen-CONT-PART-EVID sit-SS.NPURP

(2) ʔe·-no-k-la-k ʔokmaʔek-la wixwan-la ha-kxo-na-k-laknoʔo
be-CONT-PART-SG-ACC cat-NOM.SG small-NOM.SG move.SG-in-ABL-PART-EVID

ha·ʔako·n-osas-la ʔe·-k-wa·-yʔik
man-young-NOM.SG be-PART-OBV-ALL

ʔe·-t sa·xal-ʔa·-yʔik yela-k-laknoʔo
be-SS.CONS opening-DEF-ALL sit-PART-EVID

ʔokmaʔek-wa·-ʔa·-la. ʔe·-ta yace-no-k-laknoʔo
cat-OBV-DEF-NOM.SG be-SS.NPURP look-CONT-PART-EVID

ha·ʔako·n-osas-wa·-ʔa·-la-k.
man-young-OBV-DEF-SG-ACC

(3) ʔe·-l-kaʔak ha·ʔako·n-osas-wa·-ʔa·-la "hecu·-ka-k
be-3-but man-young-OBV-DEF-NOM.SG what-PL-ACC

ke-yace-no-kaʔ" no-k-laknoʔo ʔokmaʔek-wixwan-wa·-ʔa·-la-k.
1.OBJ-look-CONT-2 say-PART-EVID cat-small-OBV-DEF-SG-ACC

ʔe·-l-kaʔak ʔokmaʔek-wa·-ʔa·-la ha·cin-ʔa·-yʔik
be-3-but cat-OBV-DEF-NOM.SG near-DEF-ALL

yela-k-lakno?o ?e·-ta ya·ce-no-k-lakno?o
sit-PART-EVID be-SS.NPURP look-CONT-PART-EVID

x?el?e-k-wa·-y?ik.
sharpen-PART-OBV-ALL

(4) "hecu·-ka-k ke-ya·ce-no-ka?" no-k-lakno?o.
what-PL-ACC 1.OBJ-look-CONT-2 say-PART-EVID

?e·-l-ka?ak ?okma?ek-wa·-?a·-la c?etxan-a·to-no-k-lakno?o.
be-3-while cat-OBV-DEF-NOM.SG jump-FUT-CONT-PART-EVID

?e·-ka?ak ha·?ako·n-osas-wa·-?a·-la henko·-n-?a·-la-k
be-because man-young-OBV-DEF-NOM.SG put.on-GER-DEF-SG-ACC (='breechcloth')

wa?asay-pax henko·-ta ?e·-no-k-lakno?o.
one.side-just wear-SS.NPURP do-CONT-PART-EVID

?okma?ek-wa·-?a·-la ca·l-?a·-y?ik ya·ce-l-?ila
cat-OBV-DEF-NOM.SG ball-DEF-ALL look-3-as

c?etxan-a·to-no-k-lakno?o x?el?e-l-ka?ak ha·?ako·n-osas-wa·-?a·-l?an
jump-FUT-CONT-PART-EVID sharpen-3-while man-young-OBV-DEF-GEN

c?a·l-?a·-la hen-ti-tso?o-no-k-lakno?o.
testicle-DEF-NOM.SG TH-RED-shake-CONT-PART-EVID

(5) ?e·-kla ?okma?ek-wixwan-wa·-?a·-la ha·cin-?a·-y?ik
be-DS.NSIM cat-small-OBV-DEF-NOM.SG near-DEF-ALL

xa-yela-k-lakno?o. ?e·-l-?ok ha·?ako·n-osas-wa·-?a·-la
AUG-sit-PART-EVID be-3-as man-young-OBV-DEF-NOM.SG

x?el?e-no-k-lakno?o. ?e·-kwa ?okma?ek-wa·-?a·-la
sharpen-CONT-PART-EVID be-DS.SIM cat-OBV-DEF-NOM.SG

c?etxa-na-t ca·l-?a·-y?ik he-wle-k-lakno?o.
jump-ABL-SS.CONS testicle-DEF-ALL REFL-capture-PART-EVID

?e·-kla ha·?ako·n-osas-wa·-?a·-la ?okma?ek-wixwan-wa·-?a·-la-k
be-DS.NSIM man-young-OBV-DEF-NOM.SG cat-small-OBV-DEF-SG-ACC

he·c-ʔa·-yʔik	yakaw-ka·-na-k-laknoʔo.
this.way-DEF-ALL	kick-throw-ABL-PART-EVID

The Man and the Cat: Free English Translation

[1] A young Tonkawa man who was living in a large camp was making arrows from spikes—he was sitting there, sharpening arrows from spikes. [2] As he did, a little cat came in to where the young man was [sitting], and the cat sat down in the doorway, looking at the young man. [3] Even so, the young man said to the little cat: "What are you looking at me for?" But the cat sat there near him, watching him while he was sharpening. [4] "What are you looking at me for?" he said, as the cat was about to jump, because the young man was wearing just one side of his breechcloth. As the cat looked at his balls, he was about to jump because the young man's balls were shaking and shaking. [5] So the little cat sat right next to him, and while the man was sharpening, the cat jumped and caught his balls. Then the young man kicked the little cat away.

Works Cited

Campbell, L., T. Kaufman, and T. C. Smith-Stark. 1986. "Meso-America as a Linguistic Area." *Language* 62: 530–70.

Gatschet, Albert S. 1876. "Remarks on the Tonkawa Language." *Proceedings of the American Philosophical Society* 16, no. 98: 318–27.

———. 1884. "Tonkawa Texts." MS no. 8001. Bureau of American Ethnology. Washington, D.C.

Goddard, Ives. 1979. "The Languages of South Texas and the Lower Rio Grande." In *The Languages of Native America: Historical and Comparative Assessment*, edited by Lyle Campbell and Marianne Mithun, 355–89. Austin: University of Texas Press.

Gouskova, M., 2007. "The Reduplicative Template in Tonkawa." *Phonology* 24, no. 3: 367–96.

Greenberg, J. H. 1987. *Language in the Americas.* Stanford: Stanford University Press.

Haas, Mary. 1958. A New Linguistic Relationship in North America: Algonkian and the Gulf Languages. *Southwestern Journal of Anthropology* 14, no. 3: 231–64.

———. 1959. "Tonkawa and Algonquian." *Anthropological Linguistics* 1, no. 2: 1–6.

———. 1967. "On the Relations of Tonkawa." In *Studies in Southwestern Ethnolinguistics: Meaning and History in the Languages of the American Southwest,* edited by Dell Hymes, William E. Bittle, and Harry Hoijer, 310–20. The Hague: Mouton.

———. 1993. Tonkawa and Algonkian. *Anthropological Linguistics* 35, nos. 1–4: 15–20.

Harris, A. C. 2006. "Revisiting Anaphoric Islands." *Language* 82, no. 1: 114–30.

Haspelmath, M. 2011. "The Indeterminacy of Word Segmentation and the Nature of Morphology and Syntax." *Folia Linguistica* 45, no. 1: 31–80.

Hoijer, Harry. 1933. *Tonkawa, an Indian Language of Texas.* Edited by Franz Boaz. Handbook of American Indian Languages, Vol. 3. New York: Columbia University Press.

———. 1949a. *An Analytical Dictionary of the Tonkawa Language.* University of California Publications in Linguistics 5, no. 1. Berkeley: University of California Press.

———. 1949b. "Tonkawa Syntactic Suffixes and Anaphoric Particles." *Southwestern Journal of Anthropology* 5, no. 1 (Spring): 37–55.

———. 1972. *Tonkawa Texts.* Berkeley: University of California Press.

Hymes, Dell. 1987. "Tonkawa Poetics: John Rush Buffalo's 'Coyote and Eagle's Daughter.'" In *Native American Discourse: Poetics and Rhetoric,* edited by Joel Sherzer and Anthony C. Woodbury, 17–61. Cambridge: Cambridge University Press.

Jones, William K. 1969. *Notes on the History and Material Culture of the Tonkawa Indians.* Smithsonian Contributions to Anthropology 2, no. 5. Washington, D.C.: Smithsonian Press.

Kisseberth, C. W. 1970. "Vowel Elision in Tonkawa and Derivational Constraints." In *Studies Presented to Robert B. Lees by His Students,* edited by Jerrold M. Sadok and Anthony L. Vanek. Papers in Linguistics, Monograph Series 1. Edmonton, Alberta, Canada: Linguistic Research.

Manaster-Ramer, Alexis. 1996a. "Sapir's Classification: Coahuiltecan." *Anthropological Linguistics* 38: 1–38.

———. 1996b. "Tonkawa and Zuni: Two Test Cases for the Greenberg Classification." *International Journal of American Linguistics* 62, no. 3: 264–88.

Mithun, Marianne. 2001. *The Languages of Native North America.* Cambridge: Cambridge University Press.

Newlin, Deborah Lamont. 1981. "The Tonkawa People: A Tribal History, from Earliest Times to 1893." Doctoral dissertation, Texas Tech University, Lubbock.

Powell, J. W. 1891. Indian Linguistic Families of America North of Mexico. *Smithsonian Institution, Bureau of American Ethnology, Annual Report* 7 (1885–86): 7–142. Washington, D.C.: United States Government Printing Office.

Roach, Peter. 1982. "On the Distinction between 'Stress-Timed' and 'Syllable-Timed' Languages." *Linguistic Controversies* 73: 79.

Sadock, Jerrold. 1980. "Noun Incorporation in Greenlandic: A Case of Syntactic Word Formation." *Language* 56, no. 2: 300–319.

———. 1986. "Some Notes on Noun Incorporation." *Language* 62, no. 1: 19–31.

Sapir, Edward. 1920. "The Hokan and Coahuiltecan Languages." *International Journal of American Linguistics* 1: 280–90.

Sjoberg, Andrée. 1953. "The Culture of the Tonkawa: A Texas Indian Tribe." *Texas Journal of Science* 5, no. 3: 280–304.

Swanton, John R. 1940. *Linguistic Material from the Tribes of Southern Texas and Northeastern Mexico.* Smithsonian Institution Bureau of Ethnography, Bulletin No. 127. Washington, D.C.: Smithsonian Institution.

Wier, Thomas. 2012. "Obviation and Reference-Tracking in Tonkawa." Paper presented at the Society for the Study of the Indigenous Languages of the Americas in Portland, Oregon: https://www.academia.edu/2056229/Obviation_and_Reference-tracking_in_Tonkawa_a_comparative_study.

———. n.d. "Templatic Dependencies and Notions of Wordhood in Tonkawa." MS available online: https://freeuni.academia.edu/ThomasWier.

Index

Page references to illustrations are in *italic* type.